THE COMPLETE BOOK OF FOOD

THE COMPLETE BOOK OF FOOD

A Nutritional, Medical, &
Culinary Guide

CAROL ANN RINZLER

With an Introduction by
Jane Brody

Foreword by Michael D. Jensen, M.D.

WORLD ALMANAC
AN IMPRINT OF PHAROS BOOKS • A SCRIPPS HOWARD COMPANY
NEW YORK

Interior Design: C. Linda Dingler
Cover Design: Design Five

First published in 1987.

Distributed in the United States by Ballantine Books, a division of Random House, Inc., and in
Canada by Random House of Canada, Ltd.
Pharos Books ISBN: 0-88687-320-7
Ballantine Books ISBN: 0-345-34876-1

Library of Congress Cataloging in Publication Data:

Rinzler, Carol Ann.
     The complete book of food.

     Bibliography: p. Includes index.
     1. Food.   2. Nutrition.   I. Title.
TX353.R525   1987   641   87-60159

Printed in the United States of America.

World Almanac
An Imprint of Pharos Books
A Scripps Howard Company
200 Park Avenue
New York, NY 10166

10 9 8 7 6 5 4 3 2 1

This book is for
My agent, Phyllis Westberg, who made it work;
My editor, Beverly Jane Loo, who made it real;
And my husband, Perry Luntz, who made it possible.

CONTENTS

INTRODUCTION

You've no doubt heard of food for thought, food for love, food for strength, health food, healing food, soul food, brain food, and the like. For as long as people have inhabited this planet, edibles have been imbued with all sorts of attributes beyond satisfying hunger and sustaining life. And in many cases, popular notions about the powers of various foods and beverages have been documented by modern scientific investigations that have demonstrated, for example, the soothing qualities of chicken soup for sufferers of the common cold and the antibiotic properties of garlic.

Then there are the newer discoveries not rooted in folklore, among them the protection against cancer afforded by vegetables and fruits rich in the pigment carotene and the cancer-blockers found in members of the cabbage family; the cholesterol-lowering ability of apples, barley, beans, garlic and oats; the heart-saving qualities of fish and alcohol (in moderate amounts), and the antidiabetic properties of foods rich in dietary fiber.

But while thinking of food as preventive or cure, it is important not to lose sight of its basic values: to provide needed nutrients and a pleasurable eating experience while satisfying hunger and thirst.

In "The Complete Book of Food" Carol Ann Rinzler has put it all together, providing a handy, illuminating guide for all who shop, cook and eat. It is a "must have" for all those who want to get the very most out of the foods they eat, as well as avoid some inevitable dietary and culinary pitfalls. Ms. Rinzler tells you how to derive the maximum nutritive value from the foods you buy and ingest, with handy tips on how to select, store, prepare and in some cases serve foods to preserve their inherent worth and avoid their risks. For example, in preparing bean sprouts, you'll be cautioned to eat them within a few days of purchase and to cook them minimally to get the most food value from this vitamin C-rich food. You'll appreciate the importance of variety and moderation in your diet when you discover that broccoli, which possesses two cancer-preventing properties, also can inhibit thyroid hormone if consumed in excess.

You will also recognize that not all wholesome foods are good for all folks. Sometimes a health condition will render a food unsuitable for you. For example, beans might be restricted for those with gout and certain greens may be limited for those who must stick to a low-sodium diet. Then too, there are possible interactions—both adverse and advantageous—between certain foods and nutrients or medications. For example, citrus fruits are recommended accompaniments for iron-rich vegetables and meats since the vitamin C in the fruits enhances the absorption of iron. Those taking anticoagulant medication are advised to avoid excessive amounts of green leafy vegetables since the vitamin K in these foods may reduce the effectiveness of the drug.

You'll learn what happens to foods when they are cooked at home or processed in factories. Want to avoid olive-drab green vegetables? Steam them quickly or, better yet, cook them in the microwave with a tiny bit of water to bypass the discoloring action of acids on the green pigment chlorophyll. You'll also get the full story on methods of preserving milk—from freezing and drying to evaporating and ultrapasteurizing—that should relieve any anxieties you may have about the safety and healthfulness of processed milk.

In short, this is a book no self-respecting eater should be without. It can serve as a lifetime reference for all interested in a safe and wholesome diet.

Jane E. Brody
Personal Health Columnist
The New York Times
June, 1987.

FOREWORD

This unique book presents the most current and objective information available about the medical and nutritional aspects of food, and includes important facts about the major nutrients present (calories, protein, fat, cholesterol, carbohydrates, fiber, vitamin and mineral contributions). In addition, potentially harmful properties (high cholesterol, high fat, high sodium), as well as those parts of foods which might be potentially toxic or poisonous if inadvertantly eaten or improperly prepared are identified, as well as how foods interact—both negatively and positively.

As a physician I believe this book will be extremely helpful to both those whose doctors have asked them to comply with certain dietary restrictions or who themselves wish to improve the quality of their diet. People who are considering a special diet, such as a vegetarian one, might consider THE COMPLETE BOOK OF FOOD a handy reference book because it provides information on how to mix and match vegetable proteins to prevent protein and vitamin deficiency.

In these days of food faddism and questionable nutrition practices, this book is a splendid example of providing responsible and accurate nutritional information to the public.

Michael D. Jensen, M.D
The Mayo Clinic
Mayo Medical School

PREFACE

Think of an orange.

Think of an aspirin.

Now think how similar they are.

Both can make you better—the aspirin by relieving your headache, the orange by curing or preventing scurvy. Both have side effects. The aspirin may make your stomach bleed; the orange may give you hives. Both interact with drugs. The aspirin can make anticoagulants stronger and antidepressants weaker. The vitamin C in the orange may inactivate the active ingredient in the guaiac test for hidden blood and produce a false-negative result.

In short, they're both health products. The difference is that if you want to find out more about the aspirin's chemistry, benefits, side effects, and interactions, all you have to do is walk down to the library and check out the latest "drug book." Ask about an orange, though, and the librarian will direct you to the diet books or the cookbooks or the books on popular nutrition, but never the section on medicine.

Which is strange when you consider that all foods, like all drugs, are chemicals, and that we have always used them as medicines. The Romans sterilized wounds with wine; the Egyptians poured in honey to help them heal. The Aztecs used chocolate as an aphrodisiac. Every Jewish grandmother cured a cold with chicken soup; and every Italian mama heaped olive-oiled pasta on their platters to keep her brood in trim.

Today we recognize the germ of science in everything early man did. Wine "sterilizes" with alcohol. The hydrophilic (water-loving) honey sops up liquids from a wound, kills bacteria, and nourishes new cell growth. Chocolate's methylxanthine stimulants (caffeine, theophylline, theobromine) elevate mood. The steam from chicken soup (not to mention its aroma) stimulates the flow of liquids that clear the nasal passages. Pasta is high-fiber food, and olive oil is rich in monounsaturated fatty acids that now appear to protect the heart.

It has taken a long time for science to move beyond the parlor game of validating folklore and begin to explore the serious medical and physical effects of the natural chemicals in food. Only recently have we identified the omega-3 fatty acids in fish that appear to ameliorate all kinds of inflammatory conditions from heart diseases to psoriasis. Only now are we beginning to appreciate that the foods we eat may stimulate the production of mood-altering chemicals in the brain. What was once folklore is now science.

That's why this book was written, to pull together in one place what science now knows about the medical effects of food.

WHAT YOU WILL FIND IN THIS BOOK

The information in this book is organized into a series of 103 entries (including 277 separate foods), in alphabetical order from Apples to Zucchini. Most are described individually, but some are so similar in composition and effects that they are grouped together. For example, chives, leeks, scallions and shallots are all covered under ONIONS. Check the index for individual listings.

Each entry begins with a *Nutritional profile*, an easy-to-read chart that summarizes the relative values (low, moderate, high) of the basic constituents in the food (energy, protein, fat, carbohydrates, fiber, sodium), as well as the food's most prominent vitamins and minerals. The calculations for these *Nutritional profiles* are based on the information in the United States Department of Agriculture's comprehensive series of nutrient tables, *Composition of Foods*. Unless otherwise noted, the values are for fresh, uncooked food. (Processing may alter these values. For example, salt added in processing may change the sodium content of vegetables.)

DEFINING LOW, MODERATE, AND HIGH

There is no single source for defining what you mean when you describe a food as *low, moderate* or *high* in one nutrient or another. The definitions here are, by necessity, guidelines and averages based upon the best available information. I think you will find, however, that they agree with your own common-sense assessment of the foods you eat.

Energy value (calories per serving). While some people need more and some people need less, the National Research Council suggests that the average adult man should get approximately 2,500 calories a day; the average adult woman, about 2,000. The energy value of each food is described in terms of the amount of calories you would get from a 3.5 oz. (100 gram) serving, the portion in the USDA tables. A food that provides less than 50 calories per 3.5 oz. serving is *low* in calories. A food that provides 50 to 250 calories per 3.5 oz. serving is *moderate*. A food that provides more than 250 calories per 3.5 oz. serving is *high*.

In practical terms, of course, eating a larger (or smaller) portion of any food may change the amount of calories you get from the food. For example, if you rate bread according to the number of calories you get from a 3.5 oz. portion, it's high in calories, but a single slice of bread, which weighs about 25 grams, contains only 85 calories, a moderate amount. On the other hand, while a 3.5 oz. serving of lean beef is moderate in calories, an 8 oz. steak is high.

Proteins. Proteins that contain sufficient amounts of all the essential amino acids are called "complete" or "high quality" proteins. Proteins that are deficient in one or more of the essential amino acids are called "incomplete" or "limited" proteins. Complete proteins are found in foods of animal origin such as meat, milk, and eggs. Incomplete proteins are found in plant foods. By combining plant foods with each other or with foods of animal origin, you can improve the quality of the incomplete proteins.

The protein content of each food is described in terms of the percentage of calories in the food that comes from protein. A food that gets less than 5 percent of its calories from protein is *low* in protein. A food that gets 5-20 percent of its calories from proteins is *moderate*. A food that gets more than 20 percent of its calories from proteins is *high*.

Fat. Based on the American Heart Association's suggestion that we should get no more than 30 percent of our calories from fats, foods that derive less than 30 percent of their calories from fat are called *low* in fat. Foods that get 30-50 percent of their calories from fat are *moderate*. Foods that get more than 50 percent of their calories from fat are *high*.

Cholesterol. The American Heart Assocation recommends that we limit our consumption of cholesterol to no more than 30 mg a day or 100 mg per 1,000 calories, whichever is less. A food that provides less than 20 mg of cholesterol per 3.5 oz. (100 gram) serving is described as *low* in cholesterol. A food that provides 20-150 mg per serving is *moderate*. A food that provides more than 150 mg per serving is *high*.

Carbohydrates. The carbohydrate content of each food is described in terms of the percentage of the calories derived from carbohydrates (starches and sugars). A food that gets less than 20 percent of its calories from carbohydrates is described as *low* in carbohydrates. A food that gets 20-60 percent of its calories from carbohydrates is *moderate*. A food that gets more than 60 percent of its calories from carbohydrates is called *high*.

Fiber. Foods contain two kinds of fiber, insoluble fiber and soluble fiber. The insoluble fibers cellulose and lignin bulk up stool and may be useful in preventing constipation or cancer of the colon. The soluble fibers—pectic substance ("pectin") and gums—dissolve in water, absorb fats, and may be useful in preventing heart disease and some cancers. The fiber content of food as described in this nutritional profile refers to *crude fiber,* the amount of insoluble fiber that remains after food has been treated with chemicals that destroy its other constituents. A food that provides less than 1 gram crude fiber per 3.5 oz./100 gram serving is *low* in fiber. A food that provides 1-10 grams per serving is *high.*

Sodium. In general, a food that contains less than 50 mg sodium per serving is *low* in sodium. A food that contains 50-125 mg sodium per serving is *moderate.* A food that contains more than 125 mg sodium per serving is *high.* Obviously, consuming a larger portion of a food that is low or moderate in sodium will raise its rating.

Major vitamin contribution and Major mineral contribution. These are qualitative, not quantitative descriptions. They tell which vitamins and minerals are most prominent in the food but not how much of each the food contains.

You'll find a more detailed nutritional guide under the heading *About the nutrients in this food.* Is the food high in starch or sugars? What kinds of fiber does it contain? Are its fats highly saturated or primarily unsaturated? Are its proteins "complete," with sufficient amounts of all the essential amino acids? Does the food have any antinutrients, such as the avidin in raw egg white that inactivates biotin, or any naturally harmful chemicals, such as solanine, the nerve toxin in the green parts of potatoes and tomatoes? If so, it will be listed here.

Of course, you will want to know *The most nutritious way to serve this food.* How you serve a food or what you serve it with may improve its value. For example, the proteins in beans are deficient in the essential amino acids that are abundant in grains—and vice versa. Serving beans and grains together "completes" their proteins, a clear nutritional bonus.

If you have a medical problem or are on a special diet, you need to know about the *Diets that may restrict or exclude this food.* Sometimes the problems are not as obvious as they should be. For example, if you are sensitive to milk, you may want to avoid sausages, some of which contain milk protein as a filler or binder. Remember that this list is only a guide; for more detailed personal advice, check with your doctor.

As a consumer, you should know how to choose the freshest, safest, most nutritious food—in short, what to look for when you are *Buying this food*. Even when you know the basics (avoid lettuce that has yellowed), you may be intrigued by the chemistry (as lettuce ages, its green chlorophyll fades, allowing its yellow carotenoid pigments to show through).

At home, your challenge is to protect the food from spoiling. Some foods, like meat, must be refrigerated. Others, like dried pasta, can be stored in any cool, dry cabinet. Still others are more complicated. Tomatoes are a good example. Vine-ripened tomatoes that have not turned completely red will get juicier and tastier after a few days at room temperature, but artificially ripened tomatoes ("hard-ripe" tomatoes) will rot before they soften. that's the sort of useful information you will find under the heading *Storing this food*.

Ready to eat? Then it's time to begin *Preparing this food*. Here's where you will learn how to handle food you are about to cook or serve. Of course, that includes an explanation of the chemical reactions involved. For example, we tear greens at the very last minute to keep them crisp—and to prevent the loss of vitamin C that occurs when the torn cells release ascorbic acid oxidase, an enzyme that destroys ascorbic acid. We beat egg whites in a copper bowl whose ions will stabilize the egg-white foam. We slice onions under running water to dilute the sulfur compounds that make our eyes water. And once we've done all that, we are ready to cook.

Now the most interesting development is the chemistry of *What happens when you cook this food*. When you heat meat its sugars and proteins caramelize to form a flavorful crust. Heat also makes aroma molecules begin to move more quickly, creating scents as subtle as that of a baking apple or as harsh as boiling cabbages. Pigments combine with oxygen or other chemicals in the food; meat turns brown and string beans, olive-drab. We have all seen this happen; this section explains the "how" and "why."

If you use frozen, canned, or dried food, you should know *How other forms of processing affect this food*. Processing often changes taste and texture. Sometimes it alters the nutritional balance one way or another; canned asparagus has less vitamin C than fresh asparagus, but dried apricots are much higher in iron than fresh ones. In a few rare cases, processing may create hazards that didn't exist before. For example, dried fruit treated to prevent browning is potentially dangerous for people sensitive to sulfites.

Which leads us quite naturally to the *Medical uses and/or benefits* of food. The information under this heading is drawn from sources current as the book was written, but research in this area is so new and is expanding so rapidly that it is almost always considered a "work in progress" rather than a firm conclusion. Think of what you read here as a guide, not a final answer.

The same thing goes for the *Adverse effects associated with this food*. Allergies are a common side effect from foods. Some of us have metabolic disorders that makes us unable to digest a component in food such as lactose (milk sugar) or gluten (a protein in wheat and other grains). People with thyroid problems may have to avoid the cruciferous vegetables (cabbage, brussels sprouts, broccoli, radishes), all of which contain chemicals called goitrogens that can inhibit the production of thyroid hormones. More prosaically, if you eat too many carrots and tomatoes over a long period of time, their pigments may turn your skin orange. These are some of the side effects you'll find here.

Finally there is the question of *Food/drug interactions*, such as the ability of the calcium ions in dairy foods to bind tetracyclines into insoluble compounds your body cannot use. Like medical benefits and side effects, this is a category that is growing (and changing) every day.

When you are done, I hope that all this will give you both a new way of looking at what you eat and the ability to evaluate each food as an individual health product, just like the ones on the drugstore shelf.

Remember the orange. Remember the aspirin. Remember how similar they are.

CAROL ANN RINZLER
January 1987

ACKNOWLEDGEMENTS

As a writer who deals with technical matters, I am always grateful to the men and women who are willing to contribute their time and expertise to insuring the accuracy of my interpretation of scientific and medical data. Among them are the following people, whose patience and good humor were virtually boundless:

Harold R. Bolin of the USDA Western Regional Research Center; John L. Brady; Diane Goetz of the American Heart Association; Klaus Grohmann of Hunter College of the City University of NewYork; Joseph L. Jeraci of Cornell University; Manfred Kroger of the Pennsylvania State University; Judith Krzynowek of the National Marine Fisheries Service; Jan Lipman of the American Diabetes Association; Alfred C. Olson of the USDA Western Regional Research Center; Dennis O'Mara of the Centers for Disease Control; Joe M. Regenstein of Cornell University; Edward G. Remmers of the American Council on Science and Health; Dr. Seymour Rosenblatt; J. Scott Smith of the Pennsylvania State University; Linda Troiano; Merle L. Weaver of the USDA Western Regional Research Center; and John H. Ziegler of the Pennsylvania State University.

A NOTE TO THE READER

The material in this book regarding the medical benefits or side effects of certain foods and the possible interactions between food and drugs is drawn from sources current at the time the book was written. It is for your information only and should never be substituted for your own doctor's advice or used without his or her consent. Your doctor, the person most familiar with your medical history and current health, is always the person best qualified to advise you on medical matters, including the use or avoidance of specific foods. Please note also that the adverse effects attributed to some of the foods listed here may not happen to everyone who eats the food or every time the food is served, another reason your own doctor is your best guide to your personal nutritional requirements.

APPLES

Energy value (calories per serving):	Low
Protein:	Low
Fat:	Low
Cholesterol:	None
Carbohydrates:	High
Fiber:	High
Sodium:	Low (fresh or dried fruit) High (dried fruit treated with sodium sulfur compounds)
Major vitamin contribution:	Vitamin C
Major mineral contribution:	Potassium

ABOUT THE NUTRIENTS IN THIS FOOD

Apples are rich in sugars (glucose, fructose, and sucrose) but have only a trace of starch. They provide all the carbohydrate food fibers, cellulose, hemi-cellulose, pectins (which comprise 70 percent of the total fiber in an apple's flesh), plus the noncarbohydrate food fiber lignin, in the peel. Apples have a little protein, very little fat, and no cholesterol.

Apples have small amounts of vitamin A and the B vitamins, plus vitamin C. A 3.5-ounce apple supplies 6 mg vitamin C, 10 percent of the RDA for a healthy adult. Ounce for ounce, apples have about 70 percent as much potassium as fresh oranges.

The sour taste of all immature apples (and some varieties, even when ripe) comes from malic acid. As an apple ripens, the amount of malic acid declines and the apple becomes sweeter.

Apple seeds contain amygdalin, a naturally occurring cyanide/sugar compound that degrades into hydrogen cyanide. While accidentally swallowing an apple seed once in a while is not a serious hazard, cases of human poisoning after eating apple seeds have been reported, and swallowing only a few seeds may be lethal for a child.

THE MOST NUTRITIOUS WAY TO SERVE THIS FOOD

Fresh and unpared, to take advantage of the fiber in the peel and preserve the vitamin C, which is destroyed by the heat of cooking.

DIETS THAT MAY RESTRICT OR EXCLUDE THIS FOOD

Antiflatulence diet (raw apples)
Low-fiber diet
Sucrose-free diet

BUYING THIS FOOD

Look for: Apples that are firm and brightly colored: shiny red Macintosh, Rome, and red Delicious; clear-green Granny Smith; golden-yellow Delicious.

Avoid: Bruised apples. When an apple is damaged the injured cells release polyphenoloxidase, an enzyme that hastens the oxidation of phenols in the apple, producing brownish pigments that darken the fruit. It's easy to check loose apples; if you buy them packed in a plastic bag, turn the bag upside down and examine the fruit.

STORING THIS FOOD

Store apples in the refrigerator. Cool storage keeps them from losing the natural moisture that makes them crisp. It also keeps them from turning brown inside, near the core, a phenomenon that occurs when apples are stored at warm temperatures. Apples can be stored in a cool, dark cabinet with plenty of circulating air.

Check the apples from time to time. They store well, but the longer the storage, the greater the natural loss of moisture and the more likely the chance that even the crispest apple will begin to taste mealy.

PREPARING THIS FOOD

Don't peel or slice an apple until you are ready to use it. When you cut into the apple, you tear its cells, releasing polyphenoloxidase, an enzyme that darkens the fruit. Acid inactivates polyphenoloxidase, so you can slow the browning (but not stop it completely) by dipping raw sliced and/or peeled apples into a solution of lemon juice and water or vinegar and water or by mixing them with citrus fruits in a fruit salad. Polyphenoloxidase also works more slowly in the cold, but storing peeled apples in the refrigerator is much less effective than immersing them in an acid bath.

WHAT HAPPENS WHEN YOU COOK THIS FOOD

When you cook an unpeeled apple, insoluble cellulose and lignin will hold the peel intact through all normal cooking. The flesh of the apple, though, will fall apart as the pectin in its cell walls dissolves and the water inside its cells swells, rupturing the cell walls and turning the apples into applesauce. Commercial bakers keep the apples in their apple pies firm by treating them with calcium; home bakers have to rely on careful timing. To prevent baked apples from melting into mush, core the apple and fill the center with sugar or raisins to absorb the moisture released as the apple cooks. Cutting away a circle of peel away at the top will allow the fruit to swell without splitting the skin.

Red apple skins are colored with red anthocyanin pigments. When an apple is cooked with sugar, the anthocyanins and the sugar combine to form irreversible brownish compounds.

HOW OTHER FORMS OF PROCESSING AFFECT THIS FOOD

Juice.   Clear apple juice has been filtered to remove the pulp; the pulp is left in "natural" apple juice. Most commercial apple juice is pasteurized, then packed in vacuum-sealed packages to stop all natural enzyme action. Without pasteurization, the enzymes in the juice begin to turn sugars into alcohols, eventually producing the mildly alcoholic beverage known as "hard" cider. (Pasteurization also protects apple juice from molds that produce the neurotoxin patulin.)

MEDICAL USES AND/OR BENEFITS

As an antidiarrheal.   The pectin in apple is a natural antidiarrheal that helps solidify stool. Shaved raw apple is sometimes used as a folk remedy for diarrhea, and purified pectin is an ingredient in many over-the-counter antidiarrheals such as Kaopectate.

Lower absorption of dietary fats.   Apples are rich in pectin, which appears to interfere with the body's absorption of dietary fats. The exact mechanism by which this occurs is still unknown, but one theory is that the pectins in the apple form a gel in your stomach that sops up fats and keeps them from being absorbed by your body.

ADVERSE EFFECTS ASSOCIATED WITH THIS FOOD

Sulfite allergies (dried apples). See PRUNES.

FOOD/DRUG INTERACTIONS

*   *   *

APRICOTS

NUTRITIONAL PROFILE

Energy value (calories per serving):	Low
Protein:	Moderate
Fat:	Low
Cholesterol:	None
Carbohydrates:	High
Fiber:	Low
Sodium:	Low (fresh or dried fruit) High (dried fruit treated with sodium sulfur compounds)
Major vitamin contribution:	Vitamin A
Major mineral contribution:	Iron

ABOUT THE NUTRIENTS IN THIS FOOD

Apricots are a rich source of carotenes, the natural yellow pigments the body uses to make vitamin A. Three and a half ounces of fresh apricots provide about 2600 IU vitamin A, more than half the daily requirement for an adult. Apricots also provide vitamin C and potassium, and dried apricots are particularly rich in iron. Three and a half ounces provide one-third the daily requirement for an adult woman (about half the daily requirement for an adult man).

The bark, leaves, and inner stony pit of the apricot all contain amygdalin, a natural chemical that can break down into several components, including hydrogen cyanide (Prussic acid) in your stomach. Apricot oil, which is specially treated during processing to remove the cyanide, is marked *FFPA* to show that it is "free from Prussic acid." Cases of fatal poisoning from apricot pits have been reported, including one in a three-year-old girl who ate fifteen apricot kernels.

Extract of apricot pits, known medically as Laetrile, is used by some alternative practitioners to treat cancers. The theory behind this treatment is that the cyanide in amygdalin is released only when it comes in contact with beta-glucuronidase, an enzyme common to tumor cells, and that it does not affect healthy cells. No controlled test has proved this thesis.

THE MOST NUTRITIOUS WAY TO SERVE THIS FOOD

Ounce for ounce, dried apricots are richer in nutrients and fiber than fresh ones.

DIETS THAT MAY RESTRICT OR EXCLUDE THIS FOOD

Low-fiber diet
Low-potassium diet
Low-sodium diet (dried apricots containing sodium sulfide)
Sucrose-free diet

BUYING THIS FOOD

Look for: Firm, plump orange fruit that gives slightly when you press with your thumb.

Avoid: Bruised apricots. Like apples and potatoes, apricots contain polyphenoloxidase, an enzyme that combines with phenols in the apricots to produce brownish pigments that discolor the fruit. When apricots are bruised, cells are broken, releasing the enzyme so that brown spots form under the bruise.

Avoid apricots that are hard or mushy or withered; all are less flavorsome than ripe, firm apricots, and the withered ones will decay quickly.

Avoid greenish apricots; they are low in carotenes and will never ripen satisfactorily at home.

STORING THIS FOOD

Store ripe apricots in the refrigerator and use them within a few days. Apricots do not lose their vitamin A in storage, but they are very perishable and rot fairly quickly.

PREPARING THIS FOOD

When you peel or slice an apricot, you tear its cell walls, releasing polyphenoloxidase, an enzyme that reacts with phenols in the apricots, producing brown compounds that darken the fruit. Acids inactivate polyphenoloxidase, so you can slow down this reaction (but not stop it completely) by dipping raw sliced and/or peeled apricots into a solution of lemon juice or vinegar and water or by mixing them with citrus fruits in a fruit salad. Polyphenoloxidase also works more slowly in the cold, but storing peeled apricots in the refrigerator is much less effective than an acid bath.

To peel apricots easily, drop them into boiling water for a minute or two, then lift them out with a slotted spoon and plunge them into cold water. As with tomatoes, this works because the change in temperature damages a layer of cells under the skin so the skin slips off easily.

WHAT HAPPENS WHEN YOU COOK THIS FOOD

Cooking dissolves pectin, the primary fiber in apricots, and softens the fruit. But it does not change the color or lower the vitamin A content because carotenes are impervious to the heat of normal cooking.

HOW OTHER FORMS OF PROCESSING AFFECT THIS FOOD

Drying.   Five pounds of fresh apricots produce only a pound of dried ones. Drying removes water, not nutrients; ounce for ounce, dried apricots have twelve times the iron, seven times the fiber, and five times the vitamin A of the fresh fruit. Three and a half ounces of dried apricots provide 12,700 IU vitamin A, two and a half times the full daily requirement for a healthy adult man, and 6.3 mg of iron, one-third the daily requirement for an adult woman. In some studies with laboratory amimals, dried apricots have been as effective as liver, kidneys, and eggs in treating iron-deficiency anemia.

To keep them from turning brown as they dry, apricots may be treated with sulfur dioxide. This chemical may cause serious allergic reactions, including anaphylactic shock, in people who are sensitive to sulfites.

MEDICAL USES AND/OR BENEFITS

Potassium replacement.   Apricots are a good source of potassium. Two or three medium raw apricots contain about two-thirds the amount of potassium in a cup of orange juice. Foods rich in potassium are sometimes prescribed for people taking diuretics that lower the body's level of potassium, which is excreted in urine. However, the justification for this comes from studies in which rats were given potassium citrate or potassium chloride as supplements, and there is some debate among nutritional experts as to whether potassium gluconate, the form of potassium found in apricots, is as easily absorbed by the body.

Lowering the risk of some cancers.   According to the American Cancer Society, apricots and other foods rich in the vitamin A precursor carotene may lower the risk of cancers of the larynx, esophagus and lungs.

ADVERSE EFFECTS ASSOCIATED WITH THIS FOOD

Sulfite allergies.   See *How other forms of processing affect this food,* above.

FOOD/DRUG INTERACTIONS

*   *   *

ARTICHOKES

(Globe [French] artichoke; Jerusalem artichoke [sunchoke])

NUTRITIONAL PROFILE

Energy value (calories per serving):	Low
Protein:	Moderate
Fat:	Low
Cholesterol:	None
Carbohydrates:	High
Fiber:	Low
Sodium:	Moderate to high
Major vitamin contribution:	Vitamins A and C
Major mineral contribution:	Potassium, calcium

ABOUT THE NUTRIENTS IN THIS FOOD

Globe artichokes. These thistly plants, from which we get artichoke hearts, are a good source of vitamin C and a moderately good source of calcium, iron, and vitamin A. A 3.5-ounce serving of cooked globe artichoke provides 39 mg calcium, about 33 percent of the calcium you would get from the same size serving of whole milk, plus 12 percent of the daily requirement for vitamin C (7.4 mg).

Globe artichokes also contain cynarin, a sweet-tasting chemical that is soluble in water (including the saliva in your mouth) and can sweeten the taste of anything you eat after you eat the artichoke.

Jerusalem artichokes.   Not true artichokes, these tubers are the edible roots of a plant related to the American sunflower. Jerusalem artichokes are high in starch and indigestible carbohydrates, particularly the complex sugar known as inulin, which is made up of units of fructose. As the artichoke matures, its starches turn to sugar, making the vegetable sweeter and raising its calorie count dramatically. Just after it is dug, a small Jerusalem artichoke tastes bland and starchy and provides about 7 calories; after it has been stored for a while, it tastes sweet and delivers up to 75 calories.

THE MOST NUTRITIOUS WAY TO SERVE THIS FOOD

Jerusalem artichokes can be sliced and eaten raw, but globe artichokes should always be cooked. Raw globe artichokes contain a natural chemical that makes it hard for our bodies to digest protein; the chemical is inactivated by cooking.

DIETS THAT MAY RESTRICT OR EXCLUDE THIS FOOD

Controlled-potassium diet
Low-sodium diet
Sucrose-free diet

BUYING THIS FOOD

Look for: Compact globe artichokes that feel heavy for their size. The leaves should be tightly closed. Globe artichokes are in season all year long, and the color of their leaves may vary with the season—bright green in the spring and olive green or bronze in the winter, if they have been exposed to frost. All artichokes with greenish leaves taste equally good. Yellow leaves, however, mean that an artichoke is aging; the chlorophyll in its leaves has faded, allowing the yellow carotenes underneath to show through.

Look for: Firm, clean Jerusalem artichoke tubers with no soft or bruised spots. Like globe artichokes, Jerusalem artichokes are in season all year long.

STORING THIS FOOD

Refrigerate both globe artichokes and Jerusalem artichokes. Store them in plastic bags to protect their moisture.

Cook globe artichokes and refrigerate them in a covered container if you plan to hold them longer than a day or two.

PREPARING THIS FOOD

To clean a globe artichoke, cut off the stem and trim the tough outer leaves. Then fill a large bowl or pot with cold water and plunge the artichoke into it to rinse sand off the leaves. To core a globe artichoke, turn it upside down on a cutting board and remove the core with a grapefruit knife. To prepare a Jerusalem artichoke, scrub the root with a vegetable brush, then peel and slice.

When you slice into the base of a globe artichoke or peel and slice a Jerusalem artichoke, you tear the vegetable's cell walls, releasing polyphenoloxidase, an enzyme that converts phenols in the vegetable to brown compounds that darken the heart of the globe or the flesh of the Jerusalem artichoke. You can slow the reaction (but not stop it completely) by painting the cut surface with a solution of lemon juice or vinegar and water.

WHAT HAPPENS WHEN YOU COOK THIS FOOD

Chlorophyll, the pigment that makes green vegetables green, is sensitive to acids. When you heat a globe artichoke, the chlorophyll in its green leaves will react chemically with acids in the artichoke or in the cooking water to form pheophytin, which is brown. Artichokes also contain yellow carotenes. Together, the pheophytin and the carotenes make the cooked artichoke look bronze.

You can prevent this natural chemical reaction by cooking the artichoke so quickly that there is not time for the chlorophyll to react with the acid, by cooking it in lots of water (to dilute the acids), or by cooking the artichoke with the lid off the pot so that the volatile acids can float off into the air.

When you cook a Jerusalem artichoke, the most obvious changes are in texture. In moist heat, the starch granules in the Jerusalem artichoke absorb water. Eventually the swollen granules will rupture, and the starch and nutrients inside the artichoke's cells will be much more accessible and easier to digest.

HOW OTHER KINDS OF PROCESSING AFFECT THIS FOOD

Canning.   Globe artichoke hearts packed in brine are higher in sodium than fresh artichokes. Marinated in olive oil, they are much higher in fat.

Freezing.   Frozen artichoke hearts are comparable in nutritional value to fresh ones.

MEDICAL USES AND/OR BENEFITS
*   *   *

ADVERSE EFFECTS ASSOCIATED WITH THIS FOOD

Contact dermatitis.   Globe artichokes contain essential oils that may cause contact dermatitis in sensitive people.

FOOD/DRUG INTERACTIONS

False-positive test for occult blood in the stool.   The guiac slide test for hidden blood in feces relies on alphaguaiaconic acid, a chemical that turns blue in the presence of blood. Artichokes contain peroxidase, a natural chemical that also turns alphaguaiaconic acid blue and may produce a positive test result even when there is no blood in the stool.

ASPARAGUS

NUTRITIONAL PROFILE

Energy value (calories per serving):	Low
Protein:	High
Fat:	Low
Cholesterol:	None
Carbohydrates:	Moderate
Fiber:	Low
Sodium:	Low
Major vitamin contribution:	Vitamins A, B, C
Major mineral contribution:	Potassium, iron

ABOUT THE NUTRIENTS IN THIS FOOD

Green asparagus has some protein, a trace of fat, and a moderate amount of sugar, but no starch. It is a good source of vitamin A, vitamin C, and the B vitamins, including folic acid. One 3.5-ounce serving of fresh boiled asparagus provides 50 percent of the vitamin C, 17 percent of the vitamin A, and 15 percent or more of the riboflavin, thiamin, and niacin a healthy adult needs each day.

THE MOST NUTRITIOUS WAY TO SERVE THIS FOOD

Fresh, boiled and drained. Canned asparagus may have less than half the nutrients found in freshly cooked spears.

DIETS THAT MAY RESTRICT OR EXCLUDE THIS FOOD
Low-sodium diet (canned asparagus)
Sucrose-free diet

BUYING THIS FOOD
Look for: Bright green stalks. The tips should be purplish and tightly closed; the stalks should be firm. Asparagus is in season from March through August.

Avoid: Wilted stalks and asparagus whose buds have opened.

STORING THIS FOOD
Store fresh asparagus in the refrigerator. To keep it as crisp as possible, wrap it in a damp paper towel and then put the whole package into a plastic bag. Keeping asparagus cool helps it hold onto its vitamins. At 32° F, asparagus will retain all its folic acid for at least two weeks and nearly 80 % of its vitamin C for up to five days; at room temperature, it would lose up to 75 percent of its folic acid in three days and 50 percent of the vitamin C in twentyfour hours.

PREPARING THIS FOOD
The white part of the fresh green-asparagus stalk is woody and tasteless, so you can bend the stalk and snap it right at the line where the green begins to turn white. If the skin is very thick, peel it, but save the parings for soup stock.

WHAT HAPPENS WHEN YOU COOK THIS FOOD
Chlorophyll, the pigment that makes green vegetables green, is sensitive to acids. When you heat asparagus, its chlorophyll will react chemically with acids in the asparagus or in the cooking water to form pheophytin, which is brown. As a result, cooked asparagus is olive-drab.

You can prevent this chemical reaction by cooking the asparagus so quickly that there is no time for the chlorophyll to react with acids, or by cooking it in lots of water (which will dilute the acids), or by leaving the lid off the pot so that the volatile acids can float off into the air.

Cooking also changes the texture of asparagus: water escapes from its cells and they collapse. Adding salt to the cooking liquid slows the loss of moisture.

HOW OTHER FORMS OF PROCESSING AFFECT THIS FOOD
Canning.   The intense heat of canning makes asparagus soft, robs it of its

bright green color, and reduces the vitamin A, B, and C content by at least half. (White asparagus, which is bleached to remove the green color, contains about 5 percent of the vitamin A in fresh asparagus.) With its liquid, canned asparagus, green or white, contains about 90 times the sodium in fresh asparagus (348 mg in 3.5 oz. canned against 4 mg in 3.5 oz. fresh boiled asparagus).

MEDICAL USES AND/OR BENEFITS
*   *   *

ADVERSE EFFECTS ASSOCIATED WITH THIS FOOD
Odorous urine.   After eating asparagus, we all excrete a smelly waste product, the sulfur compound methyl mercaptan, in our urine.

FOOD/DRUG INTERACTIONS
Anticoagulants. Asparagus is high in vitamin K, a vitamin manufactured naturally by bacteria in our intestines, an adequate supply of which enables blood to clot normally. Eating foods that contain this vitamin may interfere with the effectiveness of anticoagulants such as heparin and warfarin (Coumadin, Dicumarol, Panwarfin) whose job is to thin blood and dissolve clots.

AVOCADOS

NUTRITIONAL PROFILE

Energy value
(calories per serving): Moderate

Protein: Low

Fat: High

Cholesterol: None

Carbohydrates: Moderate

Fiber: High

Sodium: Low

Major vitamin
contribution: Vitamins A and C

Major mineral
contribution: Potassium

ABOUT THE NUTRIENTS IN THIS FOOD

The calories in avocados are supplied mostly by fat, which accounts for about 16 percent of the weight of the fruit and is 71 percent monounsaturated and 13 percent polyunsaturated fatty acids. The sugar content of an avocado decreases as it ripens; immature avocados taste sweeter than ripe ones. Avocados are a good source of vitamin C; a 3.5-ounce portion provides 7.9 mg, 13 percent of the daily requirement for a healthy adult.

DIETS THAT MAY EXCLUDE OR RESTRICT THIS FOOD

Controlled-potassium diet
Low-fat diet
Sucrose-free diet

BUYING THIS FOOD

Look for: Fruit that feels heavy for its size. The California Hess is pear-shaped, with a thick bumpy skin that ranges in color from dark green to purple/black. Its flesh is oily and buttery in taste. The Florida avocado, also called alligator pear, has smooth bright green skin. Its flesh is sweeter and more watery than the Hess. Both are ripe if the fruit feels soft when pressed with the thumb. To test with minimum damage to the fruit, press at the stem end, not in the middle.

Avoid: Avocados with soft dark spots on the skin that indicate damage underneath.

STORING THIS FOOD

Store hard, unripened avocados in a warm place; a bowl on top of the refrigerator will do. Avocados are shipped before they ripen, when the flesh is hard enough to resist bruising in transit, but they ripen off the tree and will soften nicely at home.

Store soft, ripe avocados in the refrigerator to slow the natural enzyme action that turns their flesh brown as they mature even when the fruit has not been cut.

PREPARING THIS FOOD

When you peel or slice an avocado, you tear its cell walls, releasing polyphenoloxidase, an enzyme that converts phenols in the avocado to brownish compounds that darken the avocado's naturally pale green flesh. You can slow this reaction (but not stop it completely) by brushing the exposed surface of the avocado with an acid (lemon juice or vinegar). To store a cut avocado, brush it with lemon juice or vinegar, wrap it tightly in plastic, and keep it in the refrigerator—where it will eventually turn brown. Or you can store the avocado as guacamole; mixing it with lemon juice, tomatoes, onions, and mayonnaise (all of which are acid) is an efficient way to protect the color of the fruit.

WHAT HAPPENS WHEN YOU COOK THIS FOOD

*   *   *

HOW OTHER KINDS OF PROCESSING AFFECT THIS FOOD

*   *   *

MEDICAL USES AND/OR BENEFITS

*   *   *

ADVERSE EFFECTS ASSOCIATED WITH THIS FOOD
*   *   *

FOOD/DRUG INTERACTIONS

MAO inhibitors.   Monoamine oxidase (MAO) inhibitors are drugs used as antidepressants or antihypertensives. They inhibit the action of enzymes that break down the amino acid tyramine so it can be eliminated from the body. Tyramine is a pressor amine, a chemical that constricts blood vessels and raises blood pressure. If you eat a food such as avocado that contains tyramine while you are taking an MAO inhibitor you cannot eliminate the pressor amine, and the result may be abnormally high blood pressure or a hypertensive crisis (sustained elevated blood pressure).

False-positive test for tumors.   Carcinoid tumors (which may arise from tissues in the endocrine system, the intestines, or the lungs) secrete serotonin, a natural chemical that makes blood vessels expand or contract. Because serotonin is excreted in urine, these tumors are diagnosed by measuring the levels of serotonin by-products in the urine. Avocados contain large amounts of serotonin; eating them in the three days before a test for an endocrine tumor might produce a false-positive result, suggesting that you have the tumor when in fact you don't. (Other foods high in serotonin are bananas, eggplant, pineapples, plums, tomatoes, and walnuts.)

BANANAS
(Plantains)

NUTRITIONAL PROFILE

Energy value (calories per serving):	Moderate
Protein:	Low
Fat:	Low
Cholesterol:	None
Carbohydrates:	High
Fiber:	Low
Sodium:	Low
Major vitamin contribution:	B vitamins and vitamin C
Major mineral contribution:	Potassium, magnesium

ABOUT THE NUTRIENTS IN THIS FOOD

A banana begins life with more starch than sugar, but as the fruit ripens its starches turn sugar, which is why ripe bananas taste so much better than unripe ones.* The color of a banana's skin is a fair guide to its starch/sugar ratio. When the skin is yellow-green, 40 percent of its carbohydrates are starch; when the skin is fully yellow and the banana is ripe, only 8 percent of the carbohydrates are still starch. The rest (91 percent) have broken down into sugars—glucose, fructose, sucrose, the most plentiful sugar in the fruit. Its high sugar content makes the banana, in its self-contained packet, a handy energy source.

*They are also more healthful. Green bananas contain proteins that inhibit amylase, an enzyme that makes it possible for us to digest complex carbohydrates.

Bananas are a fair source of riboflavin and niacin, a moderate source of vitamin C, and a good source of vitamin B_6, potassium, and magnesium. They are low in sodium. They also contain small quantities of the indigestible food fibers cellulose, hemicellulose, and lignin and moderate amounts of pectin, the food fiber that may prevent the absorption of fats and help lower blood levels of cholesterol.

Plantains are a variety of banana. Unlike "eating" bananas, their starches do not turn to sugar as they mature. They remain a starchy food that must be cooked before being eaten. Plantains can be a good source of vitamin A; the amount of the vitamin depends on the color of the fruit—the yellower the plantain, the more vitamin A it contains. A deep-yellow plantain may provides approximately 1200 IU vitamin A in a 3.5-ounce serving, a pale-white one only 10 IU.

THE MOST NUTRITIOUS WAY TO SERVE THIS FOOD

Fresh and ripe. Green bananas contain antinutrients, proteins that inhibit the actions of amylase, an enzyme that makes it possible for us to digest starch and other complex carbohydrates. Raw bananas are richer in potassium than cooked bananas; heating depletes potassium.

Plantains must be cooked before serving.

DIETS THAT MAY RESTRICT OR EXCLUDE THIS FOOD

Controlled-potassium diet
Sucrose-free diet

BUYING THIS FOOD

Look for: Bananas that will be good when you plan to eat them. Bananas with brown specks on the skin are ripe enough to eat immediately. Bananas with creamy yellow skin will be ready in a day or two. Bananas with mostly yellow skin and a touch of green at either end can be ripened at home and used in two or three days.

Look for: Plantains that are large and firm, with green peel that may be flecked with some brown spots. As the plantain ripens, its skin turns black.

Avoid: Overripe bananas whose skin has turned brown or split open. A grayish-yellow skin means that the fruit has been damaged by cold storage. Plantains and bananas with soft spots under the skin may be rotten.

STORING THIS FOOD

Store bananas that aren't fully ripe at room temperature for a day or two.

Like avocados, bananas are picked green, shipped hard to protect them from damage en route and then sprayed with ethylene gas to ripen them quickly. Untreated bananas release ethylene naturally to ripen the fruit and turn its starches to sugar, but natural ripening takes time. Artificial ripening happens so quickly that there is no time for the starches to turn into sugar. The bananas look ripe but they may taste bland and starchy. A few days at room temperature will give the starches a chance to change into sugars.

Store ripe bananas in the refrigerator. The cold air will slow (but not stop) the natural enzyme action that ripens and eventually rots the fruit if you leave it at room temperature. Cold storage will darken the banana's skin, since the chill damages cells in the peel and releases polyphenoloxidase, an enzyme that converts phenols in the banana peel to dark brown compounds. The fruit inside will remain pale and tasty for several days.

PREPARING THIS FOOD

Do not slice or peel bananas or plantains until you are ready to use them. When you cut into the fruit, you tear its cell walls, releasing polyphenoloxidase, an enzyme that hastens the oxidation of phenols in the banana or plantain, producing brown pigments that darken the fruit. (Chilling a banana produces the same reaction because the cold damages cells in the banana peel.) You can slow the browning (but not stop it completely) by dipping raw sliced or peeled bananas into a solution of lemon juice or vinegar and water or by mixing the slices with citrus fruits in a fruit salad. Overripe, discolored bananas can be used in baking, where the color doesn't matter and their intense sweetness is an asset.

When you are ready to cook a plantain, cut off the ends, then slice down through the peel and remove the peel in strips. Do this under running water to keep the plantain from staining your hands.

WHAT HAPPENS WHEN YOU COOK THIS FOOD

When bananas are broiled or fried, they are cooked so quickly that there is very little change in color or texture. Even so, they will probably taste sweeter and have a more intense aroma then uncooked bananas. Heat liberates the volatile molecules that make the fruit taste and smell good.

When you cook a plantain, which is very high in starch, the starch granules in its flesh will absorb water, swell, and rupture so that the fruit softens and its nutrients become more available.

HOW OTHER KINDS OF PROCESSING AFFECT THIS FOOD

Drying. Drying removes water and concentrates the nutrients and calories in bananas. Bananas may be treated with compounds such sulfur dioxide to inhibit polyphenoloxidase and keep the bananas from browning as they dry. People who are sensitive to sulfites may suffer severe allergic reactions, including anaphylactic shock, if they eat these treated bananas.

Freezing.   Fresh bananas freeze well but will brown if you try to thaw them at room temperature. To protect the creamy color, thaw frozen bananas in the refrigerator and use as quickly as possible.

MEDICAL USES AND/OR BENEFITS

Potassium replacement.   Bananas and plantains are a good source of potassium. Ounce for ounce, they have nearly twice the potassium of orange juice. Foods rich in potassium are sometimes prescribed for people taking diuretics and losing potassium. However, there is some question as to whether potassium gluconate, the form of potassium found in fruits, is as easily absorbed by the body as potassium citrate or potassium chloride, the potassium given to laboratory animals in the experiments that confirmed the value of potassium supplements for people on diuretic therapy.

ADVERSE EFFECTS ASSOCIATED WITH THIS FOOD
*   *   *

FOOD/DRUG INTERACTIONS

MAO inhibitors.   Monoamine oxidase (MAO) inhibitors are drugs used as antidepressants or antihypertensives. They inhibit the action of enzymes that break down the amino acid tyramine so it can be eliminated from the body. Tyramine is a pressor amine, a chemical that constricts blood vessels and raises blood pressure. If you eat a food that contains tyramine while you are taking an MAO inhibitor you cannot eliminate the pressor amine, and the result may be abnormally high blood pressure or a hypertensive crisis (sustained elevated blood pressure). There have been some reports of such a reaction in people who ate rotten bananas or bananas stewed with the peel.

False-positive test for tumors.   Carcinoid tumors—which may arise from tissues of the endocrine system, the intestines, or the lungs—secrete serotonin, a natural chemical that makes blood vessels expand or contract. Because serotonin is excreted in urine, these tumors are diagnosed by measuring the levels of serotonin by-products in the urine. Bananas contain large amounts of serotonin; eating them in the three days before a test for an endocrine tumor might produce a false-positive result, suggesting that you have the tumor when in fact you don't. (Other foods high in serotonin are avocados, eggplant, pineapple, plums, tomatoes, and walnuts.)

BARLEY

Energy value (calories per serving):	Moderate
Protein:	Moderate
Fat:	Low
Cholesterol:	None
Carbohydrates:	High
Fiber:	Low
Sodium:	Low
Major vitamin contribution:	B vitamins
Major mineral contribution:	Iron, potassium

ABOUT THE NUTRIENTS IN THIS FOOD

Barley contains some proteins, a little fat, and a lot of complex carbohydrates (starch and food fibers). It is rich in the soluble food fiber, pectin. Its proteins are considered "incomplete" because they are deficient in lysine, and two of its important nutrients, iron and calcium, are largely unavailable because barley, like other grains, contains phytic acid—which binds the minerals into insoluble, indigestible compounds. (This presents no problem so long as your diet includes sufficient amounts of calcium and iron from other foods.)

Barley is a good source of B vitamins, potassium, phosphorus, and magnesium.

THE MOST NUTRITIOUS WAY TO SERVE THIS FOOD

With a calcium-rich food and with a food such as legumes or meat, milk, or eggs that supplies the lysine barley is missing.

*Values are for pearled barley.

DIETS THAT MAY RESTRICT OR EXCLUDE THIS FOOD
Gluten-free diet

BUYING THIS FOOD
Look for: Clean, tightly sealed boxes or plastic bags. Stains indicate that something has spilled on the box and may have seeped through to contaminate the grain inside.

STORING THIS FOOD
Store barley in air- and moistureproof containers in a cool, dark, dry cabinet. Well-protected, it will keep for several months with no loss of nutrients.

PREPARING THIS FOOD
Pick over the barley and discard any damaged or darkened grains.

WHAT HAPPENS WHEN YOU COOK THIS FOOD
Starch consists of molecules of the complex carbohydrates amylose and amylopectin packed into a starch granule. When you cook barley in water, its starch granules absorb water molecules, swell, and soften. When the temperature of the liquid reaches approximately 140° F, the amylose and amylopectin molecules inside the granules relax and unfold, breaking some of their internal bonds (bonds between atoms on the same molecule) and forming new bonds between atoms on different molecules. The result is a network that traps and holds water molecules. The starch granules swell and the barley becomes soft and bulky. If you continue to cook the barley, the starch granules will rupture, releasing some of the amylose and amylopectin molecules inside. These molecules will attract and immobilize some of the water molecules in the liquid, which is why a little barely added to a soup or stew will make the soup or stew thicker.

The B vitamins in barley are water-soluble. You can save them by serving the barley with the liquid in which it was cooked.

HOW OTHER FORMS OF PROCESSING AFFECT THIS FOOD
Pearling.   Pearled barley is barley from which the outer layer has been removed. Milling, the process by which barley is turned into flour, also removes the outer coating (bran) of the grain. Since most of the B vitamins and fiber are concentrated in the bran, both pearled and milled barley are lower in nutrients and fiber than whole barley.

Malting.   After barley is harvested, the grain may be left to germinate, a natural chemical process during which complex carbohydrates in the grain (starches and beta-glucans) change into sugar. The grain, now called *malted barley,* is used as the base for several fermented and distilled alcohol beverages, including beer and whiskey.

MEDICAL USES AND/OR BENEFITS

To reduce the levels of serum cholesterol.   Recent research suggests that foods rich in pectin may help slow the absorption of fats from the digestive tract, thus lowering blood levels of cholesterol. At the University of Wisconsin, researchers have isolated two compounds in barley that appear to lower cholesterol production in laboratory chicks. Because these compounds are found in the bran (the outer layer of the barley kernel), pearled barley may not provide the protection offered by whole barley (also known as *blocked barley*) or whole barley flour that contains most of the seed coating.

ADVERSE EFFECTS ASSOCIATED WITH THIS FOOD

*   *   *

FOOD/DRUG INTERACTIONS

*   *   *

BEAN CURD (TOFU)

NUTRITIONAL PROFILE

Energy value (calories per serving):	Moderate
Protein:	High
Fat:	Moderate
Cholesterol:	None
Carbohydrates:	Low
Fiber:	Low
Sodium:	Low
Major vitamin contribution:	B vitamins
Major mineral contribution:	Calcium, iron

ABOUT THE NUTRIENTS IN THIS FOOD

Bean curd is made by boiling soybeans with water, grinding the beans into a paste, and adding calcium sulfate that coagulates the curd and makes the bean curd a richer source of calcium than plain soybeans. (Japanese and Chinese bean curd is made without calcium sulfate; that curd is coagulated with an acid—lemon juice or vinegar.)

Bean curd supplies complete proteins which are 90 percent digestible, a figure approaching that of milk. The iron in bean curd is three times more available than the iron in whole soybeans, which are high in iron but whose iron is in a form not easily assimilated by our bodies (see SOYBEANS).

THE MOST NUTRITIOUS WAY TO SERVE THIS FOOD

Cooked. Uncooked soybean curd may harbor bacteria that can cause food poisoning.

DIETS THAT MAY RESTRICT OR EXCLUDE THIS FOOD

Controlled-protein diet (for patients with kidney disease)

BUYING THIS FOOD

Look for: Clean, covered blocks of fresh bean curd, submerged in clean water and stored in a refrigerated dairy case. Soybean curd is perishable, a moist, protein-rich food that provides a perfect medium for bacterial growth. Check the date on packages of prepacked curd.

Avoid: Unrefrigerated fresh curd or bean curd stored in a produce case (the case may not be cold enough to protect it); bean curd with a rind (which only develops when the curd is left uncovered); or bean curd whose surface is not pure, creamy white (any bright orange, yellow, blue, or green spots are almost certainly mold).

STORING THIS FOOD

Cover fresh bean curd with clean water and store it in the refrigerator. Change the water daily, using two clean spoons rather than your hands to lift the curd. Discard any moldy curd immediately (throw out the whole block, not just the moldy spot). Use fresh curd within a few days; prepacked curd should be used as indicated by the date on the bag.

PREPARING THIS FOOD

Rinse the curd and slice or cut into cubes.

WHAT HAPPENS WHEN YOU COOK THIS FOOD

Heating the soybean curd evaporates its moisture and coagulates its proteins, making the curd more dense and chewy. It also makes the bean curd safer because cooking kills microorganisms on the curd.

HOW OTHER KINDS OF PROCESSING AFFECT THIS FOOD

Freezing. Bean curd-based frozen desserts have as much fat and calories as ice creams or frozen yogurt, but their fats are primarily unsaturated and there is no cholesterol in bean curd. And, because there is no lactose in bean curd, these desserts are used as an ice cream substitute for people who cannot digest the sugar in milk.

MEDICAL USES AND/OR BENEFITS

*   *   *

ADVERSE EFFECTS ASSOCIATED WITH THIS FOOD

*   *   *

FOOD/DRUG INTERACTIONS

MAO inhibitors. Monoamine oxidase (MAO) inhibitors are drugs used as antidepressants or antihypertensives. They inhibit the action of enzymes that break down the amino acid tyramine so it can be eliminated from the body. Tyramine is a pressor amine, a chemical that constricts blood vessels and raises blood pressure. If you eat a food that contains tyramine while you are taking an MAO inhibitor you cannot eliminate the pressor amine, and the result may be abnormally high blood pressure or a hypertensive crisis (sustained elevated blood pressure). Fermented bean curd contains tyramine.

BEAN SPROUTS

See also BEANS

NUTRITIONAL PROFILE

Energy value (calories per serving):	Low
Protein:	High
Fat:	Low
Cholesterol:	None
Carbohydrates:	High
Fiber:	High
Sodium:	Low
Major vitamin contribution:	B vitamins, vitamin C
Major mineral contribution:	Iron, potassium

ABOUT THE NUTRIENTS IN THIS FOOD

As beans sprout they convert stored starches and sugars into energy needed to produce the green sprout. As a result, sprouts have less carbohydrate than beans do. They have three to five times more vitamin C than the beans from which they grew but less protein, less iron, less vitamin A, and less B vitamins.

Raw beans contain anti-nutrient chemicals that inhibit the enzymes we use to digest proteins and starches; hemagglutinens (substances that make red blood cells clump together); and "factors" that may inactivate vitamin A. These chemicals are usually destroyed when the beans are heated. Sprouted beans served *with* the bean should be cooked before serving.

THE MOST NUTRITIOUS WAY TO SERVE THIS FOOD

Fresh (the sprouts alone) or steamed (sprouted beans).

DIETS THAT MAY RESTRICT OR EXCLUDE THIS FOOD

Low-fiber, low-residue diet
Sucrose-free diet

BUYING THIS FOOD

Look for: Fresh, crisp sprouts. The tips should be moist and tender. (The shorter the sprout, the more tender it will be.) It is sometimes difficult to judge bean sprouts packed in plastic bags, but you can see through to tell if the tip of the sprout looks fresh. Sprouts sold from water-filled bowls should be refrigerated, protected from dirt and debris, and served with a spoon or tongs, *not scooped up by hand.*

Avoid: Mushy sprouts (they may be decayed) and soft ones (they have lost moisture and vitamin C).

STORING THIS FOOD

Refrigerate sprouts in a plastic bag to keep them moist and crisp. If you bought them in a plastic bag, take them out and repack them in bags large enough that they do not crush each other. To get the most vitamin C, use the sprouts within a few days.

PREPARING THIS FOOD

Rinse the sprouts thoroughly under cold running water to get rid of dirt and sand. Discard any soft or browned sprouts, then cut off the roots and add the sprouts to a salad or use as a garnish.

Do not tear or cut the sprouts until you are ready to use them. When you slice into the sprouts, you tear cells, releasing enzymes that begin to destroy vitamin C.

WHAT HAPPENS WHEN YOU COOK THIS FOOD

Cooking destroys some of the heat-sensitive vitamin C in sprouts. To save it, steam the sprouts quickly, stir-fry them, or add them uncooked just before you serve the dish.

HOW OTHER KINDS OF PROCESSING AFFECT THIS FOOD

Canning. Vitamin C is heat-sensitive, and heating the sprouts during the canning process reduces their vitamin C content.

MEDICAL USES AND/OR BENEFITS
*   *   *

ADVERSE EFFECTS ASSOCIATED WITH THIS FOOD
*   *   *

FOOD/DRUG INTERACTIONS
*   *   *

BEANS

(Black beans, chickpeas, kidney beans, navy beans, white beans)

See also BEAN CURD, BEAN SPROUTS

NUTRITIONAL PROFILE

Energy value (calories per serving):	Moderate
Protein:	High
Fat:	Low
Cholesterol:	None
Carbohydrates:	High
Fiber:	High
Sodium:	Low
Major vitamin contribution:	Vitamin B_6, folacin
Major mineral contribution:	Iron, magnesium, zinc

ABOUT THE NUTRIENTS IN THIS FOOD

Beans are seeds. Their thin outer covering is an excellent source of cellulose and the noncarbohydrate food fiber lignin, and their interior is rich in carbohydrates: pectins, gums, starch, and sugars (including the indigestible complex sugars raffinose and stachyose, which make beans "gassy" when they are fermented by bacteria in the human gut). Beans have no cholesterol and very little fat. Up to 25 percent of the calories in beans come from their proteins, which are considered "incomplete" because they are deficient in the essential amino acids methionine and cystine.*

---

*Soybeans are the only beans that contain proteins considered "complete" because they contain sufficient amounts of all the essential amino acids.

All beans are a good source of B vitamins, particularly vitamin B_6. A single half-cup serving of cooked dried beans can provide about one-fourth of an adult's daily requirement of this vitamin. Dried beans are also a good source of folacin.

Beans contain non-heme iron, the inorganic iron found in plant foods, but (like grains) beans contain phytic acid that binds their calcium and iron into insoluble, indigestible compounds. You can improve the availability of the iron in beans by eating them with meat or with a food rich in vitamin C.

Raw beans also contain antinutrient chemicals that inhibit those enzymes that make it possible for your body to digest proteins and starches and factors that inactivate vitamin A; and hemagglutinens (chemicals that make red blood cells clump together). These antinutrients are often inactivated by cooking the beans.

THE MOST NUTRITIOUS WAY TO SERVE THIS FOOD

With grains. The proteins in grains are deficient in the essential amino acids lysine and isoleucine but contain sufficient tryptophan, methionine, and cystine; the proteins in beans are exactly the opposite. Together, these foods provide "complete" proteins.

With an iron-rich food (meat) or with a vitamin C-rich food (tomatoes). Both enhance your body's ability to use the iron in the beans. The meat makes your stomach more acid (acid favors iron aborption); the vitamin C may convert the ferric iron in beans into ferrous iron, which is more easily absorbed by the body.

DIETS THAT MAY RESTRICT OR EXCLUDE THIS FOOD

Low-calcium diet
Low-fiber diet
Low-purine (antigout) diet
Sucrose-free diet

BUYING THIS FOOD

Look for: Smooth-skinned, uniformly sized, evenly colored beans that are free of stones and debris. The good news about beans sold in plastic bags is that the transparent material gives you a chance to see the beans inside; the bad news is that pyridoxine and pyridoxal, the natural forms of vitamin B_6, are very sensitive to light.

Avoid: Beans sold in bulk. The open bins expose the beans to air and light and may allow insect contamination (tiny holes in the beans indicate that an insect has burrowed into or through the bean).

STORING THIS FOOD

Store beans in air- and moistureproof containers in a cool, dark cabinet where they are protected from heat, light, and insects.

PREPARING THIS FOOD

Wash dried beans and pick them over carefully, discarding damaged or withered beans and any that float. (Only withered beans are light enough to float in water.)

Cover the beans with water, bring them to a boil, and then set them aside to soak. When you are ready to use the beans, discard the water in which beans have been soaked. Some of the indigestible sugars in the beans that cause intestinal gas when you eat the beans will leach out into the water, making the beans less "gassy."

WHAT HAPPENS WHEN YOU COOK THIS FOOD

When beans are cooked in liquid, their cells absorb water, swell, and eventually rupture, releasing the pectins and gums and nutrients inside. In addition, cooking destroys antinutrients in beans, making them more nutritious and safe to eat.

HOW OTHER KINDS OF PROCESSING AFFECT THIS FOOD

Canning.   The heat of canning destroys some of the B vitamins in the beans. Vitamin B is water-soluble. You can recover all the lost B vitamins simply by using the liquid in the can, but the liquid also contains the indigestible sugars that cause intestinal gas when you eat beans.

Preprocessing.   Preprocessed dried beans have already been soaked. They take less time to cook but are lower in B vitamins.

MEDICAL USES AND/OR BENEFITS

To reduce the levels of serum cholesterol.   The gums and pectins in dried beans and peas appear to lower blood levels of cholesterol. Currently there are two theories to explain how this may happen. The first theory is that the pectins in the beans form a gel in your stomach that sops up fats and keeps them from being absorbed by your body. The second is that bacteria in the gut feed on the bean fiber, producing short-chain fatty acids that inhibit the production of cholesterol in your liver.

As a source of carbohydrates for people with diabetes.   Beans are digested very slowly, producing only a gradual rise in blood-sugar levels. As a result, the body needs less insulin to control blood sugar after eating beans than after eating some other high-carbohydrate foods (such as bread or potato). In studies at the University of Kentucky, a bean, whole-grain, vegetable, and fruit-rich diet developed at the University of Toronto enabled patients with Type I diabetes (who do not produce any insulin themselves) to cut their daily insulin intake by 38 percent. Patients with Type II diabetes (who can produce some insulin) were able to reduce their insulin injections by 98 percent. This diet is in line with the nutritional guidelines of the American Diabetes Association, but people with diabetes should always consult with their doctors and/or dietitians before altering their diet.

As a diet aid. Although beans are high in calories, they are also high in fiber; even a small serving can make you feel full. And, because they are insulin-sparing, they delay the rise in insulin levels that makes us feel hungry again soon after eating. Research at the University of Toronto suggests the insulin-sparing effect may last for several hours after you eat the beans, perhaps until after the next meal.

ADVERSE EFFECTS ASSOCIATED WITH THIS FOOD

Intestinal gas. All legumes (beans and peas) contain raffinose and stachyose, complex sugars that human beings cannot digest. The sugars sit in the gut and are fermented by intestinal bacteria which then produce gas that distends the intestines and makes us uncomfortable. You can lessen this effect by covering the beans with water, bringing them to a boil for three to five minutes, and then setting them aside to soak for four to six hours so that the indigestible sugars leach out in the soaking water, which can be discarded. Alternatively, you may soak the beans for four hours in 9 cups of water for every cup of beans, discard the soaking water, and add new water as your recipe directs. Then cook the beans; drain them before serving.

Production of uric acid. Purines are the natural metabolic by-products of protein metabolism in the body. They eventually break down into uric acid, sharp crystals that may concentrate in joints, a condition known as gout. If uric acid crystals collect in the urine, the result may be kidney stones. Eating dried beans, which are rich in proteins, may raise the concentration of purines in your body. Although controlling the amount of purines in the diet does not significantly affect the course of gout (which is treated with allopurinol, a drug that prevents the formation of uric acid crystals), limiting these foods is still part of many gout regimens.

FOOD/DRUG INTERACTIONS

*   *   *

BEEF

NUTRITIONAL PROFILE*

Energy value (calories per serving):	Moderate
Protein:	High
Fat:	Moderate
Cholesterol:	Moderate
Carbohydrates:	None
Fiber:	None
Sodium:	Low
Major vitamin contribution:	Vitamin B_{12}, riboflavin, niacin, vitamin B_6
Major mineral contribution:	Iron, phosphorus, zinc

ABOUT THE NUTRIENTS IN THIS FOOD

Like other animal foods, beef provides "complete" proteins that supply all the essential amino acids. Beef fat contains proportionally more saturated fatty acids than pork fat, but less than lamb fat and slightly less cholesterol than an equal amount of chicken fat. There is no food fiber in beef and no carbohydrates other than the small amounts of glycogen (sugar) stored in the animal's muscles and liver.

Beef is an excellent source of B vitamins, including niacin, vitamin B_6, and vitamin B_{12}, which is found only in animal foods. Lean beef provides heme iron, the organic iron that is about five times more useful to the body than non-heme iron, the inorganic form of iron found in plant foods. Beef is also an excellent source of zinc.

*These values apply to lean, cooked beef.

THE MOST NUTRITIOUS WAY TO SERVE THIS FOOD

With a food rich in vitamin C. Ascorbic acid increases the absorption of iron from meat.

DIETS THAT MAY RESTRICT OR EXCLUDE THIS FOOD

Controlled-fat, low-cholesterol diet
Low-protein diet (for some forms of kidney disease)

BUYING THIS FOOD

Look for: Fresh, red beef. The fat should be white, not yellow.

Choose lean cuts of beef with as little internal marbling (streaks of fat) as possible. The leanest cuts are flank steak and round steak; rib steaks, brisket, and chuck have the most fat. USDA grading, which is determined by the maturity of the animal and marbling in meat, is also a guide to fat content. U.S. prime has more marbling than U.S. choice, which has more marbling than U.S. good. All are equally nutritious; the difference is how tender they are, which depends on how much fat is present.

Choose the cut of meat that is right for your recipe. Generally, the cuts from the center of the animal's back—the rib, the T-bone, the porterhouse steaks—are the most tender. They can be cooked by dry heat—broiling, roasting, pan-frying. Cuts from around the legs, the underbelly, and the neck—the shank, the brisket, the round—contain muscles used for movement. They must be tenderized by stewing or boiling, the long, moist cooking methods that break down the connective tissue that makes meat tough.

STORING THIS FOOD

Refrigerate raw beef immediately, carefully wrapped to prevent its drippings from contaminating other foods. Refrigeration prolongs the freshness of beef by slowing the natural multiplication of bacteria on the meat surface. Unchecked, these bacteria will convert proteins and other substances on the surface of the meat to a slimy film and change meat's sulfur-containing amino acids methionine and cystine into smelly chemicals called mercaptans. When the mercaptans combine with myoglobin, they produce the greenish pigment that gives spoiled meat its characteristic unpleasant appearance.

Fresh ground beef, with many surfaces where bacteria can live, should be used within 24 to 48 hours. Other cuts of beef will stay fresh in the refrigerator for three to five days.

PREPARING THIS FOOD

Trim the beef carefully. By judiciously cutting away all visible fat you can significantly reduce the amount of fat and cholesterol in each serving.

WHAT HAPPENS WHEN YOU COOK THIS FOOD

Cooking changes the appearance and flavor of beef, alters its nutritional value, makes it safer, and extends its shelf life.

Browning meat before you cook it does not "seal in the juices," but it does change the flavor by caramelizing proteins and sugars on the surface. Because beef's only sugars are the small amounts of glycogen in the muscles, we add sugars in marinades or basting liquids that may also contain acids (vinegar, lemon juice, wine) to break down muscle fibers and tenderize the meat. (Browning has one minor nutritional drawback. It breaks amino acids on the surface of the meat into smaller compounds that are no longer useful proteins.)

When beef is cooked, it loses water and shrinks. Its pigments, which combine with oxygen, are denatured (broken into fragments) by the heat and turn brown, the natural color of well-done meat.

At the same time, the fats in the beef are oxidized. Oxidized fats, whether formed in cooking or when the cooked meat is stored in the refrigerator, give cooked meat a characteristic warmed-over flavor. Cooking and storing meat under a blanket of antioxidants—catsup or a gravy made of tomatoes, peppers, and other vitamin-C-rich vegetables—reduces the oxidation of fats and the intensity of warmed-over flavor. Meat reheated in a microwave oven also has less warmed-over flavor.

An obvious nutritional benefit of cooking is the fact that heat lowers the fat content of beef by liquifying the fat so it can run off the meat. One concrete example of how well this works comes from a comparision of the fat content in regular and extra-lean ground beef. According to research at the University of Missouri in 1985, both kinds of beef lose mass when cooked, but the lean beef loses water and the regular beef loses fat and cholesterol. Thus, while regular raw ground beef has about three times as much fat (by weight) as raw ground extra-lean beef, their fat varies by only 5 percent after broiling.

Finally, cooking makes beef safer by killing *Salmonella* and other organisms in the meat. As a result, cooking also serves as a natural preservative. According to the USDA, fresh beef can be refrigerated for two or three days, then cooked and held safely for another day or two because the heat of cooking has reduced the number of bacteria on the surface of the meat and temporarily interrupted the natural cycle of deterioration.

HOW OTHER KINDS OF PROCESSING AFFECT THIS FOOD

Aging. Hanging fresh meat exposed to the air, in a refrigerated room, reduces the moisture content and shrinks the meat slightly. As the meat ages enzymes break down muscle proteins, "tenderizing" the beef.

Canning.   Canned beef does not develop a warmed-over flavor because the high temperatures used in canning food and the long cooking process alter proteins in the meat so that they act as antioxidants. Once the can is open, however, the meat should be protected from oxygen that will change the flavor of the beef.

Curing.   Salt-curing preserves meat through osmosis, the physical reaction in which liquids flow across a membrane, such as the wall of a cell, from a less dense to a more dense solution. The salt or sugar used in curing dissolves in the liquid on the surface of the meat to make a solution that is more dense than the liquid inside the cells of the meat. Water flows out of the meat and out of the cells of any microorganisms living on the meat, killing the microorganisms and protecting the meat from bacterial damage. Salt-cured meat is much higher in sodium than fresh meat.

Freezing.   Home-frozen beef is sometimes dryer when thawed than fresh beef is.* It may also be lower in B vitamins. When you freeze beef, the water inside its cells freezes into sharp ice crystals that can puncture cell membranes. When the beef thaws, moisture (and some of the B vitamins) will leak out through these torn cell walls. The loss of moisture is irreversible, but some of the vitamins can be saved by using the drippings when the meat is cooked. Freezing may also cause freezer burn—dry spots left when moisture evaporates from the surface of the meat. Waxed freezer paper is designed specifically to hold the moisture in meat; plastic wrap and aluminum foil are less effective.

Irradiation.   Irradiation kills microorganisms and may extend the meat's shelf life for several weeks. However, it does change the flavor and may alter the chemical structure of some of the fats in the meat, with consequences not yet fully understood.

Smoking.   Hanging cured or salted meat over an open fire slowly dries the meat, kills microoganisms on its surface, and gives the meat a rich, "smoky" flavor that varies with the wood used in the fire. Meats smoked over an open fire are exposed to carcinogenic chemicals in the smoke, including a-benzopyrene. Meats treated with "artificial smoke flavoring" are not, since the flavoring is commercially treated to remove tar and a-benzopyrene.

---

*Commercially prepared beef, which is frozen very quickly at very low temperatures, is less likely to show changes in texture.

MEDICAL USES AND/OR BENEFITS

Treating and/or preventing iron deficiency.   Without meat in the diet, it is virtually impossible for an adult woman to meet her iron requirement without supplements. One cooked 3.5-ounce hamburger provides about 2.9 mg iron, 16 percent of the RDA for an adult woman of childbearing age.

Possible anticarcinogenic activity.   In 1984, researchers at the University of Wisconsin identified several naturally occurring chemicals in cooked and raw hamburger that appear to inhibit the mutagenic potential of other chemicals that form naturally when beef is cooked. In tests on laboratory rats, the protective chemicals lowered the incidence of cancer among animals exposed to chemical carcinogens. The specific cancer inhibitors and their chemical structure remain to be identified.

ADVERSE EFFECTS ASSOCIATED WITH THIS FOOD

Elevated levels of serum cholesterol. Abnormally high levels of cholesterol in the blood are a risk factor in heart disease. How your diet affects the amount of cholesterol you produce is not entirely clear; dietary fat and cholesterol may not be the primary factor in determining how much and what kind of cholesterol your body makes and stores. Nonetheless, there is evidence to suggest that controlling the amount of fat and cholesterol you consume may help lower serum cholesterol levels, particularly for people whose serum levels are higher than normal. In 1986, the American Heart Association issued new guidelines suggesting that healthy people reduce their consumption of fat to 30 percent of their total daily calories and limit their cholesterol intake to 300 mg per day or 100 mg per 1000 calories, whichever is less. (Three and a half ounces of roasted beef contain 65-82 mg cholesterol.)

Antibiotic sensitivity.   Cattle in the United States are routinely given antibiotics to protect them from infection. By law, the antibiotic treatment must stop three days to several weeks before the animal is slaughtered. Theoretically, the beef should then be free of antibiotic residues, but some people who are sensitive to penicillin or tetracycline may have an allergic reaction to the meat, although this is rare.

Antibiotic-resistant Salmonella *and toxoplasmosis.*   Cattle treated with antibiotics may produce meat contaminated with antibiotic-resistant strains of *Salmonella,* and all raw beef may harbor ordinary *Salmonella* as well as *T. gondii,* the parasite that causes toxoplasmosis. Toxoplasmosis is particularly hazardous for pregnant women. It can be passed on to the fetus and may trigger a series of birth defects including blindness and mental retardation. Both *Salmonella* and the *T. gondii* can be eliminated by cooking meat thoroughly and washing all utensils, cutting boards, and counters as well as your hands with hot soapy water before touching any other food.

Decline in kidney function.   Proteins are nitrogen compounds. When metabolized they yield ammonia that is excreted through the kidneys. In laboratory animals, a sustained high-protein diet increases the flow of blood through the kidneys and accelerates the natural decline in kidney function that comes with age. Some experts suggest that this may also occur in human beings, but the thesis remains to be proved.

FOOD/DRUG INTERACTIONS

MAO inhibitors.   Monoamine oxidase (MAO) inhibitors are drugs used as antidepressants or antihypertensives. They inhibit the action of enzymes that break down tyramine, a natural by-product of protein metabolism, formed when proteins are digested or when meat is aged. Tyramine is a pressor amine, a substance that constricts blood vessels and raises blood pressure. If you eat a food rich in tyramine while you are taking an MAO inhibitor, the pressor amine cannot be eliminated from your body and the result may be a hypertensive crisis (sustained elevated blood pressure). Papain (see PAPAYA) meat tenderizers work by enzymatic action, which breaks down the proteins in beef and may produce vasoactive amines similar to tyramine.

Theophylline.   Charcoal-broiled beef appears to reduce the effectiveness of theophylline because the aromatic chemicals produced by burning fat speed up the metabolism of theophylline in the liver.

BEER
(Ale)

NUTRITIONAL PROFILE

Energy value (calories per serving):	Moderate
Protein:	Low
Fat:	None
Cholesterol:	None
Carbohydrates:	High
Fiber:	None
Sodium:	Low
Major vitamin contribution:	Riboflavin
Major mineral contribution:	Phosphorus

ABOUT THE NUTRIENTS IN THIS FOOD

Beer and ale are fermented beverages produced by yeasts that convert the sugars in malted barley and grain to ethyl alcohol.* Although they are produced by different strains of yeast and fermented at different temperatures, both beverages contain some of the nutrients present in the grains from which

---

*Because yeasts cannot digest the starches in grains, the grains to be used in making beer and ale are allowed to germinate ("malt"). When it is time to make the beer or ale, the malted grain is soaked in water, forming a mash in which the starches are split into simple sugars that can be digested (fermented) by the yeasts. If undisturbed, the fermentation will continue until all the sugars have been digested, but it can be halted at any time simply by raising or lowering the temperature of the liquid. Beer sold in bottles or cans is pasteurized to kill the yeasts and stop the fermentation. Draft beer is not pasteurized and must be refrigerated until tapped so that it will not continue to ferment in the container. The longer the shipping time, the more likely it is that draft beer will be exposed to temperature variations that may affect its quality—which is why draft beer almost always tastes best when consumed near the place where it was brewed.

they are made. For example, 12 ounces of beer contain 18 mg calcium, 44 mg phosphorus, a trace of iron, 89 mg potassium, about as much riboflavin as a cup of cooked summer squash, and nearly as much niacin as a cup of frozen green peas.

Beer has an average 410 calories per liter, half from carbohydrates and half from ethyl alcohol, which yields approximately 7 calories per gram. (One 12-ounce glass of beer contains about the same amount of alcohol as 5 ounces of wine and an ounce and a quarter of spirits. "Light" beer has about 20 percent less alcohol than regular beer.) The energy from the alcohol in beer is quickly available to your body. While most foods are broken down and absorbed from the small intestine, the molecules in alcohol are so small that they can be absorbed into the bloodstream directly from the stomach as well.

DIETS THAT MAY RESTRICT OR EXCLUDE THIS FOOD
Bland ("ulcer") diet
Gluten-free diet
Low-purine (antigout) diet

BUYING THIS FOOD
Look for: A popular brand that sells steadily and will be fresh when you buy it.

Avoid: Dusty or warm bottles and cans.

STORING THIS FOOD
Store beer in a cool place. Beer tastes best when consumed within two months of the day it is made. Since you cannot be certain how long the it took to ship the beer to the store or how long it has been sitting on the grocery shelves, buy only as much beer as you plan to use within a week or two.

Protect bottled beer and open bottles or cans of beer from direct sunlight, which can change sulfur compounds in beer into isopentyl mercaptan, the smelly chemical that gives stale beer its characteristic unpleasant odor.

WHEN YOU ARE READY TO SERVE THIS FOOD
Serve beer only in absolutely clean glasses or mugs. Even the slightest bit of grease on the side of the glass will kill the foam immediately. Wash beer glasses with detergent, not soap, and let them drain dry rather than drying them with a towel that might carry grease from your hands to the glass. If you like a long-lasting head on your beer, serve the brew in tall, tapering glasses whose wide surface lets the foam spread out and stabilize.

For full flavor, serve beer and ales cool but not ice-cold. Very low temperatures immobilize the molecules that give beer and ale their flavor and aroma.

WHAT HAPPENS WHEN YOU COOK THIS FOOD

When beer is heated (in a stew or as a basting liquid), the alcohol evaporates but the flavoring agents remain intact. Alcohol, an acid, reacts with metal ions from an aluminum or iron pot to form dark compounds that discolor the pot or the dish you are cooking in. To prevent this, prepare dishes made with beer in glass or enameled pots.

HOW OTHER FORMS OF PROCESSING AFFECT THIS FOOD

*   *   *

MEDICAL USES AND/OR BENEFITS

Alcohol and serum cholesterol. Drinking alcoholic beverages (including beer) affects the body's metabolism of fats. It appears to decrease the production and storage of low-density lipoproteins (LDLs), which hold cholesterol in the body, and increase the production and storage of high-density lipoproteins (HDLs), which carry cholesterol out of the body. Research into the effects of alcohol consumption on the levels of cholesterol in the blood is still in the experimental stage.

Stimulating the appetite. Alcoholic beverages stimulate the production of saliva and the gastric acids that cause the stomach contractions we call hunger pangs. Moderate amounts of alcoholic beverages, which may help stimulate appetite, are often prescribed for geriatric patients, convalescents, and people who do not have ulcers or other chronic gastric problems that might be exacerbated by the alcohol.

Dilation of blood vessels. Alcohol dilates the capillaries (the tiny blood vessels just under the skin), and moderate amounts of alcoholic beverages produce a pleasant flush that temporarily warms the drinker. But drinking is not an effective way to warm up in cold weather since the warm blood that flows up to the capillaries will cool down on the surface of your skin and make you even colder when it circulates back into the center of your body. Then an alcohol flush will make you perspire, so that you lose more heat. Excessive amounts of beverage alcohol may depress the mechanism that regulates body temperature.

ADVERSE EFFECTS ASSOCIATED WITH THIS FOOD

Hangover. Alcohol is absorbed from the stomach and small intestine and carried by the bloodstream to the liver, where it is oxidized to acetaldehyde by alcohol dehydrogenase (ADH), the enzyme our bodies use to metabolize the alcohol we produce when we digest carbohydrates. The acetaldehyde is converted to acetyl coenzyme A and either eliminated from the body or used in the synthesis of cholesterol, fatty acids, and body tissues. Although individuals vary widely in their capacity to metabolize alcohol, on average, normal healthy adults can metabolize the alcohol in one quart of beer in approximately five to six hours. If they drink more than that, they will have more alcohol than the body's natural supply of ADH can handle. The unmetabolized alcohol will pile up in the bloodstream, interfering with the liver's metabolic functions. Since alcohol decreases the reabsorption of water from the kidneys and may inhibit the secretion of an antidiuretic hormone, they will begin to urinate copiously, losing magnesium, calcium, and zinc but retaining more irritating uric acid. The level of lactic acid in the body will increase, making them feel tired and out of sorts; their acid-base balance will be out of kilter; the blood vessels in their heads will swell and throb; and their stomachs, with linings irritated by the alcohol, will ache. The ultimate result is a "hangover" whose symptoms will disappear only when enough time has passed to allow their bodies to marshal the ADH needed to metabolize the extra alcohol in their blood.

Fetal alcohol syndrome.   Fetal alcohol syndrome is a specific pattern of birth defects—low birth weight, heart defects, facial malformations, and mental retardation—first recognized in a study of babies born to alcoholic women who consumed more than six drinks a day while pregnant. Subsequent research has found a consistent pattern of milder defects in babies born to women who consume three to four drinks a day or five drinks on any one occasion while pregnant. To date, there is no evidence of a consistent pattern of birth defects in babies born to women who consume less than one drink a day while pregnant, but two studies at Columbia University have suggested that as few as two drinks a week while pregnant may raise a woman's risk of miscarriage. ("One drink" means 12 ounces of beer, 5 ounces of wine, or 1.25 ounces of distilled spirits.)

FOOD/DRUG INTERACTIONS

Anticoagulants.   Alcohol interferes with the metabolism of anticoagulants and may intensify their effect.

Antihypertensives.   Alcohol, which lowers blood pressure, may dangerously intensify the effects of diuretics and beta blockers.

Aspirin and nonsteroidal anti-inflammatory drugs.   Like alcohol, these analgesics irritate the lining of the stomach and may cause gastric bleeding. Combining alcohol with drugs intensifies the effect.

Disulfiram (Antabuse).   Taken with alcohol, disulfiram causes flushing, nausea, low blood pressure, faintness, respiratory problems, and confusion. The severity of the reaction generally depends on how much alcohol you drink, how much disulfiram is in your body, and how long ago you took it. Disulfiram is used to help recovering alcoholics avoid alcohol. (If taken with alcohol, metronidazole [Flagyl], procarbazine [Matulane], quinacrine [Atabrine], chlorpropamide (Diabinase), and some species of mushrooms may produce a mild disulfiramlike reaction.)

Insulin and oral hypoglycemics.   Alcohol lowers blood sugar and interferes with the metabolism of oral antidiabetics; the combination may cause severe hypoglycemia.

MAO inhibitors.   Monoamine oxidase (MAO) inhibitors are drugs used as antidepressants or antihypertensives. They inhibit the action of enzymes that break down tyramine, a pressor amine that constricts blood vessels and raises blood pressure. If you eat a food that contains tyramine while you are taking an MAO inhibitor, the pressor amine cannot be eliminated from your body, and the result may be a hypertensive crisis (sustained elevated blood pressure). Fermentation in producing beer and ale does not ordinarily produce tyramine, but some patients have reported tyramine reactions from imported beers. Beer and ale are usually excluded from the diet when you are using MAO inhibitors.

Sedatives and other central nervous system depressants.   Alcohol intensifies the sedative effects of tranquilizers, sleeping pills, antidepressants, some sinus and cold remedies, analgesics, and medication for motion sickness and, depending on the dose, may cause drowsiness, sedation, respiratory depression, coma, or death.

BEETS

NUTRITIONAL PROFILE

Energy value (calories per serving):	Low
Protein:	Moderate
Fat:	Low
Cholesterol:	None
Carbohydrates:	High
Fiber:	Low
Sodium:	Moderate
Major vitamin contribution:	Vitamin C
Major mineral contribution:	Potassium

ABOUT THE NUTRIENTS IN THIS FOOD

Beets are storage roots rich in complex carbohydrates—starch, sugars, and the indigestible food fibers cellulose and hemicellulose. They have some vitamin C and some B vitamins, but because their red color comes from anthocyanin pigments, not carotene, they have only negligible amounts of vitamin A.

THE MOST NUTRITIOUS WAY TO SERVE THIS FOOD

Cooked, to dissolve the stiff cell walls and make the nutrients inside available.

DIETS THAT MAY RESTRICT OR EXCLUDE THIS FOOD

Anti-kidney-stone diet (beets contain oxalates that bind calcium and may contribute to the formation of calcium oxalate kidney stones)

Low-sodium diet
Sucrose-free diet

BUYING THIS FOOD

Look for: Smooth round globes with fresh, crisp green leaves on top.

Avoid: Beets with soft spots or blemishes that suggest decay underneath.

STORING THIS FOOD

Protect the nutrients in beets by storing the vegetables in a cool place, such as the vegetable crisper in your refrigertor. When stored, the beet root converts its starch into sugars; the longer it is stored, the sweeter it becomes.

Remove the green tops from beets before storing and store the beet greens like other leafy vegetables, in plastic bags in the refrigerator to keep them from drying out and losing vitamins (also see GREENS).

Use both beets and beet greens within a week.

PREPARING THIS FOOD

Scrub the globes with a vegetable brush under cold running water. You can cook them whole, slice them, or peel them before (or after) cooking.

WHAT HAPPENS WHEN YOU COOK THIS FOOD

Betacyanin and betaxanthin, the red betalain pigments in beets, are water-soluble. (That's why borscht is a scarlet soup.) Betacyanins and betaxanthins turn more intensely red when you add acids; think of scarlet sweet-and-sour beets in lemon juice or vinegar with sugar. They turn slightly blue in a basic (alkaline) solution such as baking soda and water.

Like carrots, beets have such stiff cell walls that it is hard for the human digestive tract to extract the nutrients inside. Cooking will not soften the cellulose in the beet's cell walls, but it will dissolve enough hemicellulose so that digestive juices are able to penetrate. Cooking also activates flavor molecules in beets, making them taste better.

HOW OTHER KINDS OF PROCESSING AFFECT THIS FOOD

Canning. Beets lose neither their color nor their texture in canning.

MEDICAL USES AND/OR BENEFITS

*   *   *

ADVERSE EFFECTS ASSOCIATED WITH THIS FOOD

Pigmented urine and feces. The ability to metabolize betacyanins and betaxanthins is a genetic trait. People with two recessive genes for this trait cannot break down these red pigments, which will be excreted, bright red, in urine. Eating beets can also turn feces red, but it will not cause a false-positive result in a test for occult blood in the stool.

Nitrosamine formation.   Beets, celery, eggplant, lettuce, radishes, spinach, and collard and turnip greens contain nitrates that convert naturally into nitrites in your stomach—where some of the nitrites combine with amines to form nitrosamines, some of which are known carcinogens. This natural chemical reaction presents no known problems for a healthy adult. However, when these vegetables are cooked and left standing for a while at room temperature, microorganisms that convert nitrates to nitrites begin to multiply, and the amount of nitrites in the food rises. The resulting higher-nitrite foods may be dangerous for infants (see SPINACH).

FOOD/DRUG INTERACTIONS
*   *   *

BLACKBERRIES
(Boysenberries, dewberries, youngberries)

NUTRITIONAL PROFILE

Energy value (calories per serving):	Low
Protein:	Low
Fat:	Low
Cholesterol:	None
Carbohydrates:	High
Fiber:	High
Sodium:	Low
Major vitamin contribution:	Vitamin A
Major mineral contribution:	Calcium

ABOUT THE NUTRIENTS IN THIS FOOD

Blackberries have no starch but do contain sugars and dietary fiber, primarily pectin, which dissolves as the fruit matures. Unripe blackberries contain more pectin than ripe ones.

Three and a half ounces of fresh blackberries supply 21 mg vitamin C, one-third the RDA for a healthy adult.

THE MOST NUTRITIOUS WAY TO SERVE THIS FOOD

Fresh or lightly cooked.

DIETS THAT MAY EXCLUDE OR RESTRICT THIS FOOD

Sucrose-free diet (permitted on sucrose-restricted diet)

BUYING THIS FOOD

Look for: Plump, firm dark berries with no hulls. A firm, well-rounded berry is still moist and fresh; older berries lose moisture, which is why their skin wrinkles.

Avoid: Baskets of berries with juice stains or liquid leaking out of the berries. The stains and leaks are signs that there are crushed—and possibly moldy—berries inside.

STORING THIS FOOD
Cover berries and refrigerate them. Then use them in a day or two.

Do not wash berries before storing. The moisture collects in spaces on the surface of the berries which may mold in the refrigerator. Also, handling the berries may damage their cells, releasing enzymes that can destroy vitamins.

PREPARING THIS FOOD
Rinse the berries under cool running water, then drain them and pick them over carefully to remove all stems and leaves.

WHAT HAPPENS WHEN YOU COOK THIS FOOD
Cooking destroys some of the vitamin C in fresh blackberries and lets water-soluble B vitamins leach out. Cooked berries are likely to be mushy because the heat and water dissolve their pectin and the skin of the berry collapses. Cooking may also change the color of blackberries, which contain soluble red anthocyanin pigments that stain cooking water and turn blue in basic (alkaline) solutions. Adding lemon juice to a blueberry pie stabilizes these pigments; it is a practical way to keep the berries a deep, dark reddish-blue.

HOW OTHER KINDS OF PROCESSING AFFECT THIS FOOD
Canning.   The intense heat used in canning fruits reduces the vitamin C content of blackberries. Berries packed in juice have more nutrients, ounce for ounce, than berries packed in either water or syrup.

MEDICAL USES AND/OR BENEFITS
*   *   *

ADVERSE EFFECTS ASSOCIATED WITH THIS FOOD
Hives and angioedmea (swelling of the face, lips, and eyes).   These are common allergic responses to berries, virtually all of which have been known to trigger allergic reactions.

FOOD/DRUG INTERACTIONS
*   *   *

BLUEBERRIES
(Huckleberries)

NUTRITIONAL PROFILE

Energy value (calories per serving):	Low
Protein:	Low
Fat:	Low
Cholesterol:	None
Carbohydrates:	High
Fiber:	High
Sodium:	Low
Major vitamin contribution:	Vitamin A
Major mineral contribution:	Calcium

ABOUT THE NUTRIENTS IN THIS FOOD

Blueberries have some protein and a little fat. They have no starch but do contain sugars and dietary fiber—primarily pectin, which dissolves as the fruit matures—and lignin in the seeds. (The difference between blueberries and huckleberries is the size of their seeds; blueberries have smaller ones than huckleberries.)

Three and a half ounces of fresh blueberries supplies 13 mg vitamin C, about 22 percent of the RDA for a healthy adult.

THE MOST NUTRITIOUS WAY TO SERVE THIS FOOD

Fresh, raw, or lightly cooked.

DIETS THAT MAY EXCLUDE OR RESTRICT THIS FOOD
Sucrose-free diet

BUYING THIS FOOD
Look for: Plump, firm dark-blue berries. The whitish color on the berries is a natural protective coating.

Avoid: Baskets of berries with juice stains or liquid leaking out of the berries. The stains and leaks are signs that there are crushed (and possibly moldy) berries inside.

STORING THIS FOOD
Cover berries and refrigerate them. Then use them in a day or two.

Do not wash berries before storing. The moisture increases the chance that they will mold in the refrigerator. Also, handling the berries can damage them, tearing cells and releasing enzymes that will destroy vitamins.

Do not store blueberries in metal containers. The anthocyanin pigments in the berries can combine with metal ions to form dark, unattractive pigment/metal compounds that stain the containers and the berries.

PREPARING THIS FOOD
Rinse the berries under cool running water, then drain them and pick them over carefully to remove all stems, leaves, and hard (immature) or soft (over-ripe) berries.

WHAT HAPPENS WHEN YOU COOK THIS FOOD
Cooking destroys some of the vitamin C in fresh blueberries and lets water-soluble B vitamins leach out. Cooked berries are likely to be mushy because the berries' skin collapses when heat dissolves the pectin inside.

Blueberries may also change color when cooked. The berries are colored with blue anthocyanin pigments. Ordinarily, anthocyanin-pigmented fruits and vegetables turn reddish in acids (lemon juice, vinegar) and deeper blue in bases (baking soda). But blueberries also contain yellow pigments (anthoxanthins). In a basic (alkaline) environment, as in a batter with too much baking soda, the yellow and blue pigments will combine, turning the blueberries greenish-blue.

HOW OTHER KINDS OF PROCESSING AFFECT THIS FOOD
Canning and freezing.   The intense heat used in canning the fruit or in blanching it before freezing reduces the vitamin C content of blueberries by half.

MEDICAL USES AND/OR BENEFITS
*   *   *

ADVERSE EFFECTS ASSOCIATED WITH THIS FOOD
Hives and angioedmea (swelling of the face, lips, and eyes). These are common allergic responses to berries, virtually all of which have been reported to trigger these reactions.

FOOD/DRUG INTERACTIONS
*   *   *

BREAD

NUTRITIONAL PROFILE

Energy value (calories per serving):	Moderate
Protein:	Moderate
Fat:	Low to moderate
Cholesterol:	Low
Carbohydrates:	High
Fiber:	Moderate
Sodium:	Moderate to high
Major vitamin contribution:	B vitamins
Major mineral contribution:	Calcium, iron, potassium

ABOUT THE NUTRIENTS IN THIS FOOD

All commercially made yeast breads are approximately equal in nutritional value. Enriched white bread contains virtually the same amounts of proteins, fats, and carbohydrates as whole wheat bread, although it may contain only half the dietary fiber (see FLOUR).

The proteins in bread come from grains; they are low in the essential amino acid lysine. The most important carbohydrate in bread is starch; all breads contain some sugar. Depending on the recipe, the fats may be highly saturated (butter or hydrogenated vegetable fats) or primarily unsaturated (vegetable fat).

All bread is a good source of B vitamins (thiamin, riboflavin, niacin) and a moderately good source of calcium, magnesium, and phosphorus. (Breads made with milk contain more calcium than breads made without milk.) Although bread is made from grains and grains contain phytic acid, a natural antinutrient that binds calcium ions into insoluble, indigestible compounds, the phytic acid is inactivated by enzyme action during leavening. Bread does not bind calcium.

All commercially made breads are moderately high in sodium; some contain more sugar than others. Grains are not usually considered a good source of iodine, but commercially made breads often pick up iodine from the iodophors and iodates used to clean the plants and machines in which they are made.

Homemade breads share the basic nutritional characteristics of commercially made breads, but you can vary the recipe to suit your own taste, lowering the salt, sugar, or fat and raising the fiber content, as you prefer.

THE MOST NUTRITIOUS WAY TO SERVE THIS FOOD

As sandwiches, with cheese, milk, eggs, meat, fish, or poultry. These foods supply the essential amino acid lysine to "complete" the proteins in grains.

With beans or peas. The proteins in grains are deficient in the essential amino acids lysine and isoleucine and rich in the essential amino acids tryptophan, methionine, and cystine. The proteins in legumes (beans and peas) are exactly the opposite.

DIETS THAT MAY RESTRICT OR EXCLUDE THIS FOOD

Gluten-free diet (excludes breads made with wheat, oats, rye, buckwheat and barley flour)
Lactose-free diet
Low-fiber diet (excludes coarse whole-grain breads)
Low-sodium diet
Sucrose-free diet

BUYING THIS FOOD

Look for: Fresh bread. Check the date on closed packages of commercial bread.

STORING THIS FOOD

Store bread at room temperature, in a tightly closed plastic bag (the best protection) or in a breadbox. How long bread stays fresh depends to a great extent on how much fat it contains. Bread made with some butter or other fat will keep for about three days at room temperature. Bread made without fat (Italian bread, French bread) will dry out in just a few hours; for longer storage, wrap it in foil, put it inside a plastic bag, and freeze it. When you are ready to serve the French or Italian bread, you can remove it from the plastic bag and put the foil-wrapped loaf directly into the oven.

Throw away moldy bread. The molds that grow on bread may produce the same carcinogenic toxins (aflatoxins) as those made by molds on peanuts, milk, or rice.

Do not store fresh bread in the refrigerator; bread stales most quickly at temperatures just above freezing. The one exception: In warm, humid weather, refrigerating bread slows the growth of molds.

WHEN YOU ARE READY TO SERVE THIS FOOD

Use a serrated knife to cut bread easily.

WHAT HAPPENS WHEN YOU COOK THIS FOOD

Toasting is a chemical process that caramelizes sugars and amino acids (proteins) on the surface of the bread, turning the bread a golden brown. This chemical reaction, known both as the browning reaction and the Maillard reaction (after the French chemist who first identified it), alters the structure of the surface sugars, starches, and amino acids. The sugars become indigestible food fiber; the amino acids break into smaller fragments that are no longer nutritionally useful. Thus toast has more fiber and less protein than plain bread. However, the role of heat-generated fibers in the human diet is poorly understood. Some experts consider them inert and harmless; others believe they may be hazardous.

HOW OTHER KINDS OF PROCESSING AFFECT THIS FOOD

Freezing.   Frozen bread releases moisture that collects inside the paper, foil, or plastic bag in which it is wrapped. If you unwrap the bread before defrosting it, the moisture will be lost and the bread will be dry. Always defrost bread in its wrappings so that it can reabsorb the moisture that keeps it tasting fresh.

Drying.   Since molds require moisture, the less moisture a food contains, the less likely it is support mold growth. That is why breadcrumbs and Melba toast, which are relatively moisture-free, keep better than fresh bread. Both can be ground fine and used as a toasty-flavored thickener in place of flour or cornstarch.

MEDICAL USES AND/OR BENEFITS

*   *   *

ADVERSE EFFECTS ASSOCIATED WITH THIS FOOD

Allergic reactions and/or gastric distress.   Bread contains several ingredients that may trigger allergic reactions, aggravate digestive problems, or up-set a specific diet, among them gluten (prohibited on gluten-free diets); milk (prohibited on a lactose- and galactose-free diet) or for people who are sensi-tive to milk proteins); sugar (prohibited on a sucrose-free diet); salt (con-trolled on a sodium-restricted diet); and fats (restricted or prohibited on a controlled-fat, low-cholesterol diet).

FOOD/DRUG INTERACTIONS

*   *   *

BROCCOLI

NUTRITIONAL PROFILE

Energy value (calories per serving):	Low
Protein:	High
Fat:	Low
Cholesterol:	None
Carbohydrates:	Moderate
Fiber:	High
Sodium:	Low
Major vitamin contribution:	Vitamins C and A
Major mineral contribution:	Calcium

ABOUT THE NUTRIENTS IN THIS FOOD

Forty percent of the calories in broccoli come from plant proteins (considered "limited" or "incomplete" because they are deficient in some of the essential amino acids).

It is a fair to good source of vitamin A (from yellow carotenoids hidden under the chlorophyll that makes its stalks and florets green) and an excellent source of vitamin C. Ounce for ounce, boiled, drained fresh broccoli has 125 percent as much vitamin C as fresh orange juice. Broccoli also contains vitamin E and vitamin K, the blood-clotting vitamin manufactured by bacteria that live in our intestines.

Broccoli contains a little iron and is a good source of calcium. Ounce for ounce, it has approximately as much calcium as milk, and the calcium in broccoli is almost as easily assimilated by the body.

THE MOST NUTRITIOUS WAY TO SERVE THIS FOOD

Fresh, lightly steamed, to protect its vitamin C.

DIETS THAT MAY RESTRICT OR EXCLUDE THIS FOOD

Antiflatulence diet
Low-fiber diet
Sucrose-free diet

BUYING THIS FOOD

Look for: Broccoli with tightly closed buds. The stalk, leaves, and florets should be fresh, firm, and brightly colored. Broccoli is usually green; some varieties are tinged with purple.

Avoid: Broccoli with woody stalk or florets that are open or turning yellow. When the green chlorophyll pigments fade enough to let the yellow carotenoids underneath show through, the buds are about to bloom and the broccoli is past its prime.

STORING THIS FOOD

Pack broccoli in a plastic bag and store it in the refrigerator or in the vegetable crisper to protect its vitamin C. At 32° F, fresh broccoli can hold onto its vitamin C for as long as two weeks.

Keep broccoli out of the light; like heat, light destroys vitamin C.

PREPARING THIS FOOD

First, rinse the broccoli under cool running water to wash off any dirt and debris clinging to the florets. Then put the broccoli, florets down, into a pan of salt water (1 tsp. salt to 1 qt. water) and soak for 15 to 30 minutes to drive out insects hiding in the florets. Then cut off the leaves and trim away woody section of stalks. For fast cooking, divide the broccoli up into small florets and cut the stalk into thin slices.

WHAT HAPPENS WHEN YOU COOK THIS FOOD

The broccoli stem contains a lot of cellulose and will stay firm for a long time even through the most vigorous cooking, but the cells walls of the florets are not so strongly fortified and will soften, eventually turning to mush if you cook the broccoli long enough.

Like other cruciferous vegetables, broccoli contains mustard oils (isothiocyanates), natural chemicals that break down into a variety of smelly sulfur compounds (including hydrogen sulfide and ammonia) when the broccoli is heated. The reaction is more intense in aluminum pots. The longer you cook broccoli, the more smelly compounds there will be, although broccoli will never be as odorous as cabbage or cauliflower.

Keeping a lid on the pot will stop the smelly molecules from floating off into the air but will also accelerate the chemical reaction that turns green broccoli olive-drab.

Chlorophyll, the pigment that makes green vegetables green, is sensitive to acids. When you heat broccoli, the chlorophyll in its florets and stalk reacts chemically with acids in the broccoli or in the cooking water to form pheophytin, which is brown. The pheophytin turns cooked broccoli olive-drab or (since broccoli contains some yellow carotenes) bronze.

To keep broccoli green, you must reduce the interaction between the chlorophyll and the acids. One way to do this is to cook the broccoli in a large quantity of water, so the acids will be diluted, but this increases the loss of vitamin C.* Another alternative is to leave the lid off the pot so that the hydrogen atoms can float off into the air, but this allows the smelly sulfur compounds to escape, too. The best way is probably to steam the broccoli quickly with very little water, so it holds onto its vitamin C and cooks before there is time for reaction between chlorophyll and hydrogen atoms to occur.

HOW OTHER KINDS OF PROCESSING AFFECT THIS FOOD

Freezing.   Frozen broccoli usually contains less vitamin C than fresh broccoli. The vitamin is lost when the broccoli is blanched to inactivate catalase and peroxidase, enzymes that would otherwise continue to ripen the broccoli in the freezer. On the other hand, according to researchers at Cornell University, blanching broccoli in a microwave oven—2 cups of broccoli in 3 tablespoons of water for 3 minutes at 600-700 watts—nearly doubles the amount of vitamin C retained. In experiments at Cornell, frozen broccoli blanched in a microwave kept 90 percent of its vitamin C, compared to 56 percent for broccoli blanched in a pot of boiling water on top of a stove.

MEDICAL USES AND/OR BENEFITS

Protection against certain cancers.   According to the American Cancer Society, cruciferous vegetables and fruits and vegetables rich in vitamins A and C may lower the risk of cancers of the gastrointestinal and respiratory tracts. Although the potentially protective chemicals in the fruits and vegetables

---

*Broccoli will lose large amounts of vitamin C if you cook it in water that is cold when you start. As it boils, water releases oxygen that would otherwise destroy vitamin C, so you can cut the vitamin loss dramatically simply by letting the water boil for sixty seconds before adding the broccoli.

have not yet been identified and there is as yet no conclusive evidence to show how they work, the Society recommends adding these foods to your diet.

ADVERSE EFFECTS ASSOCIATED WITH THIS FOOD

Enlarged thyroid gland.   Cruciferous vegetables, including broccoli, contain goitrin, thiocyanate, and isothiocyanate, chemical compounds that inhibit the formation of thyroid hormones and cause the thyroid to enlarge in an attempt to produce more. These chemicals, known collectively as goitrogens, are not hazardous for healthy people who eat moderate amounts of cruciferous vegetables, but they may pose problems for people who have thyroid problems or are taking thyroid medication.

False-positive test for occult blood in the stool.   The guiac slide test for hidden blood in feces relies on alphaguaiaconic acid, a chemical that turns blue in the presence of blood. Broccoli contains peroxidase, a natural chemical that also turns alphaguaiaconic acid blue and may produce a positive test in people who do not actually have blood in the stool.

FOOD/DRUG INTERACTIONS
*   *   *

BRUSSELS SPROUTS

NUTRITIONAL PROFILE

Energy value (calories per serving):	Low
Protein:	High
Fat:	Low
Cholesterol:	None
Carbohydrates:	High
Fiber:	High
Sodium:	Low
Major vitamin contribution:	Vitamins A and C
Major mineral contribution:	Potassium, iron

ABOUT THE NUTRIENTS IN THIS FOOD

Twenty-six percent of the calories in brussels sprouts come from plant proteins (considered "limited" or "incomplete" because they are deficient in some of the essential amino acids). Brussels sprouts are also high in carbohydrates.

Brussels sprouts are an excellent source of vitamins C and A. Three and a half ounces of boiled drained brussels sprouts provide 62 mg vitamin C (100 percent of the RDA) and 719 IU vitamin A (14 percent of the RDA). The vitamin A comes from carotenes, whose yellow color is masked by the chlorophyll that makes the leaves green. The darkest leaves have the most vitamins.

Brussels sprouts also contain an antinutrient, a natural chemical that splits the thiamin (vitamin B_1) molecule so that it is no longer nutritionally useful. This thiamin inhibitor is inactivated by cooking.

THE MOST NUTRITIOUS WAY TO SERVE THIS FOOD

Fresh, lightly steamed to preserve the vitamin C and inactivate the antinutrient.

DIETS THAT MAY RESTRICT OR EXCLUDE THIS FOOD

Antiflatulence diet
Low-fiber diet

BUYING THIS FOOD

Look for: Firm, compact heads with bright, dark-green leaves, sold loose so that you can choose the sprouts one at a time. Brussels sprouts are available all year round.

Avoid: Puffy, soft sprouts with yellow or wilted leaves. The yellow carotenes in the leaves show through only when the leaves age and their green chlorophyll pigments fade. Wilting leaves and puffy, soft heads are also signs of aging.

Avoid sprouts with tiny holes in the leaves through which insects have burrowed.

STORING THIS FOOD

Store the brussels sprouts in the refrigerator. While they are most nutritious if used soon after harvesting, sprouts will keep their vitamins (including their heat-sensitive vitamin C) for several weeks in in the refrigerator.

Store the sprouts in a plastic bag or covered bowl to protect them from moisture loss.

PREPARING THIS FOOD

First, drop the sprouts into salted ice water to flush out any small bugs hiding inside. Next, trim them. Remove yellow leaves and leaves with dark spots or tiny holes, but keep as many of the darker, vitamin A-rich outer leaves as possible. Then, cut an X into the stem end of the sprouts to allow heat and water in so that the sprouts cook faster.

WHAT HAPPENS WHEN YOU COOK THIS FOOD

Brussels sprouts contain mustard oils (isothiocyanates), natural chemicals that break down into a variety of smelly sulfur compounds (including hydrogen sulfide and ammonia) when the the sprouts are heated, a reaction that is intensified in aluminum pots. The longer you cook the sprouts, the more smelly compounds there will be. Adding a slice of bread to the cooking water may lessen the odor; keeping a lid on the pot will stop the smelly molecules from floating off into the air.

But keeping the pot covered will also increase the chemical reaction that turns cooked brussels sprouts drab. Chlorophyll, the pigment that makes green vegetables green, is sensitive to acids. When you heat brussels sprouts, the chlorophyll in their green leaves reacts chemically with acids in the sprouts or in the cooking water to form pheophytin, which is brown. The pheophytin turns cooked brussels sprouts olive or, since they also contain yellow carotenes, bronze.

To keep cooked brussels sprouts green, you have to reduce the interaction between chlorophyll and acids. One way to do this is to cook the sprouts in a lot of water, so the acids will be diluted, but this increases the loss of vitamin C.* Another alternative is to leave the lid off the pot so that the hydrogen atoms can float off into the air, but this allows the smelly sulfur compounds to escape, too. The best solution is to steam the sprouts quickly in very little water, so they retain their vitamin C and cook before there is time for reaction between chlorophyll and hydrogen atoms to occur.

HOW OTHER FORMS OF PROCESSING AFFECT THIS FOOD

Freezing.   Frozen brussels sprouts contain virtually the same amounts of vitamins as fresh boiled sprouts.

MEDICAL USES AND/OR BENEFITS

Protection against certain cancers.   According to the American Cancer Society, cruciferous vegetables and vegetables rich in vitamins A and C may lower the risk of cancers of the gastrointestinal and respiratory tracts.

ADVERSE EFFECTS ASSOCIATED WITH THIS FOOD

Enlarged thyroid gland (goiter).   Cruciferous vegetables, including brussels sprouts, contain goitrin, thiocyanate, and isothiocyanate. These chemicals, known collectively as goitrogens, inhibit the formation of thyroid hormones and cause the thyroid to enlarge in an attempt to produce more. Goitrogens are not hazardous for healthy people who eat moderate amounts of cruciferous vegetables, but they may pose problems for people who have a thyroid condition or are taking thyroid medication.

---

*Brussels sprouts will lose as much as 25 percent of their vitamin C if you cook them in water that is cold when you start. As it boils, water releases oxygen that would otherwise destroy vitamin C. You can cut the vitamin loss dramatically simply by letting the water boil for sixty seconds before adding the sprouts.

Intestinal gas.   Bacteria that live naturally in the gut degrade the indigestible carbohydrates (food fiber) in brussels sprouts and produce gas that some people find distressing.

FOOD/DRUG INTERACTIONS

Anticoagulants.   Like other leaf vegetables, brussels sprouts contain vitamin K, the blood-clotting vitamin produced naturally by bacteria in our intestines. Additional intake of vitamin K may reduce the effectiveness of anticoagulants (warfarin, Coumadin, Panwarfin) so that the patient needs larger doses to produce the same results.

BUTTER

See also VEGETABLE FATS

NUTRITIONAL PROFILE

Energy value (calories per serving):	High
Protein:	Low
Fat:	High
Cholesterol:	High
Carbohydrates:	Low
Fiber:	None
Sodium:	Low (unsalted butter)
	High (salted butter)
Major vitamin contribution:	Vitamins A and D
Major mineral contribution:	Not applicable

ABOUT THE NUTRIENTS IN THIS FOOD

Fats are concentrated sources of energy. Ounce for ounce, they contain nearly twice as many calories as proteins and carbohydrates. They are digested more slowly than proteins and carbohydrates and keep us feeling full longer.

Except for fats from marine animals, animal fats (butter, lard) contain more saturated than unsaturated fatty acids and are high in cholesterol. Two-thirds (by weight) of the fatty acids in butter are saturated, one-third are monounsaturated, and there is a trace of polyunsaturated fatty acids. By comparison, 60 percent of the fatty acids in corn oil are polyunsaturated, 24 percent are monounsaturated, and 13 percent are saturated. One tablespoon of butter has 31 mg cholesterol; there is no cholesterol in vegetable oil.*

*Saturated fatty acids which are sold at room temperature, have molecules with no double bonds between carbon atoms. They cannot accommodate additional hydrogen atoms.

Butter has a trace of protein and carbohydrates and no fiber at all. It provides vitamin A (873 IU/oz.) and vitamin D. The amounts of vitamins A and D vary with the season and the animals' feed.

THE MOST NUTRITIOUS WAY TO SERVE THIS FOOD
*   *   *

DIETS THAT MAY RESTRICT OR EXCLUDE THIS FOOD
Low-cholesterol, controlled-fat diet
Sodium-restricted diet (salted butter)

BUYING THIS FOOD
Look for: Fresh butter. Check the date on the package.

STORING THIS FOOD
Store butter in the refrigerator, tightly wrapped to protect it from air and prevent it from picking up the odors of other food. Even refrigerated butter will eventually turn rancid as its fat molecules combine with oxygen to produce hydroperoxides that, in turn, break down into chemicals with an unpleasant flavor and aroma. This reaction is slowed (but not stopped) by cold. Because salt retards the combination of fats with oxygen, salted butter stays fresh longer than plain butter. (Lard, which is pork fat, must also be refrigerated. Lard has a higher proportion of unsaturated fats than the butter. Since unsaturated fats combine with oxygen more easily than saturated fats, lard becomes rancid more quickly than butter.)

PREPARING THIS FOOD
To measure a half cup of butter: Pour 4 ounces of water into an 8-ounce measuring cup, then add butter until the water rises to the 8-ounce mark. Scoop out the butter, use as directed in recipe.

WHAT HAPPENS WHEN YOU COOK THIS FOOD
Fats are very useful in cooking. They keep foods from sticking to the pot or pan; add flavor; and, as they warm, transfer heat from the pan to the food. In doughs and batters, fats separate the flour's starch granules from each other. The more closely the fat mixes with the starch, the smoother the bread or cake will be.

Heat speeds the oxidation and decomposition of fats. When fats are heated, they can catch fire spontaneously without boiling first at what is called the smoke point. Butter will burn at 250° F.

HOW OTHER KINDS OF PROCESSING AFFECT THIS FOOD

Freezing.   Freezing slows the oxidation of fats more effectively than plain refrigeration; frozen butter keeps for up to nine months.

Whipping.   When butter is whipped, air is forced in among the fat molecules to produce a foam. As a result, the whipped butter has fewer calories per serving, though not per ounce.

MEDICAL USES AND/OR BENEFITS

*   *   *

ADVERSE EFFECTS ASSOCIATED WITH THIS FOOD

Heartburn.   Excessive amounts of fats and fatty foods loosen the sphincter muscle at the base of the esophagus that keeps food from flowing back (refluxing) from the stomach into the esophagus. The result: the burning discomfort called heartburn.

Elevated levels of serum cholesterol. Abnormally high levels of cholesterol in the blood are a risk factor in heart disease. How your diet affects the amount of cholesterol you produce is not entirely clear; dietary fat and cholesterol may not be the primary factor in determining how much and what kind of cholesterol your body makes and stores. Nonetheless, there is evidence to suggest that controlling the amount of fat and cholesterol you consume may help lower serum cholesterol levels, particularly for people whose serum levels are higher than normal. In 1986 the American Heart Association issued new guidelines, suggesting that healthy adults reduce their consumption of fat to 30 percent of their total calories and limit cholesterol intake to 300 mg per day or 100 mg per 1000 calories, whichever is less. (One tablespoon of butter contains 31 mg cholesterol.)

Increased risk of hypertension and some forms of cancer.   There is a statistical but as yet unexplained correlation between consumption of fat and the risk of colon and breast cancer. The current search for a link between fat and cancer centers on an examination of the ways in which fat metabolism affects human body chemistry, including cholesterol metabolism and hormone cycles. As for hypertension, some controlled studies have shown that reducing fat consumption may lower blood pressure.

FOOD/DRUG INTERACTIONS

*   *   *

CABBAGE

(Bok choy [Chinese cabbage], green cabbage, red cabbage, Savoy cabbage)

See also BROCCOLI, BRUSSELS SPROUTS, CAULIFLOWER, RADISHES, TURNIPS

NUTRITIONAL PROFILE

Energy value (calories per serving):	Low
Protein:	Moderate
Fat:	Low
Cholesterol:	None
Carbohydrates:	High
Fiber:	Low
Sodium:	Low
Major vitamin contribution:	Vitamin C
Major mineral contribution:	Calcium (moderate)

ABOUT THE NUTRIENTS IN THIS FOOD

Cabbage contains small amounts of the indigestible food fibers cellulose, hemicellulose, pectin, and lignin, the fiber found in the structural and stringy parts of leaves.

It supplies moderate amounts of vitamin A from the carotenoids hidden under the green chlorophyll pigments in Savoy and green cabbage and the red anthocyanin pigments in red cabbage. Vitamin A is most abundant in the deep-green outer leaves; Savoy cabbage has more vitamin A than green cabbage, which has more than red cabbage. Raw cabbage is a good source of vitamin C.

Raw red cabbage contains an antinutrient enzyme that splits the thiamin molecule so that the vitamin is no longer nutritionally useful. This thiamin inhibitor is inactivated by cooking.

THE MOST NUTRITIOUS WAY TO SERVE THIS FOOD
Fresh, lightly steamed.

DIETS THAT MAY RESTRICT OR EXCLUDE THIS FOOD
Antiflatulence diet
Low-fiber diet
Sucrose-free diet

BUYING THIS FOOD
Look for: Cabbages that feel heavy for their size. The leaves should be tightly closed and attached tightly at the stem end. The outer leaves on a Savoy cabbage may curl back from the head, but the center leaves should still be relatively tightly closed.

Also look for green cabbages that still have their dark-green, vitamin-rich outer leaves.

Avoid: Green and Savoy cabbage with yellow or wilted leaves. The yellow carotene pigments show through only when the cabbage has aged and its green chlorophyll pigments have faded. Wilted leaves mean a loss of moisture and vitamins.

STORING THIS FOOD
Handle cabbage gently; bruising tears cells and activates ascorbic acid oxidase, an enzyme in the leaves that hastens the destruction of vitamin C.

Store cabbage in a cool, dark place, preferably a refrigerator. In cold storage, cabbage can retain as much as 75 percent of its vitamin C for as long as six months. Cover the cabbage to keep it from drying out and losing vitamin A.

PREPARING THIS FOOD
Do not slice the cabbage until you are ready to use it; slicing tears cabbage cells and releases the enzyme that hastens the oxidation and destruction of vitamin C.

If you plan to serve cooked green or red cabbage in wedges, don't cut out the inner core that holds the leaves together.

To separate the leaves for stuffing, immerse the entire head in boiling water for a few minutes, then lift it out and let it drain until it is cool enough to handle comfortably. The leaves should pull away easily. If not, put the cabbage back into the hot water for a few minutes.

WHAT HAPPENS WHEN YOU COOK THIS FOOD

Cabbage contains mustard oils (isothiocyanates) that break down into a variety of smelly sulfur compounds (including hydrogen sulfide and ammonia) when the the cabbage is heated, a reaction that occurs more strongly in aluminum pots. The longer you cook the cabbage, the more smelly the compounds will be. Adding a slice of bread to the cooking water may lessen the odor. Keeping a lid on the pot will stop the smelly molecules from floating off into the air, but it will also accelerate the chemical reaction that turns cooked green cabbage drab.

Chlorophyll, the pigment that makes green vegetables green, is sensitive to acids. When you heat green cabbage, the chlorophyll in its leaves reacts chemically with acids in the cabbage or in the cooking water to form pheophytin, which is brown. The pheophytin gives the cooked cabbage its olive color.

To keep cooked green cabbage green, you have to reduce the interaction between the chlorophyll and the acids. One way to do this is to cook the cabbage in a large quantity of water, so the acids will be diluted, but this increases the loss of vitamin C.* Another alternative is to leave the lid off the pot so that the volatile acids can float off into the air, but this allows the smelly sulfur compounds to escape too. The best way may be to steam the cabbage very quickly in very little water so that it keeps its vitamin C and cooks before there is time for the chlorophyll/acid reaction to occur.

Keeping red cabbage red is another problem. This cabbage is colored with red anthocyanins, pigments that turn redder in acids (lemon juice, vinegar) and blue-purple in bases (alkaline chemicals such as baking soda). Here the solution is simple: Make sweet-and-sour cabbage. But be careful not to make it in an iron or aluminum pot, since vinegar (which contains tannins) will react with these metals to create dark pigments that discolor both the pot and the vegetable. Glass, stainless-steel, or enameled pots do not produce this reaction.

HOW OTHER KINDS OF PROCESSING AFFECT THIS FOOD

Pickling: Sauerkraut is a fermented and pickled product, made by immersing the cabbage in a salt solution strong enough to kill off pathological bacte-

---

*According to USDA, if you cook three cups of cabbage in one cup of water you will lose only 10 percent of the vitamin C; reverse the ratio to four times as much water as cabbage and you will lose about 50 percent of the vitamin C. Cabbage will lose as much as 25 percent of its vitamin C if you cook it in water that is cold when you start. As it boils, water releases oxygen that would otherwise destroy vitamin C, so you can cut the vitamin loss dramatically simply by letting the water boil for sixty seconds before adding the cabbage.

ria but allow beneficial ones to survive, breaking down proteins in the cabbage and producing the lactic acid that gives sauerkraut its distinctive flavor. Sauerkraut contains more than thirty-seven times as much sodium as fresh cabbage (661 mg sodium/100 grams canned sauerkraut with liquid) but only one third the vitamin C and one-seventh the vitamin A.

Sauerkraut contains small amounts of tyramine, a chemical produced naturally when proteins are metabolized by the bacteria that ferment the cabbage. Tyramine is a pressor amine, a substance that makes blood vessels expand or contract. Ordinarily, tyramine is easily eliminated from the body, but if you are taking a monoamine oxidase (MAO) inhibitor, the picture changes. MAO inhibitors are drugs used as antidepressants (tricyclic antidepressants) or antihypertensives. They interfere with the action of natural enzymes that break down tyramine so that it can be eliminated from the body. If you eat a food that contains tyramine while you are taking an MAO inhibitor, the pressor amine cannot be eliminated from your body, and the result may be a hypertensive crisis (sustained elevated blood pressure).

MEDICAL USES AND/OR BENEFITS

Protection against some forms of cancer.   According to the American Cancer Society, cabbage and other cruciferous vegetables may lower the risk of some cancers of the gastrointestinal and respiratory tract, including chemically induced cancers such as the tumors caused by cigarette smoking or exposure to chemicals in the workplace.

ADVERSE EFFECTS ASSOCIATED WITH THIS FOOD

Enlarged thyroid gland (goiter).   Cruciferous vegetables, including cabbage, contain goitrin, thiocyanate, and isothiocyanate. These chemicals, known collectively as goitrogens, inhibit the formation of thyroid hormones and cause the thyroid to enlarge in an attempt to produce more. Goitrogens are not hazardous for healthy people who eat moderate amounts of cruciferous vegetables, but they may pose problems for people who have a thyroid condition or are taking thyroid medication.

Intestinal gas.   Bacteria that live naturally in the gut degrade the indigestible carbohydrates (food fiber) in cabbage, producing gas that some people find distressing.

FOOD/DRUG INTERACTIONS

Anticoagulants.   Like other leaf vegetables, cabbage contains vitamin K, the blood-clotting vitamin produced naturally by bacteria in our intestines. Additional intake of vitamin K may reduce the effectiveness of anticoagulants (warfarin, Coumadin, Panwarfin), so that larger doses may be required.

CAROB

NUTRITIONAL PROFILE

Energy value (calories per serving):	Moderate
Protein:	Moderate
Fat:	Low
Cholesterol:	None
Carbohydrates:	High
Fiber:	High
Sodium:	Low
Major vitamin contribution:	Niacin
Major mineral contribution:	Calcium

ABOUT THE NUTRIENTS IN THIS FOOD

Carob flour, which is milled from the dried pod of a Mediterranean evergreen tree, *Ceratonia siliqua,* looks like cocoa but has a starchy, beanlike flavor. It can be mixed with sweeteners to make a cocoalike powder or combined with fats and sweeteners to produce a candy that looks like and has the same rich mouthfeel as milk chocolate but tastes more like honey.

Ounce for ounce, carob, which is also known as locust bean gum, has more fiber and calcium but fewer calories than cocoa. Its carbohydrates include the sugars sucrose, D-mannose, and D-galactose. (D-galactose is a simple sugar that links up with other sugars to form the complex indigestible sugars raffinose and stachyose.) Carob also contains gums and pectins, the indigestible food fibers commonly found in seeds.

THE MOST NUTRITIOUS WAY TO SERVE THIS FOOD

As a substitute for cocoa or chocolate for people who are sensitive to chocolate.

DIETS THAT MAY RESTRICT OR EXCLUDE THIS FOOD

Low-carbohydrate diet
Sucrose-free or sucrose-restricted diet

BUYING THIS FOOD

Look for: Tightly sealed containers that will protect the flour from moisture and insects.

STORING THIS FOOD

Store carob flour in a cool, dark place in a container that protects it from air, moisture, and insects.

Keep carob candy cool and dry.

PREPARING THIS FOOD

Measure out carob flour by filling a cup or tablespoon and leveling it off with a knife. To substitute carob for regular flour, use ¼ cup carob flour plus ¾ cup regular flour for each cup ordinary flour. To substitute for chocolate, use 3 tablespoons of carob flour plus 2 tablespoons of water for each ounce of unsweetened chocolate. Carob flour is sweeter than unsweetened chocolate.

WHAT HAPPENS WHEN YOU COOK THIS FOOD

Unlike cocoa powder, carob flour contains virtually no fat. It will burn, not melt, if you heat it in a saucepan. When the flour is heated with water, its starch granules absorb moisture and rupture, releasing a gum that can be used as a stabilizer, thickener, or binder in processed foods and cosmetics. In cake batters, it performs just like other flours (see FLOUR).

HOW OTHER KINDS OF PROCESSING AFFECT THIS FOOD

*   *   *

MEDICAL USES AND/OR BENEFITS

Adsorbent and demulcent.   Medically, carob flour has been used as a soothing skin powder.

As a chocolate substitute.   People who are sensitive to chocolate can usually use carob instead. Like cocoa beans, carob is free of cholesterol. Unlike cocoa, which contains the central-nervous-system stimulant caffeine and the muscle stimulant theobromine, carob does not contain any stimulating methylxanthines.

ADVERSE EFFECTS ASSOCIATED WITH THIS FOOD
*   *   *

FOOD/DRUG INTERACTIONS
*   *   *

CARROTS

NUTRITIONAL PROFILE

Energy value (calories per serving):	Low
Protein:	Moderate
Fat:	Low
Cholesterol:	None
Carbohydrates:	High
Fiber:	High
Sodium:	Moderate
Major vitamin contribution:	Vitamin A
Major mineral contribution:	Potassium

ABOUT THE NUTRIENTS IN THIS FOOD

Carrots are roots. Their crisp texture comes from cell walls stiffened with the indigestible food fibers cellulose, hemicellulose, and lignin. Carrots also provide pectin, and they contain appreciable amounts of sugar (primarily sucrose), very little starch, a trace of fat, and no cholesterol.

They are an excellent source of the deep yellow carotenoids from which we produce vitamin A. Three and a half ounces of boiled, drained carrots supplies 25,000 IU vitamin A, five times the RDA for a healthy adult. Carrots also have small amounts of vitamin C, the B vitamins, and a form of calcium easily absorbed by the body.

THE MOST NUTRITIOUS WAY TO SERVE THIS FOOD

Cooked, so that the cellulose- and hemicellulose-stiffened cell walls of the carrot have partially dissolved and the nutrients inside are more readily available.

DIETS THAT MAY RESTRICT OR EXCLUDE THIS FOOD

Disaccharide-intolerance diet (for people who are sucrase- and/or invertase-deficient)
Low-fiber diet
Low-sodium diet (fresh and canned carrots)
Sucrose-free diet

BUYING THIS FOOD

Look for: Firm, bright orange-yellow carrots with fresh, crisp green tops.

Avoid: Wilted or shriveled carrots, pale carrots, or carrots with brown spots on the skin.

STORING THIS FOOD

Trim off the green tops before you store carrots. The leafy tops will wilt and rot long before the sturdy root.

Keep carrots cool. They will actually gain vitamin A during their first five months in storage. Protected from heat and light, they can hold to their vitamins at least another two and a half months.

Store carrots in perforated plastic bags or containers. Circulating air prevents the formation of the terpenoids that make the carrots taste bitter. Storing carrots near apples or other fruits that manufacture ethylene gas as they continue to ripen also encourages the development of terpenoids.

Store peeled carrots in ice water in the refrigerator to keep them crisp for as long as 48 hours.

PREPARING THIS FOOD

Scrape the carrots. Very young, tender carrots can be cleaned by scrubbing with a vegetable brush.

Soak carrots that are slightly limp in ice water to firm them up. Don't discard slightly wilted intact carrots; use them in soups or stews where texture doesn't matter.

WHAT HAPPENS WHEN YOU COOK THIS FOOD

Since carotenes do not dissolve in water and are not affected by the normal heat of cooking, carrots stay yellow and retain their vitamin A when you heat them. But cooking will dissolve some of the hemicellulose in the carrot's stiff cell walls, changing the vegetable's texture and making it easier for digestive juices to penetrate the cells and reach the nutrients inside.

HOW OTHER KINDS OF PROCESSING AFFECT THIS FOOD

Freezing.   The characteristic crunchy texture of fresh carrots depends on the integrity of its cellulose- and hemicellulose-stiffened cell walls. Freezing cooked carrots creates ice crystals that rupture these membranes so that the carrots usually seem mushy when defrosted. If possible, remove the carrots before freezing a soup or stew and add fresh or canned carrots when you defrost the dish.

MEDICAL USES AND/OR BENEFITS

Protection against vitamin A-deficiency blindness.   In the body, the vitamin A from carrots becomes 11-cis retinol, the essential element in rhodopsin, a protein found in the rods (the cells inside your eyes that let you see in dim light). Rhodopsin absorbs light, triggering the chain of chemical reactions known as vision. One raw carrot a day provides more than enough vitamin A to maintain vision in a normal healthy adult.

Protection against some forms of cancer.   According to the American Cancer Society, deep yellow foods rich in carotene may lower the risk of cancers of the larynx, esophagus, and lungs. Although the evidence is inconclusive and the mechanism by which these vegetables might work is unknown, the Society recommends adding them to your diet.

ADVERSE EFFECTS ASSOCIATED WITH THIS FOOD

Oddly pigmented skin.   The carotenoids in carrots are fat-soluble. If you eat large amounts of carrots day after day, these carotenoids will be stored in your fatty tissues, including the fat just under your skin, and eventually your skin will look yellow. If you eat large amounts of carrots *and* large amounts of tomatoes (which contain the red pigment lycopene), your skin may be tinted orange. This effect has been seen in people who ate two cups of carrots and two tomatoes a day for several months; when the excessive amounts of these vegetables were eliminated from the diet, skin color returned to normal.

False-positive test for occult blood in the stool.   The active ingredient in the guiac slide test for hidden blood in feces is alphaguaiaconic acid, a chemical that turns blue in the presence of blood. Carrots contain peroxidase, a natural chemical that also turns alphaguaiaconic acid blue and may produce a positive test in people who do not actually have blood in the stool.

FOOD/DRUG INTERACTIONS

*   *   *

CAULIFLOWER

NUTRITIONAL PROFILE

Energy value (calories per serving):	Low
Protein:	High
Fat:	Low
Cholesterol:	None
Carbohydrates:	High
Fiber:	High
Sodium:	Low
Major vitamin contribution:	B vitamins, vitamin C
Major mineral contribution:	Potassium

ABOUT THE NUTRIENTS IN THIS FOOD

Thirty-two percent of the calories in cauliflower come from plant proteins (considered "limited" or "incomplete" because they are deficient in some of the essential amino acids). Cauliflower is also a good source of fiber.

It is an excellent source of vitamin C. Three and a half ounces of raw cauliflower contain 71 mg vitamin C, 120 percent of the RDA for a normal healthy adult; an equal serving of boiled, drained cauliflower has 55 mg vitamin C, nearly 100 percent of the RDA. Cauliflower is also a source of B vitamins and potassium.

THE MOST NUTRITIOUS WAY TO SERVE THIS FOOD

Steamed quickly to retain its vitamin C.

DIETS THAT MAY RESTRICT OR EXCLUDE THIS FOOD

Antiflatulence diet
Low-fiber diet
Sucrose-free diet

BUYING THIS FOOD

Look for: Creamy white heads with tight, compact florets and fresh green leaves. The size of the cauliflower has no bearing on its nutritional value or its taste.

Avoid: Cauliflower with brown spots or patches.

STORING THIS FOOD

Keep cauliflower in a cool, humid place to safeguard its vitamin C content.

PREPARING THIS FOOD

Pull off and discard any green leaves still attached to the cauliflower and slice off the woody stem and core. Then plunge the cauliflower, head down, into a bowl of salted ice water to flush out any insects hiding in the head. To keep the cauliflower crisp when cooked, add a teaspoon of vinegar to the water. You can steam or bake the cauliflower head whole or break it up into florets for faster cooking.

WHAT HAPPENS WHEN YOU COOK THIS FOOD

Cauliflower contains mustard oils (isothiocyanates), natural chemicals that give the vegetable its taste but break down into a variety of smelly sulfur compounds (including hydrogen sulfide and ammonia) when the cauliflower is heated. The longer you cook the cauliflower, the better it will taste but the worse it will smell. Adding a slice of bread to the cooking water may lessen the odor; keeping a lid on the pot will stop the smelly molecules from floating off into the air.

Cooking cauliflower in an aluminum pot will intensify its odor and turn its creamy-white anthoxanthin pigments yellow; iron pots will turn anthoxanthins blue-green or brown. Like red and blue anthocyanin pigments (see BEETS, BLACKBERRIES, BLUEBERRIES), anthoxanthins hold their color best in acids. To keep cauliflower white, add a tablespoon of lemon juice, lime juice, vinegar, or milk to the cooking water.

Steaming or stir-frying cauliflower preserves the vitamin C that would be lost if the vegetable were cooked for a long time or in a lot of water.

HOW OTHER KINDS OF PROCESSING AFFECT THIS FOOD

Freezing.   Before it is frozen, cauliflower must be blanched to inactivate catalase and peroxidase, enzymes that would otherwise continue to ripen and eventually deteriorate the vegetable. According to researchers at Cornell University, cauliflower will lose less vitamin C if it is blanched in very little water (2 cups cauliflower in 2 tbsp. water) in a microwave-safe plastic bag in a microwave oven for four minutes at 600-700 watts. Leave the bag open an inch at the top so steam can escape and the bag does not explode.

MEDICAL USES AND/OR BENEFITS

Protection against certain cancers.   According to the American Cancer Society, cruciferous vegetables and vegetables rich in vitamins A and C may lower the risk of cancers of the gastrointestinal and respiratory tracts.

ADVERSE EFFECTS ASSOCIATED WITH THIS FOOD

Enlarged thyroid gland (goiter).   Cruciferous vegetables, including cauliflower, contain goitrin, thiocyanate, and isothiocyanate. These chemicals, known collectively as goitrogens, inhibit the formation of thyroid hormones and cause the thyroid to enlarge in an attempt to produce more. Goitrogens are not hazardous for healthy people who eat moderate amounts of cruciferous vegetables, but they may pose problems for people who have a thyroid condition or are taking thyroid medication.

Intestinal gas.   Bacteria that live naturally in the gut degrade the indigestible carbohydrates (food fiber) in cauliflower, producing intestinal gas that some people find distressing.

FOOD/DRUG INTERACTIONS

Anticoagulants.   Cauliflower contains vitamin K, the blood-clotting vitamin produced naturally by bacteria in our intestines. Additional intake of vitamin K may reduce the effectiveness of anticoagulants (warfarin, Coumadin, Panwarfin), requiring larger-than-normal doses to produce the same effect.

False-positive test for occult blood in the stool.   The active ingredient in the guiac slide test for hidden blood in feces is alphaguaiaconic acid, a chemical that turns blue in the presence of blood. Cauliflower contains peroxidase, a natural chemical that also turns alphaguaiaconic acid blue and may produce a positive test in people who do not actually have blood in the stool.

CAVIAR

NUTRITIONAL PROFILE

Energy value (calories per serving):	High
Protein:	High
Fat:	High
Cholesterol:	High
Carbohydrates:	Low
Fiber:	None
Sodium:	High
Major vitamin contribution:	B vitamins
Major mineral contribution:	Calcium, iron, phosphorus

ABOUT THE NUTRIENTS IN THIS FOOD

Caviar is a high-fat, high-cholesterol, high-protein, low-carbohydrate food. It is extremely high in sodium (650 mg/oz.) and, ounce for ounce, contains twice as much calcium as milk.

THE MOST NUTRITIOUS WAY TO SERVE THIS FOOD

*   *   *

DIETS THAT MAY RESTRICT OR EXCLUDE THIS FOOD

Low-cholesterol, controlled-fat diet
Low-salt/low-sodium diet

BUYING THIS FOOD

Look for: Shiny, translucent, large-grained gray fresh caviar (sturgeon roe) with a clean aroma.

Look for: Tightly sealed tins and jars of less expensive roe. Lumpfish roe is small-grained and usually black. Cod, salmon, carp, pike, and tuna roe are large-grained and orangey red or pinkish.

STORING THIS FOOD

Store fresh caviar in the coldest part of the refrigerator; it will spoil within hours at temperatures above 39° F.

Store jars of caviar in a cool, dark place.

PREPARING THIS FOOD

Always serve caviar in a dish (or jar) nestled in ice to keep it safe at room temperature. The roe contains so much salt that it will not freeze.

When making canapés, add the caviar last so that the oil does not spread and discolor the other ingredients.

WHAT HAPPENS WHEN YOU COOK THIS FOOD

*   *   *

HOW OTHER KINDS OF PROCESSING AFFECT THIS FOOD

Pressing.   Pressed caviar is caviar with 10 percent of its moisture removed. As a result it contains more nutrients per ounce than regular caviar and is even higher in sodium.

MEDICAL USES AND/OR BENEFITS

Omega-3 fish oils.   Caviar contains the same protective oils found in other fish (see FISH).

ADVERSE EFFECTS ASSOCIATED WITH THIS FOOD

*   *   *

FOOD/DRUG INTERACTIONS

MAO inhibitors.   Monoamine oxidase (MAO) inhibitors are drugs used as antidepressants or antihypertensives. They inhibit the action of enzymes that break down tyramine, a natural by-product of protein metabolism. Tyramine is a pressor amine, a chemical that constricts blood vessels and raises blood pressure. If you eat a food that contains tyramine while you are taking an MAO inhibitor, the pressor amine cannot be eliminated from your body and the result could be a hypertensive crisis (sustained elevated blood pressure). Caviar contains small amounts of tyramine.

CELERY
(Celeriac)

NUTRITIONAL PROFILE

Energy value (calories per serving):	Low
Protein:	Moderate
Fat:	Low
Cholesterol:	None
Carbohydrates:	High
Fiber:	Low (celery)
	High (celeriac)
Sodium:	High
Major vitamin contribution:	Vitamins A and C
Major mineral contribution:	Potassium, phosphorus

ABOUT THE NUTRIENTS IN THIS FOOD

Celery stalks get their crispness from small amounts of cellulose, hemicelluouse, and lignin (the noncarbohydrate polysaccharide found in leaves, stems, and roots). Celery has some sugar but almost no starch. It is a good source of vitamins A (derived from carotenes, whose yellow is masked by green chlorophyll pigments) and C. The darker green stalks contain the most vitamin A.

Celeriac, a starchy root of a plant similar to celery, has more starch, fiber, iron, and B vitamins, and about the same amount of vitamins A and C but less sodium and potassium.

THE MOST NUTRITIOUS WAY TO SERVE THIS FOOD

Fresh, filled with cheese to add protein.

DIETS THAT MAY RESTRICT OR EXCLUDE THIS FOOD

Low-fiber diet

Low-sodium diet

Sucrose-free diet

BUYING THIS FOOD

Look for: Crisp, medium-size pale-green celery with fresh leaves. Darker stalks have more vitamin A but are likely to be stringy.

Choose celeriac roots that are firm and small, with no sprouts on top. The larger roots contain more cellulose and lignin, which makes them woody.

Avoid: Wilted or yellowed stalks. Wilted stalks have lost moisture and are low in vitamins A and C. Yellowed stalks are no longer fresh; their chlorophyll pigments have faded enough to let the yellow carotenes show through.

Avoid bruised or rotten celery. Celery cells contain chemicals called furocoumarins (psoralens) that can become mutagenic or carcinogenic when the cell membranes are damaged and the furocoumarins are exposed to light. Bruised or rotting celery may contain up to a hundred times the psoralens in fresh celery.

STORING THIS FOOD

Handle celery carefully to avoid damaging the stalks and releasing furocoumarins.

Remove green tops from celeriac before storing the root.

Refrigerate celery and celeriac in plastic bags or in the vegetable crisper to keep them moist and crisp. They will stay fresh for about a week.

PREPARING THIS FOOD

Rinse celery under cold running water to remove all sand and dirt. Cut off the leaves, blanch them, dry them thoroughly, and rub them through a sieve or food mill. The dry powder can be used to season salt or frozen for later use in soups or stews.

Scrub celeriac under cold running water. Cut off leaves, small roots, and root buds. Peel and slice the celeriac and use it raw in salads or boil it. When you cut into the celeriac, you tear its cell walls, releasing polyphenoloxidase, an enzyme that will turn the vegetable brown. You can slow the reaction (but not stop it completely) by dipping raw sliced and/or peeled celeriac into lemon juice or vinegar and water. Refrigeration also slows the enzyme action, but not as effectively as an acid bath.

WHAT HAPPENS WHEN YOU COOK THIS FOOD

When you cook celery the green flesh will soften as the pectin inside its cells dissolves in water, but the virtually indestructible cellulose and lignin "strings" on the ribs will stay stiff. If you don't like the strings, pull them off before you cook the celery.

Cooking also changes the color of celery. Chlorophyll, the pigment that makes green vegetables green, is very sensitive to acids. When you heat celery, the chlorophyll in its stalks reacts chemically with acids in the celery or in the cooking water to form pheophytin, which is brown. The pheophytin will turn the celery olive-drab or, if the stalks have a lot of yellow carotene, bronze.

You can prevent this natural chemical reaction and keep the celery green by cooking it so quickly that there is no time for the chlorophyll to react with the acids, or by cooking it in lots of water (which will dilute the acids), or by cooking it with the lid off the pot so that the volatile acids can float off into the air.

Like other roots, celeriac softens when cooked as the hemicellulose in its cell walls dissolves and the pectin inside leaks out.

HOW OTHER KINDS OF PROCESSING AFFECT THIS FOOD

*   *   *

MEDICAL USES AND/OR BENEFITS

Protection against certain cancers.   According to the American Cancer Society, fiber-rich foods and vegetables that provide vitamins A and C may lower the risk of cancers of the gastrointestinal and respiratory tracts.

ADVERSE EFFECTS ASSOCIATED WITH THIS FOOD

Contact dermatitis.   Celery contains limonene, an essential oil known to cause contact dermatitis in sensitive individuals. (Limonene is also found in dill, caraway seeds, and the peel of lemon and limes.)

Photosensitivity.   The furocoumarins (psoralens) released by damaged or moldy celery are photosensitizers as well as potential mutagens and carcinogens. Constant contact with these chemicals can make skin very sensitive to light, a problem most common among food workers who handle large amounts of celery without wearing gloves.

Nitrate/nitrite poisoning.   Like beets, eggplant, lettuce, radish, spinach, and collard and turnip greens, celery contains nitrates that convert naturally into nitrites in your stomach and then react with the amino acids in proteins to form nitrosamines. Although some nitrosamines are known or suspected carcinogens, this natural chemical conversion presents no known problems for a healthy adult. However, when these nitrate-rich vegetables are cooked and left to stand at room temperature, bacterial enzyme action (and perhaps some enzymes in the plants) convert the nitrates to nitrites at a much faster rate than normal. These higher-nitrite foods may be hazardous for infants; several cases of "spinach poisoning" have been reported among children who ate cooked spinach that had been left standing at room temperature.

FOOD/DRUG INTERACTIONS
*   *   *

CEREALS
(Cornmeal, farina, kasha)

See also BARLEY, CORN, FLOUR, OATMEAL, RICE

NUTRITIONAL PROFILE

Energy value (calories per serving):	Moderate
Protein:	Moderate
Fat:	Low
Cholesterol:	None
Carbohydrates:	High
Fiber:	Low to high
Sodium:	Low
Major vitamin contribution:	B vitamins
Major mineral contribution:	Iron, potassium

ABOUT THE NUTRIENTS IN THIS FOOD

Farina, cornmeal, and kasha are grains that have been milled to remove the outer bran covering and make them useful to human beings, who cannot digest grains until the tough cellulose-and-lignin outer covering (the bran) has been cracked and broken open. When the grain is milled, the bran may be mixed in with the cereal or discarded. Cereals that contain the bran plus the germ (the part of a seed that sprouts) are called whole-grain cereals. Because the germ is high in fat, whole-grain cereals spoil more quickly than cereals that have been "degermed." Wheat cereals have moderate amounts of protein, but their proteins are considered "incomplete" because they are deficient in the essential amino acid lysine.

Wheat cereals provide B vitamins, iron, and potassium. On their own they have no sodium, but they pick up sodium from the water in which they are cooked.

THE MOST NUTRITIOUS WAY TO SERVE THIS FOOD

With beans, milk, cheese, or meat, any of which will provide the essential amino acid lysine to "complete" the proteins in the grains.

DIETS THAT MAY RESTRICT OR EXCLUDE THIS FOOD

Gluten-restricted, gliadin-free diet (farina, kasha)
Low-carbohydrate diet
Low-fiber, low-residue diet
Low-sodium diet (see *About the nutrients in this food,* above)

BUYING THIS FOOD

Look for: Tightly sealed boxes or canisters.

STORING THIS FOOD

Keep cereals in air- and moistureproof containers to protect them from potentially toxic fungi that grow on damp grains. Properly stored, degermed grains may keep for as long as a year. Whole-grain cereals, which contain the fatty germ, may become rancid and should be used as quickly as possible.

PREPARING THIS FOOD

*   *   *

WHAT HAPPENS WHEN YOU COOK THIS FOOD

Starch consists of molecules of the complex carbohydrates amylose and amylopectin packed into a starch granule. As you heat grains in liquid, their starch granules absorb water molecules, swell, and soften. When the temperature of the liquid reaches approximately 140° F, the amylose and amylopectin molecules inside the granules relax and unfold, breaking some of their internal bonds (between atoms on the same molecule) and forming new bonds between atoms on different molecules. The result is a network that traps and holds water molecules, making the starch granules very bulky. Eventually, the starch granules will rupture, releasing the nutrients inside so that they can be absorbed more easily by the body.*

---

*When you use a little starch in a lot of liquid, the amylose and amylopectin released when the starch granules rupture will thicken the liquid by attracting and immobilizing some of its water molecules. Amylose, a long unbranched spiral molecule, can form more bonds to water molecules than can amylopectin, a short branched molecule. Wheat flours, which have a higher ratio of amylose to amylopectin, are superior thickeners.

Ounce for ounce, cooked cereals have fewer vitamins and minerals than dry cereal simply because so much of the weight is now water. The single exception is sodium (see *About the nutrients in this food,* above).

HOW OTHER KINDS OF PROCESSING AFFECT THIS FOOD
*   *   *

MEDICAL USES AND/OR BENEFITS

As a source of carbohydrates for people with diabetes.   Plain cereals are digested very slowly, producing only a gradual rise in the level of sugar in the blood. As a result, the body needs less insulin to control blood sugar after eating unsugared cereals made from additive-free grain than after eating some other high-carbohydrate foods (such as bread or potato). In studies at the University of Kentucky, a whole-grain-, bean-, vegetable-, and fruit-rich diet developed at the University of Toronto and recommended by the American Diabetic Association enabled patients with Type I diabetes (who do not produce any insulin themselves) to cut their daily insulin intake by 38 percent. For patients with Type II diabetes (who can produce some insulin) the bean diet reduced the need for injected insulin by 98 percent. This diet is in line with the nutritional guidelines of the American Diabetes Association, although people with diabetes should always consult with their doctor and/or dietitian before altering their diets.

ADVERSE EFFECTS ASSOCIATED WITH THIS FOOD

Gluten intolerance.   Celiac disease in an allergic intestinal disorder experienced by people sensitive to gliadin, a component of gluten, the sticky elastic protein that makes it possible for breads made with wheat and rye flour to rise. (All wheat cereals contain gluten.) People with celiac disease cannot digest the nutrients in these grains; if they eat foods such as farina or kasha that contain gluten, they may suffer anemia, weight loss, bone pain, swelling, and skin disorders.

FOOD/DRUG INTERACTIONS
*   *   *

CHEESE

NUTRITIONAL PROFILE

Energy value (calories per serving):	Moderate to high
Protein:	Moderate to high
Fat:	Low to high
Cholesterol:	Low to high
Carbohydrates:	Low
Fiber:	None
Sodium:	High
Major vitamin contribution:	Vitamins A and D, B vitamins
Major mineral contribution:	Calcium

ABOUT THE NUTRIENTS IN THIS FOOD

The first step in turning the milk into cheese is the addition of lactobacillus and streptococcus organisms that digest lactose (milk sugar) and turn it into lactic acid, which coagulates casein (milk protein) into curds. The cheese-maker also adds rennet (gastric enzymes extracted from the stomachs of calves) to make the curds firmer, and the mixture is set aside to gel. The longer the curds are left to gel, the firmer the cheese will be. When the curds are firm enough, they are pressed to squeeze out the liquid (whey), then cooked to coagulate still more firmly and expel still more whey. The higher the cooking temperature, the more whey expelled and the firmer the final cheese.*

Natural cheese is cheese made directly from milk. *Processed cheese* is natural cheese melted and combined with emulsifiers. *Pasteurized process cheese foods* contain ingredients that allow them to spread smoothly; they are lower in fat and higher in moisture than processed cheese.

If the process stops here, the result is "fresh" or "green" cheese: cottage cheese, farmer cheese, cream cheese. To make ripe cheese, salt is added in order to remove still more moisture, kill off potentially hazardous bacteria, and slow (but not halt) the action of the original lactic acid organisms that continue to metabolize the proteins, fats, and sugars in the cheese into ever-smaller molecules. New organisms may be added at this point to give certain cheeses their special taste: *Penicillium roquefort* mold for roquefort, blue cheese, and Stilton, *Penicillium camembert* mold for camembert and brie. The action of these organisms will continue unchecked (although it may be slowed by refrigeration) until the cheese is either eaten—or thrown out because it has become unacceptable when the ultimate degradation of proteins produces the odorous nitrogen compound ammonia.

Many of the nutritional values of the finished cheese are similar to those of milk. For example, cheese is an excellent source of high-quality, complete proteins that provide sufficient amounts of all the essential amino acids. Cheese is moderate to high in cholesterol (depending on the variety); the fat content varies with the type of cheese.

FAT CONTENT OF CHEESE
(% of calories)

Very high (70%+)

American, blue, camembert, cheddar, Colby, cream cheese, feta, muenster, Neufchatel

Moderately high (50-70%)

Provolone, ricotta (whole milk), romano, mozzarella, ricotta (part-skim-milk)

Low (20-35%)

Cottage cheese (regular), cottage cheese (low-fat), farmer cheese

---

Source: *Composition of Food, Dairy and Egg Products.* Agriculture Handbook No. 8-1 (USDA 1976).

All cheeses, except cottage cheese, are good sources of vitamin A. Orange and yellow cheeses are colored with carotenoid pigments, including bixin (the carotenoid pigment in annatto) and synthetic beta-carotene.

Hard cheeses are an excellent source of calcium; softer cheeses are a good source; cream cheese and cottage cheese are poor sources. One and a half ounces of cheddar cheese, an ounce of Swiss cheese, or 15 ounces of low-fat

CALCIUM CONTENT OF CHEESE
(mg/oz.)

Parmesan	390 mg
Swiss (domestic)	272 mg
Cheddar	204 mg
Pasteurized process American	174 mg
Blue/Roquefort	150 mg
Camembert (domestic)	147 mg*
Cottage cheese (large-curd)	135 mg**

*per 1.33-oz. wedge
**per cup
Source: *Nutritive Value of Foods,* Home and Garden Bulletin No.72 (USDA, 1985).

cottage cheese each contain about as much calcium as one cup of whole milk. Ounce for ounce, cheese has much less thiamin (vitamin B_1), riboflavin (vitamin B_2), niacin, magnesium, and potassium than milk because these water-soluble nutrients are lost when the whey is discarded during cheese-making.

All cheese (unless otherwise labeled) is high in sodium.

THE MOST NUTRITIOUS WAY TO SERVE THIS FOOD

With grains, bread, noodles, beans, nuts, or vegetables to add the essential amino acids missing from these foods, "complete" their proteins, and make them more nutritionally valuable.

DIETS THAT MAY RESTRICT OR EXCLUDE THIS FOOD

Antiflatulence diet
Controlled-fat, low-cholesterol diet
Lactose- and galactose-free diet (lactose, a disaccharide [double sugar] is composed of one unit of galactose and one unit of glucose)
Low-calcium diet (for patients with kidney disease)
Sucrose-free diet (processed cheese)

BUYING THIS FOOD

Look for: Dated processed cheese. Check the date on the package of such natural cheeses as camembert and brie, which change significantly as they age.

Avoid: Any cheese with mold that is not, as with blue cheese, an integral part of the cheese itself.

STORING THIS FOOD

Refrigerate all cheese except unopened canned cheeses (such as camembert in tins) or grated cheeses treated with preservatives and labeled to show that they can be kept outside the refrigerator. Some sealed packages of processed cheeses can be stored at room temperature but must be refrigerated once the package is opened.

Wrap cheeses tightly to protect them from contamination by other microorganisms in the air and to keep them from drying out. Well-wrapped, refrigerated hard cheeses that have not been cut or sliced will keep for up to six months; sliced hard cheeses will keep for about two weeks. Soft cheeses (cottage cheese, ricotta, cream cheese, and Neufchatel) should be used within five to seven days. Use all packaged or processed cheeses by the date stamped on the package.

Throw out moldy cheese (unless the mold is an integral part of the cheese, as with blue cheese or Stilton).

PREPARING THIS FOOD

For easily grated cheese, chill the cheese first so it won't stick to the grater.

The molecules that give cheese its taste and aroma are largely immobilized when the cheese is cold. When serving cheese with fruit or crackers, bring it to room temperature to activate these molecules.

WHAT HAPPENS WHEN YOU COOK THIS FOOD

Heat changes the structure of proteins. The molecules are denatured, which means that they may be broken into smaller fragments or change shape or clump together. All of these changes may force moisture out of the protein tissue, which is why overcooked cheese is often stringy. Whey proteins, which do not clump or string at low temperatures, contain the sulfur atoms that give hot or burned cheese an unpleasant "cooked" odor. To avoid both strings and an unpleasant odor, add cheese to sauces at the last minute and cook just long enough to melt the cheese.

HOW OTHER KINDS OF PROCESSING AFFECT THIS FOOD

Freezing. All cheese loses moisture when frozen, so semisoft cheeses will freeze and thaw better than hard cheeses, which may be crumbly when defrosted.

Drying. The less moisture cheese contains, the less able it is to support the growth of organisms like mold. Dried cheeses keep significantly longer than ordinary cheeses.

MEDICAL USES AND/OR BENEFITS

Protection against osteoporosis.   Adequate dietary calcium early in life may offer some protection against osteoporosis ("thinning bones") later on, although the thesis remains to be proved. In one study at the University of Pittsburgh School of Health-Related Professions, researchers found that women who drank milk with every meal until they were thirty-five had bones of higher density than women who rarely drank milk.

Protection against tooth decay.   Cheddar cheese appears to have an inhibiting effect on the bacteria that cause tooth decay. The mechanism is still unclear.

ADVERSE EFFECTS ASSOCIATED WITH THIS FOOD

Allergy to milk proteins.   Milk is one of the foods most frequently implicated as a cause of allergic reactions, particularly upset stomach. However, in many cases the reaction is not a true allergy but the result of lactose intolerance (see below).

Lactose intolerance.   Lactose intolerance—the inability to digest the sugar in milk—is an inherited metabolic deficiency that affects two thirds of all adults, including 90 to 95 percent of all Orientals, 70 to 75 percent of all blacks, and 6 to 8 percent of Caucasians. These people do not have sufficient amounts of lactase, the enzyme that breaks the disaccharide lactose into its easily digested components, galactose and glucose. When they drink milk, the undigested sugar is fermented by bacteria in the gut, causing bloating, diarrhea, flatulence, and intestinal discomfort. Some milk is now sold with added lactase to digest the lactose and make the milk usable for lactase-deficient people. In making cheese, most of the lactose in milk is broken down into glucose and galactose. There is very little lactose in cheeses other than the fresh ones—cottage cheese, cream cheese, and farmer cheese.

Galactosemia.   Galactosemia is an inherited metabolic disorder in which the body lacks the enzymes needed to metabolize galactose, a component of lactose. Galactosemia is a recessive trait; you must receive the gene from both parents to develop the condition. Babies born with galactosemia will fail to thrive and may develop brain damage or cataracts if they are given milk. To prevent this, children with galactosemia are usually kept on a protective milk-free diet for several years, until their bodies have developed alternative pathways by which to metabolize galactose. Pregnant women who are known carriers of galactosemia may be advised to give up milk and milk products while pregnant lest the unmetabolized galactose in their bodies cause brain damage to the fetus (damage not detectible by amniocentesis). Genetic counseling is available to identify galactosemia carriers and assess their chances of producing a baby with the disorder.

Food poisoning.   Raw (unpasteurized) milk and cheeses made from raw milk contain various microorganisms, including *Salmonella* and *Listeria,* that are destroyed by pasteurization. *Salmonella* poisoning produces gastrointestinal symptoms that, in the very young, the elderly, and the debilitated, may be life-threatening. *Listeria* poisoning is a flulike infection that may be especially hazardous to infants, for those who are already ill, and for pregnant women, all of whom face the risk of encephalitis or blood infections if exposed to the *Listeria* bacteria.

Elevated levels of serum cholesterol. Abnormally high levels of cholesterol in the blood are a risk factor in heart disease. How your diet affects the amount of cholesterol you produce is not entirely clear; dietary fat and cholesterol may not be the primary factor in determining how much and what kind of cholesterol your body makes and stores. Nonetheless, there is evidence to suggest that controlling the amount of fat and cholesterol you consume may help

CHOLESTEROL CONTENT OF CHEESES
(mg/oz.)

American	27 mg
Blue/roquefort	21 mg
Camembert	20 mg
Cheddar	30 mg
Cottage cheese, one cup	
(creamed)	31-34 mg
(uncreamed)	10 mg
Cream cheese	31 mg
Mozzarella	
(part skim)	16 mg
Muenster	27 mg
Ricotta	9 mg
Swiss	26 mg

Source: "Provisional Table on the Fatty Acid and Cholesterol Content of Selected Foods." (USDA, 1984).

lower serum cholesterol levels, particularly for people with high levels. In 1986, the American Heart Association issued new guidelines, suggesting that healthy adults reduce their fat consumption to 30 percent of total calories and limit cholesterol intake to 300 mg per day or 100 mg per 1000 calories, whichever is less.

Penicillin sensitivity.   People who experience a sensitivity reaction the first time they take penicillin may have been sensitized by exposure to the *Penicillium* molds in the environment, including the *Penicillium* molds used to make brie, blue, camembert, roquefort, Stilton, and other "blue" cheeses.

FOOD/DRUG INTERACTIONS

Tetracycline.   The calcium ions in milk products, including cheese, bind tetracyclines into insoluble compounds. If you take tetracyclines with cheese, your body may not be able to absorb and use the drug efficiently.

MAO inhibitors.   Monoamine oxidase (MAO) inhibitors are drugs used as antidepressants or antihypertensives. They inhibit the enzymes that break down tyramine, a natural by-product of protein metabolism. Tyramine is a pressor amine, a chemical that constricts blood vessels and raises blood pressure. If you eat a food that contains tyramine while you are taking an MAO inhibitor, the pressor amine cannot be eliminated from your body and the result could be a hypertensive crisis (sustained elevated blood pressure). Many

TYRAMINE CONTENT OF CHEESES

High
   Boursault, camembert, cheddar, Emmenthaler, Stilton

Medium to high
   Blue, brick, brie, gruyère, mozzarella, parmesan, romano, roquefort

Low
   Processed American cheese

Very little or none
   Cottage and cream cheese

Sources: *The Medical Letter Handbook of Adverse Drug Interactions* (1985); *Handbook of Clinical Dietetics* (The American Dietetic Association, 1981).

cheeses contain tyramine, formed when bacteria digest the proteins in milk to make the cheese. As a general rule, there is more tyramine nearer the rind than in the interior of the cheese.

False-positive test for pheochromocytoma.   Pheochromocytomas (tumors of the adrenal glands) secrete adrenalin that is converted by the body to vanillyl-mandelic acid (VMA) and excreted in the urine. Tests for this tumor measure the level of VMA in the urine. Since cheese contains VMA, taking the test after eating cheese may result in a false-positive result. Ordinarily, cheese is prohibited for at least 72 hours before this diagnostic test.

CHERRIES

NUTRITIONAL PROFILE

Energy value (calories per serving):	Low
Protein:	Moderate
Fat:	Low
Cholesterol:	None
Carbohydrates:	High
Fiber:	Low
Sodium:	Low*
Major vitamin contribution:	Vitamin C, vitamin A (sour cherries)
Major mineral contribution:	Potassium

ABOUT THE NUTRIENTS IN THIS FOOD

Cherries contain no starch; all their carbohydrates are sugars. Sweet cherries contain more sugar and thus more carbohydrates than sour cherries, but fresh sour cherries (Montmorency is the variety most widely available in this country) contain about six times as much vitamin A as fresh sweet cherries, 366 IU/oz. versus 61 IU/oz. All fresh cherries are a good source of vitamin C. A 3.5-ounce (100-gram) serving of uncooked sweet cherries provides about 7 mg vitamin C, 12 percent of the adult daily requirement.

Like apple seeds and apricot, peach, or plum pits, cherry pits contain amygdalin, a naturally occurring cyanide/sugar compound that breaks down

*Except for maraschino cherries, which are high in sodium.

into hydrogen cyanide in the stomach. While accidentally swallowing a cherry pit once in a while is not a serious hazard, cases of human poisoning after eating apple seeds have been reported (see APPLES). *Note*: Some wild cherries are poisonous.

THE MOST NUTRITIOUS WAY TO SERVE THIS FOOD

Sweet cherries can be eaten raw to protect their vitamin C; sour ("cooking") cherries are more palatable when cooked.

DIETS THAT MAY RESTRICT OR EXCLUDE THIS FOOD

Low-sodium diet (maraschino cherries)
Sucrose-free diet

BUYING THIS FOOD

Look for: Plump, firm, brightly colored cherries with glossy skin whose color may range from pale golden yellow to deep red to almost black, depending on the variety. The stems should be green and fresh, bending easily and snapping back when released.

Avoid: Sticky cherries (they've been damaged and are leaking), red cherries with very pale skin (they're not fully ripe), and bruised cherries whose flesh will be discolored under the bruise.

STORING THIS FOOD

Store cherries in the refrigerator to keep them cold and humid, conserving their nutrients and flavor. Cherries are highly perishable; use them as quickly as possible.

PREPARING THIS FOOD

Handle cherries with care. When you bruise, peel, or slice a cherry you tear its cell walls, releasing polyphenoloxidase—an enzyme that converts phenols in the cherry into brown compounds that darken the fruit. You can slow this reaction (but not stop it completely) by dipping raw sliced or peeled cherries into an acid solution (lemon juice and water or vinegar and water) or by mixing them with citrus fruits in a fruit salad. Polyphenoloxidase also works more slowly in the cold, but storing sliced or peeled cherries in the refrigerator is much less effective than bathing them in an acid solution.

WHAT HAPPENS WHEN YOU COOK THIS FOOD

Depending on the variety, cherries get their color from either red anthocyanin pigments or yellow-to-orange-to-red carotenoids. The anthocyanins dissolve in water, turn redder in acids and bluish in bases (alkalis). The carotenoids are not affected by heat and do not dissolve in water, which is why cherries do not lose vitamin A when you cook them. Vitamin C, however, is vulnerable to heat.

HOW OTHER FORMS OF PROCESSING AFFECT THIS FOOD

Canning and freezing.   Canned and frozen cherries contain less vitamin C and vitamin A than fresh cherries. Sweetened canned or frozen cherries contain more sugar than fresh cherries.

Candying.   Candied cherries are much higher in calories and sugar than fresh cherries. Maraschino cherries contain about twice as many calories per serving as fresh cherries and are high in sodium.

MEDICAL USES AND/OR BENEFITS
*   *   *

ADVERSE EFFECTS ASSOCIATED WITH THIS FOOD
*   *   *

FOOD/DRUG INTERACTIONS
*   *   *

CHOCOLATE
(Cocoa, milk chocolate, sweet chocolate)

*NUTRITIONAL PROFILE**

Energy value (calories per serving):	Moderate
Protein:	Moderate
Fat:	Low (cocoa powder) High (chocolate)
Cholesterol:	None
Carbohydrates:	Low (chocolate) High (cocoa powder)
Fiber:	Low (chocolate) High (cocoa powder)
Sodium:	Moderate
Major vitamin contribution:	B vitamins
Major mineral contribution:	Calcium, iron, copper

ABOUT THE NUTRIENTS IN THIS FOOD

Like other seeds, cocoa beans are a good source of proteins, carbohydrates (starch), fiber (cellulose, pectins, gums, and the noncarbohydrate fiber lignin), B vitamins, and minerals.

The proteins in cocoa beans, cocoa, and plain chocolate are considered "incomplete" because they are deficient in the essential amino acids lysine and isoleucine (which are supplied by the milk in milk chocolate). Cocoa butter, the fat in cocoa beans, has no cholesterol but it is the second most highly

---

*These values apply to plain cocoa powder and plain unsweetened chocolate. Adding other foods, such as milk or sugar, changes these values. For example, there is no cholesterol in plain bitter chocolate, but there is cholesterol in milk chocolate.

saturated vegetable fat, second only to coconut oil. As a food, cocoa butter has two attractive special properties: it rarely becomes rancid and it melts at 92-95° F, the temperature of the human tongue.

Cocoa and chocolate are a good source of thiamin (Vitamin B_1), riboflavin (Vitamin B_2), and niacin plus phosphorus, iron, potassium, and copper. Cocoa and chocolate also contain oxalic acid, which binds with calcium to form calcium oxalate, an insoluble salt. That is the basis for the old wives' tale that chocolate milk is not nutritious. The fact, though, is that there is more calcium in the milk than can bind with the cocoa or chocolate syrup you add to it; chocolate-flavored milk is still a good source of calcium.

Finally, cocoa and chocolate contain the methylxanthine central-nervous-system stimulants caffeine, theophylline, and theobromine. Theobromine, the weakest CNS stimulant of the three, is also a muscle stimulant. A 5-ounce cup of drip-brewed coffee has 110 to 150 mg caffeine; a 5-ounce cup of cocoa made with a tablespoon of plain cocoa powder (⅓ oz.) has about 18 mg caffeine.

THE MOST NUTRITIOUS WAY TO SERVE THIS FOOD

With milk. The proteins in milk, which contain adequate amounts of all the essential amino acids, including lysine and isoleucine, complement the proteins in cocoa and chocolate.

DIETS THAT MAY RESTRICT OR EXCLUDE THIS FOOD

Antiflatulence diet
Low-calcium and low-oxalate diet (to prevent the formation of calcium oxalate kidney stones)
Low-calorie diet
Low-carbohydrate diet
Low-fat diet
Low-fat, controlled-cholesterol diet (milk chocolates)
Low-fiber diet
Potassium-regulated (low-potassium) diet

BUYING THIS FOOD

Look for: Tightly sealed boxes or bars. When you open a box of chocolates or unwrap a candy bar, the chocolate should be glossy and shiny. Chocolate that looks dull may be stale, or it may be inexpensively made candy without enough cocoa butter to make it gleam and give it the rich creamy mouthfeel we associate with the best chocolate. (Fine chocolate melts evenly on the tongue.) Chocolate should also smell fresh, not dry and powdery, and when you break a bar or piece of chocolate it should break cleanly, not crumble. One exception: If you have stored a bar of chocolate in the refrigerator, it may splinter if you break it without bringing it to room temperature first.

STORING THIS FOOD

Store chocolate at a constant temperature, preferably below 78° F. At higher temperatures, the fat in the chocolate will rise to the surface and, when the chocolate is cooled, the fat will solidify into a whitish powdery *bloom*. Bloom is unsightly but doesn't change the chocolate's taste or nutritional value. To get rid of bloom, melt the chocolate. The chocolate will turn dark, rich brown again when its fat recombines with the other ingredients. Chocolate with bloom makes a perfectly satisfactory chocolate sauce.

Dark chocolate (bitter chocolate, semisweet chocolate) ages for at least six months after it is made, as its flavor becomes deeper and more intense. Wrapped tightly and stored in a cool, dry cabinet, it can stay fresh for a year or more. Milk chocolate ages only for about a month after it is made and holds its peak flavor for about three to six months, depending on how carefully it is stored. Plain cocoa, with no added milk powder or sugar, will stay fresh for up to a year if you keep it tightly sealed and cool.

PREPARING THIS FOOD

*   *   *

WHAT HAPPENS WHEN YOU COOK THIS FOOD

Chocolate is high in starch; it burns easily. To melt chocolate without mishaps, put it in a bowl over a pot or bowl full of very hot water and stir gently.

Simple chemistry dictates that chocolate cakes be leavened with baking soda rather than baking powder. Chocolate is so acidic that it will upset the delicate balance of acid (cream of tartar) and base (alkali = sodium bicarbonate = baking soda) in baking powder. But it is not acidic enough to balance plain sodium bicarbonate. That's why we add an acidic sour-milk product such as buttermilk or sour cream or yogurt to a chocolate cake. Without the sour milk, the batter would be so basic that the chocolate would look red, not brown, and taste very bitter.

HOW OTHER KINDS OF PROCESSING AFFECT THIS FOOD

Freezing.   Chocolate freezes and thaws well. Pack it in a moistureproof container and defrost it in the same package to let it reabsorb moisture it gave off while frozen.

MEDICAL USES AND/OR BENEFITS

*   *   *

ADVERSE EFFECTS ASSOCIATED WITH THIS FOOD

Allergic reactions. Chocolate is often implicated as a cause of the classic allergy symptoms hives, angioedema (swelling of the face, lips, eyes), and upset stomach, plus headaches.

Apthous ulcers. Eating chocolate sometimes triggers a flare-up of apthous ulcers (canker sores) in sensitive people, but eliminating chocolate from the diet will not prevent or cure the canker sores.

Gastric upset. In people prone to heartburn, the caffeine in chocolate may provoke secretion of gastric acid. In addition, both the caffeine and the fat in chocolate may loosen the sphincter muscle that holds the esophagus shut. When this muscle loosens, the acid contents of the stomach may flow back into the esophagus, creating the uncomfortable sensation we call heartburn.

FOOD/DRUG INTERACTIONS

MAO inhibitors. Monoamine oxidase (MAO) inhibitors are drugs used as antidepressants or antihypertensives. They interrupt the action of natural enzymes that break down several nitrogen compounds, including phenylethylamine (PEA), so that they can be eliminated from the body. PEA is a weak pressor amine; it constricts blood vessels and raises blood pressure. If you eat a food rich in pressor amines while you are taking an MAO inhibitor, the chemical cannot be eliminated from your body and the result may be a hypertensive crisis (sustained elevated blood pressure).*

False-positive test for pheochromocytoma. Pheochromocytoma, a tumor of the adrenal gland, secretes adrenalin, which the body converts to VMA (vanillylmandelic acid). VMA is excreted in urine, and, until recently, the test for this tumor measured the level of VMA in the urine. In the past, chocolate and cocoa, both of which contain VMA, were eliminated from the patient's diet prior to the test lest they elevate the level of VMA in the urine and produce a false-positive result. Today, more finely drawn tests usually make this unnecessary.

---

*The evidence linking chocolate to allergic or migraine headaches is inconsistent. In some people, phenylethylamine (PEA) seems to cause headaches similar to those induced by tyramine, another pressor amine. The PEA-induced headache is unusual in that it is a delayed reaction that usually occurs twelve or more hours after the chocolate is eaten.

COCONUT

See also NUTS

ABOUT THE NUTRIENTS IN THIS FOOD

The coconut, which has some sugars but no starch, is a good source of fiber. Like other nuts, its proteins are "incomplete" because they are deficient in the essential amino acid lysine and isoleucine. The coconut's most plentiful nutrient is fat. Coconut meat is one-third fat. Unlike other vegetable fats, coconut oil has very little vitamin E and almost no polyunsaturated fatty acids. In fact, coconut oil has a higher concentration of saturated fatty acids than any other food. It has no cholesterol.

THE MOST NUTRITIOUS WAY TO SERVE THIS FOOD

Fresh, with beans, vegetables, eggs, or milk, all of which provide the essential amino acid lysine to complement the coconut's proteins.

DIETS THAT MAY RESTRICT OR EXCLUDE THIS FOOD

Low-fat diet
Low-fiber, low-residue diet
Sucrose-free diet

BUYING THIS FOOD

Look for: Coconuts that are heavy for their size. You should be able to hear the liquid sloshing around inside when you shake a coconut; if you don't, the coconut has dried out. Avoid nuts with a wet "eye" (the dark spots at the top of the nut) or with mold anywhere on the shell.

STORING THIS FOOD

Store whole fresh coconuts in the refrigerator and use them within a week. Shredded fresh coconut should be refrigerated in a covered container and used in a day or so while it is still fresh and moist.

Refrigerate dried, shredded coconut in an air- and moistureproof container once you have opened the can or bag.

PREPARING THIS FOOD

Puncture one of the "eyes" of the coconut with a sharp, pointed tool. Pour out the liquid. Then crack the coconut by hitting it with a hammer in the middle, where the shell is widest. Continue around the nut until you have cracked the shell in a circle around the middle and can separate the two halves. Pry the meat out of the shell.

To shred coconut meat, break the shell into small pieces, peel off the hard shell and the brown papery inner covering, then rub the meat against a regular food grater.

WHAT HAPPENS WHEN YOU COOK THIS FOOD

Toasting caramelizes sugars on the surface of the coconut meat and turns it golden. Toasting also reduces the moisture content of the coconut meat, concentrating the nutrients.

HOW OTHER FORMS OF PROCESSING AFFECT THIS FOOD

Drying.   Drying concentrates all the nutrients in coconut. *Unsweetened* dried shredded coconut has about twice as much protein, fat, carbohydrate, iron, and potassium as an equal amount of fresh coconut. (*Sweetened* dried shredded coconut has six times as much sugar.)

Coconut milk and cream.   Coconut cream is the liquid wrung out of fresh coconut meat; coconut milk is the liquid wrung from fresh coconut meat that has been soaked in water; coconut water is the liquid in the center of the whole coconut. Coconut milk and cream are high in fat, coconut water is not. All coconut liquids should be refrigerated if not used immediately.

MEDICAL USES AND/OR BENEFITS
*   *   *

ADVERSE EFFECTS ASSOCIATED WITH THIS FOOD

Hives and angioedema (swelling of the eyes and lips).   All nuts, including coconuts, are common allergens.

Apthous ulcers (canker sores).   All nuts, including coconuts, may trigger a flare-up of apthous ulcers in sensitive people, but eliminating nuts from the diet won't cure or prevent the canker sores.

FOOD/DRUG INTERACTIONS
*   *   *

COFFEE

NUTRITIONAL PROFILE

Energy value (calories per serving):	Low
Protein:	Trace
Fat:	Trace
Cholesterol:	None
Carbohydrates:	Trace
Fiber:	Trace
Sodium:	Low
Major vitamin contribution:	—
Major mineral contribution:	—

ABOUT THE NUTRIENTS IN THIS FOOD

Coffee beans (the roasted seeds from the fruit of the evergreen *Coffea* trees) are about 11 percent protein, 8 percent sucrose and other sugars, 10-15 percent oils, 6 percent assorted acids, and 1-2 percent caffeine. Coffee beans contain the B vitamins riboflavin and niacin, vitamin C, iron, potassium, and sodium, but brewed coffee has only negligible amounts of niacin, potassium, sodium, and iron and no vitamin C at all.

Like spinach, rhubarb, and tea, coffee contains oxalic acid (which binds calcium ions into insoluble compounds your body cannot absorb), but this is of no nutritional consequence so long as your diet contains adequate amounts of calcium-rich foods.

Coffee's best known constituent is the methylxanthine central-nervous system stimulant caffeine. How much caffeine you get in a cup of coffee depends on how the coffee was processed and brewed. Caffeine is water-soluble. *Instant, freeze-dried,* and *decaffeinated* coffees all have less caffeine than plain ground roasted coffee.

CAFFEINE CONTENT
(5 oz. cup of coffee)

Drip-brewed coffee	110-150 mg
Percolated coffee	64-124 mg
"Instant" coffee	40-108 mg
Decaffeinated coffee	2-5 mg

Source: Briggs, George M. and Calloway, Doris Howes, *Nutrition and Physical Fitness,* 11th ed. (New York: Holt, Rinehart and Winston, 1984).

THE MOST NUTRITIOUS WAY TO SERVE THIS FOOD

With a diet that contains adequate amounts of calcium.

DIETS THAT MAY RESTRICT OR EXCLUDE THIS FOOD

Bland diet
Gout diet
Ulcer diet

BUYING THIS FOOD

Look for: Ground coffee and coffee beans in tightly sealed, air- and moistureproof containers.

Avoid: Bulk coffees or coffee beans stored in open bins. When coffee is exposed to air, the volatile molecules that give it its distinctive flavor and richness escape, leaving the coffee flavorless and/or bitter.

STORING THIS FOOD

Store unopened vacuum-packed cans of ground coffee or coffee beans in a cool, dark cabinet—where they will stay fresh for six months to a year. They will lose some flavor in storage, though, because it is impossible to can coffee without trapping some flavor-destroying air inside the can.

Once the can or paper sack has been opened, the coffee or beans should be sealed as tight as possible and stored in the refrigerator. Tightly wrapped, refrigerated ground coffee will hold its freshness and flavor for about a week, whole beans for about three weeks. For longer storage, freeze the coffee or beans in an air- and moistureproof container. (You can brew coffee directly from frozen ground coffee and you can grind frozen beans without thawing them.)

PREPARING THIS FOOD

If you make your coffee with tap water, let the water run for a while to add oxygen. Soft water makes "cleaner"-tasting coffee than mineral-rich hard water. Coffee made with chlorinated water will taste better if you refrigerate the water overnight in a glass (not plastic) bottle so that the chlorine evaporates.

Never make coffee with hot tap water or water that has been boiled. Both lack oxygen, which means that your coffee will taste flat.

Always brew coffee in a scrupulously clean pot. Each time you make coffee, oils are left on the inside of the pot. If you don't scrub them off, they will turn rancid and the next pot of coffee you brew will taste bitter. To clean a coffee pot, wash it with detergent, rinse it with water in which you have dissolved a few teaspoons of baking soda, then rinse one more time with boiling water.

WHAT HAPPENS WHEN YOU COOK THIS FOOD

In making coffee, your aim is to extract flavorful solids (including coffee oils and sucrose and other sugars) from the ground beans without pulling bitter, astringent tannins along with them. How long you brew the coffee determines how much solid material you extract and how the coffee tastes. The longer the brewing time, the greater the amount of solids extracted. If you brew the coffee long enough to extract more than 30 percent of its solids, you will get bitter compounds along with the flavorful ones. (These will also develop by letting coffee sit for a long time after brewing it.)

Ordinarily, drip coffee tastes less bitter than percolator coffee because the water in a drip coffeemaker goes through the coffee only once, while the water in the percolator pot is circulated through the coffee several times. To make strong but not bitter coffee, increase the amount of coffee—not the brewing time.

HOW OTHER FORMS OF PROCESSING AFFECT THIS FOOD

Drying. Soluble coffees (freeze-dried, instant) are made by dehydrating concentrated brewed coffee. These coffees are often lower in caffeine than regular ground coffees because caffeine, which dissolves in water, is lost when the coffee is dehydrated.

Decaffeinating.   Decaffeinated coffee is made with beans from which the caffeine has been extracted, either with an organic solvent (methylene chloride) or with water. How the coffee is decaffeinated has no effect on its taste, but many people prefer water-processed decaffeinated coffee because it is not a chemically treated food. (Methylene chloride is an animal carcinogen, but the amounts that remain in coffees decaffeinated with methylene chloride are so small that the FDA does not consider them hazardous. The carcinogenic organic solvent trichloroethylene [TCE], a chemical that causes liver cancer in laboratory animals, is no longer used to decaffeinate coffee.)

MEDICAL USES AND/OR BENEFITS

As a stimulant.   Caffeine is a stimulant that may increase alertness and concentration, intensify muscle responses, speed up the heartbeat, and elevate mood (which is why it is often combined with analgesics in over-the-counter painkillers). Its effects vary widely from person to person and if you drink coffee every day its effects may be less than if you only drink it once in a while. Some people even find coffee relaxing.

Changes in blood vessels.   Caffeine dilates systemic blood vessels and constricts cerebral blood vessels, which is one possible explanation of coffee's ability to relieve headaches caused by engorged blood vessels. Conversely, it may also be why one study at the Long Beach Veterans Hospital in California showed that regular (but not decaffeinated) coffee appeared to increase pain-free exercise time in patients with angina. (Caffeine dilates the coronary arteries and increases the coronary blood flow but also increases heartbeat; medical opinion is divided as to whether or not heart patients should be allowed coffee.)

As a diuretic.   Caffeine is a mild diuretic sometimes included in over-the-counter remedies for premenstrual tension or menstrual discomfort.

ADVERSE EFFECTS ASSOCIATED WITH THIS FOOD

Stimulation of acid secretion in the stomach.   Both regular and decaffeinated coffees increase the secretion of stomach acid, which suggests that the culprit is the oil in coffee, not its caffeine.

Elevated levels of serum cholesterol.   In several studies, people who drink coffee appear to have higher levels of serum cholesterol than people who do not drink coffee. Some research suggests that the problem may occur in men who drink two or more cups of coffee a day and women who drink four or more cups a day.

Withdrawal symptoms.   Caffeine is a drug for which you develop a toler-ance; the more often you use it, the more likely you are to require a larger dose to produce the same effects and the more likely you are to experience withdrawal symptoms (headache, irritation) if you stop using it. The symp-toms of coffee-withdrawal can be relieved immediately by drinking a cup of coffee.

UNPROVED/DISPROVED ALLEGATIONS.

- *Birth defects.* There is no proved link between coffee consumption by a pregnant woman and birth defects in the child she is carrying.
- *Nursing infants.* Only 0.6-1.5 percent of the caffeine a nursing mother drinks show up in her breast milk; this amount is not considered harmful to the nursing infant.
- *Fibrocystic breast disease.* Although giving up coffee and other caffeinated beverages reduces symptoms in some women with fibrocystic breast disease, there is no proved link between caffeine and fibrocystic breast disease.
- *Hypertension.* Although coffee seems to raise blood pressure slightly in some people, it has not yet been shown to have any special effect on people with hypertension.

FOOD/DRUG INTERACTIONS

Allopurinol.   Coffee and other beverages containing methylxanthine stimu-lants (caffeine, theophylline, and theobromine) reduce the effectiveness of the antigout drug allopurinol, which is designed to inhibit xanthines.

Antibiotics.   Coffee increases stomach acidity, which reduces the rate at which ampicillin, erythromycin, griseofulvin, penicillin, and tetracyclines are absorbed when they are taken by mouth. (There is no effect when the drugs are administered by injection.)

Antiulcer medication.   Coffee increases stomach acidity and reduces the ef-fectiveness of normal doses of cimetidine and other antiulcer medication.

False-positive test for pheochromocytoma.   Pheochromocytoma, a tumor of the adrenal glands, secretes adrenalin, which is converted to VMA (vanillyl-mandelic acid) by the body and excreted in the urine. Until recently, the test for this tumor measured the levels of VMA in the patient's urine and coffee, which contains VMA, was eliminated from patients' diets lest it elevate the level of VMA in the urine, producing a false-positive test result. Today, more finely drawn tests make this unnecessary.

Iron supplements.   Caffeine binds with iron to form insoluble compounds your body cannot absorb. Ideally, iron supplements and coffee should be taken at least two hours apart.

Nonprescription drugs containing caffeine.   The caffeine in coffee may add to the stimulant effects of the caffeine in over-the-counter cold remedies, diuretics, pain relievers, stimulants, and weight-control products containing caffeine. Some cold pills contain 30 mg caffeine, some pain relievers 130, and some weight-control products as much as 280 mg caffeine. There are 110-150 mg caffeine in a 5-ounce cup of drip-brewed coffee.

Sedatives.   The caffeine in coffee may counteract the drowsiness caused by sedative drugs; this may be a boon to people who get sleepy when they take antihistamines. Coffee will not, however, "sober up" people who are experiencing the inebriating effects of alcoholic beverages.

Theophylline.   Caffeine relaxes the smooth muscle of the bronchi and may intensify the effects (and/or increase the risk of side effects) of this antiasthmatic drug.

CORN

(Hominy)

See also FLOUR, VEGETABLE OILS

NUTRITIONAL PROFILE

Energy value (calories per serving):	Moderate
Protein:	Moderate
Fat:	Low
Cholesterol:	None
Carbohydrates:	High
Fiber:	Low
Sodium:	Low
Major vitamin contribution:	B vitamins, vitamin C, vitamin A (in yellow corn)
Major mineral contribution:	Potassium

ABOUT THE NUTRIENTS IN THIS FOOD

Sweet corn is a high-carbohydrate, high-starch food. Carbohydrates (sugar, starch, food fiber) account for 81 percent of the solid material in fresh-boiled corn on the cob, which has about twenty times as much starch as sugar and contains moderate amounts of gums and pectins and small amounts of cellulose and the noncarbohydrate food fiber lignin.*

Corn is a moderately good source of plant proteins, but zein (its major protein) is deficient in the essential amino acids lysine, cystine, and trypto-

---

*The most plentiful sugar in sweet corn is glucose; hydrolysis (chemical splitting) of corn starch is the principal industrial source of glucose. Since glucose is less sweet than sucrose, sucrose and fructose are added to commercial corn syrup to make it sweeter.

phan. Corn is low in fat and its oils are composed primarily of unsaturated fatty acids.

Yellow corn, which gets its color from the xanthophyll pigments lutein and zeaxanthine plus the vitamin A-active pigments carotene and crypto-xanthin, contains a little vitamin A; white corn has very little.

All varieties of sweet corn are good sources of vitamin C. The kernels from an average cob, boiled, provide 6.2 mg vitamin C, about 10 percent of the daily requirement for a healthy adult. Corn is rich in niacin, but as much as 80 percent of it is unavailable to the human body because it is bound into insoluble carbohydrate-protein-nitrogen compounds. Corn also has some non-heme iron (the inorganic form of iron found in plants) that the body does not absorb as well as heme iron (the organic form of iron in foods of animal origin). You can get more non-heme iron from corn by eating the corn with meat or with a food rich in vitamin C.

THE MOST NUTRITIOUS WAY TO SERVE THIS FOOD

With beans (which are rich in lysine) or milk (which is rich in lysine and tryptophan), to complement the proteins in corn.

With meat or a food rich in vitamin C, to make the iron in corn more useful.

DIETS THAT MAY RESTRICT OR EXCLUDE THIS FOOD

Low-fiber diet
Sucrose-free diet

BUYING THIS FOOD

Look for: Cobs that feel cool or are stored in a refrigerated bin. Keeping corn cool helps retain its vitamin C and slows the natural conversion of the corn's sugars to starch.

Choose fresh corn with medium-sized kernels that yield slightly when you press them with your fingertip. Very small kernels are immature; very large ones are older and will taste starchy rather than sweet. Both yellow and white kernels may be equally tasty, but the husk of the corn should always be moist and green. A dry yellowish husk means that the corn is old enough for the chlorophyll pigments in the husk to have faded, letting the carotenes underneath show through.

STORING THIS FOOD

Refrigerate fresh corn. At room temperature, fresh-picked sweet corn will convert nearly half its sugar to starch within 24 hours and lose half its vitamin C in four days. In the refrigerator, it may keep all its vitamin C for up to a week and may retain its sweet taste for as long as ten days.

PREPARING THIS FOOD

Strip off the husks and silk, and brush with a vegetable brush to get rid of clinging silky threads. Rinse the corn briefly under running water, and plunge into boiling water for four to six minutes, depending on the size of the corn.

WHAT HAPPENS WHEN YOU COOK THIS FOOD

Heat denatures (breaks apart) the long-chain protein molecules in the liquid inside the corn kernel, allowing them to form a network of protein molecules that will squeeze out moisture and turn rubbery if you cook the corn too long. Heat also allows the starch granules inside the kernel to absorb water so that they swell and eventually rupture, releasing the nutrients inside. When you cook corn, the trick is to cook it just long enough to rupture its starch granules while keeping its protein molecules from turning tough and chewy.

Cooking fresh corn for several minutes in boiling water may destroy at least half of its vitamin C. At Cornell University, food scientists found that cooking fresh corn in the microwave oven (2 ears/without water if very fresh/4 minutes/600-700 watts) preserves most of the vitamin C.

HOW OTHER FORMS OF PROCESSING AFFECT THIS FOOD

Canning and freezing.   Canned corn and frozen corn both have less vitamin C than fresh-cooked corn. The vitamin is lost when the corn is heated during canning or blanched before freezing to destroy the natural enzymes that would otherwise continue to ripen it. Blanching in a microwave oven rather than in boiling water can preserve the vitamin C in frozen corn (see above).

Milling.   Milling removes the hull and germ from the corn kernel, leaving what is called *hominy*. Hominy, which is sometimes soaked in wood ash (lye) to increase its calcium content, can be dried and used as a cereal (grits) or ground into corn flour. Coarsely ground corn flour is called *cornmeal*.

Processed corn cereals.   All processed, ready-to-eat corn cereals are much higher in sodium and sugar than fresh corn.

MEDICAL USES AND/OR BENEFITS

As a wheat substitute in baking.   People who are allergic to wheat or cannot tolerate the gluten in wheat flour or wheat cereals can often use corn flour or hominy instead.

Bath powder.   Corn starch, a fine powder refined from the endosperm (inner part) of the corn kernel, can be used as an inexpensive, unperfumed body or face powder. Because it absorbs oils, it is also used as an ingredient in dry shampoos.

ADVERSE EFFECTS ASSOCIATED WITH THIS FOOD

Allergy.   Corn is one of the foods most commonly implicated as a cause of the classic food allergy symptoms: hives, angioedema (swelling of the lips and eyes), and upset stomach. The pollen of the corn plant is also an airborne allergen that can trigger hay feverlike symptoms in sensitive people.

Pellegra.   Pellegra is a niacin-deficiency disease that occurs most commonly among people for whom corn is the staple food in a diet lacking protein foods with the essential amino acid tryptophan, which can be converted to niacin in the human body. Pellegra is not an inevitable result of a diet high in corn, however, since the niacin in corn can be made more useful by soaking the corn in a solution of calcium carbonate (lime) and water. In Mexico, for example, the corn used to make tortillas is boiled in a dilute solution of calcium carbonate (from shells or limestone) and water, then washed, drained, and ground. The alkaline bath appears to release the bound niacin in corn so that it can be absorbed by the body.

FOOD/DRUG INTERACTIONS

*   *   *

CRANBERRIES

NUTRITIONAL PROFILE

Energy value (calories per serving):	Low
Protein:	Low
Fat:	Low
Cholesterol:	None
Carbohydrates:	High
Fiber:	High
Sodium:	Low
Major vitamin contribution:	Vitamin C
Major mineral contribution:	Iron, potassium

ABOUT THE NUTRIENTS IN THIS FOOD

Cranberries are nearly 90 percent water. The rest is carbohydrates (sugars and indigestible gums, pectins, and cellulose, but no starch), plus a little protein and a trace of fat. Since pectin dissolves as the fruit ripens, the older and riper the berries, the less pectin they contain. The only important vitamin in cranberries is vitamin C, 13.5 mg per 3.5 ounces of fresh, raw berries, enough to have made them useful as an antiscorbutic (a food or drug used to prevent or cure scurvy) for early sea captains sailing out of New England.

THE MOST NUTRITIOUS WAY TO SERVE THIS FOOD

Relish made of fresh, uncooked berries (to preserve the vitamin C, which is destroyed by heat) plus oranges.

DIETS THAT MAY RESTRICT OR EXCLUDE THIS FOOD

Low-fiber diet

Sucrose-free diet

BUYING THIS FOOD

Look for: Firm, round, plump, bright red berries that feel cool and dry to the touch.

Avoid: Shriveled, damp, or moldy cranberries. Moldy cranberries may be contaminated with fusarium molds, which produce toxins that can irritate skin and damage tissues by inhibiting the synthesis of DNA and protein.

STORING THIS FOOD

Store cranberries in the refrigerator. Fresh cranberries will turn brownish if stored at high temperatures, when oxygen and the vitamin C in the berries combine to destroy the anthocyanin pigments that make cranberries red.

PREPARING THIS FOOD

Wash the berries under running water, drain them, and pick them over carefully to remove shriveled, damaged, or moldy berries.

WHAT HAPPENS WHEN YOU COOK THIS FOOD

First, the heat will make the water inside the cranberry swell, so that if you cook it long enough the berry will burst. Next, the anthocyanin pigments that make cranberries red will dissolve and make the cooking water red. Anthocyanins stay bright red in acid solutions and turn bluish if the liquid is basic (alkaline). Cooking cranberries in lemon juice and sugar preserves the color as well as brightens the taste. Finally, the heat of cooking will destroy some of the vitamin C in cranberries. Cranberry sauce has about one-third the vitamin C of an equal amount of fresh cranberries.

HOW OTHER FORMS OF PROCESSING AFFECT THIS FOOD

*   *   *

MEDICAL USES AND/OR BENEFITS

Urinary antiseptic.   In 1985, researchers at Youngstown State University in Ohio found a special factor in cranberries that seems to interfere with the ability of pathogenic bacteria to cling to the surface of cells in the bladder and urinary tract. The factor has shown up in the urine of both animal and human subjects within one to three hours after drinking cranberry juice and may stay potent for as long as twelve to fifteen hours. If the Youngstown research proves out, it may well provide a scientific explanation for the long-standing use of cranberry juice as a folk remedy for urinary infections.

ADVERSE EFFECTS ASSOCIATED WITH THIS FOOD
*   *   *

FOOD/DRUG INTERACTIONS

Methenamine.   Foods than acidify urine appear to make this urinary anti-septic more effective. Cranberry juice, which produces hippuric acid, does makes urine more acid, but the Youngstown research (see *Medical uses,* above) raises questions about exactly why cranberries and/or cranberry juice are useful for patients with a urinary infection.

CUCUMBERS
(Pickles)

NUTRITIONAL PROFILE

Energy value (calories per serving):	Low
Protein:	Moderate
Fat:	Low
Cholesterol:	None
Carbohydrates:	High
Fiber:	Low
Sodium:	Low
Major vitamin contribution:	Vitamin C
Major mineral contribution:	Iron, potassium

ABOUT THE NUTRIENTS IN THIS FOOD

The combination of food fibers (gums, pectins, cellulose, and hemicellulose) in cucumbers can hold up to 30 times its own weight in water, compared to the fiber in wheat bran, which can hold only four to six times its own weight in water. Nevertheless, the cucumber has so much water and so little fiber that it is not considered a high-fiber food.

On the other hand, fresh cucumbers are a good source of vitamin C. A 3.5-ounce serving has 5 mg, about 8 percent of the RDA for a healthy adult.

THE MOST NUTRITIOUS WAY TO SERVE THIS FOOD

Raw, fresh-sliced, with the unwaxed skin.

DIETS THAT MAY RESTRICT OR EXCLUDE THIS FOOD

Antiflatulence diet
Low-fiber diet
Sucrose-free diet

BUYING THIS FOOD

Look for: Firm cucumbers with a green, unwaxed skin. In the natural state, the skin of the cucumber is neither shiny nor deep green, characteristics it picks up when the cucumber is waxed to keep it from losing moisture during shipping and storage. The wax is edible, but some people prefer not to eat it, which means missing out on fiber. To get your cucumbers without wax, ask for pickling cucumbers—note the difference in color and texture.

Choose cucumbers with a clean break at the stem end; a torn, uneven stem end means that the cucumber was pulled off the vine before it was ready. Technically, all the cucumbers we buy are immature; truly ripe cucumbers have very large, hard seeds that make the vegetable unpalatable.

Avoid: Cucumbers with yellowing skin; the vegetable is so old that its chlorophyll pigments have faded and the carotenes underneath are showing through. Puffy, soft cucumbers are are also past their prime.

STORING THIS FOOD

Store cucumbers in the refrigerator and use them as soon as possible. The cucumber has no starch to convert to sugar as it ages, so it won't get sweeter off the vine, but it will get softer as the pectins in its cell wall absorb water. You can make a soft cucumber crisp again by slicing it and soaking the slices in salted water. By osmotic action, the unsalted, lower-density water in the cucumber's cells will flow out across the cell walls out into the higher-density salted water and the cucumber will feel snappier.

PREPARING THIS FOOD

Rinse the cucumber under cold, running water. Check to see if the cucumber has been waxed by scraping the skin gently with the tip of your fingernail and then looking for waxy residue under the nail. If the skin is waxed, you can peel it off—but not until you are ready to use it, since slicing the cucumber tears its cell walls, releasing an enzyme that oxidizes and destroys vitamin C.

WHAT HAPPENS WHEN YOU COOK THIS FOOD

*   *   *

HOW OTHER FORMS OF PROCESSING AFFECT THIS FOOD

Pickling. Cucumbers are not a good source of iron, but pickles may be. If processed in iron vats, the pickles have picked up iron and will give you about 1 mg per pickle. Pickles made in stainless steel vats have no iron, nor do pickles made at home in glass or earthenware.

MEDICAL USES AND/OR BENEFITS

*   *   *

ADVERSE EFFECTS ASSOCIATED WITH THIS FOOD

Intestinal gas. Some sensitive people find cucumbers "gassy." Pickling, marinating, and heating, which inactivate enzymes in the cucumber, may reduce this gasiness for certain people—although others find pickles even more upsetting than fresh cucumbers.

FOOD/DRUG INTERACTIONS

False-positive test for occult blood in the stool. The active ingredient in the guaiac slide test for hidden blood in feces is alphaguaiaconic acid, a chemical that turns blue in the presence of blood. Alphaguaiaconic acid also turns blue in the presence of peroxidase, a chemical that occurs naturally in cucumbers. Eating cucumbers in the 72 hours before taking the guaiac test may produce a false-positive result in people who not not actually have any blood in their stool.

CURRANTS
(Gooseberries)

See also RAISINS

NUTRITIONAL PROFILE

Energy value (calories per serving):	Low
Protein:	Moderate
Fat:	Low
Cholesterol:	None
Carbohydrates:	High
Fiber:	High
Sodium:	Low
Major vitamin contribution:	Vitamin C
Major mineral contribution:	Potassium

ABOUT THE NUTRIENTS IN THIS FOOD

Nutritionally, fresh black (European) currants, the berries used to make *crème de cassis,* are more valuable than fresh red currants, white currants, and gooseberries. They have nearly twice as much vitamin A; about one and a half times the potassium, calcium, and phosphorus; and nearly 4.5 times as much vitamin C—181 mg/100 grams versus 41 mg/100 grams. (All currants and gooseberries are rich in vitamin C, which is lost when the berries are cooked to make jams and jellies.)

THE MOST NUTRITIOUS WAY TO SERVE THIS FOOD

Fresh.

DIETS THAT MAY RESTRICT OR EXCLUDE THIS FOOD
Sucrose-free diet

BUYING THIS FOOD
Look for: Plump, firm, well-colored currants. Gooseberries, which are members of the same species as currants, should have a slight golden blush.

Avoid: Sticky packages of currants or berries, moldy fruit, or fruit with lots of stems and leaves.

STORING THIS FOOD
Refrigerate ripe currants or gooseberries and use them within a day or so. Dried currants can be stored at room temperature in an air- and moisture-proof package.

PREPARING THIS FOOD
Wash fresh currants or gooseberries under cold running water, pull off stems and leaves, and drain the berries.

WHAT HAPPENS WHEN YOU COOK THIS FOOD
When fresh currants and gooseberries are heated, the water under the skin expands; if you cook them long enough, the berries will eventually burst.

HOW OTHER FORMS OF PROCESSING AFFECT THIS FOOD
Canning. The heat of canning destroys vitamin C; canned gooseberries have only about one-third the vitamin C of fresh gooseberries.

MEDICAL USES AND/OR BENEFITS
*   *   *

ADVERSE EFFECTS ASSOCIATED WITH THIS FOOD
Allergic reactions. Virtually all berries have been implicated as the cause of classic allergic symptoms—hives, angioedema (swelling of the lips and eyes), and upset stomach—in sensitive individuals.

FOOD/DRUG INTERACTIONS
*   *   *

DATES

NUTRITIONAL PROFILE

Energy value (calories per serving):	High
Protein:	Low
Fat:	Low
Cholesterol:	None
Carbohydrates:	High
Fiber:	High
Sodium:	Low* (fresh or dried fruit) High (dried fruit treated with sodium sulfur compounds)
Major vitamin contribution:	Niacin
Major mineral contribution:	Iron, potassium

ABOUT THE NUTRIENTS IN THIS FOOD

Dates are a high-carbohydrate food, rich in fiber and packed with sugar (as much as 70 percent of the total weight of the fruit). Dates are also a good source of non-heme iron, the inorganic iron found in plant foods, plus potassium, niacin, thiamin and riboflavin, but they are an unusual fruit because they have no vitamin C at all.

THE MOST NUTRITIOUS WAY TO SERVE THIS FOOD

With meat or with a vitamin C-rich food. Both enhance your body's ability to use the non-heme iron in plants (which is ordinarily much less useful than heme iron, the organic iron in foods of animal origin).

DIETS THAT MAY RESTRICT OR EXCLUDE THIS FOOD

Disaccharide-intolerance (sucrase- or invertase-deficiency) diet

*Unless treated with sodium sulfur compounds.

Low-carbohydrate diet
Low-fiber/low-residue diet
Low-potassium diet
Low-sodium diet (dried dates, if treated with sodium sulfite)
Sucrose-free diet

BUYING THIS FOOD

Look for: Soft, shiny brown dates in tightly sealed packages.

STORING THIS FOOD

Store opened packages of dates in the refrigerator, tightly wrapped to keep the fruit from drying out. (The dates sold in American markets are partly dried; they retain sufficient moisture to keep them soft and tasty.) Properly stored dates will stay fresh for several weeks.

PREPARING THIS FOOD

To slice dates neatly, chill them in the refrigerator or freezer for an hour first. The colder they are, the easier it will be to slice them.

If you're adding dates to a cake or bread batter, coat them first with flour to keep them from dropping through the batter.

WHAT HAPPENS WHEN YOU COOK THIS FOOD

The dates will absorb moisture from a cake or bread batter and soften.

HOW OTHER FORMS OF PROCESSING AFFECT THIS FOOD

*   *   *

MEDICAL USES AND/OR BENEFITS

Potassium replacement.   Dates, which are high in potassium, are sometimes used as a source of potassium for people who are using diuretics and losing potassium. There is some question, however, as to whether potassium gluconate, the potassium in fruit, is as readily absorbed by the body as the potassium chloride or potassium citrate in vitamin and mineral supplements used in the animal experiments that provided the scientific justification for potassium replacement during diuretic therapy.

ADVERSE EFFECTS ASSOCIATED WITH THIS FOOD

Sulfite sensitivity.   Dates contain polyphenoloxidase, an enzyme that oxidizes phenols in the fruit to brown compounds that turn its flesh dark in the presence of air. To keep dates from darkening when they are dried, they may be treated with sulfur compounds called sulfites (sulfur dioxide, sodium bisulfite, or sodium metabisulfite). Treated dates may trigger serious allergic reactions, including potentially fatal anaphylactic shock, in people sensitive to sulfites.

FOOD/DRUG INTERACTIONS
*   *   *

EGGPLANT

NUTRITIONAL PROFILE

Energy value (calories per serving):	Low
Protein:	Moderate
Fat:	Low
Cholesterol:	None
Carbohydrates:	High
Fiber:	High
Sodium:	Low
Major vitamin contribution:	Vitamin C (low)
Major mineral contribution:	Potassium (low)

ABOUT THE NUTRIENTS IN THIS FOOD

Eggplants have a little bit of everything—but not very much of any particular nutrient. They are low in calories and sodium, have very little fat and no cholesterol at all. Their primary virtue is their adaptability. Eggplants can be sliced and used in place of veal for a vegetarian *parmigiana* dish, ground and added to spaghetti sauce, or minced with olive oil and seasonings to serve as a "poor man's caviar."

THE MOST NUTRITIOUS WAY TO SERVE THIS FOOD

Freshly cooked (but see *Adverse effects,* below).

DIETS THAT MAY RESTRICT OR EXCLUDE THIS FOOD

Sucrose-free diet

BUYING THIS FOOD

Look for: Firm, purple to purple-black or umblemished white eggplants that are heavy for their size.

Avoid: Withered, soft, bruised, or damaged eggplants. Withered eggplants will be bitter; damaged ones will be dark inside.

STORING THIS FOOD

Handle eggplants carefully. If you bruise an eggplant, its damaged cells will release polyphenoloxidase, an enzyme that hastens the oxidation of phenols in the eggplant's flesh, producing brown compounds that darken the vegetable.

Refrigerate fresh eggplant to keep it from losing moisture and wilting.

PREPARING THIS FOOD

Do not slice or peel an eggplant until you are ready to use it, since the polyphenoloxidase in the eggplant will begin to convert phenols to brown compounds as soon as you tear the vegetable's cells. You can slow this chemical reaction (but not stop it completely) by soaking sliced eggplant in ice water—which will reduce the eggplant's already slim supply of water-soluble vitamin C and B vitamins—or by painting the slices with a solution of lemon juice or vinegar.

To remove the liquid that can make a cooked eggplant taste bitter, slice the eggplant, salt the slices, pile them on a plate, and put a second plate on top to weight the slices down. Discard the liquid that results.

WHAT HAPPENS WHEN YOU COOK THIS FOOD

A fresh eggplant's cells are full of air that escapes when you heat the vegetable. If you cook an eggplant with oil, the empty cells will soak it up. Eventually, however, the cell walls will collapse and the oil will leak out, which is why eggplant *parmigiana* often seems to be served in a pool of olive oil.

Eggplant should never be cooked in an aluminum pot, which will discolor the eggplant. If you cook the eggplant in its skin, adding lemon juice or vinegar to the dish will turn the skin, which is colored with red anthocyanin pigments, a deeper red-purple. Red anthocyanin pigments get redder in acids and turn bluish in basic (alkaline) solutions.

Cooking reduces the eggplant's supply of water-soluble vitamins, but you can save the Bs if you serve the eggplant with its juices.

HOW OTHER FORMS OF PROCESSING AFFECT THIS FOOD

*   *   *

MEDICAL USES AND/OR BENEFITS OF THIS FOOD
       *   *   *

ADVERSE EFFECTS ASSOCIATED WITH THIS FOOD

Nitrate/nitrite reactions. Eggplant—like beets, celery, lettuce, radish, spinach, and collard and turnip greens—contains nitrates that convert naturally into nitrites in your stomach, and then react with the amino acids in proteins to form nitrosamines. Although some nitrosamines are known or suspected carcinogens, this natural chemical conversion presents no known problems for a healthy adult. However, when these nitrate-rich vegetables are cooked and left to stand at room temperature, bacterial enzyme action (and perhaps some enzymes in the plants) convert the nitrates to nitrites at a much faster rate than normal. These higer-nitrite foods may be hazardous for infants; several cases of "spinach poisoning" have been reported among children who ate cooked spinach that had been left standing at room temperature.

FOOD/DRUG INTERACTIONS

MAO inhibitors.   Monoamine oxidase (MAO) inhibitors are drugs used as antidepressants or antihypertensives. They inhibit the action of enzymes that break down tyramine, a natural by-product of protein metabolism, so that it can be eliminated from the body. Tyramine is a pressor amine, a chemical that constricts blood vessels and raises blood pressure. If you eat a food rich in tyramine while you are taking an MAO inhibitor, the pressor amine cannot be eliminated from your body, and the result may be a hypertensive crisis (sustained elevated blood pressure). Eggplants contain small amounts of tyramine.

False-positive urine test for carcinoid tumors.   Carcinoid tumors (tumors that may arise in tissues of the endocrine and gastrointestinal systems) secrete serotonin, which is excreted in urine. The test for these tumors measures the level of serotonin in your urine. Eating eggplant, which is rich in serotonin, in the 72 hours before a test for a carcinoid tumor might raise the serotonin levels in your urine high enough to cause a false-positive test result. (Other fruits and vegetables rich in serotonin are bananas, tomatoes, plums, pineapple, avocados, and walnuts.)

EGGS

NUTRITIONAL PROFILE*

Energy value (calories per serving):	Moderate
Protein:	High
Fat:	High
Cholesterol:	High
Carbohydrates:	Low
Fiber:	None
Sodium:	Moderate to high
Major vitamin contribution:	Vitamin A, riboflavin, vitamin D
Major mineral contribution:	Iron, calcium

ABOUT THE NUTRIENTS IN THIS FOOD

An egg is really three different foods—white, yolk, and whole egg—each with its own distinct nutritional properties.

The white is a high-protein, low-fat food with virtually no cholesterol and only about 13 percent of the calories in an equal amount of egg yolk. The only important vitamin in egg white is riboflavin (vitamin B_2), a "visible vitamin" that gives egg white its slightly greenish tint. Egg white also contains the antinutrient avidin. The avidin in raw egg whites binds biotin into an insoluble compound your body cannot absorb, and people who eat large amounts of raw egg whites might end up with a biotin deficiency. However, since avidin is inactivated simply by cooking the egg, this is very rare.

*Values are for a whole egg.

Egg yolks are a good source of protein, but they are high in fat and cholesterol. Thirty-seven percent of the fatty acids in the yolk are saturated, and one large egg yolk has 274 mg cholesterol. The yolk is a good source of calcium, phosphorus, and heme iron, the organic form of iron found in foods of animal origin. Its carotenes make it a good source of vitamin A but, since the yolk also contains xanthophylls (caretenoid pigments with little vitamin A activity), you can't judge the vitamin content by the color. Egg yolks also supply vitamin D, thiamin (vitamin B_1), riboflavin (vitamin B_2), and niacin. Both egg whites and egg yolks are moderately high in sodium.

Together, the yolk and white make a high-protein, relatively low-calorie food, with a calcium-rich shell that can be ground and added to cooked eggs as a calcium supplement. The proteins in eggs are considered "complete," with a rating of 100 on an arbitrary scale established by the Food and Agriculture Organization of the World Health Organization to measure the relative quality of food proteins. Like the proteins in milk, they are 99 percent digestible, the most useful proteins available for human beings. Eggs have a little sugar, but no fiber.

THE MOST NUTRITIOUS WAY TO SERVE THIS FOOD

With meat or a vitamin C-rich food (citrus fruit or juice) to increase your body's absorption of the iron in the yolk.

With extra whites and fewer yolks (for example, two whites and one yolk) to reduce the fat and cholesterol content.

DIETS THAT MAY RESTRICT OR EXCLUDE THIS FOOD

Controlled-fat, low-cholesterol diet
Low-protein diet

BUYING THIS FOOD

Look for: Eggs that fit your needs. Eggs are graded by the size of the yolk and the thickness of the white, qualities that affect appearance but not nutritional values. The higher the grade, the thicker the yolk and the thicker the white will be when you cook the egg. A Grade AA egg fried sunny side up will look much more attractive than a Grade B egg prepared the same way, but both will be equally nutritious. Egg sizes (Jumbo, Extra large, Large, Medium, Small) are determined by how much the eggs weigh per dozen. The color of the egg's shell depends on the breed of the hen that laid the egg and has nothing to do with the egg's food value.

STORING THIS FOOD

Store fresh eggs in the the refrigerator in an egg-keeper section or keep them in the original carton, which is designed to keep them from breaking or absorbing strong odors through their shells. *Never* wash eggs before storing them: The water will make the egg shell more porous, allowing harmful microorganisms to enter.

Store separated leftover yolks and whites in small, tightly covered containers in the refrigerator, where they may stay fresh for up to a week. Raw eggs are very susceptible to *Salmonella* and other bacterial contamination; discard *any* egg that looks or smells the least bit unusual.

Refrigerate hard-cooked eggs, including decorated Easter eggs. They, too, are susceptible to *Salmonella* contamination and should *never* be left at room temperature.

PREPARING THIS FOOD

First, find out how fresh the eggs really are. The freshest ones are the eggs that sink and lie flat on their sides when submerged in cool water. These eggs can be used for any dish. By the time the egg is a week old, the air pocket inside, near the broad end, has expanded so that the broad end tilts up as the egg is submerged in cool water. The yolk and the white inside have begun to separate; these eggs are easier to peel when hard-cooked. A week or two later, the egg's air pocket has expanded enough to cause the broad end of the egg to point straight up when you put the egg in water. By now the egg is runny and should be used in sauces where it doesn't matter if it isn't picture-perfect. After four weeks, the egg will float. Throw it away.

When you're ready to crack an egg, rinse it first under cool running water to wash away microorganisms on the surface. You can separate eggs by hand *if you wash your hands thoroughly before handling the eggs to avoid transferring any bacteria from your skin to the eggs.* Naturally, any mechanical device used to separate eggs should also be absolutely clean.

When you whip an egg white, you change the structure of its protein molecules which unfold, breaking bonds between atoms on the same molecule and forming new bonds to atoms on adjacent molecules. The result is a network of protein molecules that hardens around air trapped in bubbles in the net. If you beat the whites too long, the foam will turn stiff enough to hold its shape even if you don't cook it, but it will be too stiff to expand naturally if you heat it, as in a soufflé. When you do cook properly whipped egg white foam, the hot air inside the bubbles will expand. Ovalbumin, an elastic protein in the white, allows the bubble walls to bulge outward until they are cooked firm and the network is stabilized as a puffy soufflé.

The bowl in which you whip the whites should be absolutely free of fat or grease, since the fat molecules will surround the protein molecules in the egg white and keep them from linking up together to form a puffy white foam. Egg whites will react with metal ions from the surface of an aluminum bowl to form dark particles that discolor the egg-white foam. You can whip eggs successfully in an enamel or glass bowl, but they will do best in a copper bowl because copper ions bind to the egg and stabilize the foam.

WHAT HAPPENS WHEN YOU COOK THIS FOOD

When you heat a whole egg, its protein molecules behave exactly as they do when you whip an egg white. They unfold, form new bonds, and create a protein network, this time with molecules of water caught in the net. As the egg cooks, the protein network tightens, sqeeezing out moisture, and the egg becomes opaque. The longer you cook the egg, the tighter the network will be. If you cook the egg too long, the protein network will contract strongly enough to force out all the moisture. That is why overcooked egg custards run and why overcooked eggs are rubbery.

If you mix eggs with milk or water before you cook them, the molecules of liquid will surround and separate the egg's protein molecules so that it takes more energy (higher heat) to make the protein molecules coagulate. Scrambled eggs made with milk are softer than plain scrambled eggs cooked at the same temperature.

When you boil an egg in its shell, the air inside expands and begins to escape through the shell as tiny bubbles. Sometimes, however, the force of the air is enough to crack the shell. Since there's no way for you to tell in advance whether any particular egg is strong enough to resist the pressure of the bubbling air, the best solution is to create a safety vent by sticking a pin through the broad end of the egg before you start to boil it. Or you can slow the rate at which the air inside the shell expands by starting the egg in cold water and letting it warm up naturally as the water warms rather than plunging it cold into boiling water—which makes the air expand so quickly that the shell is virtually certain to crack.

As the egg heats, a little bit of the protein in its white will decompose, releasing sulfur that links up with hydrogen in the egg, forming hydrogen sulfide, the gas that gives rotten eggs their distinctive smell. The hydrogen sulfide collects near the coolest part of the egg—the yolk. The yolk contains iron, which now displaces the hydrogen in the hydrogen sulfide to form a green iron-sulfide ring around the hard-cooked yolk.

HOW OTHER FORMS OF PROCESSING AFFECT THIS FOOD

Drying. Dried eggs have virtually the same nutritive value as fresh eggs. Always refrigerate dried eggs in an air- and moistureproof container. At room temperature, they will lose about a third of their vitamin A in six months.

MEDICAL USES AND/OR BENEFITS

External cosmetic effects. Beaten egg whites can be used as a facial mask to make your skin look smoother temporarily. The mask works because the egg proteins constrict as they dry on your face, pulling at the dried layer of cells on top of your skin. When you wash off the egg white, you also wash off some of these loose cells. Used in a rinse or shampoo, the protein in a beaten raw egg can make your hair look smoother and shinier temporarily by filling in chinks and notches on the hair shaft.

ADVERSE EFFECTS ASSOCIATED WITH THIS FOOD

Allergy.   Eggs are among the foods most often linked to the classic symptoms of true food allergy: abdominal pain, nausea or vomiting, cramps, dizziness, hives, angioedema (swollen lips and eyes), hay-feverlike reactions, and eczema.

In 1983, research at the University of California/San Francisco suggested that eggs may also trigger a delayed inflammatory reaction similar to arthritis.

Elevated levels of serum cholesterol.   Abnormally high levels of cholesterol in the blood are a risk factor in heart disease. How your diet affects the amount of cholesterol you produce is not entirely clear; dietary fat and cholesterol may not be the primary factor in determining how much and what kind of cholesterol your body makes and stores. Nonetheless, there is evidence to suggest that controlling the amount of fat and cholesterol you consume may help lower serum cholesterol levels, particularly for people with high levels.

In 1986 the American Heart Association issued new guidelines, suggesting that healthy adults reduce their fat consumption to 30 percent of their total calories and limit cholesterol intake to 3000 mg per day or 100 mg per 1000 calories, whichever is less. There is no cholesterol in egg white. (One boiled egg contains 450 mg cholesterol, all in the yolk.)

Food poisoning.   Raw eggs and egg-rich foods such as custards and cream pies are excellent media for microorganisms, including those that cause food poisoning. Raw eggs should always be refrigerated; egg-rich dishes should always be thoroughly cooked, stored in the refrigerator, and served either very hot or very cold.

FOOD/DRUG INTERACTIONS

Sensitivity to vaccines.   Live-virus measles vaccine, live-virus mumps vaccine, and the vaccines for influenza are grown in either chick embryo or egg culture. They may all contain minute residual amounts of egg proteins that may provoke a hypersensitivity reaction in people with a history of anaphylactic reactions to eggs (hives, swelling of the mouth and throat, difficulty breathing, a drop in blood pressure, or shock).

FIGS

NUTRITIONAL PROFILE

Energy value (calories per serving):	Moderate (fresh figs) High (dried figs)
Protein:	Low
Fat:	Low
Cholesterol:	None
Carbohydrates:	High
Fiber:	High
Sodium:	Low (fresh or dried fruit) High (dried fruit treated with sodium sulfur compounds)
Major vitamin contribution:	B vitamins
Major mineral contribution:	Iron (dried figs)

ABOUT THE NUTRIENTS IN THIS FOOD

Fresh figs and dried figs are an extraordinarily good source of carbohydrates (sugars), fiber, iron, calcium, and potassium.

Figs have no starch; 92 percent of the carbohydrates in dried figs are sugars (42 percent glucose, 31 percent fructose, 0.1 percent sucrose). The rest are dietary fibers (primarily pectins and gums, plus cellulose). Figs are also a good source of the noncarbohydrate fiber lignin.

The most important mineral in dried figs is iron, 0.6 mg/oz. (compared with 1.9 mg/oz. in beef liver). One 3.5-ounce serving of uncooked dried figs provides 2.23 mg iron, one-eighth the RDA for a healthy adult female. Ounce for ounce, dried figs have more calcium than milk, but they aren't as convenient a source of of this mineral because it takes 19 ounces of dried figs to supply the 800 mg of calcium we get from three 8-ounce glasses of whole milk.

THE MOST NUTRITIOUS WAY TO SERVE THIS FOOD

Dried (But see *Adverse effects,* below).

DIETS THAT MAY RESTRICT OR EXCLUDE THIS FOOD

Low-fiber, low-residue diets
Low-sodium (dried figs treated with sulfites)
Sucrose-free diet

BUYING THIS FOOD

Look for: Plump, soft fresh figs whose skin may be green, brown, or purple, depending on the variety. As figs ripen, the pectin in their cell walls dissolves and the figs grow softer to the touch.

Choose dried figs in tightly sealed airtight packages.

Avoid: Fresh figs that smell sour. The odor indicates that the sugars in the fig have fermented; such fruit is spoiled.

STORING THIS FOOD

Refrigerate fresh figs. Dried figs can be stored in the refrigerator or at room temperature; either way, wrap them tightly in an air- and moistureproof container to keep them from losing moisture and becoming hard. Dried figs may keep for several months.

PREPARING THIS FOOD

Wash fresh figs under cool water; use dried figs right out of the package. If you want to slice the dried figs, chill them first in the refrigerator or freezer: cold figs slice clean.

WHAT HAPPENS WHEN YOU COOK THIS FOOD

Fresh figs contain ficin, a proteolytic (protein-breaking) enzyme similar to papain in papayas and bromelin in fresh pineapple. Proteolytic enzymes split long-chain protein molecules into smaller units, which is why they help tenderize meat. Ficin is most effective at about 140-160° F, the temperature at which stews simmer, and it will continue to work after you take the stew off the stove until the food cools down. Temperatures higher than 160° F inactivate ficin; canned figs—which have been exposed to very high heat in processing—will not tenderize meat.

Both fresh and dried figs contain pectin, which dissolves when you cook the figs, making them softer. Dried figs also absorb water and swell.

HOW OTHER FORMS OF PROCESSING AFFECT THIS FOOD

Canning: Canned figs contain slightly less vitamin C, thiamin, riboflavin, and niacin than fresh figs, and no active ficin.

MEDICAL USES AND/OR BENEFITS

Iron supplementation.   Dried figs are an excellent source of iron.

As a laxative: Figs are a good source of the indigestible food fiber lignin. Cells whose walls are highly lignified retain water and, since they are impossible to digest, help bulk up the stool. In addition, ficin has some laxative effects. Together, the lignin and the ficin make figs (particularly dried figs) an efficient laxative food.

Potassium replacement.   Dried figs are a good source of potassium; four small ones contain slightly more potassium than a cup of orange juice. Foods rich in potassium are sometimes prescribed for people taking diuretics that lower the body's level of potassium, which is excreted in urine. However, there is some question as to whether potassium gluconate, the form of potassium in figs, is as useful to the body as potassium citrate or potassium chloride, the potassium in the supplements given to laboratory animals to show the value of potassium replacement during diuretic therapy.

ADVERSE EFFECTS ASSOCIATED WITH THIS FOOD

Sensitivity to sulfites.   Figs contain polyphenoloxidase, an enzyme that hastens the oxidation of phenols in the fig, creating brownish compounds that darken its flesh. Dried figs may be treated with a sulfur compound (sulfur dioxide, sodium sulfite, or sodium metabisulfite) to prevent this chemical reaction. People who are sensitive to sulfites may suffer serious allergic reactions, including potentially fatal anaphylactic shock, if they eat figs that have been treated with one of these compounds.

FOOD/DRUG INTERACTIONS

MAO inhibitors.   Monoamine oxidase (MAO) inhibitors are drugs used as antidepressants or antihypertensives. They inhibit the action of natural enzymes that break down tyramine, a nitrogen compound formed when proteins are metabolized, so it can be eliminated from the body. Tyramine is a pressor amine, a chemical that constricts blood vessels and raises blood pressure. If you eat a food rich in one of these chemicals while you are taking an MAO inhibitor, the pressor amines cannot be eliminated from your body, and the result may be a hypertensive crisis (sustained elevated blood pressure). There has been one report of such a reaction in a patient who ate canned figs while taking an MAO inhibitor.

FISH

See also SHELLFISH, SQUID

NUTRITIONAL PROFILE

Energy value (calories per serving):	Moderate
Protein:	High
Fat:	Low to moderate
Cholesterol:	Moderate
Carbohydrates:	Low
Fiber:	None
Sodium:	Low (fresh fish) High (some canned or salted fish)
Major vitamin contribution:	B vitamins, vitamins A and D (in fatty fish oils)
Major mineral contribution:	Iodine, selenium, phosphorus, potassium, iron, calcium

ABOUT THE NUTRIENTS IN THIS FOOD

Fish have no measurable carbohydrates or food fiber, but they are an excellent source of proteins considered "complete" because they contain sufficient amounts of all the essential amino acids. Most fish have proportionally less fat than meat, and most fish fats and oils are higher in unsaturated fatty acids than the fat in beef, pork, or lamb. The exact proportion of fat and saturated fatty acids varies with the kind of fish as well as when and where it is caught. Cooked tuna, for example, is 1 to 2 percent fat; the fat in canned tuna is 63 percent unsaturated fatty acids. Dark orange salmon has more fat than pale pink salmon; salmon fats and oils are about 68 percent unsaturated. Herring may be 13 to 16 percent fat; its fats and oils are 82 percent unsaturated fatty acids.

The most important nutrient in fish may be the omega-3 fatty acids, eicosapentaenoic acid (EPA) and docosahexanoic acid (DHA). EPA and DHA are the primary polyunsaturated fatty acids in the fat and oils of fish. They seem to lower the levels of low-density lipoproteins (LDL), the molecules that carry cholesterol into your bloodstream, and raise the level of high-density lipoproteins (HDL), the molecules that carry cholesterol away to be eliminated from the body. They also appear to inhibit the production of leuketrienes, natural inflammatory agents that transmit signals between cells. (All inflammatory diseases are the result of exaggerated eicosanoid signals.) Omega-3 fatty acids are most abundant in oils from fatty fish that live in cold water—herring, mackerel, salmon. The oils, which stay liquid at cold temperatures, may help insulate the fish against the cold.

OMEGA-3 FATTY ACID CONTENT OF
VARIOUS FISH

Fish	Grams/oz.
Atlantic mackerel	0.61
Chinook salmon (fresh)	0.60
Pink salmon	0.55
Coho salmon, canned	0.45
Sockeye salmon	0.45
Sardines	0.32
Rainbow trout	0.30
Lake whitefish	0.25

Source: "Food for the Heart," *American Health,* April 1985.

Fish are a good source of the B vitamins (particularly niacin), and fish oils and fatty fish are two of the few natural food sources of vitamin D. The soft bones of small fish or canned salmon, sardines, and mackerel are an excellent source of calcium.

THE MOST NUTRITIOUS WAY TO SERVE THIS FOOD

Cooked, to kill parasites and potentially pathological microorganisms living in raw fish.

Broiled, to liquify fat and eliminate the fat-soluble environmental contaminants found in some freshwater fish.

With the soft, mashed, calcium-rich bones (in canned salmon and
canned sardines).

DIETS THAT MAY RESTRICT OR EXCLUDE THIS FOOD

Low-purine (antigout) diet
Low-sodium diet (canned, salted, or smoked fish)

BUYING THIS FOOD

Look for: Fresh-smelling whole fish with shiny skin; reddish-pink, moist
gills; and clear, bulging eyes. The flesh should spring back when you press it
lightly.

Choose fish fillets that look moist, not dry.

Choose tightly sealed, solidly frozen packages of frozen fish.

Avoid: Fresh whole fish whose eyes have sunk into the head (a clear sign of
aging); fillets that look dry; and packages of frozen fish that are stained
(whatever leaked on the package may have seeped through onto the fish) or
are coated with ice crystals (the package may have defrosted and been
refrozen).

STORING THIS FOOD

Remove fish from plastic wrap as soon as you get it home. Plastic keeps out
air, encouraging the growth of bacteria that make the fish smell bad. If the
fish smells bad when you open the package, throw it out.

Refrigerate all fresh and smoked fish immediately. Fish spoils quickly
because it has a high proportion of polyunsaturated fatty acids (which pick
up oxygen much more easily than saturated or monounsaturated fatty acids).
Refrigeration also slows the action of microorganisms on the surface of the
fish that convert proteins and other substances to mucopolysaccharides, leaving a slimy film on the fish.

Keep frozen fish until you are ready to use it.

Store canned fish in a cool cabinet or in a refrigerator (but not the freezer). The cooler the temperature, the longer the shelf life.

PREPARING THIS FOOD

Fresh fish.   Rub the fish with lemon juice, then rinse it under cold running
water. The lemon juice (an acid) will convert the nitrogen compounds that
make fish smell "fishy" to compounds that break apart easily and can be
rinsed off the fish with cool running water. Rinsing your hands in lemon

juice and water will get rid of the fishy smell after you have been preparing fresh fish.

Frozen fish.   Defrost plain frozen fish in the refrigerator or under cold running water. Prepared frozen fish dishes should not be thawed before you cook them since defrosting will make the sauce or coating soggy.

Salted dried fish.   Salted dried fish should be soaked to remove the salt. How long you have to soak the fish depends on how much salt was added in processing. A reasonable average for salt cod, mackerel, haddock (finnan haddie), or herring is three to six hours, with two or three changes of water.

WHAT HAPPENS WHEN YOU COOK THIS FOOD

Heat changes the structure of proteins. It denatures the protein molecules so that they break apart into smaller fragments or change shape or clump together. These changes force moisture out of the tissues so that the fish turns opaque. The longer you cook fish, the more moisture it will lose. Cooked fish flakes because the connective tissue in fish "melts" at a relatively low temperature.

Cooking fish thoroughly destroys parasites and microorganisms that live in raw fish, making the fish safer to eat.

HOW OTHER FORMS OF PROCESSING AFFECT THIS FOOD

Marinating.   Like heat, acids coagulate the proteins in fish, squeezing out moisture. Fish marinated in citrus juices and other acids such as vinegar or wine has a firm texture and looks cooked, but the acid bath may not inactivate parasites in the fish.

Canning.   Fish is naturally low in sodium, but canned fish often contains enough added salt to make it a high-sodium food. A 3.5-ounce serving of baked, fresh red salmon, for example, has 55 mg sodium, while an equal serving of regular canned salmon has 443 mg. If the fish is canned in oil it is also much higher in calories than fresh fish.

Freezing.   When fish is frozen, ice crystals form in the flesh and tear its cells so that moisture leaks out when the fish is defrosted. Commercial flash-freezing offers some protection by freezing the fish so fast that the ice crystals stay small and do less damage, but all defrosted fish tastes drier and less palatable than fresh fish. Freezing slows but does not stop the oxidation of fats that causes fish to deteriorate.

Curing. Fish can be cured (preserved) by smoking, drying, salting, or pick-ling, all of which coagulate the muscle tissue and prevent microorganisms from growing. Each method has its own particular drawbacks. Smoking adds potentially carcinogenic chemicals. Drying reduces the water content, con-centrates the solids and nutrients, increases the calories per ounce, and raises the amount of sodium.

MEDICAL USES AND/OR BENEFITS

Protective effects of omega-3 fatty acids. In 1985, the *New England Jour-nal of Medicine* published the results of three separate studies dealing with the anti-inflammatory effects of a diet rich in saltwater-fish oils.

The first, a twenty-year project at the University of Leyden in the Netherlands, compared the eating habits of more than 800 men with their risk of heart disease and found that men who ate more than an ounce of fish a day had a 50 percent lower rate of heart attacks. (Research at Cornell Uni-versity has suggested that oils inhibit the formation of thromboxane, a blood-platelet aggregator, and that omega-3 fatty acids are converted to a com-pound similar to prostacyclin, a natural body chemical that inhibits clotting.)

The second study, at the Oregon Health Sciences University in Port-land, found that a diet high in fish oils appears to lower the levels of triglycer-ides in the blood. (A high level of triglycerides, like a high level of cholesterol, increases the risk of heart disease.)

In the third study, seven volunteers at Brigham and Women's Hospital in Boston were put on a diet high in fats from saltwater fish. At the end of six weeks, the researchers found that fish oils seemed to reduce the inflammatory response in body tissues, perhaps by inhibiting the production of leuketrienes, the natural inflammatory agents that trigger a wide range of inflammatory diseases, ranging from arthritis to hay fever.

This last study is bolstered by research at the University of Michigan which suggests that fish, like vegetables, fruit, and grain, appears to interfere with the body's production of arachidonic acid (AA), a natural inflammatory agent that makes psoriatic lesions swell and turn red. To date, there is no evi-dence that oils from freshwater fish have the same effect.

ADVERSE EFFECTS ASSOCIATED WITH THIS FOOD

Allergies. Fish is one of the foods most often implicated as a cause of the classic food-allergy symptoms, including gastric upset, hives, and angioe-dema (swelling of the lips and eyes).

Environmental contaminants. Many environmental contaminants can be stored in the fatty tissues of fish from contaminated waters. PCBs have been found in bluefish caught in New Jersey, and the states of New York, Illinois, Indiana, Michigan, and Wisconsin have issued warnings against Great Lakes brown trout, lake trout, or carp longer than 25 inches (the larger and older the fish, the more PCBs may have accumulated in its tissues). Fish that are raised or caught commercially are usually safe; the hazard lies mainly with fish caught in inland waterways by sport fisherman. Since PCBs are concentrated in the fat just under the skin, filleting the fish and then broiling or grilling it so that the fat can drip off the fish may be a healthful means of preparation.

Parasitical, viral, and bacterial infections.   Like raw meat, raw fish may carry various pathogens, including fish tapeworm and flukes in freshwater fish and *Salmonella* or other microorganisms left on the fish by infected food-handlers. Cooking the fish destroys these organisms.

Scombroid poisoning.   Bacterial decomposition that occurs after fish is caught produces a histaminelike toxin in the flesh of mackerel, tuna, bonito, and albacore. This toxin may trigger a number of symptoms, including a flushed face immediately after you eat it. The other signs of scombroid poisoning—nausea, vomiting, stomach pain, and hives—show up a few minutes later. The symptoms usually last 24 hours or less.

FOOD/DRUG INTERACTIONS
*   *   *

FLOUR

See also BREAD, CORN, OATS, PASTA, POTATOES, RICE, SOYBEANS

NUTRITIONAL PROFILE

Energy value (calories per serving):	High
Protein:	Moderate
Fat:	Low
Cholesterol:	None
Carbohydrates:	High
Fiber:	Low to high
Sodium:	Low (except self-rising flour)
Major vitamin contribution:	B vitamins
Major mineral contribution:	Iron

ABOUT THE NUTRIENTS IN THIS FOOD

Flour is the primary source of the carbohydrates (starch and fiber) in bread, pasta, and baked goods. All wheat and rye flours also provide some of the food fibers, including pectins, gums, and cellulose. Flour also contains significant amounts of protein but, like other plant foods, its proteins are "incomplete" because they are deficient in the essential amino acid lysine. The fat in the wheat germ is primarily polyunsaturated; flour contains no cholesterol. Flour is a good source of iron and the B vitamins. Iodine and iodophors used to clean the equipment in grain-processing plants may add iodine to the flour.

Whole grain flour, like other grain products, also contains an antinutrient, phytic acid—which binds calcium, iron, and zinc ions into insoluble compounds your body cannot absorb. This has no practical effect so long as your diet includes foods that provide these minerals.

Whole wheat flours.   Whole wheat flours use every part of the kernel: the fiber-rich bran with its B vitamins, the starch- and protein-rich endosperm with its iron and B vitamins, and the oily germ with its vitamin E.* Because they contain bran, whole-grain flours have much more fiber than refined white flours. However, some studies suggest that the size of the fiber particles may have some bearing on their ability to absorb moisture and "bulk up" stool and that the fiber particles found in fine-ground whole wheat flours may be too small to have a bulking effect.

Finely ground whole wheat flour is called *whole wheat cake flour;* coarsely ground whole wheat flour is called *graham flour. Cracked wheat* is a whole wheat flour that has been cut rather than ground; it has all the nutrients of whole wheat flour, but its processing makes it less likely to yield its starch in cooking. When dried and parboiled, cracked wheat is known as *bulgur,* a grain used primarily as a cereal, although it can be mixed with other flours and baked. *Gluten flour* is a low-starch, high-protein product made by drying and grinding hard-wheat flour from which the starch has been removed.

Refined ("white") flours.   Refined flours are paler than whole wheat flours because they do not contain the brown bran and germ. They have less fiber and fat and smaller amounts of vitamins and minerals than whole wheat flours, but *enriched refined flours* are fortified with B vitamins and iron. Refined flour has no phytic acid.

Some refined flours are bleached with chlorine dioxide to destroy the xanthophylls (carotenoid pigments) that give white flours a natural cream color. Unlike carotene, the carotenoid pigment that is converted to vitamin A in the body, xanthophylls have no vitamin A activity; bleaching does not lower the vitamin A levels in the flour, but it does destroy vitamin E.

There are several kinds of white flours. *All-purpose* white flour is a mixture of hard and soft wheats, high in protein and rich in gluten.+ *Cake flour* is a finely milled soft-wheat flour; it has less protein than all-purpose flour. *Self-rising* flour is flour to which baking powder has been added and is very high in sodium. *Instant flour* is all-purpose flour that has been ground extra-fine so that it will combine quickly with water. *Semolina* is a pale

---

*The bran is the kernel's hard, brown outer cover, an extraordinarily rich source of cellulose and lignin. The endosperm is the kernel's pale interior, where the vitamins abound. The germ, a small particle in the interior, is the part of the kernel that sprouts.

+Hard wheat has less starch and more protein than soft wheat. It makes a heavier, denser dough.

high-protein, low-gluten flour made from durum wheat and used to make pasta.

Rye flours. Rye flour has less gluten than wheat flour and is less elastic, which is why it makes a denser bread.*

Like whole wheat flour, dark rye flour (the flour used for pumpernickel bread) contains the bran and the germ of the rye grain; light rye flour (the flour used for ordinary rye bread) does not. *Triticale flour* is milled from triticale grain, a rye/wheat hybrid. It has more protein and less gluten than all-purpose wheat flour.

THE MOST NUTRITIOUS WAY TO SERVE THIS FOOD

With beans or a "complete" protein food (meat, fish, poultry, eggs, milk, cheese) to provide the essential amino acid lysine, in which wheat and rye flours are deficient.

DIETS THAT MAY RESTRICT OR EXCLUDE THIS FOOD

Low-calcium diet (whole grain and self-rising flours)
Low-fiber diet (whole wheat flours)
Low-gluten diet (all wheat and rye flour)
Sucrose-free diet

BUYING THIS FOOD

Look for: Tightly sealed bags or boxes. Flours in torn packages or in open bins are exposed to air and to insect contamination.

Avoid: Stained packages—the liquid that stained the package may have seeped through into the flour.

STORING THIS FOOD

Store all flours in air- and moistureproof canisters. Whole wheat flours, which contain the germ and bran of the wheat and are higher in fat than white flours, may become rancid if exposed to air; they should be used within a week after you open the package. If you plan to hold the flour for longer than that, store it in the freezer, tightly wrapped to protect it against air and moisture. You do not have to thaw the flour when you are ready to use it; just measure it out and add it directly to the other ingredients.

---

*Gluten is the sticky substance formed when kneading the dough relaxes the long-chain molecules in the proteins gliadin and glutenin so that some of their intermolecular bonds (bonds between atoms in the same molecule) break and new intramolecular bonds (bonds between atoms on different molecules) are formed.

Put a bay leaf in the flour canister to help protect against insect infections. Bay leaves are natural insect repellents.

PREPARING THIS FOOD

*   *   *

WHAT HAPPENS WHEN YOU COOK THIS FOOD

Protein reactions.   The wheat kernel contains several proteins, including gliadin and glutenin. When you mix flour with water, gliadin and glutenin clump together in a sticky mass. Kneading the dough relaxes the long gliadin and glutenin molecules, breaking internal bonds between individual atoms in each gliadin and glutenin molecule and allowing the molecules to unfold and form new bonds between atoms in different molecules. The result is a network structure made of a new gliadin-glutenin compound called *gluten.*

Gluten is very elastic. The gluten network can stretch to accommodate the gas (carbon dioxide) formed when you add yeast to bread dough or heat a cake batter made with baking powder or baking soda (sodium bicarbonate), trapping the gas and making the bread dough or cake batter rise. When you bake the dough or batter, the gluten network hardens and the bread or cake assumes its finished shape.

Starch reactions.   Starch consists of molecules of the complex carbohydrates amylose and amylopectin packed into a starch granule. When you heat flour in liquid, the starch granules absorb water molecules, swell, and soften. When the temperature of the liquid reaches approximately 140°F the amylose and amylopectin molecules inside the granules relax and unfold, breaking some of their internal bonds (bonds between atoms on the same molecule) and forming new bonds between atoms on different molecules. The result is a network that traps and holds water molecules. The starch granules then swell, thickening the liquid. If you continue to heat the liquid (or stir it too vigorously), the network will begin to break down, the liquid will leak out of the starch granules, and the sauce will separate.*

Combination reaction.   Coating food with flour takes advantage of the starch reaction (absorbing liquids) and the protein reaction (baking a hard, crisp protein crust).

---

*Amylose is a long, unbranched, spiral molecule; amylopectin is a short, compact, branched molecule. Amylose has more room for forming bonds to water. Wheat flour, which has a higher ratio of amylose to amylopectin, are superior thickeners.

HOW OTHER FORMS OF PROCESSING AFFECT THIS FOOD
*   *   *

MEDICAL USES AND/OR BENEFITS
See BREAD, PASTA.

ADVERSE EFFECTS ASSOCIATED WITH THIS FOOD

Allergic reactions.   Wheat is one of the foods most commonly implicated as a cause of allergic upset stomach, hives, and angioedema (swollen lips and eyes).

Gluten intolerance (celiac disease).   Celiac disease is an intestinal allergic disorder that makes it impossible to digest gluten and gliadin (proteins found in wheat and some other grains). Corn flour, potato flour, rice flour, and soy flour are all gluten- and gliadin-free.

Ergot poisoning.   Rye and some kinds of wheat will support ergot, a parasitic fungus related to lysergic acid (LSD). Because commercial flours are routinely checked for ergot contamination, there has not been a major outbreak of ergot poisoning from bread since a 1951 incident in France. Since baking does not destroy ergot toxins, the safest course is to avoid moldy flour altogether.

FOOD/DRUG INTERACTIONS
*   *   *

GARLIC

NUTRITIONAL PROFILE

Energy value (calories per serving):	Low
Protein:	Moderate
Fat:	Low
Cholesterol:	None
Carbohydrates:	High
Fiber:	High
Sodium:	Low
Major vitamin contribution:	Vitamin C, thiamin (vitamin B_1)
Major mineral contribution:	Potassium, iron

ABOUT THE NUTRIENTS IN THIS FOOD

Raw garlic is high in carbohydrates, with some fiber and protein but almost no fat. Garlic is rich in vitamins and minerals; the trick is to eat enough garlic to get measurable amounts. For example, an ounce of raw garlic provides 0.06 mg thiamin (twice the amount in 3.5 oz. egg white), 0.5 mg iron (0.3 percent of the RDA for an adult woman), and 9 mg vitamin C (15 percent of the RDA for a healthy adult).

Elephant garlic, a cross between an onion and garlic that may grow as large as a grapefruit, has a milder flavor than regular garlic.

DIETS THAT MAY RESTRICT OR EXCLUDE THIS FOOD

Antiflatulence diet

Bland diet
Sucrose-free diet

BUYING THIS FOOD

Look for: Firm, solid cloves with tight clinging skin. If the skin is papery and pulling away from the cloves and the head feels light for its size, the garlic has withered or rotted away inside.

THE MOST NUTRITIOUS WAY TO SERVE THIS FOOD

Fresh.

STORING THIS FOOD

Store garlic in a cool, dark, airy place to keep it from drying out or sprouting. (When garlic sprouts, diallyl disulfide—the sulfur compound that gives fresh garlic its distinctive taste and odor—goes into the new growth and the garlic itself becomes milder.) An unglazed ceramic "garlic keeper" will protect the garlic from moisture while allowing air to circulate freely around the head and cloves. Properly stored, garlic will keep for several months.

Do not refrigerate garlic unless you live in a very hot and humid climate.

PREPARING THIS FOOD

To peel garlic easily, blanch the cloves in boiling water for about 30 seconds, then drain and cool. Slice off the root end, and the skin should come right off without sticking to your fingers. Or you can put a head of fresh, raw garlic on a flat surface and hit the flat end with the flat side of a knife. The head will come apart and the skin should come off easily.

To get the most "garlicky" taste from garlic cloves, chop or mash them or extract the oil with a garlic press. When you cut into a garlic clove, you tear its cell walls, releasing an enzyme that converts sulfur compounds in the garlic into ammonia, pyruvic acid, and diallyl disulfide.

WHAT HAPPENS WHEN YOU COOK THIS FOOD

Heating garlic destroys its diallyl disulfide, which is why cooked garlic is so much milder than raw garlic.

HOW OTHER FORMS OF PROCESSING AFFECT THIS FOOD

Drying. Drying removes moisture from garlic but leaves the oils intact. Powdered garlic and garlic salt should be stored in a cool, dry place to keep their oils from turning rancid. Garlic salt is much higher in sodium than either raw garlic, garlic powder, or dried garlic flakes.

MEDICAL USES AND/OR BENEFITS

As an antibiotic.   Garlic contains alliin and allicin, two sulfur compounds with antibiotic activity.* Both in nature and in laboratory experiments (at the University of Oklahoma) garlic juice appears to inhibit a broad variety of microorganisms (bacteria, yeast, fungi), but its effects on human beings remain to be proved.

Protection against circulatory diseases.   In a number of laboratory studies, animals given garlic oil showed a decrease in blood levels of low-density lipoproteins (LDLs), the "bad" cholesterol that adheres to artery walls, and a corresponding increase in blood levels of high-density lipoproteins (HDLs), the "good" cholesterol that does not stick to artery walls. In one six-month study of human beings, daily capsules containing an amount of garlic oil equal to what you would get from ten medium-sized cloves produced the same general results: an overall 14 percent decline in cholesterol, with the level of LDL cholesterol falling 17 percent and the level of HDL cholesterol rising 41 percent. However, high doses of garlic oil may cause body odor, halitosis, nausea, diarrhea, and vomiting.

Studies of patients with heart disease have shown some increases in the activity of anticlotting substances in blood when the patients were given ten cloves of garlic a day for a month. The chemical suspected to produce the effect is ajoene, a natural derivative of allicin, now being tested on animals at the State University of New York at Albany. Because heating allicin speeds up the production of ajoene, cooked garlic may be more beneficial than raw.

Research into whether garlic or garlic oil is beneficial for people with hypertension is still preliminary.

ADVERSE EFFECTS ASSOCIATED WITH THIS FOOD

Body odor and halitosis.   Diallyl disulfide is excreted in perspiration and in the air you exhale, which is why eating garlic makes you smell garlicky.

FOOD/DRUG INTERACTIONS

*   *   *

---

*When you cut into garlic, you tear its cells, releasing an allicin precursor and allinase, an enzyme that turns the precursor into allicin.

GELATIN

NUTRITIONAL PROFILE*

Energy value (calories per serving):	Low
Protein:	High
Fat:	Low
Cholesterol:	Low
Carbohydrates:	None
Fiber:	None
Sodium:	Low
Major vitamin contribution:	—
Major mineral contribution:	—

ABOUT THE NUTRIENTS IN THIS FOOD

Although gelatin is made from the collagen (connective tissue) of cattle hides and bones or pig skin, its proteins are considered "incomplete" because they lack the essential acid tryptophan, which is destroyed when the bones and skin are treated with acid, and is deficient in several others, including lysine. In fact, gelatin's proteins are of such poor quality that, unlike other foods of animal origin (meat, milk), gelatin cannot sustain life. Laboratory rats fed a diet in which gelatin was the primary protein did not grow as they should; half died within 48 days, even though the gelatin was supplemented with some of the essential amino acids.

Plain gelatin has no carbohydrates and fiber. It is low in fat. Flavored

*Values are for prepared, unsweetened gelatin.

gelatin desserts, however, are high in carbohydrates because of the added sugar.

THE MOST NUTRITIOUS WAY TO SERVE THIS FOOD

With a protein food rich in complete proteins. Gelatin desserts whipped with milk fit the bill.

DIETS THAT MAY RESTRICT OR EXCLUDE THIS FOOD

Low-carbohydrate diet (gelatin desserts prepared with sugar)
Low-sodium diets (commercial gelatin powders)
Sucrose-free diet (gelatin desserts prepared with sugar)

BUYING THIS FOOD

Look for: Tightly sealed, clean boxes.

STORING THIS FOOD

Store gelatin boxes in a cool, dry cabinet.

PREPARING THIS FOOD

Commercial unflavored gelatin comes in premeasured 1-tablespoon packets. One tablespoon of gelatin will thicken about 2 cups of water. To combine the gelatin and water, first heat ¾ cup water to boiling. While it is heating, add the gelatin to ¼ cup cold liquid and let it absorb moisture until it is translucent. Then add the boiling water. (Flavored fruit gelatins can be dissolved directly in hot water.)

If you are going to chill the gelatin in a mold, first rinse the mold with clear, cold running water. Then rub the inside with vegetable oil to make it easy to unmold the hardened gelatin. (The oil will make the surface of the gelatin cloudy rather than shiny.)

WHAT HAPPENS WHEN YOU COOK THIS FOOD

When you mix gelatin with hot water, its protein molecules create a network that stiffens into a stable, solid gel as it squeezes out moisture. The longer the gel sits, the more intermolecular bonds it forms, the more moisture it loses and the firmer it becomes. A day-old gel is much firmer than one you've just made.*

Gelatin is used as a thickener in prepared foods and can be used at home to thicken sauces. Flavored gelatin dessert powders have less stiffening power

---

*Ficin, the proteolytic (protein-breaking) enzyme in fresh figs, and bromelin, the proteolytic enzyme in fresh pineapple, destroy the gelatin's protein network.

than plain gelatin because some of their protein has been replaced by sugar.

To build a layered gelatin mold, let each layer harden before you add the next.

HOW OTHER KINDS OF PROCESSING AFFECT THIS FOOD
*   *   *

MEDICAL USES AND/OR BENEFITS
*   *   *

ADVERSE EFFECTS ASSOCIATED WITH THIS FOOD
*   *   *

FOOD/DRUG INTERACTIONS
*   *   *

GRAPEFRUIT
(Ugli fruit)

NUTRITIONAL PROFILE

Energy value (calories per serving):	Low
Protein:	Low
Fat:	Low
Cholesterol:	None
Carbohydrates:	High
Fiber:	Low
Sodium:	Low
Major vitamin contribution:	Vitamins A (pink grapefruit) and C
Major mineral contribution:	Potassium

ABOUT THE NUTRIENTS IN THIS FOOD

Grapefruit and ugli fruit (a cross between the grapefruit and the tangerine) have some sugars and a little fiber but no starch. Like all citrus fruits, they are prized for their vitamin C. An average-size half grapefruit (3.5 inches across) provides 41 mg vitamin C, two-thirds the RDA for a healthy adult. Because most of the grapefruit's vitamin C is found in the peel and the bitter white membrane just underneath the peel, fresh grapefruit has about three times more vitamin C than an equal amount of fresh grapefruit juice.

White grapefruit is a poor source of vitamin A. Compared to other red and yellow fruits and vegetables, red (pink) grapefruit is only a moderately good source because it gets its color primarily from lycopene, a carotenoid that cannot be converted to vitamin A in your body, and has relatively few of the carotenoids with vitamin A activity. A 3.5-ounce serving of pink grape-fruit has 259–604 IU vitamin A, about 5–12 percent of the RDA for a healthy adult, depending on variety.

Grapefruit and grapefruit juice are rich in potassium, providing about 80 percent the potassium in an equal amount of fresh orange or orange juice.

Because it is a low-calorie food (about 40 calories per half grapefruit), grapefruit is often included in reducing diets. Even so, it has no magic ability to "burn fat."

THE MOST NUTRITIOUS WAY TO SERVE THIS FRUIT
Freshly cut or sectioned, with some of the vitamin C-rich white membrane.

DIETS THAT MAY RESTRICT OR EXCLUDE THIS FOOD
Sucrose-free diet

BUYING THIS FOOD
Look for: Firm fruit that is heavy for its size, which means that it will be juicy. The skin should be thin, smooth, and fine-grained. Most grapefruit have yellow skin that, depending on the variety, may be tinged with red or green. In fact, a slight greenish tint may mean that the grapefruit is high in sugar. Ugli fruit, which looks like misshapen, splotched grapefruit, is yellow with green patches and bumpy skin.

Avoid: Grapefruit or ugli fruit with puffy skin or those that feel light for their size; the flesh inside is probably dry and juiceless.

STORING THIS FOOD
Store grapefruit either at room temperature (for a few days) or in the refrigerator.

Refrigerate grapefruit juice in a tightly closed glass bottle with very lit-tle air space at the top. As you use up the juice, transfer it to a smaller bottle, again with very little air space at the top. The aim is to prevent the juice from coming into contact with oxygen, which destroys vitamin C. (Most plastic juice bottles are oxygen-permeable.) Properly stored and protected from oxy-gen, fresh grapefruit juice can hold its vitamin C for several weeks.

PREPARING THIS FOOD
Grapefruit are most flavorful at room temperature, which liberates the aro-matic molecules that give them their characteristic scent and taste.

Before cutting into the grapefruit, rinse it under cool running water to flush debris off the peel.

To section grapefruit, cut a slice from the top, then cut off the peel in strips—starting at the top and going down—or peel it in a spiral fashion. You can remove the bitter white membrane, but some of the vitamin C will go with it. Finally, slice the sections apart. Or you can simply cut the grapefruit in half and scoop out the sections with a curved, serrated grapefruit knife.

WHAT HAPPENS WHEN YOU COOK THIS FOOD

Broiling a half grapefruit or poaching grapefruit sections reduces the fruit's supply of vitamin C, which is heat-sensitive.

HOW OTHER KINDS OF PROCESSING AFFECT THIS FOOD

Commercially prepared juices. How well a commercially prepared juice retains its vitamin C depends on how it is prepared, stored, and packaged. Commercial flash-freezing preserves as much as 95 percent of the vitamin C in fresh grapefruit juices. Canned juice stored in the refrigerator may lose only 2 percent of its vitamin C in three months. Prepared, pasteurized "fresh" juices lose vitamin C because they are sold in plastic bottles or waxed-paper cartons that let oxygen in.

All commercially prepared juices taste different from fresh juice. First, frozen, canned, or pasteurized juices are almost always a blend of fruits from various crops. Second, they have all been heated to inactivate the enzymes that would otherwise rot the juice, and heating changes flavor.

MEDICAL USES AND/OR BENEFITS

Antiscorbutic. All citrus fruits are superb sources of vitamin C, the vitamin that prevents or cures scurvy, the vitamin C-deficiency disease.

Increased absorption of supplemental or dietary iron. If you eat foods rich in vitamin C along with iron supplements or foods rich in iron, the vitamin C will enhance your body's ability to absorb the iron.

Potassium replacement. Grapefruit is high in postassium. Potassium-rich foods are often prescribed for people who are taking diuretic drugs and losing potassium. However, there is some question as to whether potassium gluconate, the form of potassium in food, is as easily absorbed by the body as are potassium citrate and potassium chloride, the forms of potassium in the supplements fed to laboratory animals in the experiments that established need for potassium replacement for people on diuretic drugs.

Wound healing. Your body needs vitamin C in order to convert the amino acid proline into hydroxyproline, an essential ingredient in collagen, the protein needed to form skin, tendons, and bones. As a result people with scurvy do not heal quickly, a condition that can be remedied with vitamin C, which cures the scurvy and speeds healing. Whether taking extra vitamin C speeds healing in healthy people remains to be proved.

To reduce the levels of serum cholesterol.   A suspected but unproved function of vitamin C. In addition, citrus fruits, including grapefruit, are rich in pectin, the indigestible food fiber that appears to slow the body's absorption of fats and thus to lower the blood level of cholesterol. Half a grapefruit contains l gram of pectin.

ADVERSE EFFECTS ASSOCIATED WITH THIS FOOD

Contact dermatitis.   The essential oils in the peel of citrus fruits may cause skin irritation in sensitive people.

FOOD/DRUG INTERACTIONS
*   *   *

GRAPES

See also RAISINS, WINE

NUTRITIONAL PROFILE

Energy value (calories per serving):	Moderate
Protein:	Low
Fat:	Low
Cholesterol:	None
Carbohydrates:	High
Fiber:	Low
Sodium:	Low
Major vitamin contribution:	Vitamins A and C
Major mineral contribution:	Phosphorus

ABOUT THE NUTRIENTS IN THIS FOOD

Grapes have low to moderate amounts of fiber, potassium, vitamin A, the B vitamins, and vitamin C.

Grape skins, stems, and seeds contain tannins, astringent chemicals that coagulate proteins in the mucous membrane lining your mouth and make the membrane pucker. Most of the tannins, including the pigments (anthocyanins) that make red grapes red, are found in the skin.

Grapes also contain malic acid, which makes them taste sour when they are unripe. As grapes ripen, their malic acid content declines and their sugar content rises. Ripe eating grapes are invariably sweet. However, since grapes have no stored starches they can convert to sugar, they do not get sweeter after they are picked. All table grapes are shipped ready to eat.

DIETS THAT MAY RESTRICT OR EXCLUDE THIS FOOD
Sucrose-free diet

BUYING THIS FOOD
Look for: Plump, well-colored grapes that are firmly attached to green stems that bend easily and snap back when you let them go. Green grapes should have a slightly yellow tint or a pink blush; red grapes should be deep, dark red or purple.

Avoid: Mushy grapes, grapes with wrinkled skin, and grapes that feel sticky. They are all past their prime. So are grapes whose stems are dry and brittle.

CHARACTERISTICS OF DIFFERENT VARIETIES OF GRAPES

Red grapes

Cardinal	Large, dark red grapes, available March-August
Emperor	Large red grapes with seeds. September-March
Flame	Seedless, medium to large red grapes. June-August
Ribier	Large, blue-black grapes with seeds. July-February
Tokay	Large, bright red, seeds. August-November
Queen	Large, bright to dark red, seeds. June-August

White grapes

Almeria	Large, golden. August-October
Calmeria	Longish, light green. October-February
Perlette	Green, seedless, compact clusters. May-July
Thompson	Seedless, green to light gold. June-November

Sources: *The Fresh Approach to Grapes* (United Fruit & Vegetable Association, n.d.).

STORING THIS FOOD
Wrap grapes in a plastic bag and store them in the refrigerator. Do not wash grapes until you are ready to use them.

PREPARING THIS FOOD
Rinse the grapes under cold, running water; drain them and pick off stems and leaves. American grapes (Catawba, Concord, Delaware, Niagara, and

Scuppernong) are called slipskin grapes because the skin comes off easily. The European varieties (Emperor, Flame, Tokay, Malaga, Muscat, and Thompson seedless) have adherent skin that is hard to remove. Peeling American grapes to use in salad or to poach is a cinch. To peel the European grapes, drop them into boiling water for a few seconds, then plunge them into cold water. The change in temperature damages a layer of cells under the skin and the skin will slip off easily.

WHAT HAPPENS WHEN YOU COOK THIS FOOD
    *   *   *

HOW OTHER KINDS OF PROCESSING AFFECT THIS FOOD

Juice. Red grapes are colored with anthocyanin pigments that turn deeper red in acids and blue, purple, or yellowish in basic (alkaline) solutions. As a result, red grape juice will turn brighter red if you mix it with lemon or orange juice. Since metals (which are basic) would also change the color of the juice, the inside of grape juice cans is coated with plastic or enamel to keep the juice from touching the metal.

Winemaking. Grapes are an ideal fruit for winemaking. They have enough sugar to produce a product that is 10 percent alcohol and are acidic enough to keep unwanted microorganisms from growing during fermentation. Some wines retain some of the nutrients originally present in the grapes from which they are made. (See WINE.)

Drying. See RAISINS.

MEDICAL USES AND/OR BENEFITS
    *   *   *

ADVERSE EFFECTS ASSOCIATED WITH THIS FOOD
    *   *   *

FOOD/DRUG INTERACTIONS
    *   *   *

GREEN BEANS

(French beans, *haricots verts,* snap beans, string beans, wax beans)

NUTRITIONAL PROFILE

Energy value (calories per serving):	Low
Protein:	Moderate
Fat:	Low
Cholesterol:	None
Carbohydrates:	High
Fiber:	High
Sodium:	Low
Major vitamin contribution:	Vitamins A and C
Major mineral contribution:	Iron, potassium

ABOUT THE NUTRIENTS IN THIS FOOD

Green beans and wax beans are a moderately good source of fiber and a good source of vitamin C. One cup of boiled, drained green beans provides 12 mg vitamin C, 20 percent of the RDA for a healthy adult.

Green beans have carotene underneath their green chlorophyll, so they are also a good source of vitamin A, 666 IU (13 percent of the RDA for a healthy adult) per 3.5-oz. serving, but wax beans have only 81 IU per 3.5-oz. serving; their color comes from carotenoid pigments with very little vitamin A activity.

THE MOST NUTRITIOUS WAY TO SERVE THIS FOOD

Raw, microwaved, or steamed just to the crisp-tender stage, to preserve their vitamin C.

DIETS THAT MAY RESTRICT OR EXCLUDE THIS FOOD
Sucrose-free diet

BUYING THIS FOOD
Look for: Firm, crisp beans with clean, well-colored green or yellow skin.

Avoid: Withered or dry beans; they have been exposed to air, heat, or sunlight and are low in vitamin A.

STORING THIS FOOD
Wrap green beans and wax beans in a plastic bag and store them in the refrigerator to protect their vitamins by keeping them from drying out.

PREPARING THIS FOOD
Green beans were once better known as string beans because of the "string" running down the back of the bean. Today, that string has been bred out of most green beans, but you may still find it in wax beans and in *haricots verts,* the true French green beans.

To prepare green beans and wax beans, wash them under cool running water, pick off odd leaves or stems, snip off the ends, pull the string off wax beans or *haricots verts,* and slice or sliver the beans.

WHAT HAPPENS WHEN YOU COOK THIS FOOD
Cooking reduces the amount of vitamin C in green beans and wax beans but does not affect the vitamin A, which is insoluble in water and stable at normal cooking temperatures.

Green beans will change color when you cook them. Chlorophyll, the pigment that makes green vegetables green, is sensitive to acids. When you heat green beans, the chlorophyll in the beans will react chemically with acids in the vegetable or in the cooking water, forming pheophytin, which is brown. The pheophytin makes the beans look olive-drab.

To keep green beans green, you have to keep the chlorophyll from reacting with acids. One way to do this is to cook the beans in a large quantity of water (which will dilute the acids), but this increases the loss of vitamin C. A second alternative is to leave the lid off the pot so that the volatile acids can float off into the air. The best way may be to steam or microwave the green beans very quickly in very little water so that they hold onto their vitamin C and cook so fast that there is no time for the chlorophyll to react with the acids.

HOW OTHER KINDS OF PROCESSING AFFECT THIS FOOD
Canning and freezing.   Commercially frozen green beans and wax beans

have virtually the same nutritional value as fresh beans. Canned beans, however, usually have added salt that turns the naturally low-sodium beans into a high-sodium food. Canned green beans and wax beans have less vitamin C than fresh beans.

MEDICAL USES AND/OR BENEFITS
*   *   *

ADVERSE EFFECTS ASSOCIATED WITH THIS FOOD

Botulinum toxin poisoning. Because they are not an acid food, canned green beans and wax beans will allow the growth of *C. botulinum,* the heat-resistant bacillus that grows best in an oxygen-free environment and whose toxin causes botulism poisoning. But the idea that canned green beans are the food most likely to be contaminated with botulinum toxins is an old wives' tale. In fact, the toxin has shown up in canned or vacuum-sealed packages of beef, condiments, dairy products, fish, fruit, pork, and poultry.*

FOOD/DRUG INTERACTIONS
*   *   *

*The sodium nitrate and sodium nitrite in sausages and processed meats are there to protect against botulinum contamination.

GREENS

(Beet greens, broccoli rabe, chard [Swiss chard], collard greens, dandelion greens, kale, mustard greens, turnip greens, watercress)

See also CABBAGE, LETTUCE, SPINACH

NUTRITIONAL PROFILE

Energy value (calories per serving):	Low
Protein:	High
Fat:	Low
Cholesterol:	None
Carbohydrates:	Moderate
Fiber:	Low to high
Sodium:	Moderate to high
Major vitamin contribution:	Vitamins A and C
Major mineral contribution:	Calcium, iron

ABOUT THE NUTRIENTS IN THIS FOOD

Greens provide varying amounts of fiber, a little sugar, and almost no starch. They are an excellent source of vitamin A since they contain carotene. The yellow color of the carotene is hidden by the chlorophyll pigment that makes these vegetables green. The darker the leaf, the more vitamin A it provides. Dark leaves may have as much as fifty times more vitamin A than pale leaves.

Greens are also a good source of vitamin C, iron, and calcium. Ounce for ounce, fresh collard greens, kale, and mustard greens have about as much calcium as whole milk. Dandelion and turnip greens have more. Chard, kale, and turnip greens are rich in non-heme iron, the inorganic form of iron found in plants. However, non-heme iron is not as useful to the body as heme iron, the organic form of iron in foods of animal origin, and the oxalates in some greens bind the iron into insoluble compounds, further reducing its value. You can increase the yield of iron from greens by eating the greens with an iron-rich food (meat) or with a food rich in vitamin C.*

THE MOST NUTRITIOUS WAY TO SERVE THIS FOOD

Fresh, torn just before serving, or cooked in the least possible water for the shortest possible time—all to preserve vitamin C.

With an iron-rich food or a food rich in vitamin C to increase the absorption of iron from the greens.

DIETS THAT MAY RESTRICT OR EXCLUDE THIS FOOD

Low-oxalate diet (to prevent the formation of kidney stones caused by calcium oxalate; Swiss chard)
Low-sodium diet
Sucrose-free diet

BUYING THIS FOOD

Look for: Fresh, crisp, clean, cold, dark-green leaves. Refrigeration helps preserve vitamins A and C.

Avoid: Yellowed, blackened, wilted, or warm greens, all of which are lower in vitamins A and C.

WHAT TO LOOK FOR IN SPECIFIC GREENS

Broccoli rabe: Choose small, firm stalks, with very few buds and no open flowers.
Collard greens: Choose smooth, green, firm leaves.
Dandelion: Choose plants with large leaves and very thin stems but no flowers (flowering dandelions have tough, bitter leaves).
Kale: Choose small, deeply colored, moist leaves.
Mustard greens: Choose small, firm, tender leaves.
Swiss chard: Choose chard with crisp stalks and firm, brightly colored leaves. Chard is very perishable; limp stalks are past their prime.
Turnip greens: Choose small, firm, bright leaves.
Watercress: Choose crisp, bright-green leaves.

---

*The thin part of the leaf, which is much more nutritious than the fibrous rib down the middle, may have twenty times as much vitamin A and two to four times as much iron as the rib.

STORING THIS FOOD

Refrigerate all greens, wrapped in plastic to keep them from losing moisture and vitamins. Before you store the greens, rinse them well under cool running water and discard any bruised or damaged leaves (which would continue to deteriorate even when chilled).

PREPARING THIS FOOD

Rewash the greens under cool running water to flush off all sand, dirt, debris, and hidden insects.

If you plan to use the greens in a salad, pat them dry before you mix them with salad dressing; oil-based salad dressings will not cling to wet greens.

Do not tear or cut the greens until you are ready to use them; when you tear greens you damage cells, releasing ascorbic acid oxidase, an enzyme that destroys vitamin C.

WHAT HAPPENS WHEN YOU COOK THIS FOOD

Chlorophyll, the pigment that makes green vegetables green, is sensitive to acids. When you heat greens, the chlorophyll in the leaves reacts chemically with acids in the greens or in the cooking water, forming pheophytin, which is brown. Together, the pheophytin and the yellow carotenes in dark-green leaves give the cooked greens a bronze hue. Greens with few carotenes will look olive-drab.

To keep the cooked greens from turning bronze or olive, you have to prevent the chlorophyll from reacting with acids. One way to do this is to cook the greens in a large amount of water (which will dilute the acids), but this increases the loss of vitamin C. A second alternative is to leave the lid off the pot so that the volatile acids can float off into the air. The best way probably is to steam the greens in very little water, or, as researchers at Cornell University suggest, to microwave 2 cups of greens with about 3 tablespoons of water in a microwave safe plastic bag left open at the top so that steam can escape. These methods preserve vitamin C and cook the greens so fast that there is no time for the chlorophyll/acid reaction to occur.

HOW OTHER KINDS OF PROCESSING AFFECT THIS FOOD

*   *   *

MEDICAL USES AND/OR BENEFITS

Protection against some forms of cancer.   According to the American Cancer Society, deep-green or yellow vegetables rich in carotene and vitamin C may lower the risk of some cancers of the gastrointestinal and respiratory tracts and provide some protection against cancers caused by chemicals.

ADVERSE EFFECTS ASSOCIATED WITH THIS FOOD

Kidney stones.   In 1985, research at the Medical College of South Carolina in Charleston suggested that collard greens, which are high in oxalates, may be one cause of the high incidence of kidney stones among people in the American Southeast.

Nitrates.   Like beets, celery, eggplant, lettuce, radishes, and spinach, greens contain nitrates that convert naturally into nitrites in your stomach and then react with the amino acids in proteins to form nitrosamines. Although some nitrosamines are known or suspected carcinogens, this natural chemical conversion presents no known problems for a healthy adult. However, when these nitrate-rich vegetables are cooked and left to stand at room temperature, bacterial enzyme action (and perhaps some enzymes in the plants) convert the nitrates to nitrites at a much faster rate than normal. These higher-nitrite foods may be hazardous for infants; several cases of "spinach poisoning" have been reported among children who ate cooked spinach that had been left standing at room temperature.

FOOD/DRUG INTERACTIONS

Anticoagulants.   Like other leaf vegetables, greens contains vitamin K, the blood-clotting vitamin produced naturally by bacteria in our intestines. Excess amounts of foods high in vitamin K may reduce the effectiveness of anticoagulants (warfarin, Coumadin, Panwarfin).

GUAVAS

NUTRITIONAL PROFILE

Energy value
(calories per serving): Low

Protein: Low

Fat: Low

Cholesterol: None

Carbohydrates: High

Fiber: High

Sodium: Low

Major vitamin
contribution: Vitamins C and A

Major mineral
contribution: Potassium

ABOUT THE NUTRIENTS IN THIS FOOD

The guava is a high-carbohydrate, high-fiber food that has sugars (but almost no starch) and provides indigestible food fibers (cellulose, hemicellulose, pectins, and gums). Guavas have moderate amounts of vitamin A, a good supply of niacin, and may be extremely rich in vitamin C. Depending on the variety, the guavas commonly grown in the United States have anywhere from 11 to 52 mg vitamin C per ounce, compared to an average 13 mg/oz. for fresh Florida oranges.

THE MOST NUTRITIOUS WAY TO SERVE THIS FOOD

Fresh (for the most vitamin C) or lightly stewed.

DIETS THAT MAY RESTRICT OR EXCLUDE THIS FOOD

Low-carbohydrate, low-fiber diet
Sucrose-free diet

BUYING THIS FOOD

Look for :   Ripe guavas. Depending on the variety, the color of the skin may vary from white to yellow to dark red and the size from that of a large walnut to that of an apple. A ripe guava will yield slightly when you press it with your fingertip.

Avoid: Guavas with cracked or broken skin.

STORING THIS FOOD

Refrigerate ripe guavas.

PREPARING THIS FOOD

Wash the guava under cool running water, then slice it in half and remove the seeds. Never slice or peel the fruit until you are ready to use it. When you cut into the guava and damage its cells, you activate ascorbic acid oxidase, an enzyme that oxidizes and destroys vitamin C. The longer the enzyme is working, the more vitamin the fruit will lose.

WHAT HAPPENS WHEN YOU COOK THIS FOOD

As the guava cooks, its pectins and gums dissolve and the fruit gets softer. Cooking also destroys some water-soluble, heat-sensitive vitamin C. You can keep the loss to a minimum by cooking the guava as quickly as possible in as little water as possible. Never cook guavas (or any other vitamin C-rich foods) in a copper or iron pot; contact with metal ions hastens the loss of vitamin C.

HOW OTHER KINDS OF PROCESSING AFFECT THIS FOOD

Canning.   Canned guavas have less vitamin A and C and more sugar (syrup) than fresh guavas do, but their taste and texture is similar to home-cooked fruit.

MEDICAL USES AND/OR BENEFITS

Potassium replacement.   Guavas are a good source of potassium. Ounce for ounce, they have about 50 percent more potassium than fresh oranges. Potassium-rich foods are often prescribed for people who are taking diuretic drugs and losing large amounts of potassium. However, there is now some question at to whether potassium gluconate, the form of potassium in food, is as useful to the body as potassium citrate and potassium chloride, the forms of potassium in the supplements fed to laboratory animals in the experiments that established need for potassium replacement for people on diuretic drugs.

Protection against some forms of cancer.   According to the American Cancer Society, foods rich in vitamins A and C may provide some protection against the risk of cancers of the respiratory and intestinal tracts and cancers induced by chemicals.

ADVERSE EFFECTS ASSOCIATED WITH THIS FOOD
*   *   *

FOOD/DRUG INTERACTIONS
*   *   *

HONEY

See also SUGAR

NUTRITIONAL PROFILE

Energy value (calories per serving):	High
Protein:	Trace
Fat:	None
Cholesterol:	None
Carbohydrates:	High
Fiber:	None
Sodium:	Low
Major vitamin contribution:	Riboflavin (vitamin B_2), niacin
Major mineral contribution:	Iron, potassium

ABOUT THE NUTRIENTS IN THIS FOOD

Honey is the sweet, thick fluid produced when bees metabolize the sucrose in plant nectar. Enzymes in the honeybee's sac split the sucrose, which is a disaccharide (double sugar), into its constituent molecules, fructose and glucose. Honey is about 80 percent fructose and glucose and 17 percent water. The rest is dextrin (the molecules formed when starch molecules are split apart), a trace of protein and small amounts of iron, potassium, and B vitamins. Honey has no fat or cholesterol.

DIETS THAT MAY RESTRICT OR EXCLUDE THIS FOOD

Low-carbohydrate diet
Sucrose-free diet

BUYING THIS FOOD

Look for: Tightly sealed jars of honey. All honeys are natural products. They may be dark or light (depending on the plant from which the bees drew their nectar); color has no effect on the honey's nutritional value. Raw, unprocessed honey is thick and cloudy. Commercial honey is clear because it has been filtered. It pours more easily than raw honey because it has been heated to make it less viscous and to destroy potentially harmful bacteria and yeasts that might spoil the honey by turning its sugars into alcohol and other undesirable products.

STORING THIS FOOD

Store opened jars of honey in the refrigerator, tightly closed to keep the honey from absorbing moisture or picking up microorganisms from the air. Ordinarily, bacteria do not proliferate in honey, which is an acid solution. However, if the honey absorbs extra water or if its sugars precipitate out of solution and crystallize, the sugar/water ratio that makes honey acid will be upset and the honey will become more hospitable to microorganisms. Refrigeration offers some protection because it chills the honey and slows the growth of bacteria or mold.

PREPARING THIS FOOD

To measure honey easily, coat your measuring spoon or cup with vegetable oil: the honey will slide right out of the measure. To combine honey smoothly with dry ingredients, warm it with the liquids in the recipe first. And remember to reduce the liquid in a recipe when you substitute honey for sugar. For precise amounts, check the individual recipe.

WHAT HAPPENS WHEN YOU COOK THIS FOOD

When honey is heated, the bonds between its molecules relax and the honey becomes more liquid. If you heat it too long, however, its moisture will evaporate, the honey will become more viscous, and its sugars will burn.

In baking, honey is useful because it is more hydrophilic (water-loving) than granulated sugar. It retains moisture longer while a cake or bread is baking, and it may even extract moisture from the air into the finished product. As a result, breads and cakes made with honey stay moist longer than those made with sugar.

HOW OTHER KINDS OF PROCESSING AFFECT THIS FOOD
*   *   *

MEDICAL USES AND/OR BENEFITS
*   *   *

ADVERSE EFFECTS ASSOCIATED WITH THIS FOOD

Infant botulism. *C. botulinum*, the organism that produces toxins that cause *botulinum* poisoning, does not grow in the intestines of an adult or an older child. Botulism poisoning in adults and older children is caused by toxins produced when the *botulinum* spores, which are anerobic (require an airless environment), germinate in an oxygen-starved place like a sealed can of food. However, *botulinum* spores do grow in an infant's digestive tract, and infants have been poisoned by foods that have spores but no toxins. Since honey is sometimes contaminated with the *botulinum* spores, the Centers for Disease Control and the American Academy of Pediatrics recommend against feeding honey to any child younger than twelve months.

Wild honey poisoning. Like wild greens or wild mushrooms, wild honeys may be toxic and are best avoided in favor of the commercial product.

FOOD/DRUG INTERACTIONS

* * *

KOHLRABI

NUTRITIONAL PROFILE

Energy value (calories per serving):	Low
Protein:	High
Fat:	Low
Cholesterol:	None
Carbohydrates:	High
Fiber:	High
Sodium:	Low
Major vitamin contribution:	B vitamins, vitamin C
Major mineral contribution:	Calcium, iron, phosphorus

ABOUT THE NUTRIENTS IN THIS FOOD

The kohlrabi ("cabbage-turnip") is a member of the cabbage family, a stem rather than flowers (broccoli) or buds (head cabbage or brussels sprouts). It is a high-carbohydrate (starch), high-fiber food, an excellent source of cellulose and lignin, the woody food fibers that make up the structure of stems, leaves, roots, seed, and peel.

Kohlrabi is also an extremely good source of vitamin C. Three and a half ounces of boiled, drained kohlrabi have about 54 mg vitamin C, 90 percent of the RDA for a normal healthy adult. Kohlrabi also has thiamin (vitamin B_1), riboflavin (vitamin B_2), and iron.

THE MOST NUTRITIOUS WAY TO SERVE THIS FOOD

Steamed just until tender, to protect the vitamin C.

DIETS THAT MAY RESTRICT OR EXCLUDE THIS FOOD

Antiflatulence diet

Low-fiber, low-residue diet

Sucrose-free diet

BUYING THIS FOOD

Look for: Small vegetables with fresh-looking green leaves on top.

Avoid: Very mature kohlrabi. The older the stem, the more cellulose and lignin it contains. Very old kohlrabi may have so much fiber that it is inedible.

STORING THIS FOOD

Cut off the green tops. Then, store kohlrabi in a cold, humid place (a root cellar or the refrigerator) to keep it from drying out.

Wash and refrigerate the kohlrabi's green leaves. They can be cooked and eaten like spinach.

WHEN YOU ARE READY TO COOK THIS FOOD

Wash the kohlrabi under running water, using a vegetable brush to remove dirt and debris. Then peel the root and slice or quarter it for cooking.

WHAT HAPPENS WHEN YOU COOK THIS FOOD

Cooking softens kohlrabi by dissolving its soluble food fibers (pectins, gums). Like other cruciferous vegetables, kohlrabi contains natural sulfur compounds that break down into a variety of smelly chemicals (including hydrogen sulfide and ammonia) when the vegetables are heated. Kohlrabi is nowhere near as smelly as some of the other crucifers, but this production of smelly compounds is intensified by long cooking or by cooking the vegetable in an aluminum pot. Adding a slice of bread to the cooking water may lessen the odor; keeping a lid on the pot will stop the smelly molecules from floating off into the air.

HOW OTHER KINDS OF PROCESSING AFFECT THIS FOOD

*   *   *

MEDICAL USES AND/OR BENEFITS

Protection against certain cancers. According to the American Cancer Society, cruciferous vegetables and foods rich in vitamins A and C may lower the risk of some cancers of the respiratory and intestinal tract and chemically induced cancers.

ADVERSE EFFECTS ASSOCIATED WITH THIS FOOD

Enlarged thyroid gland (goiter). Cruciferous vegetables, including kohlrabi, contain goitrin, thiocyanate, and isothiocyanate. These chemicals, known collectively as goitrogens, inhibit the formation of thyroid hormones and cause the thyroid to enlarge in an attempt to produce more. Goitrogens are not hazardous for healthy people who eat moderate amounts of cruciferous vegetables, but they may pose problems for people who have a thyroid condition or are taking thyroid medication.

FOOD/DRUG INTERACTIONS

*   *   *

LAMB
(Chevon [goat meat], mutton)

NUTRITIONAL PROFILE*

Energy value (calories per serving):	Moderate
Protein:	High
Fat:	Moderate
Cholesterol:	Moderate to high
Carbohydrates:	None
Fiber:	None
Sodium:	Moderate
Major vitamin contribution:	B vitamins
Major mineral contribution:	Iron

ABOUT THE NUTRIENTS IN THIS FOOD

Like other animal foods, lamb provides "complete" proteins with all the essential amino acids. Lamb has a higher proportion of saturated fatty acids and more cholesterol than poultry, pork, and most cuts of beef. It has no food fiber and no carbohydrates other than the small amounts of glycogen (sugar) stored in the animal's muscles. Mutton, which is meat from a sheep more than one year old, is more muscular and thus less tender than lamb. Goat meat, labeled *chevon*, is leaner than mutton.

Lamb is an excellent source of B vitamins, particularly niacin, vitamin B_6, and vitamin B_{12} (which is plentiful in meat, fish, and poultry but is never found in fruits and vegetables). It also provides heme iron, the organic iron in foods of animal origin that is about five times more useful to the body than none-heme iron, the inorganic form of iron in plant foods. One 3.5-ounce

*Values are for lean, roasted lamb.

serving of roast lamb has about 1.2 to 2 mg iron, 6 to 11 percent of the RDA for a healthy woman of childbearing age.

THE MOST NUTRITIOUS WAY TO SERVE THIS FOOD

Broiled or roasted, to allow the fat to melt and run off the meat. Soups and stews that contain lamb should be skimmed.

With tomatoes, potatoes, and other foods rich in vitamin C to increase your body's absorption of iron from the meat.

DIETS THAT MAY RESTRICT OR EXCLUDE THIS FOOD

Controlled fat, low-cholesterol diet
Low-protein diet (for some forms of kidney disease)

BUYING THIS FOOD

Look for: Lamb that is pink to light red, with a smooth, firm texture and little fat. The color of the fat, which may vary with the breed and what the animal was fed, is not a reliable guide to quality. Meat labeled *baby lamb* or *spring lamb* comes from animals less than five months old; *lamb* comes from an animal less than a year old; *mutton* comes from an animal older than a year. The older the animal, the tougher and more sinewy the meat.

STORING THIS FOOD

Refrigerate fresh lamb immediately, carefully wrapped to prevent its drippings from contaminating other foods. Refrigeration prolongs freshness by slowing the natural multiplication of bacteria on the surface of the meat. Left on their own, these bacteria convert proteins and other substances on the surface of the meat to a slimy film and change the meat's sulfur-containing amino acids methionine and cystine into smelly chemicals called mercaptans. When the mercaptans combine with pigments in meat, they produce the greenish pigment that gives spoiled meat its characteristic unpleasant appearance.

PREPARING THIS FOOD

Trim the meat carefully. By judiciously cutting away all visible fat, you can significantly reduce the amount of fat and cholesterol in each serving. Lamb and mutton are covered with a thin paperlike white membrane called a fell. Generally, the fell is left on roasts because it acts as a natural basting envelope that makes the lamb juicier.

Do not salt lamb before you cook it; the salt will draw moisture out of the meat, making it stringy and less tender. Add salt when the meat is nearly done.

After handling raw meat, wash your knives, cutting board, counter—
and your hands—with warm soapy water to reduce the chance of transferring bacteria from the meat to other foods.

WHAT HAPPENS WHEN YOU COOK THIS FOOD

Cooking changes the lamb's flavor and appearance, lowers its fat and cholesterol content, and makes it safer by killing the bacteria that live naturally on
the surface of raw meat.

Browning lamb before you cook it won't seal in the juices, but it will
change the flavor by caramelizing proteins and sugars on the surface of the
meat. Because the only sugars in lamb are the small amounts of glycogen in
its muscles, we often add sugar in the form of marinades or basting liquids
that may also contain acids (lemon juice, vinegar, wine, yogurt) to break
down muscle fibers and tenderize the meat. (Note that browning has one minor nutritional drawback. It breaks amino acids on the surface of the meat
into smaller compounds that are no longer useful proteins.)

When lamb is heated, it loses water and shrinks. Its pigments, which
combine with oxygen, are denatured by the heat. They break into smaller
fragments and turn brown, the natural color of well-done meat. The pigments also release iron, which accelerates the oxidation of the lamb's fat. Oxidized fat is what gives cooked meat its characteristic warmed-over flavor.
Cooking and storing meat under a blanket of antioxidants—catsup or a gravy
made of tomatoes, peppers, and other vitamin C-rich vegetables—reduces the
oxidation of fats and the intensity of warmed-over flavor. So will reheating
the meat in a microwave rather than a conventional oven.

HOW OTHER KINDS OF PROCESSING AFFECT THIS FOOD

Canning.   Canned lamb does not develop a warmed-over flavor because the
high temperatures used in canning food and alter the structure of the proteins
in the meat so that the proteins act as antioxidants. Once the can is open,
however, lamb fat may begin to oxidize again.

Freezing.   Defrosted frozen lamb may be less tender than fresh lamb. It may
also be lower in B vitamins. When you freeze lamb, the water inside its cells
freezes into sharp ice crystals that can puncture cell membranes. When the
lamb thaws, moisture (and some of the B vitamins) will leak out through
these torn cell walls. Freezing may also cause freezer burn—dry spots left
when moisture evaporates from the lamb's surface. Waxed freezer paper is
designed specifically to protect the moisture in meat; plastic wrap and aluminum foil may be less effective.

MEDICAL USES AND/OR BENEFITS

Treating and/or preventing iron deficiency.   Without meat it is virtually impossible for a woman of childbearing age to get the 18 mg iron/day she requires unless she takes an iron supplement.

ADVERSE EFFECTS ASSOCIATED WITH THIS FOOD

Elevated levels of serum cholesterol.   Abnormally high levels of cholesterol in the blood are a risk factor in heart disease. How your diet affects the amount of cholesterol you produce is not entirely clear; dietary fat and cholesterol may not be the primary factor in determining how much and what kind of cholesterol your body makes and stores. Nontheless, there is evidence to suggest that controlling the amount of fat and cholesterol consumed may lower cholesterol levels, particularly for people whose levels are high. In 1986 the American Heart Association issued new guidelines suggesting that healthy adults reduce their fat consumption to 30 percent of their total calorie intake each day and limit cholesterol consumption to 300 mg per day or 100 mg per 1000 calories, whichever is less (3.5 ounces of lean roasted leg of lamb contain 88 mg cholesterol).

Decline in kidney function.   Proteins are nitrogen compounds. When metabolized, they yield ammonia that is excreted through the kidneys. In laboratory animals, a sustained high-protein diet increases the flow of blood through the kidneys. This may enlarge the kidneys and accelerate the natural decline in kidney function associated with aging. To date there is no evidence that this occurs in human beings.

FOOD/DRUG INTERACTIONS

False-positive test for occult blood in the stool.   The active ingredient in the test for hidden blood in the stool is alphaguaiaconic acid, a chemical that turns blue in the presence of blood. Because the test may react to blood in meat you have eaten, producing a positive result when you do not really have any gastrointestinal bleeding, lamb and other meats are excluded from your diet for three days before this test.

LEMONS
(Limes)

NUTRITIONAL PROFILE

Energy value (calories per serving):	Low
Protein:	Moderate
Fat:	Low
Cholesterol:	None
Carbohydrates:	High
Fiber:	Low
Sodium:	Low
Major vitamin contribution:	Vitamin C
Major mineral contribution:	Potassium

ABOUT THE NUTRIENTS IN THIS FOOD

Lemons and limes have no starch, very little sugar (1 percent in a lemon, less in a lime), no fat, and no cholesterol. They are valuable only for their considerable supply of vitamin C. An ounce of lemon juice (the yield of an average-size lemon) provides 13 mg vitamin C, 22 percent of the RDA for a healthy adult. An ounce of fresh lime juice provides 8.4 mg, about 14 percent of the RDA.

THE MOST NUTRITIOUS WAY TO SERVE THIS FOOD

Fresh squeezed, in a fruit-juice drink. Fresh juice has the most vitamin C. Fruit-juice drinks (lemonade, limeade) are the only foods that use enough lemon or lime juice to give us a useful quantity of vitamin C.

DIETS THAT MAY RESTRICT OR EXCLUDE THIS FOOD
Sucrose-free diet

BUYING THIS FOOD
Look for: Firm lemons and limes that are heavy for their size. The heavier the fruit, the juicier it will be. The skin should be thin, smooth, and fine-grained—shiny yellow for a lemon, shiny green for a lime. Deeply colored lemons and limes have a better flavor than pale ones. All lemons are egg-shaped, but the Key lime (which is the true lime) is small and round. Egg-shaped limes are hybrids.

STORING THIS FOOD
Refrigerate fresh lemons and limes. The lemons will stay fresh for a month, the limes for up to eight weeks. Sliced lemons and limes are vulnerable to oxygen, which can destroy their flavor and their vitamin C. Wrap them tightly in plastic, store them in the refrigerator, and use them as quickly as possible.

PREPARING THIS FOOD
The skin of the lemon and lime are rich in essential oils that are liberated when you cut into the peel and tear open its cells. To get the flavoring oil out of the peel, grate the top, colored part of the rind (the white membrane underneath is bitter) and wrap it in cheesecloth. Then wring out the oil onto some granulated sugar, stir thoroughly, and use the flavored sugar in baking or for making drinks. You can freeze lemon and lime peel or zest (grated peel), but it will lose some flavor while frozen.

Lemons and limes are often waxed to protect them from moisture loss enroute to the store. Before you peel or grate the fruit, scrub it with a vegetable brush to remove the wax.

WHAT HAPPENS WHEN YOU COOK THIS FOOD
Heating citrus fruits and juices reduces their supply of vitamin C, which is heat-sensitive.

HOW OTHER FORMS OF PROCESSING AFFECT THIS FOOD
Canning and freezing.   Canned or frozen lemon and lime juice are as rich in vitamin C as fresh juice. (Commercially frozen pink lemonade is plain lemon juice colored with grape juice.)

MEDICAL USES AND/OR BENEFITS
Antiscorbutic.   Lemons and limes, which are small and travel well, were carried on board British navy ships in the eighteenth century to prevent scurvy, the vitamin C-deficiency disease.

Wound healing.   Your body needs vitamin C in order to convert the amino acid proline into hydroxyproline, an essential ingredient in collagen—the protein needed to form skin, tendons, and bones. As a result, people with scurvy do not heal quickly, a condition that can be remedied with vitamin C, which cures the scurvy and speeds healing. Whether taking extra vitamin C speeds healing in healthy people remains to be proved.

ADVERSE EFFECTS ASSOCIATED WITH THIS FOOD

Contact dermatitis.   The peel of lemon and lime contains limonene, an essential oil known to cause contact dermatitis in sensitive individuals. (Limonene is also found in dill, caraway seeds, and celery.)

Photosensitivity.   Lime peel contains furocoumarins (psoralens), chemicals that are photosensitizers as well as potential mutagens and carcinogens. Contact with these chemicals can make skin very sensitive to light.

Apthous ulcers (canker sores).   Citrus fruits or juices may trigger a flare-up of canker sores in sensitive people, but eliminating these foods from the diet neither cures nor prevents canker sores.

FOOD/DRUG INTERACTIONS

Iron supplements.   Taking iron supplements with a food rich in vitamin C increases the absorption of iron from the supplement.

LENTILS

NUTRITIONAL PROFILE

Energy value (calories per serving):	Moderate
Protein:	High
Fat:	Low
Cholesterol:	None
Carbohydrates:	High
Fiber:	High
Sodium:	Moderate
Major vitamin contribution:	Vitamin B_6, folacin
Major mineral contribution:	Magnesium, iron, zinc

ABOUT THE NUTRIENTS IN THIS FOOD

Lentils are seeds. Their covering is an excellent source of the cellulose and the noncarbohydrate food fiber lignin, and their interior is a good source of carbohydrates: starch, sugars, hemicellulose, pectins, and gums. Up to 28 percent of the calories in cooked lentils comes from their proteins, which are considered "incomplete" because they are deficient in the essential amino acids methionine and cystine. Lentils have very little fat and no cholesterol.

Lentils are a good source of B vitamins, particularly vitamin B_6, niacin, and folacin. They have small amounts of calcium, phosphorus, and potassium and are rich in non-heme iron, the inorganic form of iron found in plant foods.

Lentils also contain antinutrient chemicals that inhibit the enzymes that enable your body to digest proteins and starches; factors that inactivate vitamin A; and hemagglutinins, substances that cause red blood cells to clump together. Cooking the lentils inactivates the enzyme inhibitors and the anti-vitamin A factors but not the hemagglutinins. However, the amount of hemagglutinins in the lentils is so small that is has no measurable effect.

THE MOST NUTRITIOUS WAY TO SERVE THIS FOOD

With grains. The proteins in grains are deficient in the essential amino acid lysine but contain sufficient methionine and cystine; the proteins in beans are exactly the opposite. Together these foods provide "complete" proteins with no cholesterol and very little fat.

With meat or with a food rich in vitamin C (tomatoes, peppers, potatoes). Both enhance your body's ability to absorb the non-heme iron in the lentils.

DIETS THAT MAY RESTRICT OR EXCLUDE THIS FOOD

Antiflatulence diet
Low-calcium diet
Low-carbohydrate diet
Low-fiber diet
Low-purine (antigout) diet
Sucrose-free diet

BUYING THIS FOOD

Look for: Smooth-skinned, uniform, evenly colored lentils that are free of stones and debris. The good news about beans sold in plastic bags is that the transparent material gives you a chance to see the beans inside; the bad news is that pyridoxine and pyridoxal, the natural forms of vitamin B_6, are very sensitive to light.

Avoid: Lentils sold in bulk. The open bins expose the beans to air and light and may allow insect contamination (tiny holes in the beans indicate an insect has burrowed into or through the bean).

STORING THIS FOOD

Store lentils in air- and moistureproof containers in cool, dark cabinets where they are protected from heat, light, and insects.

PREPARING THIS FOOD

Wash the lentils and pick them over carefully, discarding damaged or withered beans and any that float. (The only beans light enough to float in water are those that have withered away inside.) Lentils do not have to be soaked before cooking.

WHAT HAPPENS WHEN YOU COOK THIS FOOD

When lentils are cooked in liquid, their cells absorb water, swell, and eventually rupture, so that the nutrients inside are more available to your body.

HOW OTHER KINDS OF PROCESSING AFFECT THIS FOOD

*   *   *

MEDICAL USES AND/OR BENEFITS

To reduce the levels of serum cholesterol.   The gums and pectins in dried beans appear to lower the amount of cholesterol in the blood and may offer some protection against heart disease. There are currently two theories to explain how this may happen. The first theory is that the pectins in the beans form a gel in your stomach that sops up fats and keeps them from being absorbed by your body. The second is that bacteria in the gut feed on the bean fiber, producing short-chain fatty acids that inhibit the production of cholesterol in your liver.

As a source of carbohydrates for people with diabetes.   Beans are digested very slowly, producing only a gradual rise in blood-sugar levels. As a result, the body needs less insulin to control blood sugar after eating beans than after eating some other high-carbohydrate foods such as bread or potato. In studies at the University of Kentucky, a bean, whole-grain, vegetable, and fruit-rich diet developed at the University of Toronto and recommended by the American Diabetic Association enabled patients with Type I diabetes (who do not produce any insulin themselves) to cut their daily insulin intake by 38 percent. For patients with Type II diabetes (who can produce some insulin), the bean diet reduced the need for injected insulin by 98 percent. This diet is in line with the nutritional guidelines of the American Diabetic Association, but people with diabetes should always consult their doctors and/or dietitians before altering their diet.

As a diet aid.   Although beans are very high in calories, they have so much fiber that even a small serving can make you feel full. And, since beans are insulin-sparing (because they do not cause blood-sugar levels to rise quickly), they put off the surge of insulin that makes us feel hungry again and allow us to feel full longer. In fact, research at the University of Toronto suggests the insulin-sparing effect may last for several hours after you eat the beans, perhaps until after your next meal. When subjects were given one of two breakfasts—bread and cheese or lentils—the people who ate the lentils produced 25 percent less insulin after the meal.

ADVERSE EFFECTS ASSOCIATED WITH THIS FOOD

Intestinal gas. All dried beans, including lentils, contain raffinose and stachyose, sugars that the human body cannot digest. As a result these sugars sit in the gut, where they are fermented by the bacteria that live in our intestinal tract. The result is intestinal gas. Since the indigestible sugars are soluble in hot water, they will leach out into the water in which you cook the lentils. You can cut down on intestinal gas by draining the lentils thoroughly before you serve them.

Production of uric acid. Purines are the natural metabolic by-products of protein metabolism in the body. They eventually break down into uric acid, which can form sharp crystals that may cause gout if they collect in your joints or kidney stones if they collect in urine. Dried beans are a source of purines; eating them raises the concentration of purines in your body. Although controlling the amount of purine-producing foods in the diet may not significantly affect the course of gout (which is treated with medication such as allopurinol, which inhibits the formation of uric acid), limiting these foods is still part of many gout regimens.

FOOD/DRUG INTERACTIONS

*   *   *

LETTUCE

(Arugula, butterhead [Bibb], chicory [curly endive], cos [romaine], crisphead [iceberg], endive, leaf lettuce [green, red], raddichio)

See also GREENS, SPINACH

NUTRITIONAL PROFILE

Energy value (calories per serving):	Low
Protein:	Moderate
Fat:	Low
Cholesterol:	None
Carbohydrates:	High
Fiber:	Low
Sodium:	Low
Major vitamin contribution:	Vitamins A and C
Major mineral contribution:	Iron, calcium

ABOUT THE NUTRIENTS IN THIS FOOD

Lettuce has small amounts of food fiber, some sugar, a little protein and fat, but no cholesterol. Its most important nutrients are vitamin A and potassium. The vitamin A comes from carotenes, whose yellow is hidden by green chlorophyll pigments. The darkest green leaves have the most vitamin A. Lettuce is also a moderately good source of vitamin C, iron, calcium, and copper. The spine and ribs of a lettuce leaf have the most fiber; the vitamins and minerals are concentrated in the more delicate part of the leaf.

COMPARING THE NUTRITIONAL VALUE OF LETTUCES

- Looseleaf lettuce has about twice as much calcium as romaine, and nearly four times as much as iceberg.
- Looseleaf lettuce has about one-third more iron than romaine, nearly three times as much as iceberg, and nearly five times as much as Boston and Bibb.
- Romaine lettuce has about one-third more vitamin A than iceberg, three times as much as Boston and Bibb, and eight times as much as iceberg.
- Romaine lettuce has about one third more vitamin C than looseleaf, three times as much as Boston and Bibb, and six times as much as iceberg.

Source: *Composition of Foods, Vegetables and Vegetable Products,* Agriculture Handbook No. 8-11 (USDA 1984).

THE MOST NUTRITIOUS WAY TO SERVE THIS FOOD

Fresh, dark leaves, torn just before serving to preserve vitamin C. Given a choice among all the varieties of lettuce, pick romaine. Overall, it has larger amounts of vitamins and minerals than any other lettuce.

DIETS THAT MAY RESTRICT OR EXCLUDE THIS FOOD

Antiflatulence diet
Low-calcium diet
Low-carbohydrate diet
Low-fiber diet
Sucrose-free diet

BUYING THIS FOOD

Look for: Brightly colored heads. Iceberg lettuce should be tightly closed and heavy for its size. Loose leaf lettuces should be crisp. All lettuces should be symmetrically shaped. An asymmetric shape suggests a large hidden stem that is crowding the leaves to one side or the other.

Avoid: Lettuce with faded or yellow leaves; lettuce leaves turn yellow as they age and their green chlorophyll fades, revealing the yellow carotenes underneath. Brown or wilted leaves are a sign of aging or poor storage. Either way, the lettuce is no longer at its best.

STORING THIS FOOD

Wrap lettuce in a plastic bag and store it in the refrigerator. The colder the storage, the longer the lettuce will keep. Most lettuce will stay fresh and crisp for as long at three weeks at 32° F. Raise the temperature just six degrees to 38° F (which is about the temperature inside your refrigerator), and the lettuce may wilt in a week.

Do not discard lettuce simply because the core begins to brown or small brown speck appear on the spines of the leaves. This is a natural oxidation reaction that changes the color but doesn't affect the nutritional value of the lettuce. Trim the end of the core (or remove the core from iceberg lettuce) to slow the reaction. Throw out any lettuce that feels slimy or has bright-red, dark-brown, or black spots. The slime is the residue of bacterial decomposition; the dark spots may be mold or rot.

Do not store unwrapped lettuce near apples, pears, melons, or bananas. These fruits release ethylene gas, a natural ripening agent that will cause the lettuce to develop brown spots.

PREPARING THIS FOOD

Never slice, cut, or tear lettuce until you are ready to use it. When lettuce cells are torn, they release ascorbic acid oxidase, an enzyme that destroys vitamin C.

WHAT HAPPENS WHEN YOU COOK THIS FOOD

Chlorophyll, the pigment that makes green vegetables green, is sensitive to acids. When you heat lettuce, the chlorophyll in its leaves will react chemically with acids in the vegetable or in the cooking water, forming pheophytin, which is brown. Together, the pheophytin and the yellow carotenes in dark-green leaves will give the cooked lettuce a bronze hue. (Lighter leaves, with very little carotene, will be olive-drab.)

To keep cooked lettuce green, you have to keep the chlorophyll from reacting with acids. One way to do this is to cook the lettuce in a large quantity of water (which will dilute the acids), but this will accelerate the loss of vitamin C. A second alternative is to cook the lettuce with the lid off the pot so that the volatile acids will float off into the air. The best way may be to steam the lettuce quickly in very little water, so that it holds onto its vitamin C and cooks before the chlorophyll has time to react with the acids.

Heat also makes the water inside the lettuce cells expand. Eventually the cells rupture and the water leaks out, leaving the lettuce limp. The spines will remain stiffer because they contain more cellulose, which does not dissolve in water. Cooked lettuce has less vitamin C than fresh lettuce because heat destroys the vitamin.

HOW OTHER FORMS OF PROCESSING AFFECT THIS FOOD

*   *   *

MEDICAL USES AND/OR BENEFITS

Protection against some forms of cancer.   According to the American Cancer Society, foods rich in vitamins A and C may offer some protection against the risk of cancers of the respiratory and intestinal tract and cancers caused by chemicals.

ADVERSE EFFECTS ASSOCIATED WITH THIS FOOD

Nitrate poisoning.   Lettuce, like beets, celery, eggplant, radishes, spinach, and collard and turnip greens, contains nitrates that convert naturally into nitrites in your stomach, and then react with the amino acids in proteins to form nitrosamines. Although some nitrosamines are known or suspected carcinogens, this natural chemical conversion presents no known problems for a healthy adult. However, when these nitrate-rich vegetables are cooked and left to stand at room temperature, bacterial enzyme action (and perhaps some enzymes in the plants) convert the nitrates to nitrites at a much faster rate than normal. These higher-nitrite foods may be hazardous for infants; several cases of "spinach poisoning" have been reported among children who ate cooked spinach that had been left standing at room temperature.

FOOD/DRUG INTERACTIONS

Anticoagulants.   Like other leaf vegetables, lettuces contain vitamin K, the blood-clotting vitamin produced naturally by bacteria in our intestines. Additional intake of vitamin K may reduce the effectiveness of anticoagulants (warfarin, Coumadin, Panwarfin), so that larger doses are required.

LIMA BEANS

NUTRITIONAL PROFILE

Energy value (calories per serving):	Moderate
Protein:	High
Fat:	Low
Cholesterol:	None
Carbohydrates:	High
Fiber:	High
Sodium:	Low
Major vitamin contribution:	Vitamin B_6, folacin
Major mineral contribution:	Magnesium, iron, zinc

ABOUT THE NUTRIENTS IN THIS FOOD

The lima bean's thin covering is a particularly good source of cellulose and the noncarbohydrate food fiber lignin. Its interior is rich in carbohydrates: starch, sugars, hemicellulose, pectins, and gums. As much as 25 percent of the calories in fresh lima beans come from their proteins, which are considered "incomplete" because they are deficient in the essential amino acids methionine and cystine. Lima beans have very little fat and no cholesterol.

Lima beans supply B vitamins, particularly vitamin B_6, niacin, and folacin, and they are a good source of non-heme iron, the inorganic form of iron in plant foods. None-heme iron is less useful to the body than heme iron, the iron in meat, because plants contain phytic acids that bind iron into insoluble compounds your body cannot absorb.

Like other beans, limas contain antinutrients: chemicals that inhibit the enzymes that enable your body to digest proteins and starches; factors that inactivate vitamin A; and hemagglutinins (substances that cause red blood cells to clump together). Cooking the lima beans will inactivate these chemicals.

Lima beans also contain phaseolunatin, a cyanogenic glycoside that breaks down into hydrogen cyanide when the cells of the lima bean are damaged or torn and the phaseolunatin comes into contact with an enzyme in the bean that triggers its conversion. Dark-colored lima beans and lima beans grown outside the United States may contain larger amounts of phaseolunatin than the pale American limas. Since phaseolunatin is not destroyed by cooking, there have been serious cases of poisoning among people living in the tropics, where the high-cyanide varieties of the lima beans grow. The importation of lima beans is restricted by many countries, including the United States; beans grown and sold here are considered safe.

THE MOST NUTRITIOUS WAY TO SERVE THIS FOOD

With grains. The proteins in grains are deficient in the essential amino acid lysine but contain sufficient methionine and cystine; the proteins in beans are exactly the opposite. Together, these foods provide "complete" proteins with no cholesterol and very little fat.

With an iron-rich food (meat) or with a food rich in vitamin C (tomatoes, peppers, potatoes). Both enhance your body's ability to absorb the nonheme iron in the lima beans. The meat makes your stomach more acid, which enhances the absorption of iron, and the vitamin C may work by converting the iron in the lima beans from ferric iron (which is hard to absorb) to ferrous iron (which is absorbed more easily).

DIETS THAT MAY RESTRICT OR EXCLUDE THIS FOOD

Antiflatulence diet
Low-calcium diet
Low-carbohydrate diet
Low-fiber diet
Low-purine (antigout) diet
Sucrose-free diet

BUYING THIS FOOD

Look for: Well-filled, tender green pods of fresh limas. The shelled beans should be plump, with green or greenish white skin.

Avoid: Spotted or yellowing pods.

STORING THIS FOOD

Store fresh lima beans in the refrigerator.

PREPARING THIS FOOD

To remove the beans from the pod, first slice a thin strip down the side of the pod to which the beans are attached, then open the pod and take out the beans. Discard withered beans or beans with tiny holes (insects have burrowed through).

WHAT HAPPENS WHEN YOU COOK THIS FOOD

When lima beans are heated in water, their cellulose and lignin-stiffened cells absorb moisture, swell, and eventually rupture, releasing the vitamins, minerals, proteins, starch, and fiber inside. Cooking also makes lima beans safer by inactivating their antinutrients and hemagglutinins.

HOW OTHER KINDS OF PROCESSING AFFECT THIS FOOD

Drying.   Drying reduces the moisture and concentrates the calories and nutrients in lima beans.

Canning and freezing.   Frozen fresh lima beans contain about the same amounts of vitamins and minerals as fresh beans; canned lima beans are lower in vitamins but usually contain more sodium in the form of added salt.

MEDICAL USES AND/OR BENEFITS

To reduce the levels of serum cholesterol.   The gums and pectins in dried beans appear to lower the level of cholesterol in the blood. There are currently two theories to explain how this may happen. The first theory is that the pectins in the beans form a gel in your stomach that sops up fats so that they cannot be absorbed by your body. The second is that bacteria in the gut feed on the bean fiber, producing chemicals called short-chain fatty acids that inhibit the production of cholesterol in your liver.

As a source of carbohydrates for people with diabetes.   Beans are digested very slowly, producing only a gradual rise in blood-sugar levels. As a result, the body needs less insulin to control blood sugar after eating beans than after eating some other high-carbohydrate foods (bread or potato). In studies at the University of Kentucky, researchers put diabetic patients on a bean-grains-fruit-and-vegetables diet developed at the University of Toronto and recommended by the American Diabetes Association. On the diet, patients with Type I diabetes (whose bodies do not produce any insulin) to cut their insulin intake by 38 percent. Patients with Type II diabetes (who can produce some insulin) were able to reduce their insulin injections by 98 percent. This diet is in line with the nutritional guidelines of the American Diabetes Association, but people with diabetes should always consult their doctors and/or dietitians before altering their diet.

As a diet aid.   Although beans are very high in calories, they have so much fiber that even a small serving can make you feel full. And, since beans are insulin-sparing (because they don't cause blood-sugar levels to rise quickly), they postpone the natural surge of insulin that triggers hunger pangs. In fact, research at the University of Toronto suggests the insulin-sparing effect may last for several hours after eating beans, perhaps even until after the next meal.

ADVERSE EFFECTS ASSOCIATED WITH THIS FOOD

Intestinal gas.   All legumes (beans and peas) contain raffinose and stachyose, sugars that cannot be digested by human beings. Instead, they are fermented by bacteria living in the intestinal tract, producing the gassiness many people associate with eating beans. Since raffinose and stachyose leach out of the limas into the water when you cook lima beans, discarding the water in which you cook fresh limas beans or presoak dried ones may make them less gassy.

FOOD/DRUG INTERACTIONS

*   *   *

LIVER

NUTRITIONAL PROFILE*

Energy value (calories per serving):	Moderate
Protein:	High
Fat:	Moderate
Cholesterol:	High
Carbohydrates:	Low
Fiber:	None
Sodium:	Moderate
Major vitamin contribution:	Vitamin A, riboflavin, niacin, vitamin B_6, vitamin B_{12}, vitamin C
Major mineral contribution:	Iron, copper

ABOUT THE NUTRIENTS IN THIS FOOD

Liver is a high-cholesterol food rich in "complete" proteins (proteins that supply adequate amounts of all the essential amino acids). It has no carbohydrates other than the sugar (glycogen) normally stored in the liver and no fiber.

Liver is the single most efficient source of vitamin A (retinol),+ and one of the few natural sources of vitamin D. It is an excellent source of B vitamins, especially vitamin B_{12}, the vitamin that prevents or cures pernicious anemia, and heme iron, the organic iron in foods of animal origin. A 3.5 ounce serving of pan-fried beef liver has 6.28 mg iron, 35 percent of the RDA for a healthy adult woman.

*Values are for braised beef liver.

+Carotenoids, the red and yellow pigments in some fruits and vegetables, are vitamin A precursors, chemicals that are converted to vitamin A in your body.

THE MOST NUTRITIOUS WAY TO SERVE THIS FOOD

As fresh as possible. Fresh-frozen liver, if kept properly cold, may be even fresher than "fresh" liver that has never been frozen but has been sitting for a day or two in the supermarket meat case.

DIETS THAT MAY RESTRICT OR EXCLUDE THIS FOOD

Galactose-free diet (for control of galactosemia)
Low-calcium diet
Low-cholesterol, controlled-fat diet
Low-protein, low-purine diet

BUYING THIS FOOD

Look for: Liver that has a deep, rich color and smells absolutely fresh.

STORING THIS FOOD

Keep fresh liver extremely cold; it is very perishable. It should be stored in the refrigerator for no longer than a day or two and in the freezer, at 0°F, for no longer than three to four months.

PREPARING THIS FOOD

Wipe the liver with a damp cloth. If your butcher has not already done so, pull off the outer membrane, and cut out the veins. Sheep, pork, and older beef liver are strongly flavored; to make them more palatable, soak these livers for several hours in cold milk, cold water, or a marinade, then discard the soaking liquid when you are ready to cook the liver.

WHAT HAPPENS WHEN YOU COOK THIS FOOD

When liver is heated it loses water and shrinks. Its pigments, which combine with oxygen, are denatured by the heat, breaking into smaller fragments that turn brown, the natural color of cooked meat. Since liver has virtually no collagen (the connective tissue that stays chewy unless you cook it for a long time), it should be cooked as quickly as possible to keep it from drying out. Pork liver, like all pork products, must be cooked until it is no longer pink in order to kill any trichinosis organisms in the meat.

HOW OTHER KINDS OF PROCESSING AFFECT THIS FOOD

*   *   *

MEDICAL USES AND/OR BENEFITS

As a source of iron.   Liver is an excellent source of heme iron, the organic form of iron in meat that is absorbed approximately five times more easily than non-heme iron, the inorganic iron in plants.

ADVERSE EFFECTS ASSOCIATED WITH THIS FOOD

Vitamin A poisoning. Vitamin A is stored in the liver, so this organ is an extremely rich source of retinol, the true vitamin A. In large doses, retinol is poisonous. The RDA for a healthy adult is 5000 IU. Doses of 50,000 IU a day over a period of weeks have produced symptoms of vitamin A poisoning; single doses of 2,000,000-5,000,000 IU may produce acute vitamin A poisoning (drowsiness, irritability, headache, vomiting, peeling skin). This reaction was documented in early arctic explorers who ate large amounts of polar bear liver and in people who eat the livers of large fish (shark, halibut, cod) which may contain up to 100,000 IU vitamin A per gram. In infants, as little as 7.5 to 15 mg of retinol a day for 30 days has produced vomiting and bulging fontanel. In 1980 there was a report of chronic vitamin A intoxication in infants fed 120 gram (4 ounces) of chicken liver plus vitamin supplements containing 2000 IU vitamin A, yellow vegetable and fruits, and vitamin A-enriched milk every day for four months. Liver should not be eaten every day unless specifically directed by a physician.

Production of uric acid. Purines are the natural metabolic by-products of protein metabolism in the body. They eventually break down into uric acid, which can form sharp crystals that may cause gout if they collect in your joints or kidney stones if they collect in urine. Liver is a source of purines; eating liver raises the concentration of purines in your body. Although controlling the amount of purine-producing foods in the diet may not significantly affect the course of gout (treated with medication such as allopurinol, which inhibits the formation of uric acid), limiting foods that raise the levels of purines is still part of many gout regimens.

Elevated levels of serum cholesterol. Abnormally high levels of cholesterol in the blood are a risk factor in heart disease. How your diet affects the amount of cholesterol you produce is not entirely clear; dietary fat and cholesterol may not be the primary factor in determining how much and what kind of cholesterol your body makes and stores. Nonetheless, there is evidence to suggest that controlling the amount of fat and cholesterol you consume may help lower serum cholesterol levels, particularly for people whose serum levels are higher than normal. In 1986 the American Heart Association issued new guidelines suggesting that healthy people reduce their consumption of fat to 30 percent of their total daily calories and limit their cholesterol intake to 300 mg per day or 100 mg per 1000 calories, whichever is less. (A 3.5-ounce serving of fried beef liver has 434 mg cholesterol.)

FOOD/DRUG INTERACTIONS

MAO inhibitors. Monoamine oxidase (MAO) inhibitors are drugs used as antidepressants or antihypertensives. They inhibit the enzymes that break down tyramine so that it can be eliminated from your body. Tyramine, which is formed when proteins deteriorate, is a pressor amine, a chemical that constricts blood vessels and raises blood pressure. If you eat a food rich in tyramine while you are taking an MAO inhibitor, the pressor amine cannot be eliminated from your body, and the result may be a hypertensive crisis (sustained elevated blood pressure). Liver, which is extremely perishable, contains enzymes that break down its proteins quickly if the liver is not properly refrigerated or if it ages. Fresh or canned pâtés made with wine may contain more tyramine than fresh liver.

MANGOES

NUTRITIONAL PROFILE

Energy value (calories per serving):	Moderate
Protein:	Low
Fat:	Low
Cholesterol:	None
Carbohydrates:	High
Fiber:	Low
Sodium:	Low
Major vitamin contribution:	Vitamins A and C
Major mineral contribution:	Potassium

ABOUT THE NUTRIENTS IN THIS FOOD

Mangoes are an excellent source of vitamins A and C. One 3.5-ounce mango provides 28 mg vitamin C (47 percent of the RDA for a healthy adult) and 3900 IU vitamin A (78 percent of the RDA for a healthy adult), derived from the carotene and other carotenoid pigments that make the mango yellow-orange.

Unripe mangoes contain antinutrients, protein compounds that inhibit amylases (the enzymes that make it possible for us to digest starches) and catalase (the iron-containing enzyme that protects our cells by splitting potentially damaging peroxides in our body into safe water and oxygen). As the fruit ripens the enzyme inhibitors are inactivated.

THE MOST NUTRITIOUS WAY TO SERVE THIS FOOD
Ripe, chilled, and freshly cut.

DIETS THAT MAY RESTRICT OR EXCLUDE THIS FOOD
Sucrose-free diet

BUYING THIS FOOD
Look for: Flattish, oval fruit. The skin should be yellow-green or yellow-green flecked with red; the riper the mango, the more yellow and red there will be. A ripe mango will give slightly when you press it with your finger.

Avoid: Mangoes with gray, pitted, or spotted skin; they may be rotten inside.

STORING THIS FOOD
Store mangoes at room temperature if they aren't fully ripe when you buy them; they will continue to ripen. When the mangoes are soft (ripe), refrigerate them and use them within two or three days. Once you have sliced a mango, wrap it in plastic and store it in the refrigerator.

PREPARING THIS FOOD
Chill mangoes before you serve them. At room temperature they have a distinctly unpleasant taste and a fragrance some people compare to turpentine. The flavor of the mango doesn't develop fully until the fruit is completely ripe. If you cut into a mango and find that it's not ripe yet, poach it in sugar syrup. That way it will taste fine.

Eating a mango is an adventure. The long, oval pit clings to the flesh, and to get at the fruit you have to peel away the skin and then slice off the flesh.

WHAT HAPPENS WHEN YOU COOK THIS FOOD
When you poach a mango, its cells absorb water and the fruit softens.

HOW OTHER KINDS OF PROCESSING AFFECT THIS FOOD
*   *   *

MEDICAL USES AND/OR BENEFITS
Protection against some forms of cancer. According to the American Cancer Society, foods rich in vitamins A and C may offer some protection against cancers of the respiratory and intestinal tracts as well as against cancers induced by chemicals.

ADVERSE EFFECTS ASSOCIATED WITH THIS FOOD

Contact dermatitis.   The skin of the mango contains urushiol, the chemical that may cause contact dermatitis when you touch poison ivy, poison oak, and poison sumac.

FOOD/DRUG INTERACTIONS

*   *   *

MELONS

(Cantaloupe, casaba, honeydew, Persian, watermelon)

NUTRITIONAL PROFILE

Energy value (calories per serving):	Low
Protein:	Low
Fat:	Low
Cholesterol:	None
Carbohydrates:	High
Fiber:	Low
Sodium:	Low
Major vitamin contribution:	Vitamins A and C
Major mineral contribution:	Potassium

ABOUT THE NUTRIENTS IN THIS FOOD

All melons have small amounts of protein, fats, and fiber. The yellow melons (cantaloupe, Persian, and cranshaw melons) contain carotene and carotenoid pigments that your body can convert to A. Cantaloupes, for example, are an extraordinarily good source of vitamin A. One 3.5-ounce slice provides about 3200 IU, 64 percent of the RDA for a healthy adult. A similar slice of watermelon, which is colored with lycopene, a red carotenoid that cannot be converted into vitamin A, has slightly more than one-tenth as much vitamin A. Cantaloupe, cranshaw, and honeydew melons are good sources of vitamin C.

THE MOST NUTRITIOUS WAY TO SERVE THIS FOOD

Fresh and ripe.

DIETS THAT MAY RESTRICT OR EXCLUDE THIS FOOD

Low-carbohydrate diet

Low-fiber diet

Sucrose-free diet

BUYING THIS FOOD

Look for: Vine-ripened melons if possible. You can identify a vine-ripened melon by checking the stem end. If the scar is clean and sunken, it means that the stem was pulled out of a ripe melon. Ripe melons also have a deep aroma: the more intense the fragrance, the sweeter the melon.

Cantaloupes should be round and firm, with cream-colored, coarse "netting" that stands up all over the fruit. The rind at the stem end of the melon should give slightly when you press it and there should be a rich, melony aroma. *Casabas* should have a deep-yellow rind that gives at the stem end when you press it. Ripe casabas smell pleasant and melony. *Honeydews* should have a smooth cream-colored or a yellowish-white rind. If the rind is completely white or tinged with green, the melon is not ripe. Like cantaloupes, *Persian melons* have a rind covered with "netting." As the Persian ripens, the color of its rind lightens. A ripe Persian will give when you press it. *Watermelons* should should have a firm, smooth rind with a cream or yellowish undercolor. If the undercoat is white or greenish, the melon is not ripe. When you shake a ripe watermelon, the seeds inside will rattle; when you thump its rind, you should hear a slightly hollow sound.

STORING THIS FOOD

Hold whole melons at room temperature for a few days. Melons have no stored starches to convert to sugar, so they can't get sweeter once they are picked, but they will begin to soften as enzymes begin to dissolve pectin in the cell walls. As the cell walls dissolve, the melons release the aromatic molecules that make them smell sweet and ripe.

Refrigerate ripe melons to slow the natural deterioration of the fruit. Sliced melons should be wrapped in plastic to keep them from losing moisture or from absorbing odors from other foods.

PREPARING THIS FOOD

Chill the melon, wash it under running water to flush dirt off the rind, slice, and serve.

WHAT HAPPENS WHEN YOU COOK THIS FOOD

*   *   *

HOW OTHER KINDS OF PROCESSING AFFECT THIS FOOD
*   *   *

MEDICAL USES AND/OR BENEFITS

Protection against some forms of cancer. According to the American Cancer Society, deep-yellow fruits such as the cantaloupe that are rich sources of vitamin A may offer some protection against cancers of the larynx, esophagus, and lungs.

ADVERSE EFFECTS ASSOCIATED WITH THIS FOOD
*   *   *

FOOD/DRUG INTERACTIONS
*   *   *

MILK
(Goat's milk)

NUTRITIONAL PROFILE*

Energy value (calories per serving):	Moderate
Protein:	High
Fat:	Moderate
Cholesterol:	Moderate
Carbohydrates:	Moderate
Fiber:	None
Sodium:	Moderate
Major vitamin contribution:	Vitamins A and D, B vitamins
Major mineral contribution:	Calcium, iodine

ABOUT THE NUTRIENTS IN THIS FOOD

Cow's milk and goat's milk are high-protein foods with less sugar and more protein than human milk. About 82 percent of the protein in milk is casein, a protein found only in milk. The rest are whey proteins, principally lactalbumin and lactoglubulin. Milk's proteins are considered "complete" because they supply all the essential amino acids. Lactose, the sugar found in most mammal milks, is a disaccharide (double sugar). Each molecule of lactose is made of one molecule of glucose and one molecule of galactose.

About half the calories in whole milk come from milkfat, which is composed primarily of saturated fatty acids. Milkfat, which is lighter than water, will rise to the top and can be skimmed off. *Whole milk* is 3.5 percent

*Values are for whole milk.

milkfat. Depending on how much fat is skimmed off, what remains is either *low-fat* (1-2 percent fat) or *skimmed* (0.5 percent fat) milk. *Homogenized milk* is whole milk processed through machinery that reduces its fat globules to particles small enough to remain suspended in the liquid rather than float to the top.

Whole milk gets is creamy color from carotenoid pigments (principally beta-carotene) that provide small amounts of vitamin A. Since vitamin A is fat-soluble, it disappears with the fat skimmed from whole milk. Low-fat and skimmed milks are fortified with added vitamin A; all milk sold in this country is fortified with vitamin D.

Milk is a good source of thiamin (vitamin B_1), and vitamin B_6, riboflavin (vitamin B_2), a "visible vitamin" whose green pigment, masked by the carotenes in whole milk, gives skimmed milk and whey a greenish cast.

Milk is our best source of calcium. Even though some plant foods such as beans have more calcium per ounce, the calcium in plants is bound into insoluble compounds by phytic acids while the calcium in milk is completely available to our bodies. No calcium is lost when milk is skimmed.

Iodine and copper are unexpected bonuses in milk. The iodine comes from supplements given the milk cows and perhaps, from iodates and iodophors used to clean the machinery in milk-processing plants; milk picks up copper from the utensils in which it is pasteurized.

COMPARING THE NUTRIENTS IN 100 GRAMS (3.5 OZ.) OF WHOLE MILK

	Cow's milk	Goat's milk	Human milk
Calories	61	69	70
Protein (gm)	3.3	3.6	1.0
Fat (gm)	3.3	4.1	4.4
Cholesterol (mg)	14	11	14
Carbohydrates [sugar] (gm)	4.7	4.5	6.9
Calcium (mg)	119	134	32
Vitamin A (IU)	126	185	241

Source: "Composition of Foods: Dairy and Egg Products," Agriculture Handbook No 8-1 (USDA, 1976).

THE MOST NUTRITIOUS WAY TO SERVE THIS FOOD

For children: Whole milk. According to the American Academy of Pediatrics, feeding children skim or low-fat milk instead of whole milk will deprive them of some of the essential constituents of the fatty acids in milk, including various immunological factors. A 1984 study at the School of Public Health at the University of Michigan also suggested that children fed low-fat milk rather than whole milk were five times more at risk for serious gastrointestinal illness.

For adults: Low-fat or skim milk.

DIETS THAT MAY RESTRICT OR EXCLUDE THIS FOOD
Lactose- and galactose-free diet
Low-calcium diet
Low-cholesterol, controlled-fat diet

BUYING THIS FOOD
Look for: Tightly sealed, dry, refrigerated cartons that feel cold to the touch. Check the date on the carton and pick the latest one you can find.

STORING THIS FOOD
Refrigerate fresh milk and cream in tightly closed containers to keep the milk from picking up odors from other foods in the refrigerator. Never leave milk cartons standing at room temperature.

Protect milk from bright light, including direct sunlight, daylight, and fluorescent light, whose energy can "cook" the milk and change its taste by altering the structure of its protein molecules. Light may also destroy vitamin A, riboflavin (vitamin B_2), vitamin C, and vitamin B_6. Milk stored in glass bottles exposed to direct sunlight may lose as much as 70 percent of its riboflavin in just two hours. Opaque plastic cartons reduce the flow of light into the milk but do not block it completely.

PREPARING THIS FOOD
Chill, pour, and serve. *Never* pour unused milk or cream back into the original container. Doing that might introduce bacteria that can contaminate all the other milk in the bottle or carton.

WHAT HAPPENS WHEN YOU COOK THIS FOOD
When milk is warmed, its tightly-curled protein molecules relax and unfold, breaking internal bonds (bonds between atoms on the same molecule) and forming new, intermolecular bonds between atoms on neighboring molecules. The newly linked protein molecules create a network with water molecules caught in the net. As the milk cooks, the network tightens, squeezing out the water molecules and forming the lumps we call curds.

Casein, the proteins that combine with calcium to form the "skin" on top of hot milk, will also form curds if you lower the pH of the milk by adding an acid—lemon juice, fruit, vegetables, vinegar, or wine. Whey proteins do not coagulate when you make the milk more acid, but they precipitate (fall to the bottom of the pot) when the milk heated to a temperature above 170° F. If the bottom of the pot gets hotter, the whey proteins will scorch and the milk will smell burnt.

HOW OTHER KINDS OF PROCESSING AFFECT THIS FOOD

Freezing.   Milk that has been frozen and defrosted has less vitamin C and B vitamins than fresh milk. Freezing also changes the taste and texture of milk. First, it breaks up milk's protein molecules. When the milk is defrosted, they clump together so that the the milk no longer tastes perfectly smooth. Second, freezing slows but does not stop the natural oxidation of milk's fat molecules. The longer milk is frozen, the more fat molecules will oxidize and the stronger the milk will taste.

Drying.   Dried milk tastes cooked because it has been heated to evaporate its moisture. Unopened packages of dried milk should be stored in a cool, dry cabinet where they may hold their flavor and nutrients for several months. Once a package of dried milk is opened, its contents should be stored in a container, keeping out the moisture that will encourage bacterial growth and change the taste of the milk. Once the dried milk is reconstituted, it should be refrigerated.

Condensed and evaporated milk.   Evaporated and condensed milks have been cooked to evaporate moisture; condensed milk has added sugar. Both evaporated and condensed milk have a cooked flavor. They also have less vitamin C and vitamin B6 than fresh milk.

Unopened cans of condensed or evaporated milk should be stored in a cool, dark cabinet. Unopened cans of evaporated milk will keep for one month at 90° F, one to two years at 70° F, and two years or more at 39° F. At the same temperatures, unopened cans of condensed milk will keep for three months, four to nine months, and two years. Once a can of milk is opened, the milk should be poured into a clean container and refrigerated.

Heat treatments that make milk safer.   Raw (unpasteurized) milk may contain a variety of microorganisms, including pathogenic and harmless bacteria, plus yeasts and molds that are destroyed when the milk is pasteurized (heated to 145° F for 30 minutes or 160° F for 15 seconds). Ultrapasteurized milk has been heated to 280° F for two seconds or more. The higher temperature destroys more microorganisms than pasteurization and prolongs the shelf life of the milk and cream (which must be refrigerated). Ultra-high-temperature sterilization heats the milk to 280°-302° F for two to six seconds. The milk or cream is then packed into presterilized containers and aseptically sealed so that bacteria that might spoil the milk cannot enter. Aseptically packaged milk, which is widely available in Europe, can be stored on an unrefrigerated grocery or kitchen shelf for as long as three months without spoiling or losing any of its vitamins. (None of these treatments will protect milk indefinitely, of course. They simply put off the milk's inevitable deterioration by reducing the initial microbial population.)

MEDICAL USES AND/OR BENEFITS

Protection against rickets.   Virtually all fresh sweet milk in this country is fortified with vitamin D to prevent the vitamin D-deficiency disease rickets.

Protective effects of calcium.   Adequate dietary calcium early in life may offer some protection against osteoporosis ("thinning bones") later on, although the thesis remains to be proved. In one study at the University of Pittsburgh School of Health-Related Professions, researchers found that women who drank milk with every meal until they were thirty-five had bones of higher density than women who rarely drank milk.

ADVERSE EFFECTS ASSOCIATED WITH THIS FOOD

Allergy to milk proteins. Milk and milk products are among the foods most often implicated as a cause of the classic symptoms of food allergy—upset stomach, hives, and angioedemia (swelling of the face, lips and tongue).

Lactose intolerance.   Lactose intolerance—the inability to digest the sugar in milk—is not an allergy. It is an inherited metabolic deficiency that affects two-thirds of all adults, including 90 to 95 percent of all Orientals, 70 to 75 percent of all blacks, and 6 to 8 percent of Caucasians. These people do not have sufficient amounts of lactase, the enzyme that breaks lactose (a disaccharide) into its easily digested components, galactose and glucose. When they drink milk, the undigested sugar is fermented by bacteria in the gut, causing bloating, diarrhea, flatulence, and intestinal discomfort. Some milk is now sold with added lactase to digest the lactose and make the milk usable for lactase-deficient people.

Galactosemia.   Galactosemia is an inherited metabolic disorder in which the body lacks the enzymes needed to metabolize galactose, a component of lactose. Galactosemia is a recessive trait; you must get the gene from both parents to develop the condition. Babies born with galactosemia will fail to thrive and may develop brain damage or cataracts if they are given milk. To prevent this, children with galactosemia are usually kept on a protective milk-free diet for several years, until their bodies have developed alternative pathways by which to metabolize galactose. Pregnant women who are known carriers of galactosemia may be advised to give up milk while pregnant lest the unmetabolized galactose in their bodies cause brain damage to the fetus (damage that is not detectible by amniocentesis). Genetic counseling is available to identify galactosemia carriers and assess their chances of producing a baby with the disorder.

Food poisoning. Raw (unpasteurized) milk may be contaminated with *Salmonella* and/or *Listeria* organisms. Poisoning with *Salmonella* organisms may cause nausea, vomiting, and diarrhea—which can be debilitating and potentially serious in infants, the elderly, and people who are ill. *Listeria* poisoning is a flulike illness that may be particularly hazardous for pregnant women or invalids who are at risk of encephalitis, meningitis, or infections of the bloodstream. *Listeria* may also be found in milk foods made from infected raw milk. *Salmonella* will also grow in pasteurized milk if the milk is not refrigerated.

Elevated levels of serum cholesterol. Abnormally high levels of cholesterol in the blood are a risk factor in heart disease. How your diet affects the amount of cholesterol you produce is not entirely clear; dietary fat and cholesterol may not be the primary factor in determining how much and what kind of cholesterol your body makes and stores. Nonetheless, there is evidence to suggest that controlling the amount of fat and cholesterol you consume may help lower serum cholesterol levels, particularly for people with high levels. In 1986 the American Heart Association issued new nutritional guidelines, suggesting that healthy adults reduce their consumption of fat to 30 percent of their overall calories and limit cholesterol intake to 300 mg per day or 100 mg per 1000 calories, whichever is less. (One cup of whole milk contains 33 mg cholesterol, one cup skim milk 5 mg.)

FOOD/DRUG INTERACTIONS

Tetracyclines. The calcium ions in milk bind to tetracyclines (Declomycin, Minocin, Rondomycin, Terramycin, Vibramycin, and so on), forming insoluble compounds your body cannot absorb. Taking tetracyclines with milk makes them less effective.

Antacids containing calcium carbonate. People who take calcium carbonate antacids with homogenized milk fortified with vitamin D (which facilitates the absorption of calcium) may end up with milk-alkali syndrome, a potentially serious kidney disorder caused by the accumulation of excessive amounts of calcium in the blood. Milk-alkali syndrome, which is rare, subsides gradually when the patient stops taking either the antacid or the milk.

MUSHROOMS

NUTRITIONAL PROFILE

Energy value (calories per serving):	Low
Protein:	High
Fat:	Low
Cholesterol:	None
Carbohydrates:	High
Fiber:	High
Sodium:	Low
Major vitamin contribution:	Vitamin B_2 (riboflavin) and vitamin D
Major mineral contribution:	Potassium

ABOUT THE NUTRIENTS IN THIS FOOD

Mushrooms are a good source of riboflavin (vitamin B_2). They have only small amounts of the other vitamins and minerals, but are high in protein, carbohydrates, and fibers.

THE MOST NUTRITIOUS WAY TO SERVE THIS FOOD

Fresh, in salads.

DIETS THAT MAY RESTRICT OR EXCLUDE THIS FOOD

Sucrose-free diet

BUYING THIS FOOD

Look for: Smooth, plump, uniformly cream-colored button mushrooms. The cap should be closed tightly, hiding the gills. As mushrooms age, they turn darker; they also lose moisture and shrink, which is why the caps spring open, revealing the pink or tan gills. (Black gills are also an indication of age.) Older mushrooms are more intensely flavored than young ones, but they also have a shorter shelf life. And they also have less sugar than truly fresh mushrooms. By the fourth day after mushrooms are picked, about half their sugar and starch will have turned to chitin, a polymer (a compound with many molecules) similar to cellulose. That is why older mushrooms are "crisper" than fresh ones.

Avoid: Any wild mushrooms. Stick to commercially grown mushrooms from reputable growers.

STORING THIS FOOD

Refrigerate fresh mushrooms in containers that allow air to circulate among the mushrooms. The aim is to prevent moisture from collecting on the mushrooms; damp mushrooms deteriorate quickly. Mushrooms should never be stored in plastic bags.

PREPARING THIS FOOD

Rinse the mushrooms under cold running water and rub them dry with a soft paper towel or scrub them with a soft mushroom brush to remove dirt on the cap.

You can clean mushrooms quickly simply by peeling the cap, but that will make them less tasty. The mushroom's flavor comes from an unusually large amount of glutamic acid in the skin. Glutamic acid is the natural version of the flavor enhancer we know as MSG (monosodium glutamate).

Slicing mushrooms hastens the loss of riboflavin. According to the United Fresh Fruit and Vegetable Association, boiled whole mushrooms may retain as much as 82 percent of their riboflavin, sliced mushrooms only 66 percent. Slicing also changes the color of mushrooms. When you cut the mushroom, you tear its cells, releasing polyphenoloxidase, an enzyme that hastens the oxidation of phenols in the mushroom, producing brownish particles that make the white mushroom dark. You can slow this natural reaction (but not stop it entirely) by coating the mushrooms with an acid—lemon juice, vinegar, or a salad dressing that contains one or the other.

Button mushrooms lose moisture and shrink when you cook them. If you choose to cut off their stems before you cook them, leave a small stub to help the mushroom hold its shape.

WHAT HAPPENS WHEN YOU COOK THIS FOOD

The B vitamins in mushrooms are all water-soluble. They will leach out into the cooking water, which should be added to your recipe along with the mushrooms.

Cooking toughens the stem of button mushrooms but does not affect their nutritional value since riboflavin is not destroyed by heat and remains stable in a neutral solution or an acid one such as a tomato sauce or a stew with tomatoes and bell peppers.

HOW OTHER KINDS OF PROCESSING AFFECT THIS FOOD

Canning.   Canned mushrooms with their liquid may contain up to 100 times as much sodium as fresh mushrooms. Riboflavin, the most important nutrient in mushrooms, is not destroyed by heat, but it will leach out into the salty liquid. Riboflavin is sensitive to light; mushrooms in glass jars should be stored in a cool, dark cabinet.

Drying.   Dried mushrooms should be sold and stored in a tightly closed package that protects the mushrooms from moisture, and they should be kept in a cool, dark place out of direct sunlight. They should be stored in the refrigerator only if the refrigerator is less humid than the kitchen cabinet. Properly stored dried mushrooms may remain usable for as long as six months. To use dried mushrooms, cover them with boiling water and let them stand for about fifteen minutes. Then rinse them thoroughly to get rid of sand and debris in the folds of the mushroom.

MEDICAL USES AND/OR BENEFITS

*   *   *

ADVERSE EFFECTS ASSOCIATED WITH THIS FOOD

Mushroom poisoning.   About a hundred of the more than 1000 varieties of mushrooms are poisonous. In the United States, nearly 90 percent of all mushroom poisoning is due to two species of *Amanita* mushrooms, *Amanita muscaria* and *Amanita phalloides. Amanita muscaria* contains muscarine, a parasympathetic-nervous-system poison that can cause tearing, salivation, sweating, vomiting, cramps and diarrhea, dizziness, confusion, coma, and convulsions. These symptoms may show up anywhere from a few minutes to two hours after you eat the mushrooms. Muscarine poisoning is potentially fatal. Phalloidine, the toxin in *Amanita phalloide* mushrooms, is a liver poison whose symptoms include all those attributed to muscarine poisoning, plus jaundice from liver damage. These symptoms may not show up until two to three days after you eat the mushrooms. Phalloidine is a potentially lethal poison; the death rate for phalloidine poisoning is 50 percent.

FOOD/DRUG INTERACTIONS

False-positive test for occult blood in the stool.   The active ingredient in the guaiac slide test for hidden blood in feces is alphaguaiaconic acid, a chemical that turns blue in the presence of blood. Alphaguaiaconic acid also turns blue in the presence of peroxidase, a chemical that occurs naturally in mushrooms. Eating mushrooms in the 72 hours before taking the guaiac test may produce a false-positive result in people who not actually have any blood in their stool.

Alcohol/disulfiram interaction.   Disulfiram (Antabuse) is a drug used to treat alcoholism. It causes flushing, difficulty in breathing, nausea, chest pain, vomiting and rapid heart beat if taken with alcohol. Some mushrooms, including the cultivated edible varieties, may contain naturally-occuring disulfiram. If taken with alcohol, these mushrooms may cause symptoms of a disulfiram-alcohol reaction in sensitive individuals. Since disulfiram lingers in your system, the symptoms may appear half an hour after you drink alcohol, even if you ate the mushrooms as much as four or five days ago.

NUTS

(Almonds, Brazil nuts, cashews, chestnuts, macadamias, pecans, pistachios, walnuts)

See also COCONUTS, PEANUTS, VEGETABLE OILS

NUTRITIONAL PROFILE

Energy value (calories per serving):	High
Protein:	Moderate
Fat:	High
Cholesterol:	None
Carbohydrates:	Low
Fiber:	High
Sodium:	Low*
Major vitamin contribution:	B vitamins, vitamin E
Major mineral contribution:	Iron, phosphorus

ABOUT THE NUTRIENTS IN THIS FOOD

Nuts are high-protein, high-fat, high-carbohydrate, high-fiber food especially rich in the indigestible food fibers cellulose and lignin.

A single 1-1.5-ounce serving of nuts delivers 5 to 9 grams of protein, about 10 percent of the RDA for a healthy adult. But the proteins in nuts are considered "incomplete" because they are deficient in the essential amino acid lysine, and nuts are too high in fat to qualify as a good source of dietary protein. Plain nuts or nuts roasted without extra fat may be more than 70 percent fat as compared to beans, which are also high in proteins, carbohydrates, and fiber and have less than 2 percent fat.

Nuts have no cholesterol. Their fats are highly unsaturated, a good

*Unsalted nuts. Salted nuts are high in sodium.

source of vitamin E. If the nuts are exposed to air, the carbon atoms in the molecules of unsaturated fatty acids will pick up oxygen atoms. This natural oxidation of the saturated fatty acids, which turns the nuts rancid, can be slowed by protecting the nuts from air, heat, and light but it can never be completely stopped. Eventually, all nuts will become rancid.

Nuts are also a good source of B vitamins, calcium, potassium, and are considered a good source of iron.

Plain raw or roasted nuts are low in sodium; salted nuts are a high-sodium food.

THE MOST NUTRITIOUS WAY TO SERVE THIS FOOD

With peanuts or with beans. Both are legumes, which provide the essential amino acid lysine needed to "complete" the proteins in nuts. Adding raisins adds iron.

DIETS THAT MAY RESTRICT OR EXCLUDE THIS FOOD

Antiflatulence diet
Low-calcium diet
Low-fat diet
Low-fiber, low-residue diet
Low-oxalate diet (for people who form calcium oxalate kidney stones; almonds and cashews)
Low-protein diet
Low-sodium diet (salted nuts)

BUYING THIS FOOD

Look for: Fresh nuts with clean, undamaged shells. The nuts should feel heavy for their size; nuts that feel light may be withered inside.

Choose crisp, fresh shelled nuts. They should taste fresh and snap when you bite into them. As nuts age, their oils oxidize and become rancid; old nuts will have an off taste. If nuts sold in bulk are exposed to air, heat, and light, their fats will oxidize more quickly than the fats in packaged nuts. Check the date on the bottom of the can or jar to be sure packaged nuts are fresh.

Avoid: Moldy, shriveled, or discolored nuts. The molds that grow on nuts may produce potentially carcinogenic aflatoxins that have been linked to liver cancer.

STORING THIS FOOD

Store nuts in a cool, dry, dark place in a container that protects them from the air, heat, light, and moisture.

Pack nuts in a moistureproof container and store them in the freezer if you don't plan to use them right away. The cold will slow down the oxidation of fats and the nuts will stay fresh longer. For example, shelled pecans stay fresh up to one year in the freezer against about two months on a cool, dark kitchen shelf.

Check the nuts occasionally; throw out any moldy nuts or any that have shriveled.

Do not shell nuts until you are ready to use them. The shell is a natural protective shield.

PREPARING THIS FOOD

Almonds.   To peel shelled almonds, boil the nuts, drain them, and plunge them into cold water. The skin should slip off easily.

Brazil nuts.   Brazil nuts are easy to open if you chill them first. To slice shelled Brazil nuts, boil the nuts in water for five minutes, then cool and slice. Or you can shave them into slivers with a potato peeler.

Cashews.   Always cook raw cashews before you shell them. Between the shell and the raw nut is a thin layer of urushiol, the irritating oil also found in poison oak and poison ivy. The oil is inactivated by heat.

Chestnuts.   Slice an X in the flat end of the chestnut and peel off the heavy outer skin. To remove the thin inner skin, bake the chestnuts on a cookie sheet in a 400° F oven for about twenty minutes or cover them with boiling water and simmer them for fifteen minutes. Then drain the nuts and slip off the skins.

Macadamia nuts.   To open macadamia nuts, wrap them, one at a time, in a heavy cloth napkin or towel, put the package on a wooden breadboard, and hit the nut with a hammer.

Pecans and walnuts.   Crack the nut with a nutcracker.

Pistachios.   Open the nuts with your fingers, not your teeth.

WHAT HAPPENS WHEN YOU COOK THIS FOOD
   *   *   *

HOW OTHER KINDS OF PROCESSING AFFECT THIS FOOD

Vacuum packaging.   Canned nuts and nuts in glass jars stay fresh longer than nuts sold in bulk because they are protected from the oxygen that combines with oils and turns them rancid. Nuts in sealed cans and jars may stay fresh for as long as a year if stored in a cool, dark place. Once the can or jar is opened, the oils will begin to oxidize and eventually become rancid.

MEDICAL USES AND/OR BENEFITS

*   *   *

ADVERSE EFFECTS ASSOCIATED WITH THIS FOOD

Allergic reactions.   Nuts are among the foods most often implicated as a cause of the classic symptoms of food allergy: upset stomach, hives, and angioedema (swelling of the lips and eyes).

Flare-up of apthous ulcers (canker sores).   Eating nuts may trigger an episode of canker sores in susceptible people, but avoiding nuts will not prevent or cure an attack.

FOOD/DRUG INTERACTIONS

False-positive urine test for carcinoid syndrome.   Carcinoid tumors, which may arise from the tissues of the endocrine or gastrointestinal systems, secrete serotonin, a nitrogen compound that makes blood vessels expand or contract. The test for these tumors measures the amount of serotonin in the blood. Eating walnuts, which are high in serotonin, in the 72 hours before taking the test for a carcinoid tumor may cause a false-positive result, suggesting that you have the tumor when in fact you do not. (Other foods high in serotonin are avocados, bananas, eggplant, plums, pineapple, and tomatoes.)

OATS (OATMEAL)

NUTRITIONAL PROFILE

Energy value (calories per serving):	Moderate
Protein:	Moderate
Fat:	Low
Cholesterol:	None
Carbohydrates:	High
Fiber:	High
Sodium:	Low
Major vitamin contribution:	B vitamins
Major mineral contribution:	Iron, potassium

ABOUT THE NUTRIENTS IN THIS FOOD

What we call *oats* is actually oatmeal, oats that have been rolled (ground) into a meal, then steamed to break down some of their starches, formed into flakes, and dried. Steel-cut oats have been ground in a special steel machine; oat flour is finely ground oatmeal.

Unlike cows and other ruminants, human beings cannot break through the cellulose and lignin covering on raw grain to reach the nutrients inside. Cooking unprocessed oats to the point where they are useful to human beings can take as long as 24 hours. The virtue of rolled oats is that they have been precooked and can be prepared in five minutes or less. Instant oatmeals, like other "instant" cereals, are treated with phosphates to allow them to absorb water more quickly.

All oatmeals are high-carbohydrate foods, rich in starch, with a trace of sugar. They are an excellent source of indigestible food fibers including the complex carbohydrates, beta-glucans. They have moderate amounts of proteins. The proteins in oatmeal are considered "incomplete" because they are deficient in the essential amino acid lysine. Oats have no cholesterol, but oatmeal may have as much as five times the fat in rye and wheat flours. Since oats also contain an enzyme that speeds the oxidation of fats, oatmeal would become rancid very quickly if it were not for the fact that rolling and steaming the oats to make the meal also inactivates the destructive enzyme.

Oats provide B vitamins, iron, and potassium. Uncooked oatmeal made solely of oats (no additives) has no sodium, but the water you add in cooking may turn the cereal into a moderate- or high-sodium food.

THE MOST NUTRITIOUS WAY TO SERVE THIS FOOD

With beans, milk, cheese, or meat, any of which will provide the essential amino acid lysine to "complete" the proteins in the oatmeal.

DIETS THAT MAY RESTRICT OR EXCLUDE THIS FOOD

Gluten-restricted, gliadin-free diet
Low-carbohydrate diet
Low-fiber, low-residue diet
Low-sodium diet

BUYING THIS FOOD

Look for: Tightly sealed boxes or canisters.

Avoid: Bulk cereals; grains in open bins may be exposed to moisture, mold, and insect contamination.

STORING THIS FOOD

Keep oats in air- and moistureproof containers to protect them from potentially toxic fungi that grow on damp grains. Properly stored and dry, rolled oats may keep for as long as a year. Whole-grain oats (oats with the outer fatty covering) may oxidize and become rancid more quickly.

PREPARING THIS FOOD

*   *   *

WHAT HAPPENS WHEN YOU COOK THIS FOOD

Starch consists of molecules of the complex carbohydrates amylose and amylopectin packed into a starch granule. As you heat oatmeal in liquid, its starch granules absorb water molecules, swell, and soften. When the temperature of the liquid reaches approximately 140°F, the amylose and amylopectin molecules inside the granules relax and unfold, breaking some of their internal bonds (bonds between atoms on the same molecule) and forming new bonds between atoms on different molecules. The result is a network that traps and holds water molecules, making the starch granules even more bulky and thickening the liquid. Eventually the starch granules rupture, releasing the nutrients inside so that they can be absorbed more easily by the body. Oatmeal also contains hydrophilic (water-loving) gums and pectins, including beta-glucans, that attract and hold water molecules, immobilizing them so that the liquid thickens. (The beta-glucans give oatmeal its characteristic sticky texture.)

Ounce for ounce, cooked oatmeal has smaller amounts of vitamins and minerals than dry oatmeal simply because so much of its weight is now water. The single exception is sodium. Plain, uncooked oatmeal, with no additives, has no sodium; cooked oatmeal, made with water or milk, does.

HOW OTHER KINDS OF PROCESSING AFFECT THIS FOOD
*   *   *

MEDICAL USES AND/OR BENEFITS

To reduce the levels of serum cholesterol.   The gums and pectins in oatmeal appear to lower the amount of cholesterol in the blood and offer some protection against heart disease. There are currently two theories to explain how this may happen. The first theory is that the pectins in the oats form a gel in your stomach that sops up fats keeps them from being absorbed by your body. The second is that bacteria in the gut may feed on the beta-glucans in the oats and produce short-chain fatty acids that inhibit the production of cholesterol in your liver.

As a source of carbohydrates for people with diabetes.   Cereal grains are digested very slowly, producing only a gradual rise in the level of sugar in the blood. As a result, the body needs less insulin to control blood sugar after eating plain, unadorned cereal grains than after eating some other high-carbohydrate foods (bread or potato). In studies at the University of Kentucky, a whole-grain, bean, vegetable, and fruit-rich diet developed at the University of Toronto and recommended by the American Diabetes Association enabled patients with Type I diabetes (who do not produce any insulin themselves), to cut their daily insulin intake by 38 percent. For patients with Type II diabetes (who can produce some insulin), the bean diet reduced the need for injected insulin by 98 percent. This diet is in line with the nutritional guidelines of the American Diabetes Association, but people with diabetes should always check with their doctor and/or dietitian before altering their diet.

Protection against some forms of cancer.   In 1986 researchers at the University of Lund in Sweden suggested that the pectins and gels in oat bran may bind with quinolines, the potentially carcinogenic nitrogen compounds formed when meat is cooked at high heat and its amino acids are split apart, preventing the quinolines from inducing the gastrointestinal cancers associated with burnt meat products.

ADVERSE EFFECTS ASSOCIATED WITH THIS FOOD

Gluten intolerance.   Celiac disease is an intestinal allergic disorder whose victims are sensitive to gluten and gliadin, proteins in wheat and rye. People with celiac disease cannot digest the nutrients in these grains; if they eat foods containing gluten, they may suffer anemia, weight loss, bone pain, swelling, and skin disorders. Oats contain small amounts of gliadin. Corn flour, potato flour, rice flour, and soy flour are all gluten- and gliadin-free.

FOOD/DRUG INTERACTIONS

*   *   *

OKRA

NUTRITIONAL PROFILE

Energy value (calories per serving):	Low
Protein:	High
Fat:	Low
Cholesterol:	None
Carbohydrates:	High
Fiber:	High
Sodium:	Low
Major vitamin contribution:	Vitamins A and C
Major mineral contribution:	Potassium

ABOUT THE NUTRIENTS IN THIS FOOD

The okra we use as a vegetable consists of the unripe seed capsules of the okra plant. Okra is a high-carbohydrate food that contains starch plus considerable amounts of fiber, including gums and pectins. Together, the starch and pectins make okra an excellent thickener for soups and stews. Okra also provides some calcium, B vitamins, and vitamin C.

THE MOST NUTRITIOUS WAY TO SERVE THIS FOOD

In a soup or stew.

DIETS THAT MAY RESTRICT OR EXCLUDE THIS FOOD

Sucrose-free diet

BUYING THIS FOOD

Look for: Young, green tender pods of okra no more than 4 inches long.

STORING THIS FOOD

Keep okra in the refrigerator.

PREPARING THIS FOOD

Wash the okra under cold running water, then use it whole or sliced thickly.

WHAT HAPPENS WHEN YOU COOK THIS FOOD

When okra is heated in water, its starch granules absorb water molecules and swell. Eventually, they rupture, releasing amylose and amylopectin molecules as well as gums and pectic substances, all of which attract and immobilize water molecules, thickening the soup or stew.

HOW OTHER KINDS OF PROCESSING AFFECT THIS FOOD

Canning and freezing.   Canned and frozen okra have less vitamin C per serving than fresh okra.

MEDICAL USES AND/OR BENEFITS

To reduce the levels of serum cholesterol.   Eating foods rich in gums and pectins appears to lower the levels of serum cholesterol. There are currently two theories to explain how this may happen. The first theory is that the pectins form a gel in your stomach that sops up fats and keeps them from being absorbed by your body. The second is that bacteria in the gut feed on the gums and pectins, producing short-chain fatty acids that inhibit the production of cholesterol in your liver.

ADVERSE EFFECTS ASSOCIATED WITH THIS FOOD

*   *   *

FOOD/DRUG INTERACTIONS

*   *   *

OLIVES

See also VEGETABLE OILS

NUTRITIONAL PROFILE

Energy value (calories per serving):	Moderate
Protein:	Low
Fat:	High
Cholesterol:	None
Carbohydrates:	Low
Fiber:	High
Sodium:	High
Major vitamin contribution:	Vitamin A
Major mineral contribution:	Iron

ABOUT THE NUTRIENTS IN THIS FOOD

Green olives are olives that were picked before they ripened. Black olives were picked ripe and dipped in an iron solution to stabilize their color. After they are picked, green olives and black olives are soaked in a mild solution of sodium hydroxide and then washed thoroughly in water to remove oleuropein, a naturally bitter carbohydrate. Then green olives may be allowed to ferment before they are packed in a brine solution. Black olives are not allowed to ferment before packaging, which is why they taste milder than most green olives. (Green olives that do not ferment before packing taste as mild as black olives.)

Greek and Italian olives are black olives that taste sharp because they have not been soaked to remove their oleuropein. They are salt-cured and

(100 GRAMS) OLIVES

	Green olives	Ripe (black) olives	Greek olives
Calories	116	166	338
Protein (gm)	1.4	1.1	2.2
Fat (gm)	15.4	22.2	35.8
Carbohydrates (gm)	1.3	2.9	8.7
Sodium (mg)	2,400	755	3,288
Iron (mg)	1.6	1.6	(-)*

*Not available

Source: *Nutritive Value of Foods,* Home and Garden Bulletin No 72 (USDA, 1985) and Watt, Bernice K., and Merrill, Annabel L., *Composition of Foods,* Agriculture Handbook No. 8 (USDA, 1975).

sold in bulk, covered with olive oil that protects them from oxygen and helps preserve them.

All olives are high in fat and sodium and moderately high in iron.

THE MOST NUTRITIOUS WAY TO SERVE THIS FOOD

Black olives have less sodium than either green olives or salt-cured Greek or Italian olives.

DIETS THAT MAY RESTRICT OR EXCLUDE THIS FOOD

Low-fat diet
Low-sodium diet

BUYING THIS FOOD

Look for: Tightly sealed bottles or cans. Small olives are less woody than large ones. Green olives have a more astringent taste than black olives. Greek olives, available only in bulk, have a sharp, spicy taste. Pitted olives are the best buy if you want to slice the olives into a salad, otherwise olives with pits are less-expensive, better buy.

STORING THIS FOOD

Store unopened cans or jars of olives on a cool, dry shelf. Once you open a can of olives, take the olives out of the can and refrigerate them in a clean glass container.

PREPARING THIS FOOD

Olives will taste less salty if you bathe them in olive oil before you use them.

WHAT HAPPENS WHEN YOU COOK THIS FOOD

*   *   *

HOW OTHER KINDS OF PROCESSING AFFECT THIS FOOD

Pressing.   Olives are pressed to produce olive oil, one of the few vegetable oils with a distinctive taste and aroma. Olive oils are graded according to the pressing from which they come and the amount of free oleic acid they contain. (The presence of free oleic acid means that the oil's molecules have begun to break down.) Virgin olive oil is oil from the first pressing of the olives. Pure olive oil is a mixture of oils from the first and second pressings. Virgin olive oil may contain as much as 4 percent free oleic acid. Fine virgin olive oil may contain 3 percent free oleic acid, superfine virgin olive oil 1.5 percent, and extra virgin olive oil 1 percent.

Olive oil is a more concentrated source of alpha-tocopherol (vitamin E) than olives. Because it is high in unsaturated fatty acids, whose carbon atoms have double bonds that can make room for more oxygen atoms, olive oil oxidizes and turns rancid fairly quickly if exposed to heat or light. To protect the oil, store it in a cool, dark cabinet.

MEDICAL USES AND/OR BENEFITS

Protection against heart disease.   The oils in olives are composed primarily of monounsaturated fatty acids. Polyunsaturated fatty acids appear to lower the levels of high-density lipoproteins (HDLs) that carry cholesterol out of the blood and low-density lipoproteins (LDLs) that are believed to deposit cholesterol in the arteries. Monounsaturated fatty acids, on the other hand, lower the level of LDLs while maintaining high levels of HDLs.

ADVERSE EFFECTS ASSOCIATED WITH THIS FOOD

*   *   *

FOOD/DRUG INTERACTIONS

*   *   *

ONIONS

(Chives, leeks, scallions [green onions], shallots)

See also GARLIC

NUTRITIONAL PROFILE

Energy value (calories per serving):	Low
Protein:	Moderate
Fat:	Low
Cholesterol:	None
Carbohydrates:	High
Fiber:	High
Sodium:	Low
Major vitamin contribution:	Vitamin C
Major mineral contribution:	Calcium, iron

ABOUT THE NUTRIENTS IN THIS FOOD

All members of the onion family have moderate amounts of sucrose and other sugars, some protein, very little fat, and no starch or cholesterol. The most nutritious are the immature ones called *scallions* if they are picked before the bulbs have developed and *green onions* or *spring onions* if they are picked with small bulbs in place. Green onions have three to four times the vitamin C and up to 5,000 times the vitamin A in shallots or red, white, or yellow onions. The vitamin A comes from their green tops, whose yellow carotenes are masked by their green chlorophyll pigments. Red onions are colored with red anthocyanins; shallots, yellow onions, white onions, and the white bulbs of the leeks, green onions, and scallions are colored with creamy pale-yellow anthoxanthins. Neither of these natural pigments provides any vitamin A. (Chives and leeks are not onions but are members of the same plant family.)

COMPARING THE NUTRIENTS IN RAW ONIONS, LEEKS, AND SHALLOTS (per ounce)

	Yellow, red, & white onions	Green onions (tops & bulbs)	Leeks*	Shallots
Vitamin C (mg) RDA: 60 mg+	2.4	12.8	3.4	2.2
Vitamin A (IU) RDA: 5000 IU	0	1,428	27	(NA)
Iron (mg) RDA: 18 mg#	0.1	0.5	0.6	0.3

+ For a normal, healthy adult.
* Bulbs and white parts of the leaf
# For an adult woman in the childbearing years; the RDA for a healthy adult male is 10 mg.

Source: *Composition of Foods: Vegetables and Vegetable Products,* Agriculture Handbook No. 8-11 (USDA, 1984).

THE MOST NUTRITIOUS WAY TO SERVE THIS FOOD

Whole fresh green onions or green onions chopped (green portions and all) and added to a salad or other dish.

DIETS THAT MAY RESTRICT OR EXCLUDE THIS FOOD

Antiflatulence diet
Low-fiber diet
Low-sucrose or sucrose-free diet

BUYING THIS FOOD

Look for: Firm, clean shallots; yellow, white, or red onions with smooth, dry, crisp skin free of any black mold spots. Leeks and green onions should have crisp green tops and clean white bulbs.

Avoid: Onions that are sprouting or soft or whose skin is wet—all signs of internal decay.

STORING THIS FOOD

Store shallots and red, yellow, and white onions in a cool cabinet room or root cellar where the temperature is 60° F or lower and there is plenty of circulating air to keep the onions dry and prevent them from sprouting. Properly stored, onions should stay fresh for three to four weeks; at 55° F they may retain all their vitamin C for as long as six months.

Cut the roots from green onions, scallions, and leeks; trim off any damaged tops; and refrigerate the vegetables in a tightly closed plastic bag. Check daily and remove tops that have wilted.

PREPARING THIS FOOD

When you cut into an onion, you tear its cell walls and release a sulfur compound called propanethial-S-oxide that floats up into the air. The chemical, identified in 1985 by researchers at the University of St. Louis (Missouri), turns into sulfuric acid when it comes into contact with water, which it why it stings if it gets into your eyes. You can prevent this by slicing fresh onions under running water, diluting the propanethial-S-oxide before it can float up into the air.

Another way to inactivate propanethial-S-oxide is to chill the onion in the refrigerator for an hour or so before you slice it. The cold temperature slows the movement of the atoms in the sulfur compound so that they do not float up into the air around your eyes.

To peel the brown papery outer skin from an onion or a shallot, heat the vegetable in boiling water, then lift it out with a slotted spoon and put it in cold water. The skin should come off easily.

WHAT HAPPENS WHEN YOU COOK THIS FOOD

Heat converts an onion's sulfurous flavor and aroma compounds into sugars, which is why cooked onions taste sweet. When you "brown" onions, the sugars and amino acids on their surface caramelize to a deep rich brown and the flavor intensifies. This browning of sugars and amino acids is called the Maillard reaction, after the French chemist who first identified it.

Onions may also change color when cooked. Onions get their creamy color from anthoxanthins, pale-yellow pigments that turn brown if they combine with metal ions. (That's why onions discolor if you cook them in an aluminum or iron pot or slice them with a carbon-steel knife.) Red onions contain anthocyanin pigments that turn redder in acid (lemon juice, vinegar) and bluish in a basic (alkaline) solution. And the chlorophyll molecules that make the tops of green onions green are sensitive to acids. When heated, chlorophyll reacts with acids in the vegetable or in the cooking water to produce pheophytin, which is brown. The pheophytin makes green onion tops olive-drab. To keep green onions green, you have to reduce the interaction between the the chlorophyll and the acids. You can do this by leaving the top off the pot so that the acids float off into the air or by steaming the onions in little or no water or by cooking them so quickly that there is no time for the reaction to occur.

HOW OTHER KINDS OF PROCESSING AFFECT THIS FOOD

Drying.   Drying onions into flakes removes the moisture and concentrates the nutrients. Ounce for ounce, dried onions have approximately nine times the vitamin C, eight times the thiamin, ten times the riboflavin, nine times the niacin, five times the iron, and eleven times as much potassium as fresh onions.

MEDICAL USES AND/OR BENEFITS

Protection against heart disease.   In a number of laboratory studies, first in India and then in the United States, the oils in onions appear to lower blood levels of low-density lipoproteins (LDLs), the molecules that carry cholesterol into the bloodstream and raise the levels of high-density lipoproteins (HDLs), the molecules that carry cholesterol out of the body.

As a herbicide.   The strong aroma of the essential oils in onions (and garlic bulbs) planted among garden plants will repel some pests.

ADVERSE EFFECTS ASSOCIATED WITH THIS FOOD

Halitosis.   The onion's sulfur compounds can leave a penetrating odor on your breath unless you brush after eating. Fresh onions are smellier than cooked ones, since cooking breaks down the sulfur compounds.

FOOD/DRUG INTERACTIONS
*   *   *

ORANGES

NUTRITIONAL PROFILE

Energy value (calories per serving):	Low
Protein:	Low
Fat:	Low
Cholesterol:	None
Carbohydrates:	High
Fiber:	Low
Sodium:	Low
Major vitamin contribution:	Vitamin C
Major mineral contribution:	Potassium

ABOUT THE NUTRIENTS IN THIS FOOD

Oranges have sugars but no starch. They are a good source of pectins, and they have small amounts of the other indigestible food fibers. Their most important contribution to our diet is vitamin C, which is concentrated in the white layer just under the peel. A single orange, 2.5 inches in diameter, provides an average 53 mg vitamin C, 88 percent of the RDA for a healthy adult. (Half a cup of fresh juice provides 62 mg, 103 percent of the RDA.) Oranges and orange juice are good sources of potassium, moderate sources of vitamin A.

THE MOST NUTRITIOUS WAY TO SERVE THIS FOOD

Freshly sliced, quartered or squeezed.

DIETS THAT MAY RESTRICT OR EXCLUDE THIS FOOD
Sucrose-free diet

BUYING THIS FOOD
Look for: Firm fruit that is heavy for its size; the heavier the orange, the juicier it is likely to be. The skin on juice oranges (Valencias from Florida) should be thin, smooth, and fine-grained. The skin on navel oranges, the large seedless "eating orange," is thicker; it comes off easily when you peel the orange.*

STORING THIS FOOD
Refrigerate oranges if you plan to keep them for longer than a week or two, which is how long they will stay fresh at room temperature.

Refrigerate fresh orange juice in a tightly closed glass bottle. The key to preserving vitamin C is to protect the juice from heat and air (which might seep in through plastic bottles). The juice should fill the bottle as high as possible, so that there is very little space at the top for oxygen to gather. Stored this way, the juice may hold its vitamin C for two weeks. Frozen juice should be kept frozen until you are ready to use it; once reconstituted, it should be handled like fresh juice.

PREPARING THIS FOOD
Oranges may be waxed to prevent moisture loss and protect them in shipping. If you plan to grate orange rind and use it for flavoring, scrub the orange first to remove the wax. Do not grate deeper than the colored part of the skin; if you hit the white underneath, you will be getting bitter-tasting components in with the rind.

To collect natural flavoring oils from the oranges, grate the orange, wrap the grated peel in cheesecloth, let it sit for a while at room temperature, then squeeze the oil out through the cheesecloth onto some sugar that can then be added to a cake batter or sprinkled over fruit.

Orange peel contains volatile fragrant oils whose molecules are liberated when the skin is torn and its cell walls ruptured. These molecules are also more fragrant at room temperature than when cold. "Eating oranges" have a

*Oranges look most appetizing when they are a deep, vibrant orange, but on the tree a mature orange is usually green-skinned. It will turn orange only if it is chilled and the cold temperature destroys green chlorophyll pigments, allowing the yellow carotenoids underneath to show through. In a warm climate, like the Mideast, oranges are always green, but in the United States oranges are green only if they are picked in the fall before the first cold snap or if they are picked early in the spring when the tree is flooded with chlorophyll to nourish the coming new growth. Green oranges will also change color if they are exposed to ethylene gas which, like cold, breaks down the chlorophyll in the orange's skin. (Ethylene is a natural chemical found in all fruits that encourages them to ripen.) Oranges may also be dyed with food coloring.

much truer aroma and flavor if you let them come to room temperature before peeling and serving.

WHAT HAPPENS WHEN YOU COOK THIS FOOD

Heat destroys the vitamin C but not the flavoring oils in an orange. When oranges or orange peel are cooked, they add flavor but no noticeable amounts of vitamin C.

HOW OTHER FORMS OF PROCESSING AFFECT THIS FOOD

Commercially prepared juices.   How well a commercially prepared juice holds its vitamin C depends on how it is prepared, stored, and packaged. Sealed cans of orange juice stored in the refrigerator may lose only 2 percent of their vitamin C in three months. Prepared, pasteurized "fresh" juices in glass bottles hold their vitamin C better than the same juice sold in plastic bottles or waxed paper cartons that let oxygen pass through.

All commercially prepared juices taste different from fresh juice. There are two reasons for this. The first is that frozen, canned, or pasteurized juices are almost always a blend of fruits from various crops. The second is that they have all been heated to inactivate the enzymes that would otherwise rot the juice; heating alters flavor.

Canned oranges and orange juice retain most of their vitamin C. As soon as the can is opened, the oranges or juice should be removed and transferred to a glass container to prevent the fruit or juice from absorbing lead used to seal the can. The absorption of lead is triggered by oxygen, which enters the can when the seal is broken. No lead is absorbed while the can is intact.

Drying.   Orange peel may be dried for use as a candy or flavoring. Dried orange peel may be treated with sulfites (sodium sulfite, sodium bisulfite, and the like) to keep it from darkening. In sensitive people, sulfites can trigger serious allergic reactions, including potentially fatal anaphylactic shock.

MEDICAL USES AND/OR BENEFITS

Antiscorbutics.   All citrus fruits are excellent sources of vitamin C, used to cure or prevent the vitamin C-deficiency disease scurvy. Your body also needs vitamin C in order to convert the amino acid proline into hydroxyproline, an essential ingredient in collagen, the protein needed to form skin, tendons, and bones. People with scurvy do not heal quickly, a condition that can be cured by feeding them foods rich in vitamin C. Whether taking extra vitamin C speeds healing in healthy people remains to be proved. Oranges and other citrus fruits also contain rutin, hesperidin, and other natural chemicals known collectively as flavenoids ("bioflavenoids"). In experiments with laboratory animals, flavenoids appear to strengthen capillaries, the tiny blood vessels just under the skin. To date this effect has not been demonstrated in human beings.

Enhanced absorption of iron from plant foods.   Non-heme iron, the inorganic form of iron found in plant foods, is poorly absorbed by the body because it is bound into insoluble compounds by natural chemicals in the plants. Vitamin C appears to make non-heme iron more available to your body, perhaps by converting it from ferric iron to ferrous iron, which is more easily absorbed. Eating vitamin C-rich foods along with plant foods rich in iron can increase the amount of iron you get from the plant—the nutritional justification for a breakfast of orange juice and cereal or bread. (See also BEANS, BREAD, CEREAL, FLOUR, OATS.)

Potassium replacement.   Potassium-rich foods such as oranges and orange juice are often prescribed for people who are taking diuretic drugs and losing potassium. However, there is some question as to whether potassium gluconate, the form of potassium in oranges, is as easily absorbed by the body as potassium citrate or potassium chloride, the form of potassium used in the laboratory experiments with rats that established the value of potassium supplementation for people using diuretics.

Protection against some forms of cancer.   According to the American Cancer Society, foods rich in vitamins A and C may offer some protection against cancers of the respiratory and digestive tracts and cancers induced by chemicals.

To reduce the levels of serum cholesterol.   A suspected but unproved function of vitamin C. In addition, citrus fruits, including oranges, are rich in pectin, the indigestible food fiber that appears to slow the body's absorption of fats and thus to lower the blood level of cholesterol. There are presently two theories to explain how this may happen. The first is that the pectins dissolve into a gel that sops up fats in your stomach so that your body cannot absorb them. The second is that bacteria in the gut digest the fiber and then produce short-chain fatty acids that slow the liver's natural production of cholesterol.

ADVERSE EFFECTS ASSOCIATED WITH THIS FOOD

Flare-up of apthous ulcers.   In sensitive people, eating citrus fruits may trigger an attack of apthous ulcers (canker sores), but eliminating citrus fruit from the diet neither cures nor prevents canker sores.

Contact dermatitis.   Although there is ample anecdotal evidence to suggest that many people are sensitive to natural chemicals in an orange's flesh or peel, the offending substances have never been conclusively identified.

FOOD/DRUG INTERACTIONS

False-negative test for hidden blood in the stool.   The active ingredient in the guaiac slide test for hidden blood in feces is alphaguaiaconic acid, a chemical that turns blue in the presence of blood. Citrus fruits or vitamin supplements containing more than 250 mg ascorbic acid may produce excess ascorbic acid in the feces, which inhibits the ability of alphaguaiaconic acid to react with blood may produce a false-negative test result that fails to disclose the presence of a tumor in the colon.

PAPAYA

NUTRITIONAL PROFILE

Energy value (calories per serving):	Low
Protein:	Low
Fat:	Low
Cholesterol:	None
Carbohydrates:	High
Fiber:	Low
Sodium:	Low
Major vitamin contribution:	Vitamins A and C
Major mineral contribution:	Potassium

ABOUT THE NUTRIENTS IN THIS FOOD

Papayas (which are also known as paw-paws) are high in sugar, but they have no starch and very little insoluble fiber. They are an excellent source of vitamins C and A. A single 3.5-ounce serving provides 61.8 mg vitamin C (103 percent of the RDA for a healthy adult) and 2014 IU vitamin A (40 percent of the RDA). Papayas are rich in potassium.

Unripe papayas and the leaves of the papaya plant contain papain, a proteolytic (protein-dissolving) enzyme that breaks long protein molecules into smaller fragments. You can tenderize meat by cooking it wrapped in papaya leaves or by dusting it with a meat tenderizer of commercially extracted papain dried to a powder. (Soybeans, *haricots,* garden peas, broad beans, wheat flours, and egg white all contain proteins that inactivate papain.)

THE MOST NUTRITIOUS WAY TO SERVE THIS FOOD
Fresh, sliced.

DIETS THAT MAY RESTRICT OR EXCLUDE THIS FOOD
Sucrose-free diet

BUYING THIS FOOD
Look for: Medium-size, pear-shaped fruit whose skin is turning yellow. (The yellower the skin, the riper the fruit.) Papayas ripen from the bottom up, toward the stem. Always look for fruit that is yellow at least halfway up.

STORING THIS FOOD
Store papayas at room temperature until they are fully ripe, which means that they have turned golden all over and are soft enough to give when you press the stem end.

Store ripe papayas in the refrigerator.

PREPARING THIS FOOD
Wash the papaya under cool running water, then cut it in half, spoon out the seeds, and sprinkle it with lemon or lime juice.

The seeds of the papaya taste like peppercorns. They can be dried and ground as a seasoning or simply sprinkled, whole, on a salad.

WHAT HAPPENS WHEN YOU COOK THIS FOOD
*   *   *

HOW OTHER KINDS OF PROCESSING AFFECT THIS FOOD
Extraction of papain. Commercial meat tenderizers contain papain extracted from fresh papaya and dried to a powder. The powder is a much more efficient tenderizer than either fresh papaya or papaya leaves. At the strength usually found in these powders, papain can "digest" (tenderize) up to 35 times its weight in meat. Like bromelain (the proteolytic enzyme in fresh pineapple) and ficin (the proteolytic enzyme in fresh figs), papain breaks down proteins only at a temperature between 140° F and 170° F. It won't work when the temperature is higher or lower.

Meat treated with a papain tenderizer may interact with monoamine oxidase (MAO) inhibitors, drugs used as antidepressants or antihypertensives. Papain meat tenderizers work by breaking up the long chains of protein molecules. When these chains are broken, one by-product may be tyramine. Tyramine is a pressor amine, a chemical that constricts blood vessels and raises blood pressure. Ordinarily, tyramine is itself broken down and eliminated from the body by enzyme action, but MAO inhibitors interfere with the enzymes (monoamine oxidases) that degrade tyramine. If you eat a food rich in tyramine while you are taking an MAO inhibitor, the pressor amine cannot be eliminated from your body and the result may be a hypertensive crisis (sustained elevated blood pressure).

MEDICAL USES AND/OR BENEFITS

First aid for insect stings. Some experts recommend applying a paste of meat tenderizer and water to reduce the pain and itch of a mosquito bite by destroying the proteins injected with the insect venom. *Note:* This "home remedy" is *never* recommended for people who are sensitive to *any* insect venom.

ADVERSE EFFECTS ASSOCIATED WITH THIS FOOD

Irritated skin. Because it can break down proteins, papain (and/or fresh papayas) may cause dermatitis, including a hivelike reaction. This is not an allergic response: it can happen to anyone.

FOOD/DRUG INTERACTIONS

*   *   *

PARSNIPS

NUTRITIONAL PROFILE

Energy value (calories per serving):	Moderate
Protein:	Moderate
Fat:	Low
Cholesterol:	None
Carbohydrates:	High
Fiber:	High
Sodium:	Low
Major vitamin contribution:	Vitamin C
Major mineral contribution:	Potassium, calcium

ABOUT THE NUTRIENTS IN THIS FOOD

Parsnips are roots, a good source of starch, plus the carbohydrate food fibers gums, pectins, cellulose, and hemicelluose. They are moderately high in vitamin C; a 3.5-ounce serving of drained boiled parsnips has 13 mg. vitamin C, about 22 percent of the RDA for a healthy adult. They are also a moderately good source of calcium. Ounce for ounce, boiled parsnips have about 31 percent as much calcium as whole milk.

THE MOST NUTRITIOUS WAY TO SERVE THIS FOOD

Boiled and drained.

DIETS THAT MAY RESTRICT OR EXCLUDE THIS FOOD

Low-fiber diet
Sucrose-free diet

BUYING THIS FOOD

Look for: Smooth, well-shaped, cream or tan small-to-medium roots. The larger the root, the woodier and coarser it will be.

Avoid: Discolored parsnips. Parsnips that are darker in spots may have been frozen on the way to market. Gray spots or soft spots warn of rot inside the root.

STORING THIS FOOD

Keep parsnips cold and humid so they won't dry out. Store them in a root cellar or in the refrigerator. In storage, parsnips will convert some of their starch to sugar. As a rule of thumb, the sweeter the parsnip, the longer it has been stored.

PREPARING THIS FOOD

Scrub the parsnips with a vegetable brush under cool running water or simply peel them—but not until you are ready to use them. When you peel or slice a parsnip, you tear its cell walls, releasing polyphenoloxidase, an enzyme that hastens the combination of oxygen with phenols in the parsnips, turning the vegetable brown. You can slow this reaction (but not stop it completely) by dipping raw peeled or sliced parsnips into an acid solution (lemon juice and water, vinegar and water). Polyphenoloxidase also works more slowly in the cold, but storing peeled parsnips in the refrigerator is much less effective than an acid bath.

You can keep parsnips from darkening in a stew by blanching them before you add them to the dish. Boil the unpeeled parsnips for about 15 minutes to inactivate the polyphenoloxidase, then add them to the stew. If you prefer, you can freeze blanched parsnips for future use.

WHAT HAPPENS WHEN YOU COOK THIS FOOD

Heat dissolves the pectic substances in the parsnip's cell walls, making the vegetable softer. At the same time, the parsnip's starch granules absorb water, swell, and eventually rupture, releasing nutrients inside and making the vegetables easier to digest.

HOW OTHER KINDS OF PROCESSING AFFECT THIS FOOD

Freezing.   When parsnips are frozen, liquids inside the vegetable's cell form ice crystals that may tear the cells, allowing moisture to escape when you thaw the parsnips. As a result, when roots like carrots, potatoes, and parsnips are frozen and thawed, their texture is mushy rather than crisp.

MEDICAL USES AND/OR BENEFITS
*   *   *

ADVERSE EFFECTS ASSOCIATED WITH THIS FOOD

Photosensitivity. Like celery and parsley, parsnips contain psoralens, natural chemicals that make the skin sensitive to light. Psoralens are not inactivated by cooking; they are present in both raw and cooked parsnips.

In laboratory animals, psoralens applied to the skin are known to trigger cancers when the animals are exposed to light. Among human beings, their only documented side effect is the skin inflammation common among food workers who handle and process vegetables without wearing protective gloves. In 1981, however, scientists at the U.S. Department of Agriculture's Veterinary Toxicology and Entomology Research Laboratory in College Station, Texas, suggested that detailed epidemiological studies might link physiological effects to eating parsnips as well as handling them. The connection remains to be proved.

FOOD/DRUG INTERACTIONS
*   *   *

PASTA

See also FLOUR

NUTRITIONAL PROFILE

Energy value (calories per serving):	Moderate
Protein:	Moderate
Fat:	Low
Cholesterol:	None
Carbohydrates:	High
Fiber:	Low
Sodium:	Low*
Major vitamin contribution:	B vitamins
Major mineral contribution:	Iron

ABOUT THE NUTRIENTS IN THIS FOOD

The basic ingredients in pasta are water plus flour or semolina (the coarsely milled inner part of the wheat kernel called the endosperm). *Whole wheat pasta,* which is darker than ordinary pasta, is made with whole wheat flour. *Egg noodles* are made with flour and water plus eggs. *Spinach pasta* adds dried spinach for taste and color. *High-protein pasta* is fortified with soy flour. *Light pasta* is treated to absorb more water than regular pasta. *Imitation pasta* is made with flour ground from Jerusalem artichokes rather than wheat. *Rice noodles* are made with rice flour, *cellophane noodles* with flour ground from sprouted mung beans.

All pasta is high-carbohydrate (starch) food. Since semolina is virtually all protein, the more semolina the pasta contains, the more protein it pro-

*Dry pasta.

vides. The proteins in pasta are considered "incomplete" because they are deficient in the essential amino acids in lysine and isoleucine. Pasta made without eggs has no fat and no cholesterol.

All pasta is a good source of the B vitamins thiamin (viamin B_1) and riboflavin (vitamin B_2). Pasta made with flour also contains non-heme iron, the inorganic form of iron found in plants, which is three to six times less available than the iron in foods of animal origin.

THE MOST NUTRITIOUS WAY TO SERVE THIS FOOD

With meat, eggs, or milk products (cheese), which supply lysine and isoleucine to "complement" the proteins in the pasta.

With beans or peas. Grains are deficient in the essential amino acids lysine and isoleucine but contain sufficient amounts of tryptophan, methionine, and cystine. Beans and peas are just the opposite. Together, their proteins are complementary.

With a food rich in iron (meat) or a food rich in vitamin C (tomatoes). Both enhance your body's ability to absorb the iron in pasta. The meat makes your stomach more acid (which favors the absorption of iron); the vitamin C converts the iron from ferric iron (which is hard to absorb) to ferrous iron (which is more available to your body).

DIETS THAT MAY RESTRICT OR EXCLUDE THIS FOOD

Gluten-restricted, gliadin-free diet (all pastas made with wheat flour)

BUYING THIS FOOD

Look for: Tightly sealed packages. If you can see into the box, pick the pasta that looks smooth and shiny. Dry or dusty pasta is stale; so is pasta that is crumbling. The yellower the pasta, the more durum wheat it contains. (Egg noodles get their yellow from eggs.) Whole wheat pasta is brown.

STORING THIS FOOD

Store pasta in air- and moistureproof glass or plastic containers. Pasta will stay fresh for about a year, egg noodles for six months.

PREPARING THIS FOOD

To cook pasta most efficiently, start with salted water. At sea level, water boils at 212° F (100° C), the temperature at which its molecules have enough energy to escape from the surface as steam. If you add salt, the water molecules will need to pick up more energy to push the salt molecules aside and escape from the surface. In effect, adding salt forces the water to boil at a higher temperature, which means the pasta will cook more quickly.

The water should be boiling furiously before you add the pasta so that it can penetrate the pasta's starch granules as fast as possible. Add the pasta slowly so that the water continues to boil and the pasta cooks evenly.

WHAT HAPPENS WHEN YOU COOK THIS FOOD

Starch consists of molecules of the complex carbohydrates amylose and amylopectin packed into a starch granule. When you boil pasta, water molecules force their way into the starch granules. When the water reaches a temperature of approximately 140° F, the amylose and amylopectin molecules inside the starch granules relax and unfold, forming new bonds between atoms on different molecules and creating a network inside the starch granule that traps water molecules. The granules bulk up and the pasta gets thicker. In fact, the starch granules can hold so much water that plain flour-and-water pastas like spaghetti, macaroni, and lasagna will actually double in size.

The longer you cook the pasta, the more likely it is that the starch granules will absorb too much water and rupture, releasing some of their starch and making the pasta sticky. One way to keep the pieces of pasta from sticking together is to cook them in a large pot, which gives them room to boil without hitting their neighbors. Or you might add a tablespoon of olive oil to make the pasta slick enough to slide apart. If you plan to refrigerate the cooked pasta, drain it, rinse it in warm water (to wash off the starch on the outside), and toss it with olive oil.

HOW OTHER KINDS OF PROCESSING AFFECT THIS FOOD

Canning and freezing.   When pasta is canned or frozen in sauce, its starch granules continue to absorb the liquid and the pasta becomes progressively more limp.

MEDICAL USES AND/OR BENEFITS

As a source of increased energy for athletes.   When we eat carbohydrates, our bodies break them down into glycogen, which is stored in our muscles. When we need energy we convert the stored glycogen to glucose, the fuel on which our bodies run. Athletes who engage in the kind of strenuous exercise that can lead to exhaustion in 45 minutes need more glycogen than people who lead sedentary lives. Without the extra glycogen, they will run out of energy in midgame or midmarathon. One way to increase the amount of glycogen in the muscles is to increase the amount of high-carbohydrate foods, such as pasta, in the diet, a regimen known as carbohydrate loading. The classic carbohydrate-loading diet developed in Scandanavia in the 1960s calls for two days on a very low-carbohydrate diet plus very heavy exercise to deplete the muscles' normal store of glycogen, followed by three days of very little exercise and a diet which is 70 to 90 percent carbohydrates. Because so many athletes are reluctant to stop exercising for three days before an event, a modified version of this regime, developed at Ball State University in Indiana, suggests two days on a normal diet with normal to heavy exercise, then three days on a diet very high in carbohydrates while exercise tapers down to nothing on the day before the event. According to a number of studies by sports-medicine researchers, both versions of the carbohydrate-loading diet appear to increase the amount of glycogen in the athlete's muscles and thus to increase long-term stamina.

As a source of carbohydrates for people with diabetes.   Pasta is digested very slowly, producing only a gradual rise in blood-sugar levels. As a result, the body needs less insulin to control blood sugar after eating pasta than after eating some other high-carbohydrate foods (rice, bread, or corn). In studies at the University of Kentucky, a bean, whole-grain, vegetable, and fruit-rich diet developed at the University of Toronto and recommended by the American Diabetes Association enabled patients with Type I diabetes (who do not produce any insulin themselves) to cut their daily insulin intake by 38 percent. For patients with Type II diabetes (who can produce some insulin), the bean diet reduced the need for injected insulin by 98 percent. This diet is in line with the nutritional guidelines of the American Diabetes Association, but people with diabetes should always consult their doctor and/or dietitian before altering their diet.

ADVERSE EFFECTS ASSOCIATED WITH THIS FOOD

Food allergy.   Wheat is among the foods most often implicated as a cause of the classic food allergy symptoms—upset stomach, hives, skin rashes, angioedema (swelling of the face, eyes, and lips).

Gluten intolerance (celiac disease).   Celiac disease is an intestinal allergic disorder that results in an inability to absorb the nutrients in gluten and gliadin. People with celiac disease cannot absorb the nutrients in wheat or wheat products, such as pasta. Corn flour, potato flour, rice flour, and soy flour are gluten- and gliadin-free. So are pasta products made of flour ground from Jerusalem artichokes.

FOOD/DRUG INTERACTIONS
*   *   *

PEACHES
(Nectarines)

NUTRITIONAL PROFILE

Energy value (calories per serving):	Low
Protein:	Moderate
Fat:	Low
Cholesterol:	None
Carbohydrates:	High
Fiber:	Low
Sodium:	Low (fresh or dried fruit)
	High (dried fruit treated with sodium sulfur compounds)
Major vitamin contribution:	Vitamin A
Major mineral contribution:	Potassium

ABOUT THE NUTRIENTS IN THIS FOOD

Peaches have moderate amounts of dietary fiber, pectins and gums. As peaches ripen, the pectins in their cell walls dissolve and the fruit get softer. Since the pectin in the walls of the cells of freestone peaches is more soluble than the pectins in cling peaches, ripe freestones are softer and more easily damaged than cling peaches, while cling peaches stay firmer, even after they are cooked.

Peaches have a trace of protein and virtually no fat. There is some starch in unripe peaches, but it turns to sugar as the fruit ripens. Nectarines, which have been called "peaches without fuzz," have slightly more calories per ounce.

Both peaches and nectarines are colored with yellow carotenoid pigments your body can convert to vitamin A. One 3.5-ounce peach provides 535 IU vitamin A, 10 percent of the RDA for a healthy adult; a similarly sized nectarine has 736 IU, 15 percent of the RDA. Nectarines and peaches are also a good source of potassium; they provide moderate amounts of vitamin C.

Like apple seeds and apricot pits, the leaves and bark of the peach tree as well as the "nut" inside the peach pit contain amygdalin, a naturally occurring cyanide/sugar compound that breaks down into hydrogen cyanide in your stomach. Accidentally swallowing a peach pit once in a while is not a serious hazard, but cases of human poisoning after eating peach pits have been reported (see APPLES).

THE MOST NUTRITIOUS WAY TO SERVE THIS FOOD
Fresh and ripe.

DIETS THAT MAY RESTRICT OR EXCLUDE THIS FOOD
Sucrose-free diet

BUYING THIS FOOD
Look for: Peaches and nectarines with rich cream or yellow skin. The red "blush" characteristic of some varieties of peaches is not a reliable guide to ripeness. A better guide is the way the fruit feels and smells. Ripe peaches and nectarines have a warm, intense aroma and feel firm, with a slight softness along the line running up the length of the fruit.

Avoid: Green or hard unripe peaches and nectarines. As peaches and nectarines ripen enzymes convert their insoluble pectic substances to soluble pectins and decrease their concentration of bitter phenols. The longer the peach is left on the tree, the lower the concentration of phenols will be, which is why late-season peaches and nectarines are the sweetest. Once you pick the peach or nectarine, the enzyme action stops completely. The fruit may shrivel, but it cannot continue to ripen.

STORING THIS FOOD
Store firm ripe peaches and nectarines at room temperature until they soften. Once they have softened, put them in the refrigerator. The cold will stop the enzymatic action that dissolves pectins in the fruit and softens it.

PREPARING THIS FOOD
To peel peaches, immerse them in hot water for a few seconds, then lift them out and plunge them into cold water. The hot water destroys a layer of cells under the skin, allowing the skin to slip off easily.

Don't peel or slice peaches and nectarines until you are ready to use them. When you cut into them, you tear their cell walls, releasing polyphenoloxidase, an enzyme that promotes the oxidation of phenols, forming brownish compounds that darken the fruit. You can slow the reaction (but not stop it completely) by chilling the fruit or by dipping it in an acid solution (lemon juice and water or vinegar and water) or by mixing the sliced peaches and nectarines into a fruit salad with citrus fruits.

WHAT HAPPENS WHEN YOU COOK THIS FOOD

When you cook peaches or nectarines, pectin in the cell walls dissolves and the fruit softens. As noted above, cling peaches will stay firmer than freestones. Cooking peaches and nectarines also destroys polyphenoloxidase and keeps the fruit from darkening.

HOW OTHER FORMS OF PROCESSING AFFECT THIS FOOD

Drying.   Like other dried fruits, dried peaches may be treated with sulfites (sodium sulfite) that inhibit polyphenoloxidase and keep the peaches from darkening. People who are sensitive to sulfites may suffer serious allergic reactions, including potentially lethal anaphylactic shock, if they eat dried peaches treated with these compounds.

MEDICAL USES AND/OR BENEFITS

Lowering the risk of some cancers.   According to the American Cancer Society, deep-yellow foods rich in vitamin A may help lower the risk of some cancers of the larynx, esophagus, and lungs.

Potassium replacement.   Peaches and nectarines are a good source of potassium. Ounce for ounce, they have as much potassium as oranges. Foods rich in potassium are sometimes prescribed for people who are taking diuretics and losing potassium. However, there is now some question as to whether potassium gluconate, the form of potassium in fruit, is as available to the body as the forms of potassium given laboratory animals in the experiments that established the need for potassium supplementation for patients on diuretic therapy.

ADVERSE EFFECTS ASSOCIATED WITH THIS FOOD

Sulfite allergies.   See *How other kinds of processing affect this food,* above.

FOOD/DRUG INTERACTIONS

*   *   *

PEANUTS

NUTRITIONAL PROFILE

Energy value (calories per serving):	Moderate to high
Protein:	High
Fat:	High
Cholesterol:	None
Carbohydrates:	Low
Fiber:	High
Sodium:	Low
Major vitamin contribution:	Vitamin E and B vitamins
Major mineral contribution:	Iron, potassium

ABOUT THE NUTRIENTS IN THIS FOOD

Peanuts are unusual among legumes (beans, peas) in that they store fat rather than starch. As a result, while they are high-fiber foods, they contain fewer carbohydrates than dried beans or peas.

Peanuts have about twice as much starch as sugar. They are a good source of cellulose, hemicellulose, pectins, and gums as well as the noncarbohydrate food fiber lignin, which is found in stems, leaves, seeds, and seed coverings such as the skin on fresh or roasted peanuts.

Peanuts are high in protein, but their proteins are considered "incomplete" because they are deficient in the essential amino acids tryptophan, methionine, and cystine. The fats in peanuts are primarily unsaturated fatty acids. Peanuts have no cholesterol.

*Values are for dry-roasted, unsalted peanuts.

Peanuts are an excellent source of vitamin E. Raw peanuts, with the skin on, are a good source of thiamin (vitamin B_1), but much of the thiamin, as well as vitamin B_6, is lost when peanuts are roasted. All peanuts are a good source of riboflavin (vitamin B_2) and folacin.

Peanuts are high in potassium. Ounce for ounce, they have nearly three times as much potassium as fresh oranges. They are also a good source of non-heme iron, the inorganic form of iron found in plant foods. A 3.5-ounce serving of roasted peanuts, with the skin on, provides 2.2 mg iron, 12 percent of the RDA for a healthy adult woman.

THE MOST NUTRITIOUS WAY TO USE THIS FOOD

With grains. The proteins in peanuts and other legumes are deficient in the essential amino acids tryptophan, methionine, and cystine but contain sufficient amounts of the essential amino acids lysine and isoleucine. The proteins in grains are exactly the opposite. Together they complement each other and produce "complete" proteins, which is the reason a peanut-butter sandwich is nutritionally sound.

With meat or a food rich in vitamin C. Both will increase the absorption of iron from the peanuts. Meat increases the acidity of the stomach (iron is absorbed better in an acid environment); vitamin C may change the iron in the peanuts from ferrous iron (which is hard to absorb) to ferric iron (which is easier to absorb).

DIETS THAT MAY RESTRICT OR EXCLUDE THIS FOOD

Low-residue diet
Low-purine (antigout diet)
Low-sodium diet (salted peanuts, peanut butters)
Sucrose-free diet

HOW TO BUY THIS FOOD

Look for: Tightly sealed jars or cans of processed peanuts. Peanuts are rich in polyunsaturated fatty acids that combine easily with oxygen and turn rancid if the peanuts are not protected from air and heat.

Choose unshelled loose peanuts rather than shelled ones. The shell is a natural shield against light and air.

STORING THIS FOOD

Store shelled or unshelled peanuts in a cool, dark cabinet. Keep them dry to protect them against mold. If you plan to hold them for longer than a month, refrigerate them in a tightly closed container.

PREPARING THIS FOOD

Pick over the peanuts and discard any that are moldy. Moldy peanuts may be contaminated with carcinogenic mold toxins called aflatoxins.

WHAT HAPPENS WHEN YOU COOK THIS FOOD

Heat destroys the thiamin (vitamin B_1) in peanuts. Roasted peanuts are much lower in thiamin than fresh peanuts.

HOW OTHER KINDS OF PROCESSING AFFECT THIS FOOD

Peanut butter.   Peanut butters may not be as nutritious as plain peanuts. Commercially processed peanut butters may contain salt, sugar, and extra oils and fats that are not as low in saturated fatty acids as peanut oil. Commercial processors usually remove the fatty germ of the peanut so that the butters will not become rancid as quickly as they might with the germ left in. Peanut butter can be stored, tightly closed, at room temperature. If you store the butter in the refrigerator, the oils may separate out; when you are ready to use it, simply stir with a knife to mix the oils and solids.

MEDICAL USES AND/OR BENEFITS

*   *   *

ADVERSE EFFECTS ASSOCIATED WITH THIS FOOD

Allergic reactions.   Peanuts are among the foods most often implicated as triggering the classic symptoms of food allergy: gastric upset, hives, and angioedema (swelling of the lips, eyes, face, and tongue). In addition, research at the University of California, San Francisco, in 1985 suggested that peanuts might provoke a delayed allergic reaction of joint inflammation similar to arthritis.

Production of uric acid.   Purines are the natural metabolic by-products of protein metabolism in the body. They eventually break down into uric acid, which may form sharp crystals that may cause gout if they collect in your joints or kidney stones if they collect in urine. Fresh and roasted peanuts are a source of purines; eating them raises the concentration of purines in your body. Although controlling the amount of purine-producing foods in the diet may not significantly affect the course of gout (which is treated with medication such as allopurinol, which inhibits the formation of uric acid), limiting these foods is still part of many gout regimens.

FOOD/DRUG INTERACTIONS

*   *   *

PEARS

NUTRITIONAL PROFILE

Energy value (calories per serving):	Moderate
Protein:	Low
Fat:	Low
Cholesterol:	None
Carbohydrates:	High
Fiber:	High
Sodium:	Low (fresh or dried fruit) High (dried fruit treated with sodium sulfur compounds)
Major vitamin contribution:	Vitamin C
Major mineral contribution:	Potassium

ABOUT THE NUTRIENTS IN THIS FOOD

Pears are a good source of food fiber—pectin, gums, cellulose, hemicelluose, and the noncarbohydrate food fiber lignin, which is found in the sclerenchyma cells that make up the gritty particles in the pear's flesh. The pear's starches turn to sugar as it ripens; only a trace of starch remains in ripe pears. Pears have moderate amounts of vitamin C, which is concentrated in the skin.

Like apple seeds and peach pits, the seeds of pears contain amygdalin, a cyanide/sugar compound that breaks down into hydrogen cyanide in your stomach. Accidentally swallowing a pear seed once in a while is not necessarily hazardous, but there have been reports of serious poisoning among people who have eaten several apple seeds (see APPLES).

THE MOST NUTRITIOUS WAY TO USE THIS FOOD

Fresh and ripe, with the skin (for the extra fiber and vitamin C).

DIETS THAT MAY RESTRICT OR EXCLUDE THIS FOOD

Sucrose-free diet

BUYING THIS FOOD

Look for: Large, firm, ripe pears. Most fruit and vegetables get softer after they are picked because their pectic enzymes begin to dissolve the pectin in their cell walls. With pears, this reaction occurs if the pear is left on the tree to ripen, which is why tree-ripened pears sometimes taste mushy. The best-tasting pears are ones that are picked immature and allowed to ripen in storage or on your grocer's shelf.

Choose a brightly colored pear. The color of a ripe pear varies with the variety. Bartlett pears have clear yellow skin or yellow skin with a reddish blush and smooth, juicy flesh. The skin of the Anjou pear ranges from yellow to green with some russet shades in between; the flesh is juicy and spicy. Bosc pears are dark yellow with a reddish cast. They have a long tapering neck and yellowish-white flesh. Comice pears are larger than the others, with greenish-yellow skin that may have a reddish cast. The flesh is fine, sweet, and juicy.

Bosc, Anjou, and Bartlett are good varieties for eating and cooking; comice and seckel are for eating only.

Avoid: Cut, shriveled, or bruised pears. They are probably discolored inside.

STORING THIS FOOD

Store pears at room temperature for a few days if they are not fully ripe when you buy them. Pears ripen from inside out, so you should never let a pear ripen until it is really soft on the surface. A ripe pear will yield when you press it lightly with your palm.

Do not store pears in sealed plastic bags either in or out of the refrigerator. Without oxygen circulating freely around the pear, the fruit will begin to "breathe" internally, creating compounds that turn the core brown and make brownish spots under the skin.

PREPARING THIS FOOD

Handle pears with care; never peel or slice them until you are ready to use them. When you bruise a pear or slice into it, you tear its cells, releasing polyphenoloxidase, an enzyme that hastens the oxidation of phenols in the fruit, producing clumps of brownish compounds that darken the pear's flesh. You can slow this natural reaction (but not stop it completely) by chilling the pears, brushing the cut surface with an acid solution (lemon juice and water, vinegar and water), or mixing the peeled, sliced fruit into a fresh fruit salad with citrus fruits (they are full of vitamin C, a natural antioxidant).

WHAT HAPPENS WHEN YOU COOK THIS FOOD

Like other fruits and vegetables, pears have cell walls made of cellulose, hemicellulose, and pectic substances. As the fruit cooks and its pectins dissolve, it gets softer. But no amount of cooking will dissolve the lignin particles in the pear flesh. In fact, the softer the pear, the easier it is to taste the lignin particles.

HOW OTHER FORMS OF PROCESSING AFFECT THIS FOOD

Drying.   Fresh pears are sometimes treated with sulfur compounds such as sulfur dioxide to inactivate polyphenoloxidase and keep the pears from darkening when they are exposed to air while drying. People who are sensitive to sulfites may suffer serious allergic reactions, including anaphylactic shock, if they eat these treated dried pears.

Sealed packages of dried pears may be stored at room temperature for up to six months. Once the package is opened, the pears should be refrigerated in a tightly closed container that will protect them from air and moisture.

MEDICAL USES AND/OR BENEFITS

Potassium replacement.   Pears are a moderately good source of potassium. One 3.5-ounce Bartlett has about as much the potassium as 3 ounces of fresh orange juice. Foods rich in potassium are sometimes prescribed for people taking diuretics that lower the body's level of potassium, which is excreted in urine. However, there is some question as to whether potassium gluconate, the form of potassium found in pears and other fresh fruit, is as useful to the body as potassium citrate and potassium chloride, the forms of potassium given to laboratory animals in the experiments which showed that people taking diuretic drugs would benefit from potassium supplements.

ADVERSE EFFECTS ASSOCIATED WITH THIS FOOD

Allergic reactions to sulfur.   See *How other kinds of processing affect this food,* above.

FOOD/DRUG INTERACTIONS

*   *   *

PEAS
(Snow-pea pods [sugar peas], split peas)

NUTRITIONAL PROFILE

Energy value (calories per serving):	Moderate
Protein:	High
Fat:	Low
Cholesterol:	None
Carbohydrates:	High
Fiber:	High
Sodium:	Low
Major vitamin contribution:	Vitamins A and C
Major mineral contribution:	Iron

ABOUT THE NUTRIENTS IN THIS FOOD

Peas start out high in sugar but convert it to starch as they age. Within a few hours after they are picked, peas may convert as much as 40 percent of their sugars to starch. Sugar peas (also known as snow-pea pods) are eaten immature. Fresh peas are a moderately good source of food fiber: pectins, gums, hemicellulose, and cellulose and the noncarbohydrate food fiber lignin.

Peas are a high-protein food. A 3.5-ounce serving of fresh green peas has 5.4 grams of protein, 9 percent of the RDA for a healthy adult. The proteins in peas, like the proteins in other vegetables, are considered "incomplete" because they are deficient in some of the essential amino acids, in this case tryptophan, methionine, and cystine. Peas have very little fat and no cholesterol.

Peas are an excellent source of vitamin A, which comes from yellow carotenoids hidden under their green chlorophyll pigments. As peas age, the chlorophyll fades and the yellow shows through. Peas are also a good source of non-heme iron, the inorganic form of iron found in plants.

THE MOST NUTRITIOUS WAY TO USE THIS FOOD

With grains. The proteins in peas and other legumes are deficient in the essential amino acids tryptophan, methionine, and cystine but contain sufficient amounts of the essential amino acids lysine and isoleucine. The proteins in grains are exactly the opposite. Together, they complement each other and produce "complete" proteins.

DIETS THAT MAY RESTRICT OR EXCLUDE THIS FOOD

Low-residue diet
Low-purine (antigout) diet
Sucrose-free diet

HOW TO BUY THIS FOOD

Look for: Fresh, firm bright-green pods, loose fresh peas, or snow-pea pods. The pods should feel velvety; fresh pea pods should look full, with round fat peas inside.

Avoid: Flat or wilted fresh pea pods (the peas inside are usually immature), fresh pea pods with gray flecks (the peas inside are usually overly mature and starchy), or yellowed fresh or snow-pea pods.

STORING THIS FOOD

Refrigerate fresh peas in the pod and use them quickly. As peas age their sugars turn to starch; the older the peas, the less sweet. Snow-pea pods should also be stored in the refrigerator.

Do not wash pea pods before you store them. Damp pods are likely to mold.

PREPARING THIS FOOD

To prepare fresh peas, wash the pods, cut off the end, pull away the string running down the side, and shell the peas. To prepare snow-pea pods, wash them under cold running water, pull away the string, snip off the ends, then stir-fry or boil quickly to keep them crisp.

WHAT HAPPENS WHEN YOU COOK THIS FOOD

Chlorophyll, the pigment that makes green vegetables green, is sensitive to acids. When you heat green peas, the chlorophyll in the peas reacts chemically with the acids in the vegetable or in the cooking water, forming pheophytin, which is brown. The pheophytin turns the cooked peas olive-drab.

To keep cooked peas green, you have to keep the chlorophyll from reacting with acids. One way to do this is to cook the peas in lots of water, which will dilute the acids. A second alternative is to leave the lid off the pot when you cook the peas so that the volatile acids can float off into the air. Or you can steam the peas in very little water or stir-fry them so fast that they cook before the chlorophyll has time to react with the acids. No matter how you cook the peas, save the cooking liquid. It contains the peas' water-soluble B vitamins.

HOW OTHER KINDS OF PROCESSING AFFECT THIS FOOD

Drying.   Fresh green garden peas are immature seeds. The peas used to make dried split peas are mature seeds, may have twice as much starch as fresh peas, and are an extremely good source of protein. A cup and a half of dried split peas, which will weigh about 14 ounces (400 grams) when cooked, has 20 to 25 grams protein, half the RDA for a healthy adult. Split peas don't have to be soaked before cooking; in fact, soaking drains the B vitamins. When buying split peas, look for well-colored peas in a tightly sealed box or bag. Store the peas in an air- and moistureproof container in a cool, dry cupboard. When you are ready to use them, pick the peas over, discarding any damaged, broken, or withered ones along with any pebbles or other foreign matter.

MEDICAL USES AND/OR BENEFITS

To reduce the levels of serum cholesterol.   The gums and pectins in peas and split peas appear to lower the amount of cholesterol in the blood and offer some protection against heart disease. There are currently two theories to explain how this may happen. The first theory is that the pectins form a gel in your stomach that sops up fats and keeps them from being absorbed by your body. The second is that bacteria in the gut feed on fiber in the peas, producing short-chain fatty acids that inhibit the production of cholesterol in your liver.

As a source of carbohydrates for people with diabetes.   Legumes are digested very slowly, producing only a gradual rise in blood-sugar levels. As a result, the body needs less insulin to control blood sugar after eating beans than after eating some other high-carbohydrate foods (bread or potato). In studies at the University of Kentucky, a bean, whole-grain, vegetable, and fruit-rich diet developed at the University of Toronto enabled patients with Type I diabetes (who do not produce any insulin themselves) to cut their daily insulin intake by 38 percent. For patients with Type II diabetes (who can produce some insulin) the diet reduced the need for injected insulin by 98 percent. This diet is in line with the nutritional guidelines of the American Diabetes Association, but people with diabetes should always consult with their doctors and/or dietitians before altering their diet.

ADVERSE EFFECTS ASSOCIATED WITH THIS FOOD

Production of uric acid.   Purines are the natural metabolic by-products of protein metabolism in the body. They eventually break down into uric acid, forming sharp crystals that may cause gout if they collect in your joints or kidney stones if they collect in urine. Fresh and dried peas are a source of purines; eating them raises the concentration of purines in your body. Although controlling the amount of purine-producing foods in the diet may not significantly affect the course of gout (which is treated with medication such as allopurinol, which inhibits the formation of uric acid), limiting these foods is still part of many gout regimens.

FOOD/DRUG INTERACTIONS

*   *   *

PEPPERS

(Bell peppers, chili peppers, jalapeño peppers, pimentos)

NUTRITIONAL PROFILE

Energy value (calories per serving):	Low
Protein:	Moderate
Fat:	Low
Cholesterol:	None
Carbohydrates:	High
Fiber:	High
Sodium:	Low
Major vitamin contribution:	Vitamins A and C
Major mineral contribution:	Iron, potassium

ABOUT THE NUTRIENTS IN THIS FOOD

Sweet peppers, also known as bell peppers, are green when immature and red, yellow, or purple when ripe. *Hot peppers* are distinguished from sweet peppers by their shape (they are longer and skinnier) and by their burning taste. Like bell peppers, jalapeños, chili peppers, and cayennes will turn red as they ripen.

All peppers are rich in vitamin C. Three and a half ounces of fresh green pepper have 128 mg vitamin C, twice the RDA for a healthy adult. A similar serving of fresh hot peppers has 1.5 times as much. All peppers contain red or yellow carotenoid pigments your body can convert to vitamin A, but mature peppers have ten times as much vitamin A as green peppers (1600 IU/oz. vs 151 IU/oz.). One tablespoon of chili powder has approximately 2600 IU vitamin A, 52 percent of the RDA for a healthy adult.

Fresh peppers hold their nutrients well, even at room temperature. For example, green peppers stored at room temperature retained 85 percent of their vitamin C after 48 hours.

THE MOST NUTRITIOUS WAY TO SERVE THIS FOOD

Bell peppers: Fresh sliced or chopped on a salad.

Hot peppers: Seeded, in a soup or stew.

DIETS THAT MAY RESTRICT OR EXCLUDE THIS FOOD

Antiflatulence diet
Bland diet
Sucrose-free diet

BUYING THIS FOOD

Look for: Firm peppers that feel thick and fleshy. Their skin should be brightly colored green, red, yellow, or purple.

Avoid: Dull-colored peppers; they may be immature. If the skin is wrinkled, the peppers have lost moisture; soft spots suggest decay inside.

STORING THIS FOOD

Refrigerate fresh peppers in the vegetable crisper to preserve their moisture and vitamin C.

PREPARING THIS FOOD

Sweet bell peppers.   Wash the peppers under cold running water, slice, and remove the seeds and membranes (which are irritating). If you plan to cook the peppers, peel them; the skin will otherwise curl up into a hard, unpalatable strip. Immerse the pepper in hot water, then lift it out and plunge it into cold water. The hot water bath damages a layer of cells under the skin so that the skin is very easy to peel off. Roasting the peppers produces the same result.

Hot peppers.   Never handle any variety of hot peppers without protective gloves. Hot peppers contain large amounts of the irritating chemicals capsaicin, nordyhydrocapsaicin, and dihydrocapsaicin. These chemicals, which will burn unprotected skin, do not dissolve in water; you cannot simply wash them off. Capsaicin and its chemical cousins do dissolve in milkfat or alcohol, which is why either milk or beer will soothe the burning taste of a dish spiced with curry or chili.

WHAT HAPPENS WHEN YOU COOK THIS FOOD

Chlorophyll, the pigment that makes green vegetables green, is sensitive to acids. When you heat green peppers, the chlorophyll in the flesh will react chemically with acids in the pepper or in the cooking water, forming pheophytin, which is brown. The pheophytin makes a cooked pepper olive-drab or (if the pepper has a lot of yellow carotenes) bronze.

To keep cooked green peppers green, you have to keep the chlorophyll from reacting with acids. One way to do this is to cook peppers in a large quantity of water (which dilutes the acids), but this increases the loss of vitamin C. A second alternative is to cook them in a pot with the lid off so that the volatile acids float off into the air. Or you can stir-fry the peppers, cooking them so fast that there is almost no time for the chlorophyll/acid reaction to occur.

When long cooking is inevitable, as with stuffed sweet green peppers, the only remedy is to smother the peppers in sauce so that it doesn't matter what color the peppers are. (Red and yellow peppers won't fade; their carotenoid pigments are impervious to heat.)

Because vitamin C is sensitive to heat, cooked peppers have less than fresh peppers. But peppers have so much vitamin C to begin with that even cooked peppers are a good source of this nutrient.

HOW OTHER KINDS OF PROCESSING AFFECT THIS FOOD

* * *

MEDICAL USES AND/OR BENEFITS

Relieving the congestion of a cold. Hot spices, including hot pepper, irritate the mucous membranes lining your nose and throat and the bronchi in your lungs, making the tissues "weep." The watery secretions may make it easier for you to cough up mucus or blow your nose, thus helping to relieve your congestion for a while.

ADVERSE EFFECTS ASSOCIATED WITH THIS FOOD

Irritant dermatitis. See *Preparing this food* (Hot peppers), above.

Painful urination. The irritating oils in peppers are eliminated through urination. They may cause temporary irritation of the urinary tract.

FOOD/DRUG INTERACTIONS

* * *

PERSIMMONS

NUTRITIONAL PROFILE

Energy value (calories):	Moderate
Protein:	Low
Fat:	Low
Cholesterol:	None
Carbohydrates:	High
Fiber:	High
Sodium:	Low
Major vitamin contribution:	Vitamins A and C
Major mineral contribution:	Potassium

ABOUT THE NUTRIENTS IN THIS FOOD

There are two kinds of persimmon, the imported Japanese variety (sometimes called a "kaki") and the smaller, more seedy native American persimmon. The American fruit is more valuable nutritionally, with twice the carbohydrates, sixteen times the iron, twice the potassium, and nine times as much vitamin C as the Japanese fruit. One 3.5-ounce serving of American persimmons has 66 mg vitamin C, 110 percent the RDA for a healthy adult.

THE MOST NUTRITIOUS WAY TO SERVE THIS FOOD

Fresh and ripe.

DIETS THAT MAY RESTRICT OR EXCLUDE THIS FOOD

Sucrose-free diet

BUYING THIS FOOD

Look for: Firm, plump fruit with brightly colored, smooth unbroken skin. The bright-green stem cap should be firmly anchored to the fruit.

STORING THIS FOOD

Let persimmons ripen at room temperature until they are soft, then store them in the refrigerator. Oriental persimmons, which are more astringent than the American varieties, will lose some of their sharpness if you store them in a plastic bag with an apple. The apple releases ethylene gas, which ripens and mellows the persimmon.

PREPARING THIS FOOD

Wash the persimmon and pull off its stem cap. Then peel and slice the persimmon or put it through a food mill to mash the flesh and remove the seeds.

WHAT HAPPENS WHEN YOU COOK THIS FOOD

*   *   *

HOW OTHER KINDS OF PROCESSING AFFECT THIS FOOD

*   *   *

MEDICAL USES AND/OR BENEFITS

Potassium replacement.   American persimmons are a good source of potassium. Ounce for ounce, the persimmon has 60 percent more potassium than orange juice. Foods rich in potassium are sometimes prescribed for people who are using diuretic drugs and losing potassium. However, there is some question as to whether potassium gluconate, the form of potassium in fresh fruit like persimmons and oranges, is as easily absorbed as potassium citrate or potassium chloride, the forms of potassium given laboratory animals in the experiments designed to show the value of potassium supplements for people on diuretics.

Protection against some forms of cancer.   According to the American Cancer Society, foods rich in vitamins A and C may offer some protection against the risk of cancers of the larynx, esophagus, and lungs.

ADVERSE EFFECTS ASSOCIATED WITH THIS FOOD

*   *   *

FOOD/DRUG INTERACTIONS

*   *   *

PINEAPPLE

NUTRITIONAL PROFILE

Energy value (calories per serving):	Low
Protein:	Low
Fat:	Low
Cholesterol:	None
Carbohydrates:	High
Fiber:	Low
Sodium:	Low (fresh or dried fruit) High (dried fruit treated with sodium sulfur compounds)
Major vitamin contribution:	Vitamin C
Major mineral contribution:	Potassium

ABOUT THE NUTRIENTS IN THIS FOOD

Pineapples have moderate amounts of soluble fiber (primarily pectins and gums). They are high in sugar but have no starch and only minuscule amounts of protein and fat. Their most important nutrient is vitamin C. A 3.5-ounce serving of fresh pineapple provides 15.4 mg vitamin C, 26 percent of the RDA for a healthy adult.

The pineapple fruit and the stem of the pineapple plant contain bromelain, a proteolytic (protein-dissolving) enzyme similar to papain (in unripe papayas) and ficin (in fresh figs). Bromelain is a natural meat tenderizer that breaks down the protein molecules in meat when you add the fruit to a stew or baste a roast with the juice. Bromelain only works at a temperature between 140° and 170° F. It is destroyed by boiling the fruit. To get the maximum effect in stewing, keep the pot simmering, not boiling. If you add fresh pineapple to gelatin, the bromelain will break down the proteins in the gelatin and the dish will not set. To add fresh pineapple to a gelatin mold, boil the fruit first.

DIETS THAT MAY RESTRICT OR EXCLUDE THIS FOOD
Sucrose-free diet

BUYING THIS FOOD
Look for: Large pineapples. The leaves in the crown on top should be fresh and green, the pineapple should feel heavy for its size (which means it's juicy), it should have a rich pineapple aroma, and you should hear a solid "thunk" when you tap a finger against the side. While the pineapple's shell generally loses chlorophyll and turns more golden as the fruit ripens, some varieties of pineapple have more chlorophyll and stay green longer than others, so the color of the shell is not a reliable guide to ripeness.

STORING THIS FOOD
Store pineapples either at room temperature or in the refrigerator. Neither will have any effect on the sweetness of the fruit. Fruits and vegetables get sweeter after they are picked by converting stored starches to sugars. Since the pineapple has no stored starch and gets its sugar from it leaves, it is as sweet as it ever will be on the day it is picked. It will get softer while stored, though, as its pectic enzymes break down pectins in its cell walls.

PREPARING THIS FOOD
To sweeten and soften fresh pineapple, peel and slice the fruit (or cut it into chunks), sprinkle it with sugar, and chill it in the refrigerator. The sugar and water on the pineapple's surface is a denser solution than the liquid inside the pineapple's cells. As a result liquid flows out of the cells. Without liquid to hold them rigid, the cell walls will collapse inward and the pineapple will be softer. This physical phenomenon—the flow of liquids across a membrane from a less dense to a more dense environment—is called osmosis.

WHAT HAPPENS WHEN YOU COOK THIS FOOD
As you cook pineapple, the pectic substances in its cell walls dissolve and the pineapple softens. Boiling pineapple also inactivates its bromelain. (For pineapple's effects on other foods, see *About the nutrients in this food,* above.)

HOW OTHER KINDS OF PROCESSING AFFECT THIS FOOD
Drying.   Drying concentrates the calories and nutrients in pineapple. Fresh pineapple may be treated with a sulfur compound such as sulfur dioxide to

protect its vitamin C and keep it from darkening as it dries. In people sensitive to sulfites, these compounds may provoke serious allergic reactions, including potentially fatal anaphylactic shock.

MEDICAL USES AND/OR BENEFITS
*   *   *

ADVERSE EFFECTS ASSOCIATED WITH THIS FOOD

Dermatitis.   Bromelain, which breaks down proteins, may cause irritant dermatitis. Pineapples may also cause allergic dermatitis. (Irritant dermatitis may occur in anyone who touches a pineapple; allergic dermatitis occurs only in an individual who is sensitive to a particular substance.)

Sulfur allergies.   See *How other kinds of processing affect this food,* above.

FOOD/DRUG INTERACTIONS

False-positive test for carcinoid tumors.   Carcinoid tumors, which may arise from tissues in the endocrine or gastrointestinal system, secrete serotonin, a natural chemical that makes blood vessels expand or contract. Because serotonin is excreted in urine, these tumors are diagnosed by measuring serotonin levels by products in the urine. Pineapples contain large amounts of serotonin; eating them in the three days before a test for an endocrine tumor might produce a false-positive result, suggesting that you have the tumor when in fact you don't. (Other foods high in serotonin are avocados, bananas, eggplant, plums, tomatoes, and walnuts.)

PLUMS

See also PRUNES

See also PRUNES

NUTRITIONAL PROFILE

Energy value (calories per serving):	Moderate
Protein:	Low
Fat:	Low
Cholesterol:	None
Carbohydrates:	High
Fiber:	Low
Sodium:	Low
Major vitamin contribution:	Vitamins A and C
Major mineral contribution:	Potassium

ABOUT THE NUTRIENTS IN THIS FOOD

Plums are high in sugar. They have no starch, and only moderate amounts of soluble gums and pectins in the flesh, plus small amounts of cellulose and the noncarbohydrate food fiber lignin in the peel. Plums have very little protein and only a trace of fat. They are a good source of vitamins A and C and potassium. Like apple seeds and peach and apricot pits, the seed inside a plum pit contains amygdalin, a natural cyanide/sugar compound that breaks down into hydrogen cyanide in your stomach (see APPLES).

THE MOST NUTRITIOUS WAY TO SERVE THIS FOOD

Fresh and ripe, with the peel.

DIETS THAT MAY RESTRICT OR EXCLUDE THIS FOOD
Sucrose-free diet

BUYING THIS FOOD

Look for: Firm, brightly colored fruit that are slightly soft to the touch, yielding a bit when you press them with your finger.

COMPARING VARIETIES OF PLUMS

Damson	Dark skin and flesh (for preserves only)
Friar	Dark-red skin, deep-yellow flesh
Greengage	Green-yellow skin and yellow flesh
Italian ("prune" plums)	Small, oval, with blue-purple skin and firm golden flesh
Laroda	Large; yellow skin with a red blush and yellow flesh
Red Beauty	Bright red skin, firm yellow flesh
Santa Rosa	Red-purple skin, yellow flesh (very tart)

Sources: "Guide to Selection and Care of Fresh Fruit" and "The fresh approach to plums," United Fresh Fruit and Vegetable Association (n.d.); Rombauer, Irma S. and Becker, Marion Rombauer, *The Joy of Cooking* (Indianapolis: Bobbs-Merrill, 1984).

STORING THIS FOOD

Store firm plums at room temperature. Plums have no stored starch to convert to sugars, so they won't get sweeter after they are picked, but they will soften as their pectic enzymes disssolve some of the pectin stiffening their cell walls. When the plums are soft enough, refrigerate them to stop the enzyme action.

PREPARING THIS FOOD

Wash and serve fresh plums or split them, remove the pit, and slice the plums for fruit salad. Plums can be stewed in the skin; if you prefer them skinless, put them in boiling water for a few minutes, then lift them out with a slotted spoon and plunge them into cold water. The hot water will damage a layer of cells under the skin, the plum will swell, and its skin will split and peel off easily.

WHAT HAPPENS WHEN YOU COOK THIS FOOD

When you cook a plum, its water-soluble pectins and hemicellulose will dissolve and the flesh will soften.

Cooking may also change the color of plums with red, purple, or blue-red skin colored with anthocyanin pigments that are sensitive to acids or bases (alkalis). The colors get more intensely red or purple in acids (lemon juice) and less so in bases (baking soda). And, cooking plums (which are acid) in an aluminum pot can create acid/metal compounds that discolor either the pot or the plum.

HOW OTHER KINDS OF PROCESSING AFFECT THIS FOOD

Drying.   See PRUNES.

MEDICAL USES AND/OR BENEFITS

*   *   *

ADVERSE EFFECTS ASSOCIATED WITH THIS FOOD

*   *   *

FOOD/DRUG INTERACTIONS

False-positive test for carcinoid tumors.   Carcinoid tumors, tumors that may arise from tissues of the endocrine or gastrointestinal systems, secrete serotonin, a chemical that makes blood vessels expand or contract. Because serotonin is excreted in urine, these tumors are diagnosed by measuring the serotonin levels in the patient's urine. Plums contain large amounts of serotonin. Eating plums in the 72 hours before the test might give a false-positive result, suggesting that you have an endocrine tumor when in fact you do not. (Other foods rich in serotonin include avocados, bananas, eggplant, pineapple, tomatoes, and walnuts.)

POMEGRANATES

NUTRITIONAL PROFILE

Energy value (calories per serving):	Moderate
Protein:	Low
Fat:	Low
Cholesterol:	None
Carbohydrates:	High
Fiber:	Low
Sodium:	Low
Major vitamin contribution:	Vitamin C
Major mineral contribution:	Potassium

ABOUT THE NUTRIENTS IN THIS FOOD

Pomegranates are rich in sugar. The juice—which we get by crushing or crunching the jellylike substance that clings to the pomegranate's seeds—contains no starch, no fiber, a little protein, a trace of fat, and moderate amounts of vitamin C and the B vitamins. Pomegranate juice is also a good source of potassium.

THE MOST NUTRITIOUS WAY TO SERVE THIS FOOD

Fresh cut or juiced.

DIETS THAT MAY RESTRICT OR EXCLUDE THIS FOOD

Sucrose-free diet

BUYING THIS FOOD

Look for: A pomegranate that feels heavy for its size (which means it's juicy). The rind should be bright red.

Avoid: Pale pomegranates or pomegranates that look dry or wrinkled.

STORING THIS FOOD

Store pomegranates in the refrigerator and use within a week.

PREPARING THIS FOOD

Slice through the stem end of the pomegranate and pull off the top—carefully, to avoid splashing red pomegranate juice all over yourself. Then slice the pomegranate into wedges and pull the wedges apart. Once you cut the pomegranate apart you can handle it in one of two ways, the messy way and the neat way. The messy way is to pull the seeds out of the pomegranate, crush them in your teeth to get the juice, and then spit out the crushed seeds. The neat way is to put the seeds through a strainer, collect the juice, and discard the seeds.

WHAT HAPPENS WHEN YOU COOK THIS FOOD

*   *   *

HOW OTHER KINDS OF PROCESSING AFFECT THIS FOOD

*   *   *

MEDICAL USES AND/OR BENEFITS

*   *   *

ADVERSE EFFECTS ASSOCIATED WITH THIS FOOD

*   *   *

FOOD/DRUG INTERACTIONS

*   *   *

PORK

See also SAUSAGES

NUTRITIONAL PROFILE*

Energy value (calories per serving):	Moderate
Protein:	High
Fat:	Moderate
Cholesterol:	Moderate
Carbohydrates:	None
Fiber:	None
Sodium:	Moderate
Major vitamin contribution:	Thiamin (vitamin B_1), niacin, vitamin B_6
Major mineral contribution:	Iron

ABOUT THE NUTRIENTS IN THIS FOOD

Pork, like other foods of animal origin, is rich in complete proteins that provide sufficient amounts of all the essential amino acids. Its fat is higher in unsaturated fatty acids than the fat in beef, veal, or lamb. Pork fat is 64 percent unsaturated fatty acids, while beef and veal fat are 52 percent unsaturated fatty acids and lamb fat is 44 percent unsaturated fatty acids. Pork's cholesterol content is similar to that of beef.

Pork is a good source of B vitamins but provides less iron than beef. A 3.5-ounce serving of roast pork has 0.9 mg iron (5 percent of the RDA for a healthy adult woman), while a 3.5-ounce serving of roast beef has 2.3 mg (13 percent of the RDA). The iron in pork, like the iron in beef, is heme iron, the organic form of iron found in foods of animal origin. Heme iron is five times

*Values are for lean broiled meat.

more available to the body than non-heme iron, the inorganic iron in plant foods.

THE MOST NUTRITIOUS WAY TO SERVE THIS FOOD

Lean pork, thoroughly cooked.

DIETS THAT MAY RESTRICT OR EXCLUDE THIS FOOD

Controlled-fat, low-cholesterol diet
Low-protein diet

BUYING THIS FOOD

Look for: Firm, fresh pork that is light pink or reddish and has very little visible fat. If there are any bone ends showing, they should be red, not white; the whiter the bone ends, the older the animal from which the meat was taken.

Avoid: Packages with a lot of liquid leakage. Meat that has lost moisture is likely to be dry and tough.

STORING THIS FOOD

Refrigerate fresh pork immediately. Refrigeration prolongs the freshness of pork by slowing the natural multiplication of bacteria on the surface of meat. Left to their own devices, these bacteria convert proteins and other substances on the surface of the meat to a slimy film and, eventually, they will convert the meat's sulfur-containing amino acids methionine and cystine into smelly chemicals called mercaptans. When the mercaptans combine with myoglobin, they produce the greenish pigment that gives spoiled meat its characteristic unpleasant appearance.

Refrigeration slows this whole chain of events so that fresh roasts and chops usually stay fresh for three to five days. For longer storage, store the pork in the freezer where the very low temperatures will slow the bacteria even more.

Store unopened smoked or cured pork products in the refrigerator in the original wrapper and use according to the date and directions on the package.

PREPARING THIS FOOD

Trim the pork carefully. You can significantly reduce the amount of fat and cholesterol in each serving by judiciously cutting away all visible fat.

Do not add salt to the pork before you cook it; the salt will draw moisture out of the meat, making it stringy and tough. Add salt near the end of the cooking process.

After handling raw meat, wash your knives, cutting board, counter—and your hands—with hot soapy water to reduce the chance of transferring microorganisms from the pork to other foods.

WHAT HAPPENS WHEN YOU COOK THIS FOOD

Cooking changes the way pork looks and tastes, alters its nutritional value, makes it safer, and extends its shelf life.

Browning meat before you cook it does not seal in the juices, but it does change the flavor by caramelizing proteins and sugars on the surface. Because the only sugars that occur naturally in pork are the small amounts of glycogen in its muscles, we add sugars in the form of marinades or basting liquids that may also contain acids (vinegar, lemon juice, wine) to break down muscle fibers and tenderize the meat. Browning has one minor nutritional drawback. It breaks amino acids on the surface of the meat into smaller compounds that are no longer useful proteins.)

When pork is heated, it loses water and shrinks. Its pigments, which combine with oxygen, are denatured (broken into smaller fragments) by the heat and turn brown, the natural color of cooked meat. This color change is more dramatic in beef (which starts out red) than in pork (which starts out gray-pink). In fact, you can pretty much judge beef's doneness from its color, but you must use a meat thermometer to measure the internal temperature of the meat before you can say it is thoroughly cooked.

Pork is considered done (and safe to eat) when it reaches an average uniform internal temperature of 170° F, hot enough to kill *Trichinella spiralis,* the organism that causes trichinosis.*

Killing these organisms is one obvious benefit of heating pork thoroughly. Another benefit: Heat liquifies the fat on the meat so that it simply runs off the meat. The unsaturated fatty acids that remain in the meat, continue to oxidize as the meat cooks. Oxidized fats give cooked meat a characteristic warmed-over flavor. You can reduce the warmed-over flavor by cooking and storing the meat under a blanket of catsup or a gravy made from tomatoes, peppers, and other vitamin C-rich vegetables, all natural antioxidants that slow the oxidation of the fats.

---

*Cooking pork in a microwave oven requires careful attention to the temperature. In 1982, researchers at Iowa State University found live trichinae in nine of 51 experimentally infected samples of pork that had been cooked in different brands and models of microwave ovens according to directions from the manufacturers and from the Pork Producers Council. In each case, while the internal temperature of the meat rose to 170° F, moisture evaporating on the surface of the meat kept the temperature there too low to kill the trichinae. In a second study, in 1983, the researchers recommended that pork cooked in a microwave oven be cooked in a special transparent plastic cooking bag to prevent the evaporation of moisture on the surface of the meat. Subsequent laboratory tests at Iowa showed that pork roasts microwaved in these bags reached temperatures high enough to kill trichinae on all surfaces of the meat.

HOW OTHER KINDS OF PROCESSING AFFECT THIS FOOD

Freezing.   Freezing changes the flavor and texture of fresh pork. When fresh pork is frozen, the water in its cells turn into ice crystals that can tear the cell walls so that liquids leak out when the pork is thawed. That's why defrosted pork, like defrosted beef, veal, or lamb, may be drier and less tender than fresh meat.

Curing, smoking, and aging.   Curing preserves meat by osmotic action. The dry salt or a salt solution draws liquid out the cells of the meat and the cells of any microorganisms living on the meat.* *Smoking*—hanging meat over an open fire—gives meat a rich, "smoky" flavor that varies with the wood used in the fire. Meats smoked over an open fire are exposed to carcinogenic chemicals in the smoke, including a-benzopyrene. Meats treated with artificial smoke flavoring are not, since the flavoring is commercially treated to remove tar and a-benzopyrene. Cured and smoked meats sometimes have less moisture and proportionally more fat than fresh meat. They are also saltier. *Aging*—letting the meat hang exposed to air—further reduces the moisture content and shrinks the meat.

Irradiation.   In 1985 the Food and Drug Administration approved the use of low doses of radiation to kill *Trichinella spiralis* in fresh pork. Irradiation does not eliminate other harmful organisms, such as *Salmonella.* Irradiated pork should be treated like any other fresh meat product, which means washing all implements, surfaces, and your hands with hot soapy water after preparing the meat. Irradiation reduces the amount of thiamin (vitamin B_1) in fresh pork.

MEDICAL USES AND/OR BENEFITS

*   *   *

ADVERSE EFFECTS ASSOCIATED WITH THIS FOOD

Trichinosis.   You get trichinosis by eating meat that contains cysts of *Trichinella spiralis,* a parasitic roundworm that lives in animals that eat meat. Pigs are not the only animals that carry trichinosis. It can show up in any animal that eats uncooked flesh infested with the worms. In the arctic, for example, explorers got trichinosis from polar bear meat.

When we swallow encysted *Trichinella* larvae, the wall of the cyst

---

*Osmosis is the physical phenomenon by which liquids flow across a membrane, like a cell wall, from a less dense to a more dense environment. Since salt or salty liquid is denser than the liquid inside cells, it pulls out moisture. Pork becomes dryer and the microorganisms, which cannot live without water, die after preparing the meat. Irradiation destroys the thiamin (vitamin B_1) in fresh pork.

breaks down in our stomach, freeing the larvae, which burrow into the membranes of the stomach and gut, where they mature within two days. The mature *Trichinellae* burrow into the intestinal wall, where the females begin to discharge larvae that are carried into the bloodstream and throughout the body, infesting and eventually destroying muscle fibers. The worms can damage the retina and other tissues in the eye. Untreated, trichinosis can cause death from paralysis of the respiratory muscles.

In this country, trichinosis has not been a widespread problem, because we have been conditioned to cook meat thoroughly enough to destroy the *Trichinella* organism. Nonetheless, 60 cases were reported to the Centers for Disease Control in 1984, and as many as 4 percent of all Americans may have the cysts in their muscles, although they have never developed the disease. (Because the symptoms of trichinosis—aches, fever, dizziness—are so similar to flu symptoms, it is estimated that only one in every 3000 cases is actually diagnosed.)*

Elevated levels of serum cholesterol.   Abnormally high levels of cholesterol in the blood are a risk factor in heart disease. How your diet affects the amount of cholesterol you produce is not entirely clear; dietary fat and cholesterol may not be the primary factor in determining how much and what kind of cholesterol your body makes and stores. Nonetheless, there is evidence to suggest that controlling the amount of fat and cholesterol you consume may help lower serum cholesterol levels, particularly for people with high levels. In 1986 the American Heart Association issued new nutritional guidelines, suggesting that healthy adults reduce their consumption of fat to 30 percent of their daily calories and limit cholesterol intake to 300 mg per day or 100 mg per 1000 calories, whichever is less (3.5 ounces of lean, broiled pork chop contains 99 mg cholesterol).

FOOD/DRUG INTERACTIONS
*   *   *

*Contrary to common belief, as of 1986 the USDA does not inspect fresh pork for *Trichinella spiralis*. As a result, other countries, including Common Market countries, will not accept our fresh pork for import.

POTATOES

See also SWEET POTATOES

NUTRITIONAL PROFILE

Energy value (calories per serving):	Moderate
Protein:	Moderate
Fat:	Low
Cholesterol:	None
Carbohydrates:	High
Fiber:	Low
Sodium:	Low
Major vitamin contribution:	Vitamins C and B_6
Major mineral contribution:	Potassium

ABOUT THE NUTRIENTS IN THIS FOOD

Potatoes are high-carbohydrate food with much starch and a little sugar. In storage, the potato's starch turns to sugar, so the longer a potato is stored, the sweeter (and more unpalatable) it will taste. Potatoes have cellulose, hemicellulose, pectins, and gums plus lignin, the noncarbohydrate food fiber found in plant stems, leaves, and peel.

The proteins in potatoes are considered incomplete because they are deficient in the essential amino acids methionine and cystine. Potatoes have very little fat and no cholesterol at all.

Potatoes are a good source of vitamin C. A 3.5-ounce baked potato provides 12.9 mg vitamin C, 22 percent of the RDA for a healthy adult. Potatoes are rich in B vitamins, particularly thiamin (vitamin B_1) and niacin, and they are a good source of potassium.

Potatoes also contain solanine, a natural toxin. Solanine, which is produced in the green parts of the potato (the leaves, the stem, and any green spots on the skin), is a nerve poison. It interferes with your body's ability to use acetylcholinesterase, a chemical that facilitates the transmission of impulses between body cells.

Potatoes that are exposed to light will produce solanine more quickly than potatoes stored in the dark, but all potatoes produce some solanine all the time. Solanine does not dissolve in water, nor is it destroyed by heat; any solanine present in a raw potato will still be there after you cook it.

The federal government does not permit the sale of potatoes containing more than 200 ppm (parts per million) solanine. The potatoes we buy usually contain about 100 ppm. At that level, a healthy adult might have to eat 4.5 pounds of potatoes at one sitting to experience the first gastrointestinal or neurological symptoms of poisoning. However, there have been cases of illness and death from solanine poisoning reported. The safest course is to throw out all potatoes with green spots on the skin or sprouting "eyes."

DIETS THAT MAY EXCLUDE OR RESTRICT THIS FOOD
Low-carbohydrate diet
Low-salt diet (canned potatoes, potato chips, potato sticks, and the like)
Sucrose-free diet

THE MOST NUTRITIOUS WAY TO SERVE THIS FOOD
With meat, milk, or grains, all of which provide the essential amino acids methionine and cystine needed to complete the proteins in the potatoes.
With the skin, which is a valuable source of food fiber.

BUYING THIS FOOD
Look for: Firm potatoes with unscarred, unblemished skin. Different varieties of potatoes have skins of different thickness. This has no effect at all on the nutritional value of the potato.

Avoid: Potatoes with peeling skin (an immature vegetable that won't store well); potatoes with wrinkled or blemished skin (there may be decay inside); potatoes with green spots or sprouts growing out of the eyes (higher than normal levels of solanine); or moldy potatoes (potentially hazardous toxins).

STORING THIS FOOD
Store potatoes in a dark, dry cabinet or root cellar to prevent sprouting and protect them from mold. The temperature should be cool, but not cold, since temperatures below 50° F encourage the conversion of the potato's starches to

sugar. If the potatoes are accidentally frozen, they will develop black rings inside.

Use potatoes as quickly as possible. Vitamin C is sensitive to oxygen, so the longer potatoes are stored, the less vitamin C they will have.

Do not wash potatoes before you store them or store them in the refrigerator; dampness encourages the growth of molds.

PREPARING THIS FOOD

Discard potatoes with green spots, sprouting eyes, or patches of mold on the skin, and scrub the rest with a stiff vegetable brush under cool running water. When you peel and slice potatoes, throw out any that have rot or mold inside.

Don't peel or slice potatoes until you are ready to use them. When you cut into a potato and tear its cell walls you release polyphenoloxidase, an enzyme that hastens the oxidation of phenols in the potato, creating the brownish compounds that darken a fresh-cut potato. You can slow this reaction (but not stop it completely) by soaking the peeled sliced fresh potatoes in ice water, but many of the vitamins in the potatoes will leach out into the soaking water. Another alternative is to dip the sliced potatoes in an acid solution (lemon juice and water, vinegar and water), but this will alter the taste.

WHAT HAPPENS WHEN YOU COOK THIS FOOD

Starch consists of granules packed with the molecules of amylose and amylopectin. When you cook a potato, its starch granules absorb water molecules that cling to the amylose and amylopectin molecules, making the granules swell. If the granules absorb enough water, they will rupture, releasing the nutrients inside. If you are cooking potatoes in a stew or soup, the amylose and amylopectin molecules that escape from the ruptured starch granule will attract and hold water molecules in the liquid, thickening the dish.

However you prepare them, cooked potatoes have more nutrients available than raw potatoes do. They may also be a different color. Like onions and cauliflower, potatoes contain pale anthoxanthin pigments that react with metal ions to form blue, green, or brown compounds. That's why potatoes may turn yellowish if you cook them in an aluminum or iron pot or slice them with a carbon-steel knife. To keep potatoes pale, cook them in a glass or enameled pot.

HOW OTHER FORMS OF PROCESSING AFFECT THIS FOOD

Freezing. A potato's cells are like a box whose stiff walls are held rigidly in place by the water inside the cell. When you freeze a cooked potato, the water in its cells forms ice crystals that can tear the cell walls, allowing liquid to leak out when the potatoes are defrosted, which is why defrosted potatoes taste mushy. Commercial processors get around this by partially dehydrating potatoes before they are frozen or by freezing potatoes in a sauce that gives an interesting flavor to take you mind off the texture.

Dehydrating.   Potato "flakes" and "granules" have fewer vitamins and minerals than fresh potatoes; potato chips and sticks are usually much higher in salt.

Potato salad.   Commercially prepared potato salads may be treated with a sulfite such as sulfur dioxide to inactivate polyphenoloxidase and keep the potatoes from darkening. People who are sensitive to sulfites may suffer serious allergic reactions, including potentially fatal anaphylactic shock if they eat potato salads treated with these chemicals.

MEDICAL USES AND/OR BENEFITS

To soothe a skin rash.   Potato starch, like corn starch, may be used as a dusting powder or added to a lukewarm bath to soothe a wet, "weepy" skin rash. The starch, which is very drying, should never be used on a dry rash or without a doctor's advice.

As an antiscorbutic.   Raw potatoes, which are high in vitamin C, were once used as an antiscorbutic, a substance that prevents or cures the vitamin C-deficiency disease scurvy. Today we have much more effective means of preventing scurvy.

ADVERSE EFFECTS ASSOCIATED WITH THIS FOOD

Allergic reactions to sulfite.   See *How other forms of processing affect this food,* above.

Solanine poisoning.   See *About the nutrients in this food,* above.

FOOD/DRUG INTERACTIONS

*   *   *

POULTRY
(Chicken, duck, goose, turkey)

NUTRITIONAL PROFILE*

Energy value (calories per serving):	Moderate
Protein:	High
Fat:	Low to high
Cholesterol:	Moderate (chicken, turkey) High (duck, goose)
Carbohydrates:	None
Fiber:	None
Sodium:	Moderate
Major vitamin contribution:	Riboflavin (vitamin B_2), vitamin B_6, vitamin B_{12}, niacin
Major mineral contribution:	Zinc, magnesium

ABOUT THE NUTRIENTS IN THIS FOOD

All poultry provides generous amounts of high-quality, "complete" proteins (proteins with adequate amounts of all the essential amino acids). One 3.5-7ounce serving has 20 to 25 grams of protein, nearly 50 percent of the RDA for a healthy adult.

Most poultry has less fat than beef, veal, pork, or lamb. Its fat is proportionally higher in unsaturated fatty acids, but cooked chicken and turkey have about the same amount of cholesterol as cooked lean beef (74-79 mg/ 3.5 oz.).

Poultry is a good source of the B vitamins and heme iron, the organic form of iron found in foods of animal origin that is five times more available to the body than non-heme iron, the inorganic form of iron in plant foods.

*Values are for roasted mixed dark and white meat.

THE MOST NUTRITIOUS WAY TO SERVE THIS FOOD

Broiled or roasted, with the skin removed to reduce the fat. Soups and stews should be skimmed.

DIETS THAT MAY RESTRICT OR EXCLUDE THIS FOOD

Controlled-fat, low cholesterol diet (duck, goose)
Low-protein diet

BUYING THIS FOOD

Look for: Poultry with fresh, unblemished skin and clear unblemished meat. If you buy whole fresh chickens that have not been prepacked, try to bend the breastbone—the more flexible it is, the younger the bird and the more lean and tender the flesh.

Choose the bird that fits your needs. Young birds (broiler, fryer, capon, rock cornish hen, duckling, young turkey, young hen, and young tom) are good for broiling, frying, and roasting. Older birds (hen, stewing chicken, fowl, mature duck, turkey, goose) have tougher muscle fiber, which requires long stewing or steaming to tenderize the meat.

Avoid: Poultry whose skin is dry or discolored.

STORING THIS FOOD

Refrigerate fresh poultry immediately. Refrigeration prolongs freshness by slowing the natural multiplication of bacteria on the surface of the chicken, turkey, duck, or goose. Left unchecked, these bacteria will convert proteins and other substances on the surface of the poultry to mucopolysaccharides, a slimy film. They will also convert the sulfur-containing amino acids methionine and cystine into smelly sulfur compounds called mercaptans, which give spoiled poultry a characteristic unpleasant odor. The bacteria multiply most on poultry wrapped in plastic, which is why it often smells bad when you unwrap it at home. Never use, store or freeze any poultry that does not smell absolutely fresh. Throw it out or return it to the store.

Cover fresh poultry and refrigerate it in a dish that keeps it from dripping and contaminating other foods or the refrigerator. Properly wrapped fresh poultry will keep for one or two days at 40° F. For longer storage, freeze the poultry.

PREPARING THIS FOOD

Wash the poultry under cool running water to flush off the bacteria on its surface. There are more bacteria on an animal's skin than in its flesh. Since we buy poultry with the skin on, it has a much higher population of bacteria (including the ones that cause *Salmonella* food poisoning) than beef, veal, pork, and lamb. Beef and pork may have a few hundred bacteria per square centimeter; chicken will have several thousand.

Discard any poultry that feels slimy to the touch. If you are preparing duck or goose, pull as much fat out of the abdominal cavity as possible. To cut down on the fat in chicken, remove the skin before cooking.

After preparing fresh poultry, always wash your implements, the counter, and your hands with hot soapy water to avoid contaminating other foods with bacteria from the poultry.

WHAT HAPPENS WHEN YOU COOK THIS FOOD

Cooking changes the way poultry looks and tastes, alters its nutritional content, and makes it safer to eat.

Heat changes the structure of the poultry's proteins. It denatures the protein molecules so that they break apart into smaller fragments or change shape or clump together. These changes force moisture out of the tissues so that the poultry turns opaque as it cooks. As it loses water, the poultry also loses water-soluble B vitamins, which drip out into the pan. Since they are not destroyed by heat, they can be saved by using the skimmed pan drippings for gravy. Cooking also caramelizes proteins and the small amounts of sugar on the bird's surface, a "browning" reaction that gives the skin of the bird its characteristic sweet taste. As moisture escapes from the skin, it turns crisp. At the same time, the heat liquifies the fat in the bird, which runs off into the pan, lowering the fat and cholesterol content.

Finally, cooking kills the *Salmonella* and other microorganisms on the skin and flesh of poultry. For maximum safety, poultry should be cooked to a uniform internal temperature of 180° F. If you are cooking your poultry in a microwave oven, check to be sure that the surface of the bird—which is cooled by evaporating moisture—is as hot as the inside, otherwise bacteria on the skin may remain alive.

HOW OTHER KINDS OF PROCESSING AFFECT THIS FOOD

Freezing.   When poultry is frozen, the water in its cells turns into ice crystals which rupture the cell walls. When you thaw the poultry, liquid escapes from the cells and the chicken, turkey, duck, or goose may taste dry and stringy.

The unsaturated fatty acids in poultry will continue to oxidize (and eventually turn rancid) while the bird is frozen. Poultry cut into pieces will spoil more quickly than a whole bird because it has more surfaces exposed to the air. Fresh whole chicken and turkey will keep for up to twelve months at 0° F; chicken pieces will keep for nine months; turkey pieces and whole duck and goose for six months.

Smoking. Smoking (which means slowly roasting a bird in the smoke from an open fire) gives poultry a rich taste that varies according to the wood used in the fire. Birds smoked over an open fire may pick up carcinogenic chemicals from the smoke, including a-benzopyrene, the most prominent carcinogen in tobacco smoke. Artificial smoke flavoring is commercially treated to remove tar and a-benzopyrene. Smoked poultry has less moisture and proportionally more fat than fresh poultry.

"Self-basting" turkeys. To make these birds "self-basting," fat or oil is inserted under the skin of the breast before the bird is packed or frozen. As the bird cooks, the fat warms, melts, and oozes out, basting the turkey. "Self-basting" turkeys are higher in fat than other turkeys; depending on what kind of fat is inserted into the breast, they may also be higher in cholesterol.

MEDICAL USES AND/OR BENEFITS

To relieve the congestion of a cold. Hot chicken soup, the quintessential folk remedy, does appear to relieve the congestion that comes with a head cold. Exactly why remains a mystery but some researchers have suggested that the hot steam from the soup helps liquify mucus and clear the nasal passages.

ADVERSE EFFECTS ASSOCIATED WITH THIS FOOD

Elevated levels of serum cholesterol. Abnormally high levels of cholesterol in the blood are a risk factor in heart disease. How your diet affects the amount of cholesterol you produce is not entirely clear; dietary fat and cholesterol may not be the primary factor in determining how much and what kind of cholesterol your body makes and stores. Nonetheless, there is evidence to suggest that controlling the amount of fat and cholesterol you consume may help lower serum cholesterol levels, particularly for people with high levels. In 1986 the American Heart Association issued new guidelines suggesting that healthy adults reduce their consumption of fat to 30 percent of their total calories and limit cholesterol intake to 300 mg per day or 100 mg per 1000 calories, whichever is less. (Duck, which is considered a high-cholesterol food, has approximately 190 mg/3.5-oz. serving.)

FOOD/DRUG INTERACTIONS

* * *

PRUNES

See also PLUMS

NUTRITIONAL PROFILE*

Energy value (calories per serving):	Moderate
Protein:	Low
Fat:	Low
Cholesterol:	None
Carbohydrates:	High
Fiber:	High
Sodium:	Low (fresh or dried fruit) High (dried fruit treated with sodium sulfur compounds)
Major vitamin contribution:	Vitamin A
Major mineral contribution:	Iron, Potassium

ABOUT THE NUTRIENTS IN THIS FOOD

Prunes are high-fiber food. Ounce for ounce, they have more food fiber than dry beans. Prunes are also high-sugar fruit. Thirty percent of the weight of a prune is glucose, 15 percent is fructose, and 2 percent is sucrose. Prunes have very little fat and no cholesterol.

Prunes are an excellent source of vitamin A. A 3.5-ounce serving of uncooked dried prunes has 1987 IU, nearly 40 percent of the RDA for a healthy adult. They are also a good source of B vitamins and an excellent source of non-heme iron, the form of iron found in plants. Ounce for ounce, they provide more than one-third as much iron as an equal serving of liver. Prunes are also a good source of potassium.

*Values are for dried, uncooked prunes

THE MOST NUTRITIOUS WAY TO SERVE THIS FOOD

With meat or a food rich in vitamin C to increase the absorption of iron from the prunes. Meat makes the stomach more acid (iron is absorbed better in an acid medium), while vitamin C changes the iron from ferric iron to ferrous iron, a more easily absorbed form.

DIETS THAT MAY RESTRICT OR EXCLUDE THIS FOOD

Antiflatulence diet
Low-fiber diet
Low-residue diet
Low-potassium diet
Low-sodium diet (prunes treated with sodium bisulfite, sodium metabisulfite, sodium sulfite)
Sucrose-free diet

BUYING THIS FOOD

Look for: Tightly sealed boxes or bags of fruit that are protected from air, moisture, and insects. Prunes come in different sizes, but size has no bearing on taste or quality. Pitted prunes are more convenient but also more expensive than prunes with their pits still in place.

STORING THIS FOOD

Store prunes in a tightly closed container at room temperature, where they may stay fresh for up to six months. Check periodically to be sure that there is no insect infestation and no mold.

PREPARING THIS FOOD

Do not soak prunes before you cook them. The sugars that make prunes so distinctively sweet are soluble and will leach out into the soaking water.

WHAT HAPPENS WHEN YOU COOK THIS FOOD

When you stew dried prunes, their water-soluble pectins and hemicellulose dissolve and their cells absorb water. Uncooked dried "nugget"-type prunes are 2.5 percent water; when stewed, they are 50.7 percent water. Uncooked "softened" dried prunes are 28 percent water; when stewed, they are 66.4 percent water. Since the water displaces nutrients, ounce for ounce stewed prunes (of either type) may have only one-third as much vitamin C and B vitamins, vitamin A, iron, and fiber as uncooked prunes.

HOW OTHER FORMS OF PROCESSING AFFECT THIS FOOD

*   *   *

MEDICAL USES AND/OR BENEFITS

To relieve or prevent constipation.   Prunes are a high-fiber food that helps relieve constipation. However, since prune juice, which has only a trace of fiber, is also a laxative, some food chemists suggest that what makes the prune such an effective laxative is not its fiber but another constituent, an unidentified derivative of the organic chemical isatin, which is related to another natural substance, biscodyl. Biscodyl, which is the active ingredient in some over-the-counter laxative tablets and suppositories, is a contact laxative that induces the secretion of fluid in the bowel and stimulates contractions of the intestines that push waste through the colon more quickly and efficiently.

Protection against the risk of some forms of cancer.   According to the American Cancer Society, foods high in fiber and vitamin A may offer some protection against cancers of the gastrointestinal and respiratory tracts as well as cancers induced by chemicals.

Potassium replacement.   Prunes and prune juice are a good source of potassium. Ounce for ounce, uncooked dried prunes have four times as much potassium as fresh oranges, and canned or bottled prune juice has approximately 30 percent more potassium than fresh orange juice. Prunes (like other potassium-rich foods) may be prescribed for people who are taking diuretic drugs and losing potassium. However, there is some question as to whether potassium gluconate, the form of potassium in prunes, is as easily absorbed as potassium citrate and potassium chloride, the forms of potassium used in the experiments with laboratory animals which demonstrated the value of potassium supplements for people on diuretics. Furthermore, diuretic drugs are most often used for people who have hypertension and must follow a low-sodium diet, which would almost certainly exclude prunes treated with a sodium/sulfur compound

ADVERSE EFFECTS ASSOCIATED WITH THIS FOOD

Allergic reactions to sulfite.   When they are dried, prune plums may be treated with sulfites (sulfur dioxide, sodium bisulfite, and the like) to inactivate polyphenoloxidase, an enzyme that hastens the oxidation of phenols in the prunes, forming brownish compounds that darken the fruit. People who are sensitive to sulfite may suffer serious allergic reactions, including potentially fatal anaphylactic shock, if they eat prunes treated with sulfites. Also, prunes treated with sulfite compounds are high in sodium.

FOOD/DRUG INTERACTIONS

*   *   *

PUMPKIN

See also WINTER SQUASH

NUTRITIONAL PROFILE

Energy value (calories per serving):	Low
Protein:	Moderate
Fat:	Low
Cholesterol:	None
Carbohydrates:	High
Fiber:	High
Sodium:	Low
Major vitamin contribution:	Vitamin A, B vitamins
Major mineral contribution:	Potassium

ABOUT THE NUTRIENTS IN THIS FOOD

Pumpkins are really two foods: the orange-yellow flesh (whose nutritional profile appears above) and the brown edible seeds.

Like the flesh of other winter squashes, the pumpkin's has moderate amounts of sugar, some starch, some fiber, a little protein and fat. Pumpkins are packed with yellow-orange carotenoids that your body can convert to vitamin A. One 3.5-ounce serving of canned pumpkin may provide as much as 22,056 IU vitamin A, 440 percent of the RDA for a healthy adult.

The pumpkin's seeds are edible and highly nutritious, rich in protein, high in unsaturated vegetable oil (the source of vitamin E), and an excellent source of B vitamins and iron. A one-ounce serving of dry pumpkin seeds, used as a garnish or as a snack, provides 7 grams of protein (an amount equal to a similar serving of meat, fish, poultry, milk, or eggs), 4.2 mg iron (23 percent of the RDA for an adult woman), and twice as much thiamin as an equal serving of pumpkin itself. The seeds are also high in food fiber, including the indigestible noncarbohydrate fiber lignin, found in stems, leaves, peel, and seed coverings.

THE MOST NUTRITIOUS WAY TO SERVE THIS FOOD

Pumpkin.   Baked. Boiled pumpkin absorbs water, which displaces nutrients; ounce for ounce, baked pumpkin has more nutrients than boiled pumpkin.

Pumpkin seeds.   Oven-toasted without salt.

DIETS THAT MAY RESTRICT OR EXCLUDE THIS FOOD

Low-fat (the seeds)
Low-fiber (particularly the seeds)
Sucrose-free diet

BUYING THIS FOOD

Look for: A pumpkin with a bright-orange, blemish-free rind. The pumpkin should feel heavy for its size.

STORING THIS FOOD

Store pumpkins in a cool, dry place and use within a month. Vitamin A is vulnerable to oxygen; the longer the pumpkin is stored, the less vitamin A it will have.

PREPARING THIS FOOD

Wash the pumpkin under cold running water, then cut it in half or in quarters or in smaller portions, as you wish. Pull off the stringy parts and collect and set aside the seeds. Leave the rind on if you plan to bake large pieces of the pumpkin; peel it off for boiling. (If the pumpkin is small enough and/or your oven is large enough, you can simply scoop out the strings and seeds and bake the pumpkin whole, as you would a large acorn squash.)

WHAT HAPPENS WHEN YOU COOK THIS FOOD

Pumpkin.   When you bake a pumpkin, the soluble food fibers in its cell walls dissolve and the pumpkin gets softer. If you bake it too long, the moisture inside the cells will begin to evaporate and the pumpkin will shrink. When you boil pumpkin, it's just the opposite. The cell walls still soften, but its cells absorb water and the vegetable swells. (Boil it too long, though, and the cells will rupture, moisture will escape, and the pumpkin once again will shrink.)

Baking also caramelizes sugars on the cut surface of the pumpkin, browning the vegetable. Since the pumpkin is not extraordinarily high in sugars, we help this along by dusting it with brown sugar before baking. Either way, the pumpkin will retain its color and its vitamin A since its carotenoids are impervious to the normal heat of cooking.

Pumpkin seeds.   When you toast pumpkin seeds, their moisture evaporates and they turn crisp and brown. (Commercially toasted pumpkin seeds are usually salted and must be considered high-sodium food.)

HOW OTHER KINDS OF PROCESSING AFFECT THIS FOOD
Canning.   According to the USDA, canned "pumpkin" may be a mixture of pumpkin and other yellow-orange winter squash, all of which are similar in nutritional value.

MEDICAL USES AND/OR BENEFITS
Protection against some forms of cancer.   According to the American Cancer Society, deep-yellow foods are rich in carotene, a form of vitamin A that may lower the risk of cancers of the larynx, esophagus, and lungs.

ADVERSE EFFECTS ASSOCIATED WITH THIS FOOD
*   *   *

FOOD/DRUG INTERACTIONS
*   *   *

QUINCES

NUTRITIONAL PROFILE

Energy value (calories per serving):	Moderate
Protein:	Low
Fat:	Low
Cholesterol:	None
Carbohydrates:	High
Fiber:	High
Sodium:	Low
Major vitamin contribution:	Vitamin C
Major mineral contribution:	Potassium

ABOUT THE NUTRIENTS IN THIS FOOD

Quinces, which look like pears and are (like pears) members of the same family as apples, are high in sugar, with moderate amounts of food fiber. (Like apples, they are a good source of pectins.) Fresh quinces are rich in vitamin C, but, since quince is always cooked before it is served and vitamin C is heat-sensitive, it has only moderate amounts of vitamin C when it reaches your plate. Quinces are a moderately good source of potassium.

The seeds of the quince, like apple seeds, pear seeds, and apricot, cherry, peach, and plum pits, contain amygdalin, a natural cyanide/sugar compound that breaks down into hydrogen cyanide in your stomach (see APPLES).

THE MOST NUTRITIOUS WAY TO SERVE THIS FOOD

Baked without sugar to save calories.

DIETS THAT MAY RESTRICT OR EXCLUDE THIS FOOD

Sucrose-free diet

BUYING THIS FOOD

Look for: Firm, round, or pear-shape fruit with a pale-yellow, fuzzy skin.

Avoid: Small, knobby fruit or fruit with bruised skin.

STORING THIS FOOD

Store quinces in the refrigerator and use them within two weeks.

PREPARING THIS FOOD

Wash the quince under cold running water, wipe off the fuzz, cut off the stem and the blossom ends, core the fruit, and bake or stew it.

WHAT HAPPENS WHEN YOU COOK THIS FOOD

When you cook a quince, heat and the acids in the fruit convert the quince's colorless leucoanthocyanin pigments to red anthocyanins, turning its flesh from pale yellow to pink or red. Cooking also tranforms the raw quince's strong, unpleasant, astringent taste to a more mellow flavor, halfway between that of an apple and a pear.

HOW OTHER FORMS OF PROCESSING AFFECT THIS FOOD

*   *   *

MEDICAL USES AND/OR BENEFITS

To reduce levels of serum cholesterol.   Quinces, like apples, are very high in pectins that seem to lower the amount of cholesterol in the blood and offer some protection against heart disease. There are currently two theories to explain how this may happen. The first theory is that the pectins in the fruit form a gel in your stomach that sops up fats and keeps them from being absorbed by your body. The second is that bacteria in the gut feed on the fiber, producing short-chain fatty acids that inhibit the production of cholesterol in your liver.

ADVERSE EFFECTS ASSOCIATED WITH THIS FOOD

*   *   *

FOOD/DRUG INTERACTIONS

*   *   *

RADISHES
(Daikon, horseradish)

NUTRITIONAL PROFILE

Energy value (calories per serving):	Low
Protein:	High
Fat:	Low
Cholesterol:	None
Carbohydrates:	High
Fiber:	Low
Sodium:	Low
Major vitamin contribution:	Vitamin C
Major mineral contribution:	Iron, potassium

ABOUT THE NUTRIENTS IN THIS FOOD

Radishes are roots, members of the cabbage family. They have moderate amounts of starch and sugar. All varieties of radish—the daikon, the common red "eating" radish, and the horseradish—are excellent sources of vitamin C. Ounce for ounce, they have about 42 percent as much vitamin C as fresh oranges. (Radishes have about 7 mg of vitamin C per ounce compared to about 15 mg per ounce in a fresh orange.)

THE MOST NUTRITIOUS WAY TO SERVE THIS FOOD

Fresh, crisp red or daikon radishes; freshly grated fresh horseradish or recently opened prepared horseradish.

DIETS THAT MAY RESTRICT OR EXCLUDE THIS FOOD
Antiflatulence diet
Sucrose-free diet

BUYING THIS FOOD
Look for: Firm, well-shaped radishes. The skin should be clear, clean, and free of blemishes. If there are green tops on the radish, they should be crisp and fresh. If you are buying radishes in plastic bags, check them carefully through the plastic to see that they are free of mold.

Avoid: Misshapen radishes, spongy radishes, or radishes with soft spots (which suggest decay or discoloration underneath), and withered or dry radishes (they have lost vitamin C, which is sensitive to oxygen).

STORING THIS FOOD
Cut off any green tops and refrigerate fresh radishes in plastic bags to keep them from drying out.

PREPARING THIS FOOD
Scrub the radishes under cold running water. Cut off the tops and the roots. Don't slice or grate radishes until you are ready to use them. When you cut into a radish, you tear its cells, releasing moisture—which converts an otherwise mild chemical called sinigrin into an irritant mustard oil that gives radishes their hot taste.

WHAT HAPPENS WHEN YOU COOK THIS FOOD
*   *   *

HOW OTHER KINDS OF PROCESSING AFFECT THIS FOOD
Prepared horseradish.   Prepared horseradish should be used within a few weeks after you open the bottle. The longer it is exposed to air, the more bitter (rather than spicy) its mustard oils will be.

MEDICAL USES AND/OR BENEFITS
Protection against some forms of cancer.   According to the American Cancer Society, epidemiological studies suggest that cruciferous vegetables (including radishes) may contain natural substances that lower the risk of some cancers of the gastrointestinal and respiratory tracts, including chemically induced cancers such as the tumors caused by cigarette smoking or exposure to chemicals in the workplace.

ADVERSE EFFECTS ASSOCIATED WITH THIS FOOD

Enlarged thyroid gland (goiter).   Cruciferous vegetables, including radishes, contain goitrin, thiocyanate, and isothiocyanate. These chemicals, known collectively as goitrogens, inhibit the formation of thyroid hormones and cause the thyroid to enlarge in an attempt to produce more. Goitrogens are not hazardous for healthy people who eat moderate amounts of cruciferous vegetables, but they may pose problems for people who have a thyroid disorder.

FOOD/DRUG INTERACTIONS

False-positive test for occult blood in the stool.   The active ingredient in the guaiac slide test for hidden blood in feces, alphaguaiaconic acid, a chemical that turns blue in the presence of blood. Alphaguaiaconic acid also turns blue in the presence of peroxidase, a chemical that occurs naturally in radishes. Eating radishes in the 72 hours before taking the guaiac test may produce a false-positive result in people who do not actually have any blood in their stool.

RAISINS

("Currants")
See also GRAPES

NUTRITIONAL PROFILE

Energy value (calories per serving):	High
Protein:	Low
Fat:	Low
Cholesterol:	None
Carbohydrates:	High
Fiber:	High
Sodium:	Low (fresh or dried fruit) High (dried fruit treated with sodium sulfur compounds)
Major vitamin contribution:	B vitamins
Major mineral contribution:	Iron, potassium

ABOUT THE NUTRIENTS IN THIS FOOD

Raisins with seeds you can actually taste are dried Muscat grapes. Raisins dried from Thompson grapes have tiny seeds that are almost imperceptible. Raisins dried from Sultana grapes have no seeds at all. "Currants" are *not* dried currants; they are dried, dark-skinned black Corinth grapes.

All raisins are high-carbohydrate food, extraordinarily rich in sugars with no starch at all. They are also rich in food fiber, primarily gums, pectins, and hemicellulose. Raisins have some proteins and a little fat.

Raisins are a good source of B vitamins and potassium, but they have virtually no vitamin C. This vitamin, which is oxygen-sensitive, disappears when the raisins are dried. Raisins are also rich in non-heme iron, the inorganic form of iron found in plant foods. Ounce for ounce, seedless raisins have as much iron as cooked hamburger and nearly one-third the iron in cooked liver.

THE MOST NUTRITIOUS WAY TO SERVE THIS FOOD

With meat or with a food rich in vitamin C. Non-heme iron is five times less available to the body than heme iron, the organic form of iron found in meat, fish, poultry, milk, and eggs. Eating raisins with meat or vitamin C increases the amount you absorb because meat increases the secretion of stomach acid (iron is more easily absorbed in an acid environment), while vitamin C may change iron from ferric iron (which is hard for your body to absorb) to ferrous iron (which your body absorbs more easily).

DIETS THAT MAY RESTRICT OR EXCLUDE THIS FOOD

Low-fiber diet
Sucrose-free diet

BUYING THIS FOOD

Look for: Tightly sealed packages that protect the raisins from air (which will make them dry and hard) and insects.

STORING THIS FOOD

Store sealed packages of raisins in a cool, dark cabinet, where they may stay fresh for as long as a year. Once the package is opened, the raisins should be stored in an air- and moistureproof container at room temperature and used within a few months. Check periodically for mold or insect infestation.

PREPARING THIS FOOD

To use raisins in a bread or cake, "plump" them first by soaking them in water (or wine, rum, or brandy for a fruit cake) for about fifteen minutes. Otherwise the raisins will be hard and dry when the cake or bread is baked.

WHAT HAPPENS WHEN YOU COOK THIS FOOD

If you cook raisins in water, their pectins and gum will dissolve and the raisins will soften. They will also absorb liquids and swell up. Cook them long enough and the water will leak out again, allowing the raisins to collapse.

HOW OTHER KINDS OF PROCESSING AFFECT THIS FOOD

*   *   *

MEDICAL USES AND/OR BENEFITS

Iron supplementation. See *About the nutrients,* above.

ADVERSE REACTIONS ASSOCIATED WITH THIS FOOD

Cavities.   Raisins contain large amounts of fermentable, sticky sugars. According to a 1985 study in the *Journal of the American Dental Association,* raisins are one of the snack foods most likely to support the growth of the bacteria that cause cavities, but you can reduce the risk by brushing thoroughly after eating raisins.

Sulfite allergies.   To keep light grapes from drying to a dark-brown color, the grapes are treated with sulfites such as sulfur dioxide. People who are sensitive to sulfite may experience serious allergic reactions, including potentially fatal anaphylactic shock, if they eat raisins treated with sulfites.

FOOD/DRUG INTERACTIONS

MAO inhibitors.   Monoamine oxidase (MAO) inhibitors are drugs used as antidepressants or antihypertensives. They inhibit the action of natural enzymes that break down tyramine so that that it can be eliminated from the body. Tyramine is a pressor amine, a chemical that constricts blood vessels and raises blood pressure. Tyramine, a natural by-product of protein metabolism, occurs naturally in many foods, particularly fermented or aged foods. If you eat a food rich in tyramine while you are taking an MAO inhibitor, the pressor amines cannot be efficiently eliminated from your body and the result may be a hypertensive crisis (sustained elevated blood pressure). There has been one report of an adverse side effect (severe headache) in a patient who ate two small packages of dark raisins while using an MAO inhibitor.

RHUBARB

NUTRITIONAL PROFILE

Energy value
(calories per serving): Low

Protein: Low

Fat: Low

Cholesterol: None

Carbohydrates: High

Fiber: Low

Sodium: Low

Major vitamin
contribution: Vitamins C and A

Major mineral
contribution: Potassium

ABOUT THE NUTRIENTS IN THIS FOOD

Despite its crunchy stringiness, rhubarb provides only small amounts of fiber, including the insoluble cellulose and lignin in the stiff cells of its stalk and "strings" and the soluble pectins in the flesh. Rhubarb has some sugar, no starch, and only a trace of protein and fat.

Rhubarb is a moderately good source of vitamin C; a 3.5-ounce serving of cooked frozen rhubarb with sugar added has 3.3 mg vitamin C, 5 percent of the RDA for a healthy adult. It has some calcium, but oxalic acid (one of the natural chemicals that gives rhubarb its astringent flavor) binds the calcium into calcium oxalate, an insoluble compound your body cannot absorb.

Rhubarb also contains astringent tannins and phenols that coagulate proteins on the surface of the mucous membrane lining of your mouth, which is why your mouth puckers when you eat rhubarb. Tannins, which are also found in tea, red wines, and many unripe fruits, may be constipating.

THE MOST NUTRITIOUS WAY TO SERVE THIS FOOD

Cooked. Only the stalks of the rhubarb are used as food; *the leaves are poisonous, whether raw or cooked.*

DIETS THAT MAY RESTRICT OR EXCLUDE THIS FOOD

Low-oxalate diet (for people who form calcium oxalate kidney stones)
Sucrose-free diet

BUYING THIS FOOD

Look for: Crisp, bright, fresh stalks of rhubarb. Although color is not necessarily a guide to quality, the deeper the red, the more flavorful the stalks are likely to be. The medium-size stalks are generally more tender than large ones, which, like large stalks of celery, may be stringy.

STORING THIS FOOD

Wrap rhubarb in plastic and store it in the refrigerator to keep cool and humid. Rhubarb is fairly perishable; use it within a few days after you buy it.

PREPARING THIS FOOD

Remove and discard all leaves on the rhubarb stalk. *Rhubarb leaves are not edible; they are poisonous, raw or cooked.*

Wash the rhubarb under cool running water. Trim the end and cut off any discolored parts. If the stalks are tough, peel them to get rid of hard "strings." (Most of the rhubarb we buy is grown in hothouses and bred to have a thin skin that doesn't have to be peeled.)

WHAT HAPPENS WHEN YOU COOK THIS FOOD

Rhubarb is colored with red anthocyanin pigments that turn redder in acid and turn bluish in bases (alkalis) and brownish if you cook them with sugar at very high heat. If you cook rhubarb in an aluminum or iron pot, metal ions flaking off the pot will interact with acids in the fruit to form brown compounds that darken both the pot and the rhubarb.

HOW OTHER KINDS OF PROCESSING AFFECT THIS FOOD

*   *   *

MEDICAL USES AND/OR BENEFITS

*   *   *

ADVERSE EFFECTS ASSOCIATED WITH THIS FOOD

Kidney stones.   More than 50 percent of all kidney stones are composed of calcium oxalate or calcium oxalate plus phosphate. People with a metabolic disorder that leads them to excrete large amounts of oxalates in their urine or who have had ileal disease or who eat large amounts of foods high in oxalic acid are the ones most likely to form these stones. Rhubarb, like beets, cocoa, nuts, parsley, spinach, and tea, is high in oxalic acid.

FOOD/DRUG INTERACTIONS

   *   *   *

RICE
(Wild rice)

NUTRITIONAL PROFILE

Energy value (calories per serving):	Moderate
Protein:	Moderate
Fat:	Low
Cholesterol:	None
Carbohydrates:	High
Fiber:	Low
Sodium:	Low*
Major vitamin contribution:	B vitamins
Major mineral contribution:	Iron, calcium

ABOUT THE NUTRIENTS IN THIS FOOD

Brown rice is rice that retains its outer bran and its germ. *White rice* has been milled to remove the bran and germ. *Wild rice* is not a true member of the rice family but the seed of a native American grass. Since it is expensive to gather and mill, wild rice is usually mixed with white rice to make it more economical.

All rice is high-carbohydrate food, rich in starch, with some of all the carbohydrate food fibers (cellulose, hemicellulose, pectins, and gums). Brown rice, which still has its bran, also has the noncarbohydrate food fiber lignin, found in stems, leaves, and seed coverings.

*Dry, uncooked rice is low in sodium. Cooked rice has absorbed liquid; its sodium content depends on the sodium content of the liquid in which it's cooked.

The proteins in rice are considered "incomplete" because they are limited in the essential amino acids lysine and isoleucine. White rice has only a trace of fat. Brown rice, with its fatty germ, gets 4 percent of its calories from fat. There is no cholesterol in rice.

Brown rice has more vitamins and minerals than plain milled white rice, but enriched white rice may have even more nutrients than the natural brown product. All rice is a good source of B vitamins, and it is rich in calcium and non-heme iron, the inorganic form of iron found in plant foods. However, since rice (like other grains) contains phytic acids that bind its iron and calcium into insoluble compounds, it is not necessarily a good source of these minerals.

THE MOST NUTRITIOUS WAY TO SERVE THIS FOOD

With legumes (beans, peas). The proteins in rice are deficient in the essential amino acids lysine and isoleucine and rich in the essential amino acids tryptophan, methionine, and cystine. The proteins in legumes are exactly the opposite. Combining the two foods in one dish "complements" or "completes" their proteins.

With meat or a food rich in vitamin C (tomatoes, peppers). Both will increase the availability of the iron in the rice. Meat increases the secretion of stomach acids (iron is absorbed better in an acid environment); vitamin C changes the iron in the rice from ferric iron (which is hard to absorb) to ferrous iron (which is easier to absorb).

DIETS THAT MAY RESTRICT OR EXCLUDE THIS FOOD

Low-calcium diet (brown rice, wild rice)
Low-fiber diet
Sucrose-free diet

BUYING THIS FOOD

Look for: Tightly sealed packages that protect the rice from air and moisture, which can oxidize the fats in the rice and turn them rancid.

Choose the rice that meets your needs. *Long-grain rice,* which has less starch than *short-grain* ("Oriental") rice, will be fluffier and less sticky when cooked. *Brown rice* has a distinctive nutty taste that can overwhelm delicate foods or "fight" with other strong flavors.

Avoid: Stained boxes of rice, even if they are still sealed. Whatever spilled on the box may have seeped through the cardboard onto the rice inside.

STORING THIS FOOD

Store rice in air- and moistureproof containers in a cool, dark cabinet to keep it dry and protect its fats from oxygen. White rice may stay fresh for as long as a year. Brown rice, which retains its bran and germ and thus has more fats than white rice, may stay fresh for only a few months before its fats (inevitably) oxidize. All rice spoils more quickly in hot, humid weather. Aging or rancid rice usually has a distinctive stale and musty odor.

PREPARING THIS FOOD

Should you wash rice before you cook it? Yes, if you are preparing wild rice, imported rice, or rice purchased in bulk. No, if you are preparing prepacked white or brown rice.

You wash wild rice and bulk rices to flush away debris and/or insects. You wash imported rices to rinse off the cereal or corn-syrup coating. You should pick over brown and white rices to catch the occasional pebble or stone, but washing is either worthless or detrimental.

Washing brown rice has no effect one way or the other. Since the grains are protected by their bran, the water will not flush away either starches or nutrients. Washing long-grain white rices, however, will rinse away some of the starch on the surface, which can be a plus if you want the rice to be as fluffy as possible. The down side is that washing the rice will also rinse away any nutrients remaining on plain milled rice and dissolve the starch/nutrient coating on enriched rices. Washing the starches off short-grain, Oriental rices will make the rice uncharacteristically dry rather than sticky.

WHAT HAPPENS WHEN YOU COOK THIS FOOD

Starch consists of molecules of the complex carbohydrates amylose and amylopectin packed into a starch granule. When you cook rice, the starch granules absorb water molecules. When the temperature of the water reaches approximately 140° F, the amylose and amylopectin molecules inside the starch granules relax and unfold, breaking some of their internal bonds (bonds between atoms on the same molecule) and forming new bonds between atoms on different molecules. The result is a starch network of starch molecules that traps and holds water molecules, making the starch granules even more bulky. In fact, rice holds so much water that it will double or even triple in bulk when cooked.*

If you continue to cook the rice, the starch granules will eventually break open, the liquid inside will leak out, the walls of the granules will collapse, and the rice will turn soft and mushy. At the same time, amylose and amylopectin molecules escaping from the granules will make the outside of the rice sticky—the reason why overcooked rice clumps together.

---

*Cooking rice in liquids other than water (tomato juice, bouillon, wine) keeps the rice firmer, since the grains will absorb solids along with water.

There are several ways to keep rice from clumping when you cook it. First, you can cook the rice in so much water that the grains have room to boil without bumping into each other, but you will lose B vitamins when you drain the excess water from the rice. Second, you can sauté the rice before you boil it or add a little fat to the boiling liquid. Theoretically, this should make the outside of the grains slick enough to slide off each other. But this method raises the fat content of the rice—with no guarantee that it will really keep the rice from clumping. The best method is to cook the rice in just as much water as it can absorb without rupturing its starch granules and remove the rice from the heat as soon as the water is almost all absorbed. Fluff the cooked rice with a fork as it is cooling, to separate the grains.

HOW OTHER KINDS OF PROCESSING AFFECT THIS FOOD

"Converted" rice. "Converted" rice is rice that is parboiled under pressure before it is milled. This process drives the vitamins and minerals into the grain and loosens the bran so that it slips off easily when the rice is milled. Converted rice retains more vitamins and minerals than conventionally milled white rice.

"Quick-cooking" rice. This is rice that has been cooked and dehydrated. Its hard, starchy outer covering and its starch granules have already been broken so it will reabsorb water almost instantly when you cook it.

MEDICAL USES AND/OR BENEFITS

To soothe irritated skin. Like corn starch or potato starch, powdered rice used as a dusting powder or stirred into the bath water may soothe and dry a "wet" skin rash. It is so drying, however, that it should *never* be used on a dry skin rash or on any rash without a doctor's advice.

As a substitute for wheat flour in a gluten-free diet. People with celiac disease have an inherited metabolic disorder which makes it impossible for them to digest gluten and gliadin, proteins found in wheat and some other grains. Rice and rice flour, which are free of gluten and gliadin, may be a useful substitute in some recipes.

ADVERSE EFFECTS ASSOCIATED WITH THIS FOOD

Beri-beri. Beri-beri is the thiamin (vitamin B_1)-deficiency disease. Beri-beri, which is rare today, occurs among people for whom milled white rice, stripped of its B vitamins, is a dietary mainstay. Enriching the rice prevents beri-beri.

Mold toxins.   Rice, like other grains, may support the growth of toxic molds, including *Aspergillus flavus,* which produces carcinogenic aflatoxins. Other toxins found on moldy rice include citrinin, a penicillium mold too toxic to be used as an antibiotic; rubratoxins, mold products known to cause hemorrhages in animals who eat the moldy rice; and nivalenol, a mold toxin that suppresses DNA and protein synthesis in cells. Because mold may turn the rice yellow, moldy rice is also known as yellow rice.

FOOD/DRUG INTERACTIONS
*   *   *

SAUSAGE

See also BEEF, LAMB, LIVER, PORK, POULTRY

NUTRITIONAL PROFILE

Energy value (calories per serving):	Moderate to high
Protein:	Moderate to high
Fat:	High
Cholesterol:	Moderate to high
Carbohydrates:	Low
Fiber:	None
Sodium:	High
Major vitamin contribution:	Thiamin (vitamin B_1), niacin, vitamin B_6
Major mineral contribution:	Iron, phosphorus

ABOUT THE NUTRIENTS IN THIS FOOD

Like other meat, sausage contains proteins considered "complete" because they contain adequate amounts of all the essential amino acids. But sausage is higher in fat and thus proportionally lower in protein than beef, veal, lamb, pork, or poultry. The composition of the fat (its ratio of saturated to unsaturated fatty acids) varies according to the meat used to make the sausage.

All sausage, like all meat, contains B vitamins and heme iron, the organic form of iron found in meat, fish, poultry, milk, and eggs. Liver sausage, like liver, has vitamin A and iron.

Prepared sausages are preserved with sodium nitrate and sodium nitrite, which protect the sausage meat from botulinum contamination and keep it red (but see *Adverse effects associated with this food,* below). Vitamin

C, which interferes with the chemical transformation of these preservatives into nitrosamines, is preserved in the form of added sodium ascorbate or sodium erythorbate.

Sausages may also contain a number of "hidden ingredients," that can trigger allergic reactions in sensitive individuals. Among these are coloring agents, hydrolyzed vegetable protein, gums, milk proteins, soy proteins, and sweeteners (sugars and corn syrup).

The Food and Drug Administration has established standards that determine what ingredients may be included in sausages. The following table shows the requirements for several kinds of popular sausages:

COMPARING SAUSAGE PRODUCTS: FDA STANDARDS

Beef sausage	No more than 30% fat, no by-products, no extenders, and no more than 3% added water.
Breakfast sausage	No more than 50% fat. May contain 3.5% binders/extenders and 3% added water.
Brown-and-serve sausage	No more than 35% fat; no more than 10% added water.
Frankfurter or bologna	Only skeletal meat. No more than 30% fat, 10% added water, 2% corn syrup. No more than 15% poultry meat. Frankfurters with by-products must contain at least 15% skeletal meat; frankfurters with binders may contain 3.5% nonmeat binders or 2% soy protein.
Liverwurst or liver sausage	Must contain at least 30% liver.
Pork sausage	May not contain any by-products or extenders; no more than 50% fat or 3% added water.

Source: "Meat and Poultry Products," Home and Garden Bulletin No. 236 (USDA, 1981).

THE MOST NUTRITIOUS WAY TO SERVE THIS FOOD

In moderation. For example, adding a moderate amount of sausage to a casserole with beans combines a high-fat, low-fiber meat with high-fiber, low-fat beans and allows you to enjoy the sausage's taste while using its "complete" proteins to complement the tryptophan, methionine, and cystine-limited proteins in the beans.

DIETS THAT MAY RESTRICT OR EXCLUDE THIS FOOD

Controlled-fat, low-cholesterol diet
Lactose-free diet
Low-protein diet
Low-sodium diet
Low-purine diet (liverwurst, liver sausages)
Sucrose-free diet

BUYING THIS FOOD

Look for: Fresh sausage that meets the test for any fresh meat: it should look fresh—not gray or brown or dry. Pick packaged sausage by the date on the package and the ingredient label. Check for "hidden ingredients."

STORING THIS FOOD

Refrigerate all sausages. *Fresh* (raw) *sausages* and *uncooked smoked sausages,* which are highly perishable, should be wrapped carefully to keep them from dripping and contaminating the refrigerator shelves or other foods and used within two or three days (or according to the directions on the package). Whole *cooked sausages* and *cooked smoked sausages* such as frankfurters, bologna, liverwurst, and salami may stay fresh for five or six days in the refrigerator. (Unopened packages may have a shelf life of weeks or months; check the label.) Whole *dry sausages* such as pepperoni, chorizo, and mortadella may keep months in the refrigerator, but when sliced these sausages spoil more quickly. All should be wrapped in plastic to keep others foods from absorbing their strong odors.

PREPARING THIS FOOD

If you are using fresh pork sausage, *always* wash all surfaces, utensils, and your hands with hot soapy water once you're done to keep from contaminating other foods with any microorganisms (including *Trichina spiralis)* from the raw pork. *Never* taste any raw pork sausage.

WHAT HAPPENS WHEN YOU COOK THIS FOOD

Cooking sausage changes its flavor, reduces its fat content, and makes raw sausage safer by killing any pathogenic microorganisms, including those that cause trichinosis.

Browning the sausage caramelizes proteins and sugars on the surface of the meat, giving the sausage a richer flavor. At the same time, browning breaks up protein molecules, making them less valuable nutritionally. As the sausage cooks, it loses moisture and shrinks. Its pigments, which combine with oxygen, are denatured (broken into smaller fragments) by the heat and turn brown, the natural color of cooked meat.

HOW OTHER KINDS OF PROCESSING AFFECT THIS FOOD
*   *   *

MEDICAL USES AND/OR BENEFITS
*   *   *

ADVERSE REACTIONS ASSOCIATED WITH THIS FOOD

Elevated levels of serum cholesterol.   Abnormally high levels of cholesterol in the blood are a risk factor in heart disease. How your diet affects the amount of cholesterol you produce is not entirely clear; dietary fat and cholesterol may not be the primary factor in determining how much and what kind of cholesterol your body makes and stores. Nonetheless, there is evidence to suggest that controlling the amount of fat and cholesterol you consume may help lower serum cholesterol levels, particularly for people with high levels. In 1986 the American Heart Association issued new guidelines, suggesting that healthy adults reduce their consumption of fat to 30 percent of their total daily calories and limit cholesterol intake to 300 mg per day or 100 mg per 1000 calories, whichever is less. A 3.5 oz. (100 gram) serving of dried or cooked fresh or canned beef or pork sausage may contain 50-186 mg cholesterol.

Allergy to milk proteins and/or lactose intolerance.   Milk proteins or lactose (milk sugar) are present in sausages that contain nonfat milk solids as binders, extenders, or sweeteners. Milk proteins or sugars may cause upset stomach or other reactions in people sensitive to the proteins or unable to digest lactose (see MILK).

Allergic reactions to coloring agents.   Some sausage casings may contain color additives. For the most part, these additives do not have to be listed by name on the label; they can be described simply as "artificial colors" or "natural colors." Only one, FD&C Yellow No. 5 (tartrazine), must be listed by name. Tartrazine is a known allergen that may trigger severe sensitivity reactions in people with asthma who are sensitive to aspirin.

Production of uric acid.   Purines are the natural metabolic by-products of protein metabolism in the body. They eventually break down into uric acid, which may form sharp crystals that may cause gout if they collect in your joints or kidney stones if they collect in urine. Sausages made with liver are a source of purines; eating them raises the concentration of purines in your body. Although controlling the amount of purine-producing foods in the diet may not significantly affect the course of gout (which is treated with medication such as allopurinol, which inhibits the formation of uric acid), many gout regimens still include a diet that limits the intake of purines.

MAO inhibitors.   Monoamine oxidase (MAO) inhibitors are drugs used as antidepressants or antihypertensives. They inhibit the action of natural enzymes that break down tyramine, a natural by-product of protein metabolism. Tyramine, which is also formed when protein foods are fermented or pickled, is a pressor amine, a chemical that constricts blood vessels and raises blood pressure. If you eat foods high in tyramine while you are taking an MAO inhibitor, the pressor amine cannot be eliminated from your body and the result may be a hypertensive crisis (sustained elevated blood pressure). Fermented sausages are high in tyramine.

FOOD/DRUG INTERACTIONS
*   *   *

SHELLFISH

(Abalone, clams, conch, crabs, crayfish, lobster, mussels, oysters, prawns, scallops, shrimp, snails)

NUTRITIONAL PROFILE*

Energy value (calories per serving):	Moderate
Protein:	High
Fat:	Low
Cholesterol:	Moderate to high
Carbohydrates:	Trace
Fiber:	None
Sodium:	Moderate to high
Major vitamin contribution:	B vitamins
Major mineral contribution:	Iron (clams), iodine, copper, zinc (oysters), arsenic

ABOUT THE NUTRIENTS IN THIS FOOD

Shellfish are an excellent source of high-quality proteins that are considered "complete" because they contain sufficient amounts of all the essential amino acids. Shellfish are relatively low in fat. Like other saltwater seafood, they contain omega-3 fatty acids, which appear to offer some protection against a variety of inflammatory conditions. Unlike other seafood, shellfish are relatively high in cholesterol.

All shellfish are a good source of B vitamins and heme iron, the organic form of iron found in meat, fish, poultry, milk, and eggs.

*Values are for raw or steamed shell fish.

IRON CONTENT OF SHELLFISH
(mg/100 grams)

Clams	3.4-7.5 mg
Crab	0.8 mg
Lobster	0.6-0.9 mg
Mussels	3.4 mg
Oysters	5.5-8.1 mg
Scallop	1.5 mg
Snails	3.5 mg

Source: Watt, Bernice K., and Merrill, An-nabel L., *Composition of Foods,* Agriculture Handbook No. 8 (USDA, 1975).

Shellfish are also a good source of the trace minerals copper, iodine, and zinc.

THE MOST NUTRITIOUS WAY TO SERVE THIS FOOD

Thoroughly cooked, to take advantage of the nutrients while destroying any potentially hazardous microorganisms.

DIETS THAT MAY RESTRICT OR EXCLUDE THIS FOOD

Controlled-fat, low-cholesterol diet
Low-protein diet
Low-sodium diet

BUYING THIS FOOD

Look for: Clams, mussels, and oysters shucked or live in the shell. Live clams, mussels, and oysters should be tightly shut or close with a snap when you touch them. Shucked clams, mussels, and oysters should be plump and shiny and smell absolutely fresh. There should be very little liquid in the container.

Choose live crabs that are actively moving their legs around. Lump crab-meat should be pink and white (not tan or yellowed), and it should smell absolutely fresh, as should cooked crabs.

Choose live lobsters and crayfish that look fresh, smell good, and are moving about actively. American lobsters come in four sizes: chicken (¾-1 lb.), quarter (1.25 lb.), large (1.5-2.25 lbs.), and jumbo (over 2.5 lbs.). Cooked lobsters should have a bright-red shell and a fresh aroma. If the tail curls back when you pull it down, the lobster was alive when cooked. Female lobsters, which have fluffy fins ("swimmerettes") at the juncture of tail and body, may contain roe or coral that turns red when you cook the lobster.

Choose dry, creamy, sweet-smelling scallops; unlike clams, oysters, and mussels, they can't be kept alive out of the water. Sea scallops, the large ones, may be sold fresh or frozen; bay scallops, the smaller shellfish, are usually only sold fresh.

Choose fresh shrimp and prawns that look dry and firm in the shell.

Choose tightly sealed cans of snails.

NOTE: Because of the possibility of industrial and microbial contamination of waters, live shellfish should be gathered only in waters certified by local health authorities.

STORING THIS FOOD

Refrigerate all shellfish and use as quickly as possible. Like other seafood, shellfish are extremely perishable once they are no longer alive, and their fats, which are higher in unsaturated than saturated fatty acids, will oxidize and turn rancid fairly quickly. As a general rule, live clams in the shell may keep for up to two weeks, oysters in the shell for five days, shelled scallops for a day or two, and mussels should be used the day you buy them. Regardless of these estimates, *check the shellfish frequently to see that it is still alive and unspoiled.*

Cook live crabs, crayfish, and lobsters before storing to prolong their storage time. Shrimps and prawns will also stay fresh longer if you cook them before storing them. *Check frequently to see that the shellfish are still fresh.*

PREPARING THIS FOOD

When you are ready to prepare shellfish, sniff them first. If they don't smell absolutely fresh, throw them out.

Abalone.   Tenderize the abalone meat by pounding, then trim off any dark part, and slice the fish against the grain.*

Clams.   All clams are sandy when you bring them home. To get rid of the grit, wash the closed clams thoroughly under cold running water. Then either immerse them in a salty solution (about ⅓ cup salt to a gallon of water) or sprinkle them with cornmeal and cover them with water. Refrigerate the clams. They will take in the salt water (or cornmeal) and disgorge sand.

*Some abalone are all black. Check with your fish market.

Clams covered with salt water will be clean in about half an hour, clams covered with cornmeal in about three hours. Before serving or cooking, *discard any clams that are open or do not close immediately when you touch them or remain closed or float in the water.*

Conch.   Steam the conch or crack its shell. Open the shell and pull out the meat. Cut away and discard the stomach (it's right in the middle) and the dark tail. Peel off the skin, slice the meat thin, and pound it to tenderize the meat. Rinse, pat dry, and cook.

Crabs.   To clean *hard-shell crabs,* cook them first. Then plunge the hot crabs into cold water to firm up the meat. Remove the tail, snap off the claws, and pull off the shell. Cut away the gills and the digestive organs in the middle of the body and pull the meat away from the skeleton. *Soft-shell crabs* should be washed in cold water. They are ready to cook when you buy them.

Lobsters and crayfish (live).   If you plan to boil the lobsters, you can cook them just as they come from the store. If you plan to broil a lobster, kill it first by inserting a knife into the space between the head and the body and slicing through the crustacean's spinal cord. Then split the lobster and remove the internal organs. Live crayfish that have been stored in fresh running water do not have to be eviscerated before you boil them. If you wish to eviscerate the crayfish, grasp the middle fin on the tail, twist, and pull hard to pull out the stomach and intestine.

Mussels.   In the shell, mussels, like clams, are apt to be sandy. To get rid of the grit, scrub the mussels under cold running water, then put them in a pot of cold water and let them stand for an hour or two. Discard any that float to the top. Rinse the rest once more under cold running water, trim the "beard" with scissors, and prepare as your recipe directs.

Oysters.   Unlike clams and mussels, oysters in the shell are free of sand when you buy them. To prepare them, just wash the oysters thoroughly under cold running water. Discard any that don't close tight when you touch them or that float in water. Cook them in the shell or pry open the shell, strain the liquid for any stray grit, and use the oysters with or without the shell, as you recipe directs.

Scallops.   Shelled scallops in bulk should be relatively free of liquid. Rinse them in cold running water and use as your recipe directs.

Shrimp and prawns.   Wash the shrimp or prawns in cold running water. Then cook them in the shell to enhance the flavor of a soup or stew, or peel off the shell and remove the black "vein" (actually the digestive tract) running down the back, and prepare the shellfish as your recipe directs. (The orange line sometimes found running alongside the "vein" is edible roe.)

Snails (canned).   Prepare as your recipe directs.

WHAT HAPPENS WHEN YOU COOK THIS FOOD

When you cook shellfish, heat changes the structure of its proteins. The protein molecules are "denatured," which means they may break apart into smaller fragments, change shape, or clump together. All these changes force moisture out of protein tissues, making the shellfish opaque. The loss of moisture also changes the texture of the shellfish; the longer they are cooked, the more rubbery they will become. Shellfish should be cooked long enough to turn the flesh opaque and destroy any microorganisms living on the food.

HOW OTHER KINDS OF PROCESSING AFFECT THIS FOOD

Freezing.   When you freeze shellfish, the water in their cells forms ice crystals that can tear the cell membranes so the liquids inside leak out when the shellfish is defrosted—which is the reason defrosted shellfish tastes tougher and has less B vitamins than fresh shellfish. Defrosting the shellfish slowly, in the refrigerator, lessens the loss of moisture and B vitamins. Frozen shrimp and prawns can be boiled whole, in the shells, without defrosting.

Canning.   Canning prolongs the shelf life of shellfish. Virtually all canned shellfish is higher in sodium than fresh shellfish. To reduce the sodium content, rinse the shellfish in cold water before you use it.

MEDICAL USES AND/OR BENEFITS

Protective effects of omega-3 fatty acids.   Like other saltwater seafood, shellfish contain omega-3 fatty acids. In 1985 the *New England Journal of Medicine* published the results of three separate studies dealing with the anti-inflammatory effects of a diet rich in these fats.

The first study, a twenty-year project at the University of Leyden in the Netherlands, compared the eating habits of more than 800 men at risk for heart disease and found that men who ate more than an ounce of fish a day had a 50 percent lower rate of heart attacks. (Research at Cornell University has suggested that oils inhibit the formation of thromboxane, a chemical that causes red blood cells to clump together, and that omega-3 fatty acids are converted to a compound similar to prostacyclin, a natural body chemical that inhibits clotting.)

The second study, at the Oregon Health Sciences University in Portland, found that a diet high in fish oils appears to lower the levels of triglycerides in the blood. (A high level of triglycerides, like a high level of cholesterol, increases the risk of heart disease.)

In the third study, seven volunteers at Brigham and Women's Hospital in Boston were put on a diet high in fats from saltwater fish. At the end of six weeks the researchers found that fish oils seemed to reduce the anti-inflammatory response in body tissues, perhaps by inhibiting the production of leuketrienes, the natural inflammatory agents that trigger a wide range of inflammatory diseases ranging from arthritis to hay fever.

This last study is bolstered by research at the University of Michigan which suggests that fish, like vegetables, fruit, and grain, appears to interfere with the body's production of arachidonic acid (AA), a natural inflammatory agent that makes psoriatic lesions swell and turn red.

As a source of calcium.   Ground oyster shells, which are rich in calcium carbonate, are the calcium source in many over-the-counter supplements. Calcium carbonate is a less efficient source of the mineral than calcium lactate, the form of calcium in milk; it is also likely to cause constipation.

ADVERSE EFFECTS ASSOCIATED WITH THIS FOOD

Allergic reactions.   Shellfish are among the foods most often implicated as the cause of the classic symptoms of food allergy—upset stomach, hives, and angioedema (swelling of the face, lips, and eyes). In addition, shrimp, which are often treated with sulfites to keep them from darkening, may provoke serious allergic reactions, including anaphylactic shock, in people who are sensitive to sulfites.

Elevated levels of serum cholesterol.   Abnormally high levels of cholesterol in the blood are a risk factor in heart disease. How your diet affects the amount of cholesterol you produce is not entirely clear; dietary fat and cholesterol may not be the primary factor in determining how much and what kind of cholesterol your body makes and stores. Nonetheless, there is evidence to suggest that controlling the amount of fat and cholesterol you consume may help lower serum cholesterol levels, particularly for people with high levels. In 1986 the American Heart Association issued new guidelines suggesting that healthy adults cut their consumption of fat to 30 percent of their total calories and limit cholesterol intake to 300 mg per day or 100 mg per 1000 calories, whichever is less.

CHOLESTEROL CONTENT OF SHELLFISH
(mg/100 grams)

Clams	40–65 mg.
Crab (fresh or canned)	60–120 mg.
Lobster	150 mg.
Mussels (raw)	100 mg.
Oysters (raw)	50 mg.
Prawns	200 mg.
Scallops	40 mg.
Shrimp	200 mg.

Source: National Marine Fisheries Service, Northeast Fisheries Center Laboratory, Gloucester, Massachusetts (1986); Paul, A. A., and D. A. T. Southgate (eds.), *McCance and Widdowson's The Composition of Foods,* 4th ed. (London: Her Majesty's Stationers Office, 1978).

"Red Tide" poisoning.   "Red tide" is a blanket of reddish organisms called dinoflagellates that float on the surface of the coastal waters of the Pacific and New England coasts between July and October. The dinoflagellates produce a neurological toxin that can be carried by any shellfish (clams, mussels, oysters) that eat the plankton. The toxin, which cannot be destroyed by cooking, can cause nausea, vomiting, and abdominal cramps, followed by muscle weakness and paralysis. Death may occur due to respiratory failure. These symptoms generally begin to appear within a half-hour after you eat the contaminated shellfish. Other plankton ingested by shellfish may contain a diarrheic poison that causes gastric symptoms once thought to be caused by bacterial or viral food poisoning.

Worms or parasites.   Raw shellfish, like raw meat, may be host to worms, parasites, or their eggs and cysts. These organisms are killed by cooking the shellfish until the flesh is completely opaque.

Shellfish-transmitted infectious diseases.   In the past ten years food scientists have identified an increasing number of bacteria and viruses, including the cholera organism, the hepatitis virus, and *Vibrio vulnificus* in live shellfish.

According to the Food and Drug Administration, *Vibrio cholerae* organisms introduced when wastes are thrown into the ocean are now permanent residents along some parts of the Atlantic and Gulf coasts. *Vibrio cho-*

lerae has been found all the way from Maine to Texas. Cholera-contaminated shrimp and crabs have been found in Louisiana, contaminated blue crabs in Texas, and contaminated oysters in Florida.

Shellfish may pick up the hepatitis B virus from infected waters and transmit it to man. Another shellfish-borne organism, *Vibrio vulnificus,* may cause fever, chills, and shock. The bacterium, which thrives on iron, is a serious hazard for people with hepatitis or cirrhosis of the liver, who release iron into their blood rather than storing it.

While it is true that thoroughly cooking shellfish kills these organisms, the Centers for Disease Control (which advocates cooking all shellfish before you eat it) warns that viruses will survive the customary quick steaming. The CDC further warns that raw shellfish, which pose a potential health hazard for anyone who eats them, are particularly dangerous for people with liver disease, diabetes, chronic gastrointestinal disease, or cancer.

Production of uric acid.   Purines are the natural metabolic by-products of protein metabolism in the body. They eventually break down into uric acid, which may form sharp crystals that may cause gout if they collect in your joints or kidney stones if they collect in urine. Shrimp are a source of purines; eating them raises the concentration of purines in your body. Although controlling the amount of purine-producing foods in the diet may not significantly affect the course of gout (which is treated with medication such as allopurinol, which inhibits the formation of uric acid), limiting these foods is still part of many gout regimens.

FOOD/DRUG INTERACTIONS
*   *   *

SOFT DRINKS

See also SUGAR

NUTRITIONAL PROFILE

Energy value (calories per serving):	Low to moderate
Protein:	None*
Fat:	None
Cholesterol:	None
Carbohydrates:	Moderate
Fiber:	None
Sodium:	Low to high
Major vitamin contribution:	—
Major mineral contribution:	—

ABOUT THE NUTRIENTS IN THIS FOOD

Soft drinks have no carbohydrates other than sugar, no fiber, no proteins,* no fat, no cholesterol, and—unless they are fortified—no vitamins.

"Regular" soft drinks are sweetened with sucrose ("sugar"), fructose, or corn-syrup solids. While fructose and corn-syrup solids are less expensive and more economical for the manufacturer, they are nutritionally the same as sucrose, since all of them eventually break down into units of glucose. Diet sodas contain saccharin or aspartame.+

---

*Under some conditions, aspartame, the artificial sweetener in some diet sodas, breaks down into its constituent compounds, which include the amino acid phenylalanine (see *Adverse effects associated with this food*, below).

+ Saccharin is a weak carcinogen in laboratory animals, but the Food and Drug Administration believes that the small amounts in diet sodas are harmless for human beings.

Some soft drinks are fortified with vitamin C. Some are high in sodium. (*Seltzer* is plain, carbonated water; *club soda* usually contains sodium bicarbonate.) Some contain caffeine. A 12-ounce glass of a soft drink made with caffeine contains approximately 46 mg caffeine, about 42 percent as much as you would get from a cup of drip-brewed coffee. Soft drinks may also contain assorted flavors and colors.

THE MOST NUTRITIOUS WAY TO SERVE THIS FOOD
In moderation.

DIETS THAT MAY RESTRICT OR EXCLUDE THIS FOOD
Antiflatulence diet
Low-sodium diet
Sucrose-free diet

BUYING THIS FOOD
Look for: Tightly sealed bottles and clean, undented cans. Plastic bottles are safer than glass because they can't break if you drop them, but the plastic is air-permeable. Air can pass through it, which means that after long storage carbonated sodas in plastic bottles will eventually begin to lose their sparkle.

STORING THIS FOOD
Store soft drinks in a cool place to protect the ingredients from deteriorating. Cool storage is particularly important for diet sodas sweetened with aspartame. Since sodas are stored for several weeks at high temperatures, the sweetener may break down into its components, aspartic acid, phenylalanine, and methanol. Although aspartame breaks down into these chemicals naturally in your stomach, some scientists suggest that the chemicals may be more difficult for your body to handle if they are already separated before you drink the soda (see *Adverse effects*, below).

PREPARING THIS FOOD
Carbonated soft drinks should be chilled before you serve them. Carbon dioxide, the gas that makes these sodas bubbly, is most soluble at low temperatures and in cold liquids. At warm temperatures and in warm liquids, the carbon dioxide expands and escapes as bubbles. Adding ice cubes to carbonated beverages allows the gas to escape faster because the cubes are sufaces (nucleation sites) on which the gas bubbles can collect. If you add ice cubes to a warm soda, the soda will go flat very quickly.

WHAT HAPPENS WHEN YOU COOK THIS FOOD
Carbonated soft drinks are sometimes used as sweet marinades or basting liq-

uids. When you heat them, the liquid evaporates and the sweet flavoring remains.

HOW OTHER KINDS OF PROCESSING AFFECT THIS FOOD
*   *   *

MEDICAL USES AND/OR BENEFITS
*   *   *

ADVERSE EFFECTS ASSOCIATED WITH THIS FOOD

Adverse effects of aspartame. In your stomach the artificial sweetener aspartame breaks down into its chemical components, aspartic acid, phenylalanine, and methanol. Phenylalanine, an amino acid, then breaks down into tyrosine, another amino acid. Both phenylalanine and tyrosine appear to interfere with the transmission of nerve impulses from one cell to another and some researchers believe that they may trigger changes in mood and behavior, depression, and/or seizures.

Aspartame may also be a problem for children born with phenylketonuria (PKU) and for pregnant women who were PKU infants; people with PKU cannot metabolize phenylalanine. In newborns and infants, the excess phenylalanine in the blood may damage brain cells and cause mental retardation. To prevent this, all newborns are given a simple bood or urine test to detect PKU, and PKU babies are put on a special protective diet low in phenylalanine that is usually maintained throughout childhood. In 1981, researchers at the Children's Medical Center in Boston suggested that women who had been PKU babies should return to a protective diet (which would exclude foods sweetened with aspartame) to avoid developing high blood levels of phenylalanine, which might damage brain cells in a developing fetus.

Caffeine effects.   Soft drinks containing caffeine may produce the same adverse effects as coffee. *See* COFFEE.

FOOD/DRUG INTERACTIONS

Anticoagulants. Quinine, which is an ingredient in tonic water, makes anticoagulants stronger and may trigger bleeding episodes.

Caffeine/drug interactions.   Soft drinks containing caffeine may trigger caffeine/drug interactions. Caffeine increases the secretion of stomach acid and may reduce the effectiveness of cimetidine (Tagamet) and other antiulcer drugs. It may reduce the effectiveness of allopurinol, a xanthine inhibitor used to treat gout. It increases alertness and may reduce the effectiveness of sedatives and tranquilizers.

SOYBEANS

See also BEAN CURD, BEAN SPROUTS

NUTRITIONAL PROFILE

Energy value (calories per serving):	Moderate
Protein:	High
Fat:	Moderate
Cholesterol:	None
Carbohydrates:	Moderate
Fiber:	High
Sodium:	Low
Major vitamin contribution:	B vitamins
Major mineral contribution:	Iron, potassium

ABOUT THE NUTRIENTS IN THIS FOOD

Soybeans are an excellent source of food fiber (cellulose, pectins, gums, and the noncarbohydrate food fiber lignin), starch, and sugars, including the indigestible complex sugars raffinose and stachyose which make beans "gassy" when they are fermented by bacteria in the human gut.

Soybeans are the only beans whose proteins are considered "complete"; they contain more than 100 percent of the dietary requirements of the essential amino acids lysine, methionine and cystine, threonine and tryptophan. One cup of cooked soybeans provides 22 grams of protein, about the amount found in 3 to 3.5 ounces of meat, fish, and poultry.

Unlike other legumes (beans and peas), soybeans store fat as well as starch. The oils in soybeans are primarily unsaturated fatty acids (62 percent polyunsaturated, 23 percent monounsaturated).

Soybeans are a good source of B vitamins, particularly vitamin B_6. They are rich in non-heme iron (the inorganic iron found in plant foods) but, like grains, beans contain phytic acid which binds their iron into insoluble compounds your body cannot absorb. As a result, non-heme iron is five to six times less available to the body than heme iron, the organic form of iron in meat, fish, and poultry.

Raw soybeans contain a number of antinutrients, including enzyme inhibitors (chemicals that interfere with the enzymes that make it possible for us to digest proteins); hemagglutinens (chemicals that make red blood cells clump together); and goitrogens (chemicals that make it hard for the thyroid to absorb iodine, which makes the gland swell in an effort to absorb more iodine; we call the swelling goiter). These chemicals are inactivated by cooking the soybeans.

THE MOST NUTRITIOUS WAY TO SERVE THIS FOOD

With meat or a food rich in vitamin C to increase the amount of iron you can absorb from the soybeans. Meat makes your stomach more acid (iron is absorbed more easily in an acid environment); vitamin C may convert the iron in soybeans from ferric iron (which is hard to absorb) to ferrous iron (which is easier to absorb).

DIETS THAT MAY RESTRICT OR EXCLUDE THIS FOOD

Low-calcium diet
Low-fiber diet
Low-protein diet
Low-purine (antigout) diet
Sucrose-free diet

BUYING THIS FOOD

Look for: Tightly sealed packages that protect the beans from air and moisture. The beans should be smooth-skinned, uniformly sized, evenly colored, and free of stones and debris. It is easy to check beans sold in plastic bags, but the transparent material lets in light that may destroy pyridoxine and pyridoxal, the natural forms of vitamin B_{12}.

STORING THIS FOOD

Store beans in air- and moistureproof containers in a cool, dark cabinet where they are protected from heat, light, and insects.

PREPARING THIS FOOD

Wash the beans and pick them over carefully, discarding damaged beans, withered beans, or beans that float. (The only beans light enough to float in water are those that have withered away inside.)

Soak "fresh" dried soybeans as directed on the package and then discard the water. If you use canned beans, discard the liquid in the can and rinse the beans in cool running water. In discarding this liquid you are getting rid of some of the soluble indigestible sugars that may cause intestinal gas when you eat beans.

WHAT HAPPENS WHEN YOU COOK THIS FOOD

When soybeans are cooked in liquid, their cells absorb water, swell, and eventually rupture, releasing pectins, gums, and the nutrients inside the cell. In addition, cooking destroys antinutrients in beans, making them safe to eat.

HOW OTHER KINDS OF PROCESSING AFFECT THIS FOOD

Soy sauce.   Soy sauce is made by adding salt to cooked soybeans and setting the mixture aside to ferment. Soy sauce is particularly useful in Japanese cuisines because it inactivates antinutrient enzymes in raw fish.

Like soybeans, soy sauce is high in protein (1 gm/4 tsp.). Unlike plain soybeans cooked without salt, it is high in sodium. And it may interact with monoamine oxidase (MAO) inhibitors, drugs used as antidepressants or antihypertensives. MAO inhibitors interfere with the action of enzymes that break down tyramine, a natural by-product of protein metabolism. Tyramine is a pressor amine, a chemical that constricts blood vessels and raises blood pressure. If you eat a food such as soy sauce (which is high in tyramine) while you are taking an MAO inhibitor, the pressor amine cannot be eliminated from your body and the result may be a hypertensive crisis (sustained elevated blood pressure).

Milling.   Soy flour is a powder made from soybeans. It is very high in protein (37-47 percent) and fat (0.9 percent-20 percent). It can be used as a substitute for up to 20 percent of the wheat flour in any recipe. Unlike wheat flour, it has no gluten or gliadin, which makes it useful for people who have celiac disease, a metabolic disorder that makes it impossible for them to digest these wheat proteins (*see* FLOUR).

Canning.   The heat of canning destroys some of the B vitamins in soybeans. Since the B vitamins are water-soluble, you could save them by using the liquid in the can. But the liquid also contains the indigestible sugars that cause intestinal gas when you eat beans.

Preprocessing.   Preprocessed dried soybeans have already been soaked. They take less time to cook, but they are lower in B vitamins.

MEDICAL USES AND/OR BENEFITS

To reduce the level of serum cholesterol.   The gums and pectins in dried legumes appear to lower blood levels of cholesterol. There are currently two theories to explain how this may happen. The first theory is that the pectins in the beans form a gel in your stomach that sops up fats and keeps them from being absorbed by your body. The second is that bacteria in the gut feed on the bean fiber, producing short-chain fatty acids that inhibit the production of cholesterol in your liver.

As a source of carbohydrates for people with diabetes.   Beans are digested very slowly, producing only a gradual rise in blood-sugar levels. As a result, the body needs less insulin to control blood sugar after eating beans than after eating some other high-carbohydrate foods (bread or potato). In studies at the University of Kentucky, a bean, whole-grain, vegetable, and fruit-rich diet developed at the University of Toronto and recommended by the American Diabetes Association enabled patients with Type I diabetes (who do not produce any insulin themselves) to cut their daily insulin intake by 38 percent. For patients with Type II diabetes (who can produce some insulin) the bean diet reduced the need for injected insulin by 98 percent. This diet is in line with the nutritional guidelines of the American Diabetes Association, but people with diabetes should always consult their doctor and/or dietitian before altering their diet.

As a diet aid.   Although beans are high in calories, they are also high in fiber; even a small serving can make you feel full. And, because they are insulin-sparing, they put off the rise in insulin levels that makes us feel hungry again soon after eating. Research at the University of Toronto suggests the insulin-sparing effect may last for several hours after you eat the beans, perhaps until after your next meal.

ADVERSE EFFECTS ASSOCIATED WITH THIS FOOD

Intestinal gas.   All legumes contain raffinose and stachyose, complex sugars that human beings cannot digest. The sugars sit in the gut, where they are fermented by intestinal bacteria, which then produce gas that distends the intestines and makes us uncomfortable. You can lessen this effect by covering the beans with boiling water and soaking them for four to six hours before you cook them so that the indigestible sugars leach out into the soaking water, which can be discarded. Or you may soak the beans for four hours in 9 cups of water for every cup of beans, discard the soaking water, and add new water as your recipe directs. Then cook the beans and drain them before serving.

Production of uric acid.   Purines are the natural metabolic by-products of protein metabolism in the body. They eventually break down into uric acid, which forms sharp crystals that may concentrate in joints, a condition known as gout. If uric acid crystals collect in the urine, the result may be kidney stones. Eating dried beans, which are rich in proteins, may raise the concentration of purines in your body. Although controlling the amount of purines in the diet does not significantly affect the course of gout (which is treated with allopurinol, a drug that prevents the formation of uric acid crystals), limiting these foods is still part of many gout regimens.

FOOD/DRUG INTERACTIONS
*   *   *

SPINACH

NUTRITIONAL PROFILE

Energy value (calories per serving):	Low
Protein:	High
Fat:	Low
Cholesterol:	None
Carbohydrates:	Moderate
Fiber:	Low
Sodium:	Moderate
Major vitamin contribution:	Vitamins A and C
Major mineral contribution:	Potassium

ABOUT THE NUTRIENTS IN THIS FOOD

Spinach has some sugar, a trace of starch; a moderate amount of proteins considered "incomplete" because they are deficient in the essential amino acids tryptophan, methionine, and cystine; very little fat; and no cholesterol. It has moderate amounts of cellulose, and the noncarbohydrate food fiber lignin, which is found in roots, seed coverings, stems, and the ribs of leaves.

Spinach is an extraordinarily good source of vitamin C. One 3.5-ounce serving of fresh raw spinach provides 28 mg vitamin C, 47 percent of the RDA for a healthy adult. Spinach is rich in yellow carotenes, which are converted to vitamin A in your body. One 3.5-ounce serving of fresh raw spinach provides 6700 IU vitamin A, 134 percent of the RDA; an equal amount of boiled, drained spinach has 8200 IU, 164 percent of the RDA. Spinach is also rich in riboflavin (vitamin B$_2$), which is more plentiful in the leaves than in the stems.

Spinach has a lot of calcium but it also has a lot of oxalic acid, which binds the calcium into an insoluble salt (calcium oxalate) that your body cannot absorb. The oxalic acid also binds iron; only 2 to 5 percent of spinach's seemingly plentiful supply of iron is actually available to your body.

THE MOST NUTRITIOUS WAY TO SERVE THIS FOOD

Fresh, lightly steamed, to protect its vitamin C.

With a cream sauce. The sauce, which can be made of low-fat milk, provides the essential amino acids needed to complete the proteins in the spinach.

DIETS THAT MAY RESTRICT OR EXCLUDE THIS FOOD

Low-calcium, low-oxalate diet (for people who form calcium-oxalate kidney
    stones)
Low-sodium diet
Sucrose-free diet

BUYING THIS FOOD

Look for: Fresh, crisp dark-green leaves that are free of dirt and debris.

Avoid: Yellowed leaves. These are aging leaves whose chlorophyll pigments have faded, allowing the carotenoids underneath to show through. Wilted leaves or leaves that are limp and brownish have lost vitamin C.

STORING THIS FOOD

Refrigerate loose leaves in a roomy plastic bag. If you bought the spinach already wrapped in plastic, unwrap it and divide it up into smaller packages so the leaves are not crowded or bent, then refrigerate.

PREPARING THIS FOOD

Wash the spinach thoroughly under cool running water to remove all sand and debris. Discard damaged or yellowed leaves. Trim the ribs and stems but don't remove them entirely; they are rich in food fiber. If you plan to use the spinach in a salad, refrigerate the damp leaves to make them crisp.

WHAT HAPPENS WHEN YOU COOK THIS FOOD

Chlorophyll, the pigment that makes green vegetables green, is sensitive to acids. When you heat spinach, the chlorophyll in its leaves will react with acids in the vegetable or in the cooking water, forming pheophytin, which is brown. The pheophytin turns cooked spinach olive-drab or, if the spinach leaves contain a lot of yellow carotenes, bronze.

To keep cooked spinach green, you have to keep the chlorophyll from reacting with acids. One way to do this is to cook the spinach in a lot of water (which dilutes the acids), but this increases the loss of vitamin C. Another alternative is to cook the spinach with the lid off the pot so the volatile acids can float off into the air. Or you can steam the spinach quickly in very little water so that it retains its vitamin C and cooks before there is time for the chlorophyll/acid reaction to occur.

Spinach also contains astringent tannins that react with metals to create dark pigments. If you cook the leaves in an aluminum or iron pot, these pigments will discolor the pots and the spinach. To keep the spinach from darkening, cook in an enameled or glass pot.

HOW OTHER KINDS OF PROCESSING AFFECT THIS FOOD

Canning and freezing.   Canned spinach, which is processed at high heat, is olive or bronze rather than green. Like cooked spinach, canned spinach and frozen spinach have only 50 percent of the vitamin C in fresh spinach.

MEDICAL USES AND/OR BENEFITS

Protection against the risk of some forms of cancer.   According to the American Cancer Society, vegetables rich in vitamins A and C may offer some protection against the risk of cancers of the respiratory and gastrointestinal tracts and cancers induced by chemicals.

ADVERSE EFFECTS ASSOCIATED WITH THIS FOOD

Nitrate/nitrite poisoning.   Spinach, like beets, celery, eggplant, lettuce, radish, and collard and turnip greens, contains nitrates that convert naturally into nitrites in your stomach and then react with the amino acids in proteins to form nitrosamines. Although some nitrosamines are known or suspected carcinogens, this natural chemical conversion presents no known problems for a healthy adult. However, when these nitrate-rich vegetables are cooked and left to stand at room temperature, bacterial enzyme action (and perhaps some enzymes in the plants) converts the nitrates to nitrites at a much faster rate than normal. These higher-nitrite foods may be hazardous for infants; several cases of "spinach poisoning" been reported among children who ate cooked spinach that had been left standing at room temperature.

FOOD/DRUG INTERACTIONS

Anticoagulants.   Like other leaf vegetables, spinach contains vitamin K, the blood-clotting vitamin produced naturally by bacteria in our intestines. Additional intake of vitamin K may reduce the effectiveness of anticoagulants (warfarin, Coumadin, Panwarfin) so that larger doses are required.

MAO inhibitors.   Monoamine oxidase (MAO) inhibitors are drugs used as antidepressants or antihypertensives. They interfere with the action of enzymes that break down tyramine, a chemical produced when long-chain protein molecules are broken into smaller pieces. Tyramine is a pressor amine, a chemical that constricts blood vessels and raises blood pressure. If you eat a food rich in tyramine while you are taking an MAO inhibitor, the pressor amine cannot be eliminated from your body and the result may be a hypertensive crisis (sustained elevated blood pressure). There has been at least one report of such an interaction in a patient who consumed New Zealand prickly spinach while using an MAO inhibitor.

SPIRITS
(Brandy, gin, rum, tequila, whiskey, vodka)

NUTRITIONAL PROFILE

Energy value (calories per serving):	Moderate to high
Protein:	None
Fat:	None
Cholesterol:	None
Carbohydrates:	None (except for cordials which contain added sugar)
Fiber:	None
Sodium:	Low
Major vitamin contribution:	None
Major mineral contribution:	Phosphorus

ABOUT THE NUTRIENTS IN THIS FOOD

Spirits are the clear liquids produced by distilling the fermented sugars of grains, fruit, or vegetables. The yeasts that metabolize these sugars and convert them into alcohol stop growing when the concentration of alcohol rises above 12-15 percent. In the United States, the proof of an alcoholic beverage is defined as twice its alcohol content by volume: a beverage with 20 percent alcohol by volume is 40 proof.

This is high enough for most wines, but not high enough for most whiskies, gins, vodkas, rums, brandies, and tequilas. To reach the concentration of alcohol required in these beverages, the fermented sugars are heated and distilled. Ethyl alcohol (the alcohol in beer, wine, and spirits) boils at a lower temperature than water. When the fermented sugars are heated, the ethyl alcohol escapes from the distillation vat and condenses in tubes leading from the vat to a collection vessel. The clear liquid that collects in this vessel is called *distilled spirits* or, more technically, *grain neutral spirits.*

Gins, whiskies, cordials, and many vodkas are made with spirits distilled from grains. *American whiskeys* (which include bourbon, rye, and blended whiskeys) and *Canadian, Irish,* and *Scotch whiskies* are all made from spirits aged in wood barrels. They get their flavor from the grains and their color from the barrels. (Some whiskies are also colored with caramel.)

Vodka is made from spirits distilled and filtered to remove all flavor. By law, vodkas made in America must be made with spirits distilled from grains. Imported vodkas may be made with spirits distilled either from grains or potatoes and may contain additional flavoring agents such as citric acid or pepper. *Aquavit,* for example, is essentially vodka flavored with caraway seeds. *Gin* is a clear spirit flavored with an infusion of juniper berries and other herbs (botanicals). *Cordials* (also called liqueurs) and *schnapps* are flavored spirits; most are sweetened with added sugar. Some cordials contain cream.

Rum is made with spirits distilled from sugar cane (molasses). *Tequila* is made with spirits distilled from catcus. *Brandies* are made with spirits distilled from fruit. (*Armagnac* and *cognac* are distilled from fermented grapes, *calvados* and *applejack* from fermented apples, *kirsch* from fermented cherries, *slivovitz* from fermented plums.)

Unless they contain added sugar or cream, spirits have no nutrients other than alcohol. Unlike food, which has to be metabolized before your body can use it for energy, alcohol can be absorbed into the blood-stream directly from the gastrointestinal tract. Ethyl alcohol provides 7 calories per gram.

THE MOST NUTRITIOUS WAY TO SERVE THIS FOOD

In moderation.

DIETS THAT MAY RESTRICT OR EXCLUDE THIS FOOD

Bland diet

Lactose-free diet (cream cordials made with cream or milk)

Low-purine (antigout) diet

Sucrose-free diet (sweetened spirits, such as cordials and flavored schnapps)

BUYING THIS FOOD

Look for: Tightly sealed bottles stored out of direct sunlight, whose energy might disrupt the structure of molecules in the beverage and alter its flavor.

Choose spirits sold only by licensed dealers. Products sold in these stores are manufactured under the strict supervision of the federal government.

STORING THIS FOOD

Store sealed or opened bottles of spirits in a cool, dark cabinet.

PREPARING THIS FOOD

All spirits except unflavored vodkas contain volatile molecules that give the beverage its characteristic taste and smell. Warming the liquid excites these molecules and intensifies the flavor and aroma, which is the reason we serve brandy in a round glass with a narrower top that captures the aromatic molecules as they rise toward the air when we warm the glass by holding it in our hands. Whiskies, too, though traditionally served with ice in America, will have a more intense flavor and aroma if served at room temperature.

WHAT HAPPENS WHEN YOU COOK THIS FOOD

The heat of cooking evaporates the alcohol in spirits but leaves the flavoring intact. Like other alcoholic beverages, spirits should be added to a recipe near the end of the cooking time to preserve the flavor while cooking away any alcohol bite.

Alcohol is an acid. If you cook it in an aluminum or iron pot, it will combine with metal ions to form dark compounds that discolor the pot and the food you are cooking. Any recipe made with spirits should be prepared in an enameled, glass, or stainless-steel pot.

HOW OTHER KINDS OF PROCESSING AFFECT THIS FOOD

*   *   *

MEDICAL USES AND/OR BENEFITS

Alcohol and serum cholesterol. Drinking alcoholic beverages (including spirits) affects the body's metabolism of fats. It appears to decrease the production and storage of low-density lipoproteins (LDLs), which hold cholesterol in the body, and increase the production and storage of high-density lipoproteins (HDLs), which carry cholesterol out of the body. Research into the effects of alcohol consumption on the levels of cholesterol in the blood is still in the experimental stage.

Stimulating the appetite. Alcoholic beverages stimulate the production of saliva and the gastric acids that cause the stomach contractions we call hunger pangs. Moderate amounts of alcoholic beverages, which may help stimulate appetite, are often prescribed for geriatric patients, convalescents, and people who do not have ulcers of other chronic gastric problems that might be exacerbated by the alcohol.

Dilation of blood vessels.   Alcoholic beverages dilate the tiny blood vessels just under the skin, bringing blood up to the surface. That's why moderate amounts of alcoholic beverages (0.2-l gram per kilogram of body weight, or 2 ounces of whiskey for a 150-pound adult) temporarily warm the drinker. But the warm blood that flows up to the surface of the skin will cool down there, making you even colder when it circulates back into the center of your body. Then an alcohol flush will make you perspire, so you lose more heat. Excessive amounts of beverage alcohol may depress the mechanism that regulates body temperature.

ADVERSE EFFECTS ASSOCIATED WITH THIS FOOD

Alcohol abuse.   People who consistently consume excessive amounts of alcoholic beverages or who are unable to metabolize alcohol efficiently or to deal with its physiological and psychological effects may suffer from *alcoholism,* an illness that may cause both physical and emotional problems, including cirrhosis (degeneration) of the liver, malnutrition, delirium tremens, and death.

Hangover.   Alcohol is absorbed from the stomach and small intestine and carried by the bloodstream to the liver, where it is oxidized to acetaldehyde by alcohol dehydrogenase (ADH), the enzyme our bodies use every day to metabolize the alcohol we produce when we digest carbohydrates. The acetaldehyde is converted to acetyl coenzyme A and either eliminated from the body or used in the synthesis of cholesterol, fatty acids, and body tissues. Although individuals vary widely in their capacity to metabolize alcohol, an adult of average size can metabolize the alcohol in 4 ounces (120 ml) whiskey in approximately five to six hours. If he or she drinks more than that, the amount of alcohol in the body will exceed the available supply of ADH. The surplus, unmetabolized alcohol will pile up in the bloodstream, interfering with the liver's metabolic functions. Since alcohol decreases the reabsorption of water from the kidneys and may inhibit the secretion of an antidiuretic hormone, the drinker will begin to urinate copiously, losing magnesium, calcium, and zinc but retaining uric acid, which is irritating. The level of lactic acid in the body will increase, making him or her feel tired and out of sorts; the acid-base balance will be out of kilter; the blood vessels in the head will swell and throb; and the stomach, its lining irritated by the alcohol, will ache. The ultimate result is a hangover whose symptoms will disappear only when enough time has passed to allow the body to marshal the ADH needed to metabolize the extra alcohol in the person's blood.

Migraine headache.   Some alcoholic beverages contain chemicals that inhibit PST, an enzyme that breaks down certain alcohols in spirits so that they can be eliminated from the body. If they are not broken down by PST, these alcohols will build up in the bloodstream and may trigger a migraine headache. Gin and vodka appear to be the distilled spirits least likely to trigger headaches, brandy the most likely.

Fetal alcohol syndrome.   Fetal alcohol syndrome is a specific pattern of birth defects—low birth weight, heart defects, facial malformations, learning disabilities, and mental retardation—first recognized in a study of babies born to alcoholic women who consumed more than six drinks a day while pregnant. Subsequent research has found a consistent pattern of milder defects in babies born to women who drink three to four drinks a day or five drinks on any one occasion while pregnant. To date there is no evidence of a consistent pattern of birth defects in babies born to women who consume less than one drink a day while pregnant, but two studies at Columbia University have suggested that as few as two drinks a week while pregnant may raise a woman's risk of miscarriage. (One drink is 12 ounces of beer, 5 ounces of wine, or 1.25 ounces of distilled spirits.)

FOOD/DRUG INTERACTIONS

Anticoagulants.   Alcohol makes anticoagulants stronger by inhibiting your body's ability to metabolize and eliminate them.

Antihypertensives (diuretics and beta blockers).   Alcohol, which lowers blood pressure, may dangerously intensify the effects of these drugs (see *MAO inhibitors,* below).

Aspirin and nonsteroidal anti-inflammatory drugs.   Like alcohol, these analgesics irritate the lining of the stomach and may cause gastric bleeding. Combining the two intensifies the effect.

Disulfiram (Antabuse).   Taken with alcohol, disulfiram causes flushing, nausea, low blood pressure, faintness, respiratory problems, and confusion. The severity of the reaction generally depends on how much alcohol you drink, how much disulfiram is in your body, and how long ago you took it. Disulfiram is used to help recovering alcoholics avoid alcohol. If taken with alcohol, metronidazole (Flagyl), procarbazine (Matulane), quinacrine (Atabrine), and chlorpropamide (Diabinase) may produce a mild disulfiram-like reaction.

Insulin and oral hypoglycemics.   Alcohol lowers blood sugar and interferes with the metabolism of oral antidiabetics; the combination may cause severe hypoglycemia.

MAO inhibitors.   Monoamine oxidase (MAO) inhibitors are drugs used as antidepressants or antihypertensives. They inhibit the action of natural enzymes that break down tyramine, a substance formed naturally when proteins are metabolized. Tyramine is a pressor amine, a chemical that constricts blood vessel and raises blood pressure. If you eat a food that contains tyramine while you are taking an MAO inhibitor, the pressor amine cannot be eliminated from your body and the result may be a hypertensive crisis (sustained elevated blood pressure). Brandy, a distilled spirit made from wine (which is fermented) contains tyramine. All other distilled spirits may be excluded from your diet when you are taking an MAO inhibitor because the spirits and the drug, which are both sedatives, may be hazardous in combination.

Sedatives and other central-nervous-system depressants.   Alcohol intensifies the sedative effects of tranquilizers, sleeping pills, antidepressants, some sinus and cold remedies, analgesics, and medication for motion sickness. Depending on the dose, the combination may cause drowsiness, sedation, respiratory depression, coma, or death.

SQUID (CALAMARI)
(Octopus)

NUTRITIONAL PROFILE

Energy value (calories per serving):	Moderate
Protein:	High
Fat:	Low
Cholesterol:	High
Carbohydrates:	Low
Fiber:	None
Sodium:	Moderate
Major vitamin contribution:	B vitamins
Major mineral contribution:	Iron

ABOUT THE NUTRIENTS IN THIS FOOD

Squid (also known by its Italian name, *calamari*) and octopus are cephalopods *(cephalo* = head; *pod* = foot), a class of molluscs. They are lean, muscular animals, high in protein and very low in fat.

The proteins in squid and octopus are considered "complete" because they provide all the essential amino acids. The fats are proportionally higher in cholesterol than the fat in many other forms of seafood, but they are also high (30 percent) in the omega-3 fatty acids, eicosapentaenoic acid (EPA) and docosahexanoic acid (DHA). EPA and DHA are the primary polyunsaturated fatty acids in the fat and oils of fish. They appear to lower blood

CHOLESTEROL AND OMEGA-3 FATTY ACIDS
IN 100 GRAMS SQUID AND OCTOPUS
(mg/100 grams)

	Cholesterol	Omega-3s
Loligo squid	170-450 mg*	300 mg
Illex squid	100-350 mg	300 mg
Octopus	200 mg	#

*The cholesterol content varies from animal to animal; there is no reliable way to pick a lower-cholesterol squid. However, the mantle (body) generally has less cholesterol than the tentacles.

Not available

Source: National Marine Fisheries Service, Northeast Fisheries Center, Gloucester (Mass.) Laboratories (1986).

levels of low-density lipoproteins (LDL) and increase blood levels of high-density lipoproteins (HDL).* They also appear to inhibit the production of leuketrienes, natural inflammatory agents that transmit signals between cells (see *Medical use and/or benefits,* below).

Both squid and octopus are good sources of B vitamins and provide heme iron, the organic form of iron found in meat, fish, and poultry. They are naturally low in sodium and have traces of calcium and phosphorus.

THE MOST NUTRITIOUS WAY TO SERVE THIS FOOD

Prepared with little or no added fat, to preserve the seafood's status as a low-fat food.

DIETS THAT MAY RESTRICT OR EXCLUDE THIS FOOD

Low-cholesterol diet
Low-protein diet
Low-sodium diet (frozen squid or octopus)

BUYING THIS FOOD

Look for: Fresh whole squid with clear, smooth skin. The squid should smell absolutely fresh. Squid larger than 8 inches may be tough.

Choose fresh, whole baby octopus or octopus meat that looks and smells absolutely fresh. Octopus larger than 2 to 2.5 pounds may be tough.

*LDLs are molecules that carry cholesterol into your bloodstream; HDLs are molecules that carry cholesterol away to be eliminated from the body.

STORING THIS FOOD

Refrigerate fresh, cleaned octopus or squid immediately and use it within a day or two. Frozen squid or octopus will keep for one month in a 0° F freezer.

PREPARING THIS FOOD

Note: Handle live squid or octopus with care. They bite.

Squid. Whole squid are usually sold cleaned, like any other seafood. If you are cleaning the squid yourself, your goal is to throw out everything but the empty saclike body and the tentacles. Start by removing the beak. Then reach into the body cavity and pull out all the innards, including the cartilage. (If you tear or puncture the ink sac and spill the ink, just wash it off your hands.) Cut the innards away from the body and throw them out. Peel off the skin. Squeeze the thick end of the tentacles and discard the small yellowish piece of meat that pops out. Rinse the squid meat thoroughly, inside and out, under cool running water. Stuff the sac whole for baking or cut it into rings and stew it along with chunks of the tentacles.

Octopus. Cleaned, dressed octopus needs only be rinsed thoroughly under cold running water. To prepare a small whole octopus, remove the beak, eyes, anal area, and ink sac. Cut off the tough ends of the tentacles, slice the tentacles into rounds or chunks, rinse them thoroughly under cold running water to remove all the gelatinous cartilege, and pound the meat to tenderize.

WHAT HAPPENS WHEN YOU COOK THIS FOOD

Heat changes the structure of the proteins in the squid and octopus. The proteins are denatured, which means that they break into smaller fragments or change shape or clump together. These changes cause protein tissues to lose moisture and shrink, so that the seafood becomes opaque as it cooks.

Squid cooks fairly quickly. Its thin-walled body can be fried or sautéed in less than a minute and stewed in half an hour. Octopus, on the other hand, may need to be simmered for as long as three hours. But take care: the longer you cook the octopus, the more moisture you squeeze out of its protein tissues and the more rubbery it becomes.

HOW OTHER KINDS OF PROCESSING AFFECT THIS FOOD

Freezing. Commercially processed squid are soaked in brine before freezing, which makes them much higher in sodium than fresh squid.

MEDICAL USES AND/OR BENEFITS

Protective effects of omega-3 fatty acids. In 1985 the *New England Jour-*

nal of Medicine published the results of three separate studies dealing with the effects of a diet rich in saltwater fish oils.

The first, a twenty-year project at the University of Leyden in the Netherlands, compared the eating habits of more than 800 men and their risk of heart disease and found that men who ate more than an ounce of fish a day had a 50 percent lower rate of heart attacks. (Research at Cornell University has suggested that oils inhibit the formation of thromboxane, a chemical that makes red blood cells clump together, and that omega-3 fatty acids are converted to a compound similar to prostacyclin, a natural body chemical that inhibits clotting.)

The second study, at the Oregon Health Sciences University in Portland, found that a diet high in fish oils appears to lower the levels of triglycerides in the blood. (A high level of triglycerides, like a high level of cholesterol, increases the risk of heart disease.)

In the third study, seven volunteers at Brigham and Women's Hospital in Boston were put on a diet high in fats from saltwater fish. At the end of six weeks, the researchers found that fish oils seemed to reduce the anti-inflammatory response in body tissues, perhaps by inhibiting the production of leuketrienes, the natural inflammatory agents that trigger a wide range of inflammatory diseases ranging from arthritis to hay fever.

This last study is bolstered by research at the University of Michigan which suggests that fish (like vegetables, fruit, and grain), appears to interfere with the body's production of arachidonic acid (AA), a natural inflammatory agent that makes psoriatic lesions swell and turn red.

The beneficial effects in all these studies are assumed to be due to the omega-3 fatty acids in the fish oils. Omega-3s are especially plentiful in fatty fish from cold waters. The oils in squid and octopus are proportionally high in omega-3 fatty acids (30 percent), but both contain so little fat that they provide only small amounts of omega-3s.

ADVERSE EFFECTS ASSOCIATED WITH THIS FOOD

Allergic reactions.   Shellfish are among the foods most likely to cause the classic symptoms of food allergy, including upset stomach, hives, and angioedema (swelling of the lips and eyes).

Parasitical, viral, and bacterial infections and/or food poisoning.   Like raw meat, raw shellfish may carry various pathogens, including *Salmonella* bacteria. These organisms are destroyed by thorough cooking.

Elevated levels of serum cholesterol.   People whose blood-cholesterol levels are abnormally high are considered at risk for heart disease, but experts disagree as to the effects of dietary cholesterol on serum cholesterol. Patients with hypercholesteremia, a metabolic disorder that influences cholesterol production in the liver, may benefit from a diet low in dietary cholesterol, but there is no conclusive proof that lowering a healthy person's consumption of dietary cholesterol will significantly change the amount of cholesterol he or she produces. In 1986 the American Heart Association issued new guidelines suggesting that healthy adults reduce their consumption of fat to 30 percent of total calories and limit cholesterol intake to 300 mg per day or 100 mg per 1000 calories, whichever is less (3.5 ounces of squid or octopus have 300 mg cholesterol).

FOOD/DRUG INTERACTIONS

*   *   *

STRAWBERRIES

NUTRITIONAL PROFILE

Energy value (calories per serving):	Low
Protein:	Moderate
Fat:	Low
Cholesterol:	None
Carbohydrates:	High
Fiber:	High
Sodium:	Low
Major vitamin contribution:	Vitamin C
Major mineral contribution:	Potassium

ABOUT THE NUTRIENTS IN THIS FOOD

Strawberries have moderately high amounts of sugar, no starch, and are a good source of food fiber, particularly pectin and the noncarbohydrate food fiber lignin, which is found in the tiny seeds that dot the surface of the berry.

Strawberries are an excellent source of vitamin C. Ounce for ounce, they have 24 percent more vitamin C than fresh oranges or fresh orange juice, and 50 percent more than fresh grapefruit juice. Strawberries are also a good source of potassium.

THE MOST NUTRITIOUS WAY TO SERVE THIS FOOD

Fresh and ripe, to preserve the vitamin C.

DIETS THAT MAY RESTRICT OR EXCLUDE THIS FOOD

Low-fiber diet

Sucrose-free diet

BUYING THIS FOOD

Look for: Bright red berries with fresh green caps. Pale berries are immature; berries with dark, red wet spots are overmature; berries whose caps
have browned are aging. Small berries are generally more flavorful than
large ones.

STORING THIS FOOD

Refrigerate strawberries with their caps on. When you remove the caps you
tear cells in the berries, activating ascorbic acid oxidase, an enzyme that destroys vitamin C. Keeping strawberries cool also helps keep them bright red;
the anthocyanin pigments that make strawberries red turn brown faster at
high temperatures.

PREPARING THIS FOOD

When you are ready to use the berries, rinse them thoroughly under cool running water. Then remove the caps. (If you hull the berries before you rinse
them, water may run into the berry and dilute the flavor.)

Don't slice the berries until you are ready to use them. When you slice a
strawberry, you tear cell walls, releasing ascorbic acid oxidase, the enzyme
that breaks down vitamin C. This reduces the nutritional value of the strawberries. It may also be linked to the degradation of the pigments that make
strawberries red. Acids retard the color loss; sprinkling the sliced berries with
lemon juice helps preserve color.

You can soften and sweeten strawberries by dusting them with sugar
and letting them sit for a while. The sugar dissolves in moisture on the surface of the berry, producing a solution that is more dense than the liquid inside the strawberry's cells. Then the liquid inside the cells will flow across
the cell walls to the denser sugar-water solution (a phenomenon known as osmosis); the cell walls that were held apart by the water will collapse inward,
and the strawberry will be softer.

WHAT HAPPENS WHEN YOU COOK THIS FOOD

The red anthocyanin pigments in strawberries are heat-sensitive; they break
apart and turn brown when you heat them. Adding sugar speeds up the process even further because some of the chemicals produced when sugars are
heated also break down anthocyanins. That's why strawberries cooked in

boiling, sugared water turn brown faster than strawberries steamed quickly without sugar.

Red anthocyanins also change color in acids and bases (alkalis). They are bright-red in acids such as lemon juice and bluish or purple in bases such as baking soda. If you cook strawberries in an aluminum or iron pot, their acids will react with metal ions from the surface of the pot to create dark brown compounds that darken either the pot or the fruit.

Strawberries also lose heat-sensitive vitamin C when you cook them.

HOW OTHER FORMS OF PROCESSING AFFECT THIS FOOD

Heat processing (canning; making jams, jellies, and preserves). As noted above, strawberries turn brown when you heat them with sugar. Lemon juice added to jams, jellies, and preserves makes the taste tart and helps preserve the color.

MEDICAL USES AND/OR BENEFITS

As an antiscorbutic. Strawberries, which (ounce for ounce) have more vitamin C than citrus fruits, help protect against scurvy, the vitamin C-deficiency disease.

Protection against some forms of cancer. According to the American Cancer Society, foods rich in vitamin C may lower the risk of cancers of the gastrointestinal tract.

ADVERSE EFFECTS ASSOCIATED WITH THIS FOOD

Allergic reactions. Strawberries are among the foods most often implicated as a cause of the classic food-allergy symptoms: upset stomach, hives, angioedema (swelling of the face, lips, and eyes), and a hay-feverlike reaction.

FOOD/DRUG INTERACTIONS

*   *   *

SUGAR

(Corn syrup, fructose, maple sugar, maple syrup, molasses)

See also HONEY

NUTRITIONAL PROFILE

Energy value (calories per serving):	High
Protein:	None
Fat:	None
Cholesterol:	None
Carbohydrates:	High
Fiber:	None
Sodium:	None
Major vitamin contribution:	B vitamins (molasses)
Major mineral contribution:	Iron (molasses)

ABOUT THE NUTRIENTS IN THIS FOOD

Sugars are carbohydrates, members of the class of nutrients that includes starches and some food fibers. The sugars we use in cooking—table sugar ("white sugar"), brown sugar, fructose, molasses, corn syrup—are all made of units of fructose or glucose or galactose, alone or in combination. Different sugars have different combinations of these three "building blocks."

Table sugar (also known as *granulated sugar, white sugar, refined sugar,* or simply *sugar*) is sucrose crystallized from sugar cane or sugar beets. Sucrose is a disaccharide ("double sugar") that contains one molecule of fructose and one molecule of glucose. Sucrose cannot be absorbed into your body until it is split into fructose and glucose.

Table sugar has no nutrients. They are left behind when sucrose is crystallized out of cane or beet juice. *Molasses* and *blackstrap molasses,* which are by-products of the production of table sugar, retain minute amounts of these nutrients. *Brown sugar* is table sugar to which molasses has been added; the darker the sugar, the more molasses it contains. *Confectioner's sugar* (also known as *powdered sugar*) is table sugar mixed with corn starch. *Raw sugar* (also known as *turbinado sugar*) is cane sugar with some of the molasses left in. Because of its impurities, true raw sugar cannot be sold legally in the United States. The "raw sugar" we buy in the supermarket is usually plain white sugar colored with molasses. *Maple sugar* is sucrose concentrated from the sap of the maple tree.

Fructose, which is twice as sweet as sucrose, is a monosaccharide (a "single sugar"). Unlike sucrose, which must be broken down by enzymes before you can use it, fructose can be absorbed directly into your body. Eating fructose does not trigger the insulin rush that occurs when you eat sucrose.

Corn syrup, a liquid syrup processed from corn, is made of glucose, a monosaccharide extracted from corn starch, plus some sucrose or fructose to make it sweeter. (Glucose is only half as sweet as sucrose.)

With the exception of blackstrap molasses, none of these sugars contributes any appreciable amount of any nutrient other than calories. (A tablespoon of blackstrap molasses provides about 19 mg calcium, 2 percent of the RDA for an adult, and 0.5 mg iron, 2.7 percent of the RDA for iron for a healthy adult woman.)

THE MOST NUTRITIOUS WAY TO SERVE THIS FOOD
In moderation.

DIETS THAT MAY RESTRICT OR EXCLUDE THIS FOOD
Low-calorie diet
Low-carbohydrate diet
Sucrose-free diet

BUYING THIS FOOD
Look for: Tightly sealed boxes or sacks of dry sugars. Avoid stained packages; whatever stained the outside may have seeped through into the sugar.

Choose tightly sealed bottles of liquid sugars. The liquid inside should be clear; tiny bubbles and a gray scum on the surface of the sugar suggest that it has fermented.

STORING THIS FOOD
Store solid sugars in air- and moistureproof containers in a cool, dry cabinet. Sugars are hydrophilic, which means that they will absorb moisture. If sug-

ars get wet (or pick up excess moisture from hot, humid air), they will harden or cake.

Store tightly sealed, unopened containers of liquid sugars such as corn syrup, maple syrup, and molasses at room temperature. Once the container is opened, you can store the sugar in the refrigerator to protect it from molds and keep the sugars from fermenting.

PREPARING THIS FOOD

Because they contain different amounts of water and have different levels of sweetness, sugars cannot simply be substituted equally for each other. As a general rule, one cup of white table sugar = one cup of firmly packed brown sugar = 1. 75 cup confectioner's sugar (which cannot be substituted in baking) = 2 cups corn syrup (with a reduction of liquid in baking and substitution of corn syrup for only half the sugar) = 1.3 cups molasses (with reduced liquid and no more than substitution for half the sugar in baking).

To measure granulated white sugar, pour into a cup and use a knife to level. To measure brown sugar, pack tightly into a cup. Powdered (confectioner's) sugar can be sifted or not, as the recipe dictates.

WHAT HAPPENS WHEN YOU COOK THIS FOOD

When you heat sugar its molecules separate. The sugar liquifies, then turns brown. The browning is called caramelization. When you heat sugar in water it attracts molecules of water and forms a syrup that can be thickened by heating the solution long enough to evaporate some of the water.

HOW OTHER KINDS OF PROCESSING AFFECT THIS FOOD

*   *   *

MEDICAL USES AND/OR BENEFITS

*   *   *

ADVERSE EFFECTS ASSOCIATED WITH THIS FOOD

Tooth decay.   Fermentable carbohydrates, including sugars, may cling to the teeth and nourish the bacteria that cause cavities. Regular flossing and brushing remove the sugars mechanically; fluoridated water hardens the surface of the teeth so that they are more resistant to bacterial action.

Sugar in the urine.   People with diabetes cannot use sucrose efficiently either because they do not produce enough insulin (which promotes the metabolism of carbohydrates) or because they do not have enough of the receptors to which insulin binds when it is released by the pancreas. Eating sugar will not cause diabetes, but it may exacerbate existing cases so that unmetabolized glucose will be present in urine and blood.

Heart disease.   In some people, a high-carbohydrate diet may cause an increase in the level of triglycerides (fatty acids) in the blood, but this rise is only temporary in people whose weight is normal. People who are overweight tend, as a rule, to have levels of triglycerides that are consistently higher than normal. When they lose weight the levels of triglycerides fall. The theory that sugar causes heart disease, first proposed by British researchers in the 1960s, has been successfully refuted by long-term studies from several countries that show no correlation at all between sugar intake and the incidence of coronary heart disease.

Behavioral problems.   The National Institutes of Health has conducted double-blind studies in which children were given drinks sweetened with glucose, sucrose, or saccharin without their knowing which drink had which sweetener. Theses studies show no correlation between eating the sugars and developing behavioral problems, even in children whose parents had claimed that the children were hyperactive after eating sugared foods. In fact, the children were quieter after the sugared beverages, an observation consistent with research at the Massachusetts Institute of Technology which shows that eating carbohydrates facilitates the brain's ability to absorb tryptophan and produce serotonin, a naturally calming chemical.

Hypoglycemia.   Reactive hypoglycemia, an oversecretion of insulin in response to eating sugar, is a rare condition that causes trembling, anxiety, headache, fast heartbeat, and difficulty in thinking clearly. Hypoglycemia may also be caused by the presence of a pancreatic tumor or an overdose of insulin. This is a more serious condition that, uncorrected, may lead to coma or death.

FOOD/DRUG INTERACTIONS

*   *   *

SWEET POTATOES
(Yams)

See also POTATOES

NUTRITIONAL PROFILE

Energy value (calories per serving):	Moderate
Protein:	Moderate
Fat:	Low
Cholesterol:	None
Carbohydrates:	High
Fiber:	Low
Sodium:	Low
Major vitamin contribution:	Vitamin A
Major mineral contribution:	Potassium

ABOUT THE NUTRIENTS IN THIS FOOD

Sweet potatoes are high in starch, with moderate amounts of food fiber, some protein, a trace of fat, and no cholesterol. Sweet potatoes contain alpha amylase, an enzyme that converts starches to sugars as the potato matures, when it is stored, or as it begins to heat up when you cook it.

According to research at Brigham Young University in Utah, curing sweet potatoes by storing them at 85° F for four to six days immediately after they are harvested makes the potatoes sweeter by increasing the concentration of alpha amylase. Curing also appears to heal small surface scratches and decrease the risk of rotting.

Sweet potatoes are an excellent source of vitamin A, derived from the carotene pigments that make the potato orange-yellow. The deeper the color, the higher the vitamin-A content. On average, a 3.5-ounce baked sweet potato provides 21,822 IU vitamin A, more than four times the RDA, for a healthy adult. Sweet potatoes also have vitamin C (24.6 mg, 40 percent of the RDA, in a 3.5-ounce potato), B vitamins, potassium, and iron.

True yams, which are native to Africa, are only rarely available in this country. The "yams" sold here are actually a variety of sweet potato with copper-colored skin, orange flesh, a moist texture, less vitamin A, and more vitamin C than sweet potatoes.

Raw sweet potatoes, like raw lima beans, contain cyanogenic glycosides, natural chemicals that break down into hydrogen cyanide in your stomach or when the potato is heated. If you pierce the potato while it is baking or leave the lid off the pot while it is boiling, the hydrogen cyanide (a gas) will float off harmlessly into the air.

THE MOST NUTRITIOUS WAY TO SERVE THIS FOOD
Baked or boiled.

DIETS THAT MAY RESTRICT OR EXCLUDE THIS FOOD
Sucrose-free diet

BUYING THIS FOOD
Look for: Solid, well-shaped sweet potatoes, thick in the center and tapering toward the ends. The potatoes should feel heavy for their size and the skin should be evenly colored and free of blemishes, bruises, and mold. Moldy sweet potatoes may be contaminated with a number of toxins including the liver toxin ipomeamarone and a toxic derivative, ipomeamaronol. These toxins cannot be destroyed by normal boiling or baking.

STORING THIS FOOD
Handle sweet potatoes gently to avoid bruising. When you bruise a sweet potato you tear some of its cells, releasing polyphenoloxidase, an enzyme that hastens the oxidation of phenols in the potato, creating brown compounds that darken the potato.

Store sweet potatoes in a cool (55-60° F), dark cabinet, not in the refrigerator. Like bruising, very cold temperatures damage the potato's cells, releasing polyphenoloxidase and darkening the potato.

Store home-grown sweet potatoes at 85° F for four to six days right after harvesting to sweeten them by increasing the natural conversion of starches to sugars.

PREPARING THIS FOOD

Scrub sweet potatoes under cool running water. Boiling the potatoes in their skin will save more vitamins since you will be able to peel them more closely after they are cooked. If you plan to bake the sweet potatoes, pierce the skin with a cake tester to let the steam escape as the potato cooks, and insert an aluminum "potato nail" to carry heat evenly through as it bakes.

WHAT HAPPENS WHEN YOU COOK THIS FOOD

Cooking sweetens the potato by converting some of its starches to sugars. Cooking also changes the potato's texture. When you bake a sweet potato, the water inside its cells dissolves some of the pectins in its cell walls, so the potato gets softer. As it continues to bake, moisture begins to evaporate from the cells and the potato shrinks. When you boil sweet potatoes, the initial reaction is just the opposite: at first, the starch granules in the potato absorb moisture and swell so that the potato looks bigger. If you continue to boil the potato, however, its starch granules will absorb so much water that they rupture. The water inside will leak out and the potato, once again, will shrink.

HOW OTHER KINDS OF PROCESSING AFFECT THIS FOOD

Canning. Sweet potatoes canned in water have the same nutrients as cooked fresh sweet potatoes. Sweet potatoes canned in sugar syrups have more carbohydrates and more calories.

MEDICAL USES AND/OR BENEFITS

Protection against some forms of cancer. According to the American Cancer Society, deep-yellow foods that are a rich source of vitamin A (carotene) may offer some protection against the risk of cancers of the esophagus, larynx, and lungs.

ADVERSE EFFECTS ASSOCIATED WITH THIS FOOD

*   *   *

FOOD/DRUG INTERACTIONS

*   *   *

TANGERINES
(Clementine, tangelo)

NUTRITIONAL PROFILE

Energy value (calories per serving):	Low
Protein:	Moderate
Fat:	Low
Cholesterol:	None
Carbohydrates:	High
Fiber:	Low
Sodium:	Low
Major vitamin contribution:	Vitamin C
Major mineral contribution:	Potassium

ABOUT THE NUTRIENTS IN THIS FOOD

The tangerine (also known as Mandarin orange), the tangelo (a cross between the grapefruit and the tangerine), and the clementine (a small-to-medium-size Algerian tangerine) are all high in sugar, with no starch and moderate amounts of soluble food fiber, gums and pectins. A tangerine provides about as much pectin as an apple.

Ounce for ounce, tangerines have about 60 percent as much vitamin C as oranges. While a 2.5-inch (4.7 oz.) orange provides 70 mg vitamin C, 116 percent of the RDA for a healthy adult, a 2.5-inch (3 oz.) tangerine has 26 mg, about 43 percent of the RDA.

Tangerines, tangelos, and clementines are a good source of potassium, and tangerines have more vitamin A than other citrus fruit.

THE MOST NUTRITIOUS WAY TO SERVE THIS FOOD

Freshly peeled.

DIETS THAT MAY RESTRICT OR EXCLUDE THIS FOOD

Low-fiber diet

Sucrose-free diet

BUYING THIS FOOD

Look for: Tangerines that are heavy for their size (which means they will be juicy). The skin should be deep orange, almost red, and naturally puffy and easy to peel.

Choose firm, heavy tangelos, with a thin, light-orange skin that is less puffy than the tangerine's.

Choose small-to-medium clementines with bright-orange skin. They should be heavy for their size.

STORING THIS FOOD

Store tangelos at room temperature for a few days. Refrigerate them for longer storage.

Refrigerate tangerines and clementines. Tangerines are very perishable; use them within a day or two.

PREPARING THIS FOOD

Wash the fruit under cold running water. Don't peel it until you are ready to use it; peeling tears cells and activates ascorbic acid oxidase, an enzyme that destroys vitamin C.

Although many people prefer citrus fruits very cold, bringing the tangerines, clementines, and tangelos to room temperature before you serve them liberates the aromatic molecules that make the fruit smell and taste good, intensifying the flavor and aroma.

WHAT HAPPENS WHEN YOU COOK THIS FOOD

*   *   *

HOW OTHER FORMS OF PROCESSING AFFECT THIS FOOD

Canning.   Before they are canned, Mandarin oranges are blanched briefly in steam to inactivate ascorbic acid oxidase, an enzyme that would otherwise destroy the fruit's vitamin C. Canned Mandarin oranges contain approximately as much vitamin C as fresh ones.

MEDICAL USES AND/OR BENEFITS

As an antiscorbutic.   Although tangerines, tangelos, and clementines provide less vitamin C per ounce than other citrus fruits, they are still useful in preventing scurvy, the vitamin C-deficiency disease.

Protection against some forms of cancer.   According to the American Cancer Society, foods rich in vitamin A and C may offer some protection against the risk of cancers of the respiratory and gastrointestinal tracts as well as cancers caused by chemicals.

Potassium replacement.   Tangerines, tangelos, and clementines have nearly as much potassium as oranges. Foods rich in potassium are sometimes prescribed for people taking diuretic drugs and losing potassium. However, there is some question as to whether potassium gluconate, the form of potassium found in food, is as valuable to the body as potassium citrate and potassium chloride, the forms of potassium in the supplements given to laboratory animals in the experiments that established the need for potassium replacement for people on diuretic therapy.

ADVERSE EFFECTS ASSOCIATED WITH THIS FOOD

Contact dermatitis.   The oils in the peel of the tangerine, tangelo, or clementine may be irritating to sensitive individuals.

Apthous ulcers.   Eating citrus fruit, including tangerines, tangelos, and clementines, may trigger an attack of apthous ulcers (canker sores) in sensitive people, but eliminating these foods from your diet will neither cure nor prevent an attack.

FOOD/DRUG INTERACTIONS

*   *   *

TEA

NUTRITIONAL PROFILE

Energy value (calories per serving):	Low
Protein:	None
Fat:	None
Cholesterol:	None
Carbohydrates:	Low
Fiber:	None
Sodium:	None
Major vitamin contribution:	Folacin
Major mineral contribution:	Fluoride, magnesium

ABOUT THE NUTRIENTS IN THIS FOOD

Green tea, black tea, and oolong all come from the same plant. The difference lies in the way they are processed. *Green tea* is made from leaves that are dried right after harvesting; the leaves are still green, with a delicate flavor. *Black tea* is made of leaves allowed to ferment after harvesting. During fermentation polyphenoloxidase, an enzyme in the leaves, hastens the oxidation of phenols in the leaves, creating brown pigments that darken the leaves and intensify their flavor.* *Oolong tea* is made from leaves allowed to ferment for only a short time. The leaves are brownish-green and the flavor is somewhere

---

*Polyphenoloxidase is the enzyme that turns fruits and vegetables brown when you slice or peel them. (See, for example, APPLES or POTATOES.)

between the delicate green tea and the strong black tea. (*Souchong, pekoe,* and *orange pekoe* are terms used to describe grades of black-tea leaves. Souchong leaves are round; orange pekoe leaves are thin and wiry; pekoe leaves are shorter and rounder than orange pekoe.)

All these teas are a good source of the B vitamin folacin. Five cups of green tea will provide about a quarter of the daily folacin requirement for an adult; black teas contain a little less; oolong teas contain about one-third as much folacin as green teas. Teas are rich in fluorides. They ordinarily provide about 0.3-0.5 mg fluoride per cup, and tea plants with a fluoride concentration of 100 ppm (parts per million) are not uncommon. (Fluoridated water is generally 1 ppm fluoride.) Tea also provides some magnesium and potassium.

Like coffee and chocolate, tea contains the methylxanthine stimulants caffeine, theophylline, and theobromine. (Caffeine predominates in coffee, theophylline in tea, and theobromine in chocolate.) Depending on how you brew it, a cup of tea may have anywhere from 30-110 percent as much caffeine as a cup of coffee. Steeped tea is higher in caffeine than tea made from bags or instant teas.

CAFFEINE CONTENT OF BREWED TEAS
(mg/5-oz. cup)

Tea bags (black tea)	
5-min. brew	47 mg
1-min. brew	29 mg
Loose tea	
Black, 5-min. brew	41 mg
Green, 5-min. brew	36 mg
Green (Japanese),	
5-min. brew	21 mg
Drip-brewed coffee	139 mg

Source: The American Dietetic Association, *Handbook of Clinical Dietetics* (New Haven: Yale University Press, 1981).

Tea leaves also contain antinutrient enzymes that can split the thiamin (vitamin B_1) molecule so that it is no longer nutritionally useful. This is not generally considered a problem for healthy people who eat a balanced diet and consume normal amounts of tea, but it might trigger a thiamin deficiency if you drink a lot of tea and your diet is marginal in thiamin. The tannins in tea are also potential antinutrients that bind calcium and iron into insoluble compounds your body cannot absorb. According to the National Research Council of the National Academy of Sciences, an "inordinate" consumption of tea might substantially reduce the absorption of iron from foods. Tannins also interfere with the absorption of thiamin (vitamin B_1) and vitamin B_{12}. Finally, tea contains oxalates that can bind calcium and might contribute to the formation of calcium-oxalate kidney stones in people predisposed to form stones.

THE MOST NUTRITIOUS WAY TO SERVE THIS FOOD

With milk. Milk protein (casein) binds and inactivates tannins.

DIETS THAT MAY RESTRICT OR EXCLUDE THIS FOOD

Bland diet
Low-oxalate diet (for people who form calcium oxalate kidney

BUYING THIS FOOD

Look for: Tightly sealed packages. Tea loses flavor and freshness when it is exposed to air, moisture, or light.

STORING THIS FOOD

Store tea in a cool, dark cabinet in an air- and moistureproof container, preferably a glass jar.

PREPARING THIS FOOD

When brewing tea, always start with an absolutely clean glass, china, or enamel pot and, if possible, soft, mineral-free water. The tannins in tea leaves react with metals and minerals to create the compounds that make up the film sometimes seen floating on top of a cup of tea.

WHAT HAPPENS WHEN YOU COOK THIS FOOD

When tea leaves are immersed in water they begin to release flavoring agents plus bitter tannins, the astringent chemicals that coagulate proteins on the surface of the mucous membranes lining the mouth, making the tissues pucker. The best tea is brewed at the boiling point of water, a temperature that allows the tea leaves to release flavoring agents quickly without overloading the tea with bitter tannins. If the brewing water is below the boiling point, the leaves will release their flavoring agents so slowly that by the time enough flavor molecules have been released into the brew, the ratio of bitter tannins will be so high that the tea tastes bitter. Brewing tea in water that is too hot also makes a bitter drink. At temperatures above boiling, the tannins are released so fast that they turn tea bitter in a minute or two.

You cannot judge the flavor of brewed tea by its color. Brewed black teas turn reddish-brown and brewed green teas are almost colorless, but they are both distinctively flavored. Brewing time is a much better guide, three to five minutes for the most flavorful brew. Once the tea is brewed, swirl a spoon through it before serving, to make sure the flavoring oils are evenly distributed.

HOW OTHER KINDS OF PROCESSING AFFECT THIS FOOD

Iced tea.   Hot water can dissolve more pigments from tea leaves than cold water. When tea brewed in hot water is chilled, as for iced tea, the "extra" pigments will precipitate out and the tea will look cloudy.

MEDICAL USES AND/OR BENEFITS

Methylxanthine effects.   All methylxanthines are stimulants. Theophylline and caffeine are central-nervous-system stimulants, vasoactive compounds that dilate the skeletal blood vessels and constrict blood vessels in the brain. Theophylline, which effectively relaxes the smooth muscles in the bronchi—the small passages that carry air into the lungs—is used as an asthma medication, but the relatively low concentrations of theophylline in brewed tea are too small to produce therapeutic effects.

Protection against tooth decay.   Tea contains natural fluorides that may protect against tooth decay, but if you are a steady tea drinker, the fluorides may also stain your teeth.

ADVERSE EFFECTS ASSOCIATED WITH THIS FOOD

Stimulation of the central nervous system.   Taken in excessive amounts, caffeine and theophylline may cause rapid heartbeat, restlessness, sleeplessness, and/or depression in sensitive individuals. Since different people can tolerate different amounts of caffeine and theophylline without suffering ill effects, exactly which dose produces problems varies from person to person.

Constipation.   The tannins in tea may be constipating.

FOOD/DRUG INTERACTIONS

Allopurinol.   Tea and other beverages containing the methylxanthine stimulants (caffeine, theophylline, and theobromine) reduce the effectiveness of the xanthine inhibitor, antigout drug allopurinol.

Antibiotics.   Drinking tea increases stomach acidity, which reduces the absorption of the antibiotics ampicillin, erythromycin, griseofulvin, penicillin, and tetracycline.

Anticoagulants.   Tea is high in vitamin K, the blood-clotting vitamin produced naturally by bacteria in our intestines. Using foods rich in vitamin K while you are taking an anticoagulant (warfarin, Coumadin, Panwarfin) may reduce the effectiveness of the anticoagulant, so larger doses are required.

Antiulcer medication.   Drinking tea makes the stomach more acid and may reduce the effectiveness of normal doses of cimetidine and other antiulcer medication.

Iron supplements.   Caffeine and tannic acid bind with iron to form insoluble compounds your body cannot absorb. Ideally, iron supplements and tea should be taken at least two hours apart.

Nonprescription drugs containing caffeine.   The caffeine in brewed tea may add to the stimulant effects of the caffeine in some cold remedies, diuretics, pain relievers, stimulants, and weight-control products. Some over-the-counter cold pills contain 30 mg caffeine, some pain relievers 130 mg, and some weight-control products as much as 280 mg caffeine. There are 21 to 47 mg caffeine in a 5-ounce cup of brewed tea.

Sedatives.   The caffeine in tea may counteract the drowsiness caused by sedative drugs.

Theophylline.   The theophylline and caffeine in brewed tea may intensify the effects and/or increase the risk of side effects from this antiasthmatic drug.

TOMATOES

NUTRITIONAL PROFILE

Energy value (calories per serving):	Low
Protein:	Moderate
Fat:	Low
Cholesterol:	None
Carbohydrates:	High
Fiber:	Low
Sodium:	Low
Major vitamin contribution:	Vitamin C
Major mineral contribution:	Potassium

ABOUT THE NUTRIENTS IN THIS FOOD

Tomatoes are rich in sugar (fructose, glucose, and sucrose), but they have no starch and only moderate amounts of food fiber, including cellulose and the noncarbohydrate food fiber lignin in the seeds and peel. Tomatoes have a little protein, a trace of fat, and no cholesterol at all.

Tomatoes are an excellent source of vitamin C, most of which is found in the "jelly" around each seed. One medium-size (3.5-oz.) fresh tomato has 17.6 mg vitamin C, 29 percent of the RDA for a healthy adult. Tomatoes grown outdoors have almost twice as much vitamin C as hothouse tomatoes; a garden-grown tomato picked just as it is beginning to turn yellow already has more vitamin C than fully ripened red hothouse tomatoes. Tomatoes are not an important source of vitamin A since most of their color comes from lycopene, a red carotenoid that the body cannot convert into vitamin A. Tomatoes are a good source of potassium.

The roots and leaves of the tomato plant are poisonous. They contain the nerve toxin solanine, which interferes with your body's ability to use acetylcholinesterase, a chemical that facilitates the transmission of impulses between body cells. Solanine does not dissolve in water, nor is it destroyed by heat. (Tomatoes also contain solanidine, a less-toxic derivative of solanine.)

THE MOST NUTRITIOUS WAY TO SERVE THIS FOOD

Fresh and ripe.

DIETS THAT MAY RESTRICT OR EXCLUDE THIS FOOD

Low-fiber diet
Sucrose-free diet

BUYING THIS FOOD

Look for: Smooth round or oval tomatoes. The tomatoes should feel heavy for their size; their flesh should be firm, not watery. If you plan to use the tomatoes right away, pick ripe ones whose skin is a deep orange-red. If you plan to store the tomatoes for a few days, pick tomatoes whose skin is still slightly yellow.

Choose pear-shaped Italian plum tomatoes for sauce-making. They have less water than ordinary tomatoes and more sugar.

Avoid: Bruised tomatoes or tomatoes with mold around the stem end. The damaged tomatoes may be rotten inside; the moldy ones may be contaminated with mycotoxins, poisons produced by molds.

STORING THIS FOOD

Store unripe tomatoes at room temperature until they turn fully orange-red. Tomatoes picked before they have ripened on the vine will be at their most nutritious if you let them continue to ripen at a temperature between 60° and 75° F. Keep them out of direct sunlight, which can soften the tomato without ripening it and destroy vitamins A and C. At room temperature, yellow to light-pink tomatoes should ripen in three to five days.

Refrigerate ripe tomatoes to inactivate enzymes that continue to soften the fruit by dissolving pectins in its cell walls. Fully ripe tomatoes should be used within two or three days.

PREPARING THIS FOOD

Remove and discard all leaves and stalks. Wash the tomatoes under cool running water, then slice and serve. Or peel the tomatoes by plunging them into boiling water, then transferring them on a slotted spoon into a bowl of cold water. The change in temperature damages a layer of cells just under the skin so that the skin slips off easily.

To get rid of the seeds, cut the tomato in half across the middle and squeeze the halves gently, cut side down, over a bowl. The seeds should pop out easily.

WHAT HAPPENS WHEN YOU COOK THIS FOOD

When a tomato is heated the soluble pectins in its cell walls dissolve and the flesh of the tomato turns mushy. But the seeds and peel, which are stiffened with insoluble cellulose and lignin, stay hard. This is useful if you are baking or broiling a tomato (the peel will act as a natural "cup") but not if you are making a soup or stew. If you add an unpeeled tomato to the dish the peel will split, separate from the tomato flesh, and curl up into hard little balls or strips.

Vitamin C is sensitive to heat. A cooked tomato has less vitamin C than a fresh one, but it has the same amount of vitamin A. Carotenoid pigments are impervious to the heat of normal cooking.

HOW OTHER KINDS OF PROCESSING AFFECT THIS FOOD

Artificial ripening.   Tomatoes are available all year round. In the summer, when they can be picked close to the market and have less distance to travel, they are picked vine-ripened. In the winter, when they have to travel farther, they are picked while the skin is still a bit green so they will not spoil on the way to market. On the vine, in shipping, or in your kitchen, tomatoes produce ethylene, a natural ripening agent that triggers the change from green to red skin. In winter, if the tomatoes are still green when they reach the market, they are sprayed with ethylene—which turns them red. These tomatoes are called hard-ripened (as opposed to vine-ripened). You cannot soften hard-ripened tomatoes by storing them at room temperature. They should be refrigerated to keep them from rotting.

Canning.   Most canned tomatoes are salted. Unless otherwise labeled, they should be considered high-sodium foods. (The *botulinum* organism whose toxin causes botulism thrives in an airless, nonacid environment like the inside of a vegetable can. Because tomatoes are an acid food, many people assume that canned tomatoes will not support the growth of the *botulinum* organism, but there have been reports of canned tomatoes contaminated with *botulinum* toxins. Tomatoes should therefore be treated like any other canned food. Cook them thoroughly before you use them. Throw out any unopened can that is bulging. And discard—*without tasting*—any canned tomatoes that look or smell suspicious.)

Aseptic packaging.   Tomatoes packed in aseptic boxes may taste fresher than canned tomatoes because they are cooked for a shorter time before processing.

Sun-drying.   Sun-dried tomatoes will keep for several months in the refrigerator. If they are not packed in oil, they have to be "plumped" before you can use them. Plunge them in boiling water for a few minutes, then drain, soak, chop, and use within a day or so. Or cover them with olive oil and store them in the refrigerator.

MEDICAL USES AND/OR BENEFITS

As an antiscorbutic.   Fresh tomatoes, which are rich in vitamin C, help protect against scurvy, the vitamin C-deficiency disease.

ADVERSE EFFECTS ASSOCIATED WITH THIS FOOD

Orange skin.   Lycopene, the red carotenoid pigment in tomatoes, can be stored in the fatty layer under your skin. If you eat excessive amounts of tomatoes (or tomatoes and carrots), the carotenoids may turn your palms, the soles of your feet, and even some of your other skin yellow-orange. The color (which is harmless) will disappear as soon as you cut back your consumption of these vegetables.

FOOD/DRUG INTERACTIONS

False-positive test for carcenoid tumors.   Carcenoid tumors, which may arise in tissues of the endocrine or gastrointestinal system, secrete serotonin, a natural chemical that makes blood vessels expand or contract. Because serotonin is excreted in urine, these tumors are diagnosed by measuring the levels of serotonin by products in the urine. Tomatoes contain large amounts of serotonin; eating them in the three days before a test for an endocrine tumor might produce a false-positive result, suggesting that you have the tumor when in fact you do not. (Other foods high in serotonin are avocados, bananas, eggplant, pineapple, plums, and walnuts.)

TURNIPS
(Rutabaga)

See also GREENS

See also GREENS

NUTRITIONAL PROFILE

Energy value (calories per serving):	Low
Protein:	Moderate
Fat:	Low
Cholesterol:	None
Carbohydrates:	High
Fiber:	Low
Sodium:	Moderate
Major vitamin contribution:	Vitamins C and A
Major mineral contribution:	Calcium

ABOUT THE NUTRIENTS IN THIS FOOD

White turnips and rutabagas (which are members of the same plant family) are taproots of plants belonging to the cabbage family (cruciferous vegetables). The white turnip is a creamy globe, tinged with rose at the top and capped with greens that may be used on their own as a rich source of calcium (see GREENS). The rutabaga is a large globe with bumpy tan skin and a yellow interior. The outside of the rutabaga is usually waxed to keep the vegetable from drying out on the way to market.

Both turnips and rutabagas are moderately good sources of the food fiber, pectin, and sugars. They have no starch, some protein, a trace of fat, and no cholesterol.

Nutritionally, the rutabaga is a better bargain than the white turnip. While both have vitamin C plus calcium and potassium, ounce for ounce, the rutabaga has almost twice as much as the white turnip. A 3.5-ounce serving of drained boiled rutabaga has 21.9 mg vitamin C (37 percent of the RDA) and 42 mg calcium (5 percent of the RDA).

THE MOST NUTRITIOUS WAY TO SERVE THIS FOOD

White turnips.   Raw or steamed, to preserve the vitamin C. The peeled raw turnip may be grated into a salad or eaten like an apple.

Rutabagas.   Steamed as quickly as possible, to protect the vitamin C.

DIETS THAT MAY RESTRICT OR EXCLUDE THIS FOOD

Low-fiber diet
Low-sodium diet (white turnips)
Sucrose-free diet

BUYING THIS FOOD

Look for: Firm, smooth, medium-sized white turnips with fresh green leaves on top.

Choose smoothly waxed, medium-sized rutabagas with smooth, un-scarred skin.

Avoid: White turnips with wilted greens or rutabagas with mold on the surface.

STORING THIS FOOD

Pull all the leaves off a white turnip, wash them, and store them separately in a plastic bag. (For information about preparing turnip greens, see GREENS.) Refrigerate the turnips in the vegetable crisper. Waxed rutabagas may be stored in a cool, dark cabinet.

PREPARING THIS FOOD

White turnips.   Wash the turnips under cool running water and peel to just under the line that separates the peel from the flesh.

Rutabagas.   Cut the vegetables into quarters (or smaller pieces if necessary) and then cut away the waxed rind.

WHAT HAPPENS WHEN YOU COOK THIS FOOD

When turnips and rutabagas are cooked, the pectins in their cells walls dissolve and the vegetable softens.

Like other cruciferous vegetables, turnips and rutabagas contain mustard oils bound to sugar molecules. These compounds are activated when you cook a turnip or rutabaga or cut into it, damaging its cell walls and releasing enzymes that separate the sugar and oil compounds into their smelly components (which include hydrogen sulfide, the chemical that makes rotten eggs smell rotten). Compared to the mustard oils in cabbage, brussels sprouts, and broccoli, the ones in turnips and rutabagas are very mild. They produce only a faint odor when these vegetables are cut or cooked, but the longer you cook a turnip or rutabaga, the more smelly chemicals you will produce and the stronger the taste and odor will be.

Cooking white turnips in an aluminum or iron pot will darken the turnips or discolor the pot. The turnips contain pale anthoxanthin pigments that interact with metal ions escaping from the surface of the pot to form brown or yellow compounds. Rutabagas, which get their color from carotenes that are impervious to the heat of normal cooking, stay bright-yellow in any pot.

HOW OTHER KINDS OF PROCESSING AFFECT THIS FOOD

Freezing. Crisp fruit and vegetables like apples, carrots, potatoes, turnips, and rutabagas snap when you break or bite into them because their cells are so full of moisture that they pop when the cell walls are broken. When these vegetables are cooked and frozen, the water inside their cells turns into ice crystals that tear cell membranes so that the moisture inside leaks out when the vegetable is defrosted and the cells collapse inward (which is the reason defrosted turnips and rutabagas, like defrosted carrots and potatoes, have a mushy texture).

MEDICAL USES AND/OR BENEFITS

Protection against some forms of cancer. According to the American Cancer Society, turnips and other cruciferous vegetables may lower the risk of some cancers of the gastrointestinal and respiratory tract and chemically induced cancers such as the tumors caused by cigarette smoking or exposure to chemicals in the workplace.

ADVERSE EFFECTS ASSOCIATED WITH THIS FOOD

Enlarged thyroid gland (goiter). Cruciferous vegetables, including turnips, contain goitrogens, chemicals that inhibit the formation of thyroid hormones and cause the thyroid to enlarge in an attempt to produce more. Goitrogens are not hazardous for healthy people who eat moderate amounts of cruciferous vegetables, but they may pose problems for people who have thyroid disorder. The goitrogens in turnips are progoitrin and gluconasturtin.

FOOD/DRUG INTERACTIONS

False-positive test for occult blood in the stool.   The active ingredient in the guaiac slide test for hidden blood in feces is alphaguaiaconic acid, a chemical that turns blue in the presence of blood. Alphaguaiaconic acid also turns blue in the presence of peroxidase, a chemical that occurs naturally in turnips. Eating turnips in the 72 hours before taking the guaiac test may produce a false-positive result in people who do not actually have any blood in their stool.

VARIETY MEATS

(Brain, heart, sweetbreads, tripe, kidney, tongue)

See also BEEF, LIVER, PORK, SAUSAGE, VEAL

NUTRITIONAL PROFILE

Energy value (calories per serving):	Moderate
Protein:	High
Fat:	Moderate (muscle meats) High (organ meats)
Cholesterol:	High
Carbohydrates:	None
Fiber:	None
Sodium:	Low to high
Major vitamin contribution:	Thiamin, vitamin B_6, vitamin B_{12}, niacin
Major mineral contribution:	Iron, copper

ABOUT THE NUTRIENTS IN THIS FOOD

Heart, tongue, and tripe (the muscular lining of the cow's stomach) are muscle meats. Brains, kidneys, and sweetbreads (the thymus gland) are organ meats. Like other foods of animal origin, both kinds of meats are rich sources of proteins considered "complete" because they have sufficient amounts of all the essential amino acids.

Organ meats have more fat than muscle meats. Their fat composition varies according to the animal from which they come. Ounce for ounce, beef fat has proportionally more saturated fatty acids than pork fat, slightly less cholesterol than chicken fat, and appreciably less than lamb fat. There is no food fiber in any meat and no carbohydrates other than the very small amounts of glycogen (sugar) stored in an animal's muscles and liver.

All variety meats are an excellent source of B vitamins, including niacin, vitamin B_6 and vitamin B_{12}, which is found only in animal foods. Sweetbreads are a good source of vitamin C. One 3.5-ounce serving of braised sweetbreads has 30 mg vitamin C, 50 percent of the RDA for a healthy adult. Kidneys are a good source of vitamin A, the fat-soluble vitamin stored in fatty organs. A 3.5-ounce serving of simmered beef kidneys provides 1241 IU vitamin A, 25 percent of the RDA for a healthy adult.

Variety meats are rich in heme iron, the organic form of iron in meat, fish, and poultry that is up to five times more available to the body than non-heme iron, the inorganic form of iron in plant foods. Heart, kidneys, and sweetbreads as well as tongue and tripe are high in sodium.

THE MOST NUTRITIOUS WAY TO SERVE THIS FOOD

With a food rich in vitamin C. Vitamin C changes ferrous iron in foods into the more easily absorbed ferric iron.

DIETS THAT MAY RESTRICT OR EXCLUDE THIS FOOD

Low-cholesterol, controlled-fat diet
Low-protein diet
Low-sodium diet

BUYING THIS FOOD

Look for: Refrigerated meat that feels cold to the touch and looks and smells absolutely fresh. Frozen heart or tripe should be solid, with no give to the package and no drippings staining the outside.

Choose some variety meats by size. The smaller the tongue, for example, the more tender it will be. The most tender kidneys come from young animals. On the other hand, all brains and sweetbreads are by nature tender, while all heart, tongue, and tripe (the most solidly muscular of the variety meats) require long simmering to make them tender.

STORING THIS FOOD

Refrigerate variety meats immediately. All are highly perishable and should be used within 24 hours of purchase. Refrigeration prolongs the freshness of meat by slowing the natural multiplication of bacteria on the surface. Unchecked, these bacteria will digest the proteins on the surface of the meat, leaving a slimy film in their wake, and convert the meat's sulfur-containing amino acids (tryptophan, methionine, and cystine) into smelly chemicals called mercaptans. The combination of mercaptans with myoglobin, a pigment in blood that transfers oxygen hemoglobin to muscle tissues, creates the greenish pigment that makes rotten meat look so unpleasant.

Wrap fresh meat carefully before storing to keep the drippings from spilling and contaminating other food or the refrigerator/freezer shelves.

PREPARING THIS FOOD

Brains. First wash the brains under cold running water and pull off the membranes. Then put the brains in a bowl of cold water and let them soak for a half hour. Change the water; let them soak for another half hour. Repeat the process one more time, for a total soaking time of an hour and a half. Now drain the water, put the brains in a saucepan, cover with water, add a tablespoon or two of acid (lemon juice or vinegar) to firm the brains, and cook them for 20 to 25 minutes over low heat without boiling. Drain and use as your recipe directs.

Kidneys. Pull off the white membrane and rinse the kidneys thoroughly under plenty of cold running water. Cut them in half, remove the inner core, and rinse once again. Slice them and use as your recipe directs. (Beef kidneys have a strong, distinctive flavor that can be toned down by soaking the kidneys for an hour in a solution of 1 teaspoon lemon juice to 1 cup of water before cooking.)

Heart. Cut out the blood vessels, rinse the heart thoroughly (inside and out) under cold running water, and prepare as your recipe directs.

Sweetbreads. Rinse the sweetbreads thoroughly under cold running water and soak in ice water for at least an hour, changing the water until it remains clear and free of blood. Then drain the sweetbreads and blanch them in water plus 2 teaspoons of acid (lemon juice or vinegar) to firm them. Drain the sweetbreads, cover them with ice water, and remove membranes and connective tissue. Then use as your recipe directs.

Tongue. Scrub the tongue with a vegetable brush under cold running water. Cover it with cold water, bring the water to a boil, and cook the tongue at a simmer for 30 minutes or soak and cook as directed on the package. Drain the tongue, peel off the skin, cut away the gristle and small bones, and prepare as your recipe directs. Some smoked tongues require long soaking, even overnight; check the directions on the package.

Tripe. Virtually all the tripe sold in markets today has been blanched and boiled until tender. All you have to do is wash it thoroughly under cold running water and use it as directed in your recipe. If you have to start from scratch with tripe, wash it in several changes of cold water, boil it for several hours until tender, then use as your recipe directs.

After handling any raw meat, always wash your knives, cutting board, counter—and your hands—with warm soapy water to reduce the chance of transferring microorganisms from the meat to any other food.

WHAT HAPPENS WHEN YOU COOK THIS FOOD

Heat changes the structure of proteins. It denatures protein molecules—they break apart into smaller fragments, change shape, or clump together. All these changes force moisture out of protein tissues. The longer you cook variety meats, the more moisture they will lose. The meat's pigments, also denatured by the heat, combine with oxygen and turn brown—the natural color of cooked meat.

As the meat cooks, its fats oxidize. Oxidized fats, whether formed in cooking or when the cooked meat is stored in the refrigerator, give cooked meat a characteristic warmed-over flavor the next day. Stewing and storing heart or kidneys under a blanket of antioxidants—catsup or a gravy made of tomatoes, peppers and other vitamin C-rich vegetables—reduces the oxidation of fats and the intensity of warmed-over flavor.

All variety meats must be cooked thoroughly.

HOW OTHER KINDS OF PROCESSING AFFECT THIS FOOD

Freezing.   When meat is frozen, the water inside its cells freezes into sharp ice crystals that puncture cell membranes so that water (and B vitamins) leak out of the cells when the meat is thawed. Frozen heart, kidneys, and tripe are drier when thawed than they would have been fresh. They may also be lower in B vitamins. Freezing may also cause freezer burn, dry spots left when moisture evaporates from the surface of the meat. Waxed freezer paper is designed specifically to hold the moisture in frozen meat.

MEDICAL USES AND/OR BENEFITS

As a source of heme iron.   Because the body stores excess iron in the heart, kidneys, and other organs, variety meats are an excellent source of heme iron.

ADVERSE EFFECTS ASSOCIATED WITH THIS FOOD

Production of uric acid.   Purines are natural by-products of protein metabolism. Purines break down into uric acid, which form sharp crystals that can cause gout if they collect in your joints or kidney stones if they collect in urine. Sweetbreads and kidneys are a source of purines. Eating them raises the concentration of purines in your body. Although controlling the amount of purine-producing foods in the diet may not significantly affect the course of gout (treated with medication such as allopurinol, which inhibits the formation of uric acid), limiting these foods is still part of many gout treatment regimens.

Elevated levels of serum cholesterol.   Abnormally high levels of cholesterol in the blood are a risk factor in heart disease. How your diet affects the amount of cholesterol you produce is not entirely clear; dietary fat and cholesterol may not be the primary factor in determining how much and what kind of cholesterol your body makes and stores. Nonetheless, there is evidence to suggest that controlling the amount of fat and cholesterol you consume may help lower serum cholesterol levels, particularly for people with high levels. In 1986 the American Heart Association issued new guidelines suggesting that healthy adults reduce fat consumption to 30 percent of the total calories consumed each day and limit cholesterol intake to 300 mg per day or 100 mg per 1000 calories, whichever is less.

CHOLESTEROL CONTENT OF
VARIETY MEATS
FROM BEEF
(mg/3.5 oz. serving)

Brains (simmered)	2,054 mg
Heart (simmered)	193 mg
Kidney (simmered)	387 mg
Sweetbread (braised)	294 mg
Tongue (simmered	107 mg
Tripe (raw)	95 mg

Source: *Composition of Foods: Beef Products,* Agriculture Handbook No. 8-13 (USDA, 1986).

Decline in kidney function.   Proteins are nitrogen compounds. When metabolized by your body, they yield ammonia that is excreted through the kidneys. In laboratory animals, a sustained high-protein diet increases the flow of blood through the kidneys and may accelerate the natural decline in kidney function associated with aging. To date there is no proof that this also occurs in human beings.

FOOD/DRUG INTERACTIONS
*   *   *

VEAL

Energy value (calories per serving):	Moderate
Protein:	High
Fat:	Moderate
Cholesterol:	Moderate
Carbohydrates:	None
Fiber:	None
Sodium:	Moderate
Major vitamin contribution:	Thiamin, vitamin B_6, vitamin B_{12}, niacin
Major mineral contribution:	Iron, zinc

ABOUT THE NUTRIENTS IN THIS FOOD

Veal is meat from cattle usually under three months of age, weighing less than 400 pounds.

Veal is more subtly flavored than beef from older animals. It has proportionally more protein and less fat. Like other animal foods, veal provides proteins considered "complete" because they have adequate amounts of all the essential amino acids. Veal has no food fiber and no carbohydrates other than small amounts of glycogen (sugar) stored in the animal's muscles.

Veal is an excellent source of B vitamins, including niacin, vitamin B_6, and vitamin B_{12}, which is found only in animal foods. Veal is a good source of heme iron, the organic form of iron found in foods of animal original. Heme iron is approximately five times more available to the body than non-heme iron, the inorganic form of iron found in plant foods.

*Values are for lean, roast meat.

THE MOST NUTRITIOUS WAY TO SERVE THIS FOOD

With a food rich in vitamin C. Ascorbic acid increases the absorption of iron from meat.

DIETS THAT MAY RESTRICT OR EXCLUDE THIS FOOD

Controlled-fat, low-cholesterol diet
Low-protein diet (for some forms of kidney disease)

BUYING THIS FOOD

Look for: The cut of veal that fits your recipe. Thick cuts, such as roasts, need long, slow cooking to gelatinize their connective tissue and keep the veal from drying out. A breast with bones, however, has more fat than a solid roast. Veal scallops and cutlets are the only kinds of veal that can be sauteed or broiled quickly.

STORING THIS FOOD

Refrigerate raw veal immediately, carefully wrapped to prevent its drippings from contaminating the refrigerator shelves or other foods. Refrigeration prolongs the freshness of veal by slowing the natural multiplication of bacteria on the surface of meat. Unchecked, these bacteria will convert proteins and other substances on the surface of the meat to a slimy film. Eventually, they will also convert the meat's sulfur-containing amino acids methionine and cystine into smelly chemicals called mercaptans that interact with myoglobin to create the greenish pigment that gives spoiled meat its characteristic unpleasant appearance.

Fresh veal will keep for three to five days in the refrigerator. As a general rule, large cuts of veal will keep a little longer than small ones. Ground veal, which has many surfaces where bacteria can live and work, should be used within 48 hours.

PREPARING THIS FOOD

To lighten the color of veal, cover the meat with milk and soak it overnight in the refrigerator. Or marinate it in lemon juice. Trim the meat carefully. By judiciously cutting away all visible fat you can significantly reduce the amount of fat and cholesterol in each serving.

Do not salt the veal before you cook it. The salt dissolves in water on the surface of the meat to form a liquid denser than the moisture inside the veal's cells. As a result the water inside the cells will flow out across the cell toward the denser solution, a phenomenon known as osmosis. The loss of moisture will make the veal less tender and stringy.

After handling raw meat, *always* wash your knives, cutting board, counter—and your hands—with warm soapy water to reduce the chance of transferring microorganisms from the meat to other foods.

WHAT HAPPENS WHEN YOU COOK THIS FOOD

Cooking changes the way veal looks and tastes, alters its nutritional value, makes it safer, and extends its shelf life.

Browning meat before you cook it does not seal in the juices but does change the flavor by caramelizing proteins and sugars on the surface. Since meat has no sugars other than the small amounts of glycogen in its muscles, we usually add sugars in the form of marinades or basting liquids that may also contain acids (vinegar, lemon juice, wine) to break down muscle fibers and tenderize the meat. Browning has one minor nutritional drawback. It breaks amino acids on the surface of the meat into smaller compounds that are no longer useful proteins.

Heat changes the structure of proteins. It denatures the protein molecules, which means they break up into smaller fragments or change shape or clump together. All these changes force water out of protein tissues, which is why meat gets dryer the longer it is cooked. In addition, heat denatures the pigments in meat, which combine with oxygen and turn brown.

As the veal continues to cook, its fats oxidize. Oxidized fats, whether formed in cooking or when the cooked meat is stored in the refrigerator, give cooked the meat a characteristic warmed-over flavor. You can reduce the oxidation of fats and the warmed-over flavor by cooking and storing meat under a blanket of catsup or a gravy made of tomatoes, peppers, and other vitamin C-rich vegetables—all of which are natural antioxidants.

An obvious nutritional benefit of cooking is that it liquifies the fat in the meat so that it can run off. And, of course, cooking makes veal safer by killing *Salmonella* and other organisms.

HOW OTHER KINDS OF PROCESSING AFFECT THIS FOOD

Freezing.   When you thaw frozen veal it may be less tender than fresh veal. It may also be lower in B vitamins. While the veal is frozen, the water inside its cells turn into sharp ice crystals that can puncture cell membranes. When the veal thaws, moisture (and some of the B vitamins) will leak out through these torn cell walls. The loss of moisture is irreversible.

Freezing can also cause freezer burn, the dry spots where moisture has evaporated from the surface of the meat. Waxed freezer paper is designed specifically to hold the moisture in meat.

Freezing slows the oxidation of fats and the multiplication of bacteria so that the veal stays usable longer than it would in a refrigerator. At 0° F fresh veal will keep for four to eight months. (Beef, which has fewer oxygen-sensitive unsaturated fatty acids than veal, will keep for up to a year.)

MEDICAL USES AND/OR BENEFITS
*   *   *

ADVERSE EFFECTS ASSOCIATED WITH THIS FOOD

Elevated levels of serum cholesterol.   Abnormally high levels of cholesterol in the blood are a risk factor in heart disease, but the amount of saturated fat in the diet may not be the primary factor in determining how much and what kind of cholesterol an individual produces. People with hypercholesteremia, a metabolic disorder that influences cholesterol production in the liver, may benefit from a diet low in dietary cholesterol, but there is no conclusive proof that lowering a healthy person's consumption of dietary cholesterol will significantly change the amount of cholesterol he or she produces. In 1986 the American Heart Association issued new guidelines advising healthy people to reduce their fat consumption to 30 percent of the calories they eat each day and limit their cholesterol intake to 300 mg per day or 100 mg per 1000 calories, whichever is less. (A 3.5-ounce serving of veal cutlet has 100 mg cholesterol.)

Antibiotic sensitivity.   Cattle in this country are routinely given antibiotics to protect them from infection. By law, the antibiotic treatment must stop three days before the veal is slaughtered. Theoretically, the veal should then be free of antibiotic residues, but some people who are sensitive to penicillin or tetracycline may (rarely) have an allergic reaction to the meat.

Antibiotic-resistant Salmonella *and toxoplasmosis.*   Veal treated with antibiotics may produce meat contaminated with antibiotic-resistant strains of *Salmonella,* and all raw beef may harbor *T. gondii,* the parasite that causes toxoplasmosis. Toxoplasmosis is particularly hazardous for pregnant women. It can be passed on to the fetus and may trigger a series of birth defects, including blindness and mental retardation. Both the drug-resistant *Salmonella* and *T. gondii* can be eliminated by cooking meat thoroughly and washing all utensils, cutting boards, and counters as well as your hands with hot soapy water before touching any other food.

Decline in kidney function.   Proteins are nitrogen compounds. When metabolized they yield ammonia, which is eventually is excreted through the kidneys. In laboratory animals, a sustained high-protein diet increases the flow of blood through the kidneys and may accelerate the decline in kidney function associated with aging. There is no proof yet that this occurs in humans.

FOOD/DRUG INTERACTIONS

MAO inhibitors.   Monoamine oxidase (MAO) inhibitors are drugs used as antidepressants or antihypertensives. They inhibit the action of enzymes that break down tyramine, a natural by-product of protein metabolism, so it can be eliminated from the body. Tyramine is a pressor amine, a substance that constricts blood vessels and raises blood pressure. If you eat a food rich in tyramine while you are taking an MAO inhibitor, the pressor amine cannot be eliminated from your body, and the result may be a hypertensive crisis (sustained elevated blood pressure). Papain (see PAPAYA) tenderizers, which work by enzymatic action that breaks down the proteins in meat, may produce vasoactive compounds similar to tyramine. Meat treated with papain tenderizers may be excluded from your diet when you are using an MAO inhibitor.

VEGETABLE OILS

(Coconut oil, corn oil, cottonseed oil, olive oil, peanut oil, safflower oil, sesame oil, soybean oil)

NUTRITIONAL PROFILE

Energy value (calories per serving):	High
Protein:	None
Fat:	High
Cholesterol:	None
Carbohydrates:	None
Fiber:	None
Sodium:	None
Major vitamin contribution:	Vitamin E
Major mineral contribution:	None

ABOUT THE NUTRIENTS IN THIS FOOD

Vegetable oils are derived from nuts, seeds, and vegetables. They are concentrated sources of energy. Gram for gram, fats contain twice as many calories as proteins and carbohydrates; because they are digested more slowly, they produce a feeling of satiety and keep us from being hungry again quickly.

Fats are similar to proteins in that some of their constituents cannot be manufactured by the human body. Proteins provide essential amino acids we cannot produce on our own. Fats provide the essential fatty acids linoleic acid and arachidonic acid. Our bodies cannot manufacture linoleic acid, but we can make arachidonic acid from the linoleic acid we get from foods. The best sources of linoleic acid are vegetable oils other than olive oil and coconut oil. The best sources of arachidonic acid are the fats in dairy foods, meat, fish, and poultry.

Vegetable oils are also our best source of vitamin E, a natural antioxidant. (*Vitamin E* is the collective name for a group of chemicals known as tocopherols.)

Vegetable oils are composed primarily of unsaturated fatty acids, fatty acids whose molecule can accommodate extra hydrogen atoms. Monounsaturated fatty acids can accommodate two extra hydrogen atoms; polyunsaturated fatty acids can accommodate four or more hydrogen atoms. Most of the fatty acids in olive oil and peanut oil are monounsaturated; most of the fatty acids in corn oil, safflower oil, and soybean oil are polyunsaturated.

FATTY ACID COMPOSITION OF VARIOUS DIETARY FATS

	% saturated	% monounsaturated	% polyunsaturated
Corn oil	13%	25%	62%
Olive oil	14%	77%	9%
Peanut oil	15%	48%	34%
Safflower oil	13%	12%	78%
Soybean oil partially hydrogenated)	15%	45%	39%
Butter	66%	31%	4%

Source: "Provisional table on the fatty acid and cholesterol count of selected foods" (USDA, 1984).

THE MOST NUTRITIOUS WAY TO SERVE THIS FOOD
In moderation.

DIETS THAT MAY RESTRICT OR EXCLUDE THIS FOOD
Low-fat diet

BUYING THIS FOOD
Look for: Tightly sealed bottles of vegetable oil, protected from light and heat.

STORING THIS FOOD
Store vegetable oils in a cool, dark cabinet to protect them from light, heat, and air. When exposed to air, fatty acids become rancid, which means that they combine with oxygen to form hydroperoxides, natural substances that

taste bad, smell bad, and may destroy the vitamin E in the oil. The higher the proportion of polyunsaturated fatty acids in the oil, the more quickly it will turn rancid. Many salad and cooking oils contain antioxidant preservatives (BHT, BHA) to slow this reaction.

PREPARING THIS FOOD
*   *   *

WHAT HAPPENS WHEN YOU COOK THIS FOOD

Heat promotes the oxidation of fats, a chemical reaction accelerated by cooking fats in iron pots. Cooked fats are safe at normal temperatures, but when they are used over and over, they may break down into components known as free radicals—which are suspected carcinogens.

Most fats begin to decompose well below 500° F, and they may catch fire spontaneously with no warning without boiling first. The point at which they decompose and burn is called the smoking point. Vegetable shortening will burn at 375° F, vegetable oils at close to 450° F. Safflower, soybean, cottonseed, and corn oils have higher smoking points than peanut and sesame oils.

HOW OTHER KINDS OF PROCESSING AFFECT THIS FOOD

Margarine and shortening.   Margarine is made of hydrogenated vegetable oils (oils to which hydrogen atoms have been added). Adding hydrogen atoms hardens the oils into a semi-solid material than can be molded into bars or packed in tubs as margarine or shortening. Hydrogenation also changes the structure of some of the polyunsaturated fatty acids in the oils from a form known as "cis fatty acids" to a form known as "trans fatty acids." Questions have been raised as to the safety of trans fatty acids, but there is no proof so far that they are more likely than cis fatty acids to cause atherosclerosis. Margarines may also contain coloring agents (to make the margarine look like butter), emulsifiers, and milk or animal fats (including butter).

Margarine should be refrigerated, closely wrapped to keep it from picking up odors from other foods. It will keep for about two weeks in the refrigerator before its fatty acids oxidize to produce off odors and taste. Shortening can be stored, tightly covered, at room temperature.

MEDICAL USES AND/OR BENEFITS

Protection against coronary artery disease.   People whose serum cholesterol levels are abnormally high are considered at risk for heart disease. Vegetable oils rich in unsaturated fatty acids appear to lower levels of serum cholesterol. Polyunsaturated fatty acids lower all forms of cholesterol, including the "good cholesterol," the high-density lipoproteins (HDLs) that remove cholesterol from the bloodstream. Monounsaturated fatty acids lower cholesterol levels as effectively as polyunsaturates, but they protect the HDL fractions and thus may be more protective than polyunsaturated fatty acids. In 1986 the American Heart Association issued new guidelines suggesting that consumers reduce total fat intake to 30 percent of the calories consumed each day and limit cholesterol intake to 300 mg per day, or 100 mg per 1,000 calories, whichever is less.

ADVERSE EFFECTS ASSOCIATED WITH THIS FOOD
*   *   *

FOOD/DRUG INTERACTIONS
*   *   *

WATER

NUTRITIONAL PROFILE

Energy value (calories per serving):	None
Protein:	None
Fat:	None
Cholesterol:	None
Carbohydrates:	None
Fiber:	None
Sodium:	Low to high
Major vitamin contribution:	None
Major mineral contribution:	Sodium, calcium, magnesium, fluorides

ABOUT THE NUTRIENTS IN THIS FOOD

Water has no nutrients other than the minerals it picks up from the earth or the pipes through which it flows or that are added by a bottler to give the water a specific taste. *Hard* water contains dissolved calcium and magnesium salts, usually in the form of bicarbonates, sulfates, and chlorides. *Soft* water has very little calcium and magnesium, but it may still contain sodium. According to figures published in 1986 in the *Journal of the American Dietetic Association,* one out of every four water supplies in the United States has more than 50 mg sodium per quart of water; five out of every hundred have 250 mg sodium per quart. Some bottled mineral waters may contain as much as 200 to 400 mg sodium in an 8-ounce glass.

The only absolutely pure water is *distilled water,* which has been vaporized, condensed, and collected free of any impurities. *Spring water* is water that flows up to the earth's surface on its own from an underground spring. *Well water* is water that must be reached through a hole drilled into the ground. *Naturally sparkling water* is spring water with naturally occurring carbon dioxide. *Sparkling water,* artificially carbonated with added carbon dioxide, is known as *seltzer. Club soda* is sparkling water flavored with salts, including sodium bicarbonate.

THE MOST NUTRITIOUS WAY TO SERVE THIS FOOD

Filtered, if required, to remove impurities. (Bacteria may multiply on an ordinary faucet filter. Change the filter frequently to protect your drinking water.)

DIETS THAT MAY RESTRICT OR EXCLUDE THIS FOOD

Low-sodium diets ("softened" water, some bottled waters)

BUYING THIS FOOD

Look for: Tightly sealed bottles, preferably with a protective foil seal under the cap. If you are on a low-sodium diet, read the label on bottled waters carefully. Many bottled mineral waters contain sodium chloride or sodium bicarbonate.

STORING THIS FOOD

Store bottled water in a cool, dark cabinet. Water bottled in glass will keep longer than water bottled in plastic, which may begin to pick up the taste of the container after about two weeks.

Improve the taste of heavily chlorinated tap water by refrigerating it overnight in a glass bottle. The chlorine will evaporate and the water will taste fresh.

PREPARING THIS FOOD

Let cold tap water run for a minute or two before you use it; the air it picks up while it runs will make it taste better.

WHAT HAPPENS WHEN YOU COOK THIS FOOD

The molecules in a solid material are tightly packed together in an orderly crystal structure. The molecules in a gas have no particular order, which is why a gas will expand to fill the space available. A liquid is somewhere in between. The attractive forces that hold its molecules together are weaker than those between the molecules in a solid but stronger than those between the molecules in a gas. When you heat a liquid, you excite its molecules (increase their thermal energy) and disrupt the forces holding them together. As the molecules continue to absorb energy, they separate from each other and begin to escape from the liquid. When the concentration of the molecules escaping from the liquids equals the pressure of air above the surface, the liquid will *boil* and its molecules will *vaporize,* converting the liquid to a gas that floats off the surface as the liquid *evaporates.*

At sea level, plain water boils at 212° F (100° C), the temperature at which its molecules have absorbed enough energy to begin to escape from the surface as steam. If you add salt to the water before it starts to boil, the water molecules will need to pick up extra energy in order to overcome the greater attractive forces between the salt and water molecules. Since the energy comes from heat, adding salt raises the boiling point of the water. Salted water boils at a higher temperature than plain water does. That is why pasta, rice, and other foods cook more quickly in boiling salted water than in plain boiling water.

HOW OTHER KINDS OF PROCESSING AFFECT THIS FOOD

Freezing.   Water is the only compound that expands when it freezes. A water molecule is shaped roughly like an open triangle, with an oxygen atom at the center and a hydrogen atom at the end of either arm. When water is frozen, its molecules move more slowly, and each hydrogen atom forms a temporary bond to the oxygen atom on a nearby water molecule. The phenomenon, known as hydrogen bonding, creates a rigid structure in which the molecules stretch out rather than pack closely together, as normally happens when a substance is cooled. An ounce of frozen water (ice) takes up more room than an ounce of liquid water.

"Softening."   Home water softeners that filter out "hard" calcium carbonate and replace it with sodium may increase the sodium content of tap water by as much as 100 mg per quart.

MEDICAL USES AND/OR BENEFITS

Antacid, diuretic, and laxative effects. Mineral waters are natural mild diuretics and, because they contain sodium bicarbonate, naturally antacid. Any kind of water, taken warm about a half hour before breakfast, appears to be mildly laxative, perhaps because it stimulates contractions of the muscles in the digestive tract.

Protection against cavities. Fluorine is a natural element, present in soil and rocks. Fluoridated drinking water provides fluoride ions that are incorporated into the crystalline structure of dental enamel and bones, making our teeth more resistant to decay and possibly offering some protection against osteoporosis. A concentration of one part fluoride ions to one million parts water (1 ppm) is considered both safe and protective. In some parts of the American Southwest, however, the ground water is naturally fluoridated to levels as high as 10 ppm. At levels higher than 2 ppm, the fluoride ions may stain your teeth with white patches and brown stains. If you continue to drink highly fluoridated drinking water it may eventually pit the enamel surface of your teeth and/or cause abnormal hardening of the bones.

●

Protection against hypertension and heart disease.   Two major studies, one at the University of Missouri and one at Dartmouth Medical School, have suggested that people whose drinking water is "hard" (more than 15-50 ppm calcium and magnesium salts) appear to have lower rates of coronary heart disease than people whose drinking water is "soft" (less than 15-50 ppm calcium and magnesium salts). Exactly how hard water might protect against heart disease remains to be explained.

ADVERSE EFFECTS ASSOCIATED WITH THIS FOOD

Contaminants.   Drinking water may pick up a variety of chemical contaminants as it travels through the ground or through pipes. To date, more than 300 chemical contaminants, including arsenic, asbestos, nitrates and nitrites, pesticides, and lead, have been identified in the water systems of various American cities. Even chlorine, which is added to the water supply to eliminate potentially hazardous microorganisms, can be a problem. The free chlorine generated during the purification process may react with organic compounds in the water to produce trihalomethanes, such a chloroform, which are suspected carcinogens or mutagens (substances that alter the structure of DNA). To prevent this, the Environmental Protection Agency (EPA) monitors chlorinated water supplies to make sure that the level of trihalomethanes remains below 0.10 mg/liter (100 parts per billion), a level currently considered safe for human consumption.

Water overload.   On an average day, a healthy adult may lose 2500 ml (milliliters) water through breathing, perspiring, urinating, and defecating. Since an ounce is equal to 30 ml, we can replace the fluid we lose with eight 10-ounce glasses of water or any combination of water plus other liquids and/or foods with a high water content. If we take in much more water than we need to replace what we lose, the excess water will dilute the liquid inside our cells, lowering the normal concentration of electrolytes (sodium, potassium, chloride). Because a proper ratio of electrolytes is vital to the transmission of impulses from cell to cell, a continued excessive intake of fluid may cause water intoxication, a condition whose symptoms include lethargy, muscle spasms, convulsions, coma, and/or death. Healthy people whose kidneys are able to eliminate a temporary water overload are unlikely to suffer from water intoxication, but diets that require excessive water consumption may be hazardous for epileptics and others at risk of seizures.

FOOD/DRUG INTERACTIONS

* * *

WINE

NUTRITIONAL PROFILE*

Energy value (calories per serving):	Moderate
Protein:	Low
Fat:	None
Cholesterol:	None
Carbohydrates:	Low
Fiber:	None
Sodium:	Low
Major vitamin contribution:	B vitamins
Major mineral contribution:	Potassium

ABOUT THE NUTRIENTS IN THIS FOOD

Wine is a beverage produced by yeasts that digest the sugars in fruits and turn them into alcohol. Grapes are particularly well suited to winemaking because they are sweet enough to produce a beverage that is at least 10 percent alcohol and acid enough to encourage the growth of the friendly yeasts while discouraging the growth of potentially harmful bacteria.

Table wines are wines with an alcohol content lower than 15 percent.+ *Dessert wines* are sweet wines whose alcohol content ranges between 15 and 24 percent. *Sherry, madeira,* and *port* are *fortified wines,* wines to which

*Values are for table wines.

+In the United States, "proof" is twice the alcohol content. A wine that is 15 percent alcohol by volume is 30 proof.

brandy or spirits have been added. *Sparkling wines,* such as champagne, are bottled with a precisely measured yeast-and-sugar solution that ferments in the bottle to produce carbon dioxide bubbles.

Wines contain carbohydrates, a trace of protein, and small amounts of vitamins and minerals but no fats. Unlike food, which has to be metabolized before your body can use it for energy, the alcohol in wine can be absorbed into the bloodstream directly from the gastrointestinal tract. Ethyl alcohol (the alcohol in alcohol beverages) provides 7 calories per gram.

Quercitin and quercitrin, the pale yellow pigments that make white wine "white," turn browner as they age. The darker the wine, the older it is. Red wine's ruby color comes from red anthocyanin pigments in red grape skins. As red wines age, their red pigments react with tannins in the wine and turn brown.

THE MOST NUTRITIOUS WAY TO SERVE THIS FOOD
In moderation.

DIETS THAT MAY RESTRICT OR EXCLUDE THIS FOOD
Bland diet
Lactose-free diet
Low-purine (antigout) diet
Low-sodium diet (cooking wines)
Sucrose-free diet

BUYING THIS FOOD
Look for: Tightly sealed bottles stored away from direct sunlight, whose energy might disrupt the structure of molecules in the beverage and alter its flavor.

Choose wines sold only by licensed dealers. Products sold in these stores are manufactured under the strict supervision of the federal government.

STORING THIS FOOD
All wine should be stored in tightly sealed bottles in a cool, dry, dark place, protected from direct light—whose energy might disrupt the structure of the flavor molecules in the wine. (Most wine bottles are tinted amber or green to screen out ultraviolet light.)

After it is bottled, wine continues to react with the small amount of oxygen in the container, a phenomenon known as aging. Red wines improve ("mature") in the bottle; their taste is deeper and mellower after a year or two, and some continue to age for as long as fifteen years. Keep the bottle on its side so that the wine flows down and keeps the cork wet. A wet cork expands to seal the bottle even more tightly and keep extra air from coming into the bottle and oxidizing the wine to vinegar. (Bottles with plastic corks or screw tops can be stored upright. Their seals are air-tight.)

Store leftover wine in a small bottle with a tight cap and as little air space as possible. Use leftover table wines as soon as possible (or let them oxidize to vinegar). Appetizer and dessert wines, which are higher in alcohol content than table wines, may taste good for as long as a month after the bottle is opened.

PREPARING THIS FOOD

All wines contain volatile molecules that give the beverage its characteristic taste and smell. Warming the liquid excites these molecules and intensifies the flavor and aroma. While dry white or rosé wines are usually chilled before serving, sweet white wines and the more flavorful reds are best served at room temperature.

Stand a bottle of wine upright for a day before serving it, so that the sediment (dregs) will settle to the bottom. When you open a bottle of wine, handle it gently to avoid stirring up the sediment.

WHAT HAPPENS WHEN YOU COOK THIS FOOD

When you heat wine, its alcohol evaporates but its flavor remains. Since evaporation concentrates the flavor, be sure the wine you're using tastes good enough to drink; cooking won't improve the flavor of a bad wine. In cooking with wine, when you add the wine depends on what you want it to do. As a tenderizer, add the wine when you start cooking the dish. For flavor, add it near the end of the cooking process. For maximum flavor, reduce (evaporate) the wine slightly before you add it.

Alcohol is an acid. If you cook it in an aluminum or iron pot, it will react with metal ions to form dark compounds that discolor the pot and the food. Recipes made with wine should be prepared in an enameled, glass, or stainless steel pot.

HOW OTHER KINDS OF PROCESSING AFFECT THIS FOOD

*   *   *

MEDICAL USES AND/OR BENEFITS

To reduce the level of serum cholesterol. Alcohol beverages, including wine, affect the body's metabolism of fats and appear to decrease the production or storage of low-density lipoproteins (LDL) while increasing the production and storage of high-density lipoproteins (HDL). Research into the effects of alcohol consumption on cholesterol levels is still in the experimental stage.

Stimulating the appetite.   Alcohol beverages stimulate the production of saliva and gastric acids that cause the stomach contractions we call hunger pangs. Moderate amounts, which may help stimulate appetite, are often prescribed for geriatric patients, convalescents, and people who do not have ulcers or other chronic gastric problems.

Dilation of blood vessels.   Alcohol dilates the tiny blood vessels just under the skin, bringing blood up to the surface. That's why moderate amounts of alcohol beverages (0.2-1 gram per kilogram of body weight—that is, 6.6 ounces of wine for a 150-pound adult) temporarily warms the drinker. But the warm blood that flows up to the surface of the skin will cool down there, making you even colder when it circulates back into the center of your body. Then an alcohol flush will make you perspire, so that you lose more heat. Excessive amounts of beverage alcohol may depress the mechanism that regulates body temperature.

ADVERSE EFFECTS ASSOCIATED WITH THIS FOOD

Alcohol abuse.   People who consistently consume excessive amounts of alcohol beverages or who are unable to metabolize alcohol efficiently or to deal with its physiological and psychological effects may suffer from alcoholism, an illness that may cause both physical and emotional problems, including cirrhosis (degeneration) of the liver, malnutrition, delirium tremens, and death.

Hangover.   Alcohol is absorbed from the stomach and small intestine and carried by the bloodstream to the liver, where it is oxidized to acetaldehyde by alcohol dehydrogenase (ADH), the enzyme our bodies use every day to metabolize the alcohol we produce when we digest carbohydrates. The acetaldehyde is converted to acetyl coenzyme A and either eliminated from the body or used in the synthesis of cholesterol, fatty acids, and body tissues. Although individuals vary widely in their capacity to metabolize alcohol, an adult of average size can metabolize the alcohol in 13 ounces (400 ml) of wine in approximately five to six hours. If he or she drinks more than that, the amount of alcohol in the body will exceed the available supply of ADH. The surplus, unmetabolized alcohol will pile up in the bloodstream, interfering with the liver's metabolic functions. Since alcohol decreases the reabsorption of water from the kidneys and may inhibit the secretion of an antidiuretic hormone, the drinker will begin to urinate copiously, losing magnesium, calcium, and zinc but retaining more irritating uric acid. The level of lactic acid in the body will increase, making him or her feel tired and out of sorts; the acid-base balance will be out of kilter; the blood vessels of the head will swell and throb; and the stomach, its lining irritated by the alcohol, will ache. The ultimate result is a "hangover" whose symptoms will disappear only when enough time has passed to allow the body to marshal the ADH needed to metabolize the extra alcohol in the blood.

Fetal alcohol syndrome.   Fetal alcohol syndrome is a specific pattern of birth defects—low birth weight, heart defects, facial malformations, learning disabilities, and mental retardation—first recognized in a study of babies born to alcoholic women who consumed more than six drinks a day while pregnant. Subsequent research has found a consistent pattern of milder defects in babies born to women who have three to four drinks a day or five drinks on any one occasion while pregnant. There is no evidence yet of a consistent pattern of birth defects in babies born to women who consume less than one drink a day while pregnant, but two studies at Columbia University have suggested that as few as two drinks a week may raise a pregnant woman's risk of miscarriage. ("One drink" is 12 ounces of beer, 5 ounces of wine, or 1.25 ounces of distilled spirits.)

Sulfite allergy.   Sulfur dioxide (a sulfite) is sometimes used as a preservative to control the growth of "wild" microorganisms that might turn wine to vinegar. People who are sensitive to sulfites may experience severe allergic reactions, including anaphylactic shock, if they drink these wines.

Migraine headaches.   When grapes are fermented, their long protein molecules are broken into smaller fragments. One of these fragments, tyramine, inhibits PST, an enzyme that that deactivates phenols (alcohols). The resulting build-up of phenols in your bloodstream may trigger a headache. All wines have some tyramine, but the most serious offenders appear to be red wines, particularly chianti.

FOOD/DRUG INTERACTIONS

Anticoagulants.   Alcohol interferes with the metabolism of anticoagulants. Larger amounts of the drug remain in the body and its effects are increased.

Antihypertensives (diuretics and beta blockers).   Alcohol, which lowers blood pressure, may dangerously intensify the effects of these drugs (see *MAO inhibitors,* below).

Aspirin and nonsteroidal anti-inflammatory drugs.   Like alcohol, these analgesics irritate the lining of the stomach and may cause gastric bleeding. Combining the two intensifies the effect.

Disulfiram (Antabuse).   Disulfiram is a drug used to help recovering alcoholics avoid alcohol beverages. Taken with alcohol, disulfiram causes flushing, nausea, low blood pressure, faintness, respiratory problems, and confusion. The severity of the reaction generally depends on how much alcohol you drink, how much disulfiram is in your body and how long ago you took it. If taken with alcohol, metronidazole (Flagyl), procarbazine (Matulane), quinacrine (Atabrine), chlorpropamide (Diabinase), and some species of mushrooms produce a mild disulfiramlike reaction.

Insulin and oral hypoglycemics.   Alcohol lowers blood sugar and interferes with the metabolism of oral antidiabetics; the combination may cause severe hypoglycemia.

MAO inhibitors.   Monoamine oxidase (MAO) inhibitors are drugs used as antidepressants or antihypertensives. They inhibit the action of natural enzymes that break down tyramine, a natural substance formed when long-chain protein molecules are metabolized or fermented and broken into smaller fragments. Tyramine is a pressor amine, a chemical that constricts blood vessels and raises blood pressure. If you eat a food that contains tyramine while you are taking an MAO inhibitor, the pressor amine cannot be eliminated from your body and the result may be a hypertensive crisis (sustained elevated blood pressure). Red wines (particularly chiantis) and sherry contain significant amounts of tyramine.

Sedatives and other central-nervous-system depressants.   Taken together, alcohol intensifies the sedative effects of tranquilizers, sleeping pills, antidepressants, sinus and cold remedies, analgesics, and medication for motion sickness. The combination may cause drowsiness, sedation, respiratory depression, coma, or death.

WINTER SQUASH
(Acorn, butternut, Hubbard, spaghetti squash)
See also PUMPKIN

NUTRITIONAL PROFILE

Energy value (calories per serving):	Low
Protein:	Moderate
Fat:	Low
Cholesterol:	None
Carbohydrates:	High
Fiber:	Low
Sodium:	Low
Major vitamin contribution:	Vitamins A and C, B vitamins
Major mineral contribution:	Calcium, potassium

ABOUT THE NUTRIENTS IN THIS FOOD

Winter squash has sugar, some fiber (mostly gums and some pectins, with a bit of cellulose), a little protein and fat, and no cholesterol.

All the winter squash are good sources of vitamin A, which comes from the carotenoids that make their flesh bright yellow. The darker the yellow, the more vitamin A in the squash.

Winter squash also provide moderate amounts of vitamin C, the B vitamins, iron, and potassium.

THE MOST NUTRITIOUS WAY TO SERVE THIS FOOD

Baked. Ounce for ounce, most baked squash has more vitamin A than boiled squash.

COMPARING THE VITAMIN A IN COOKED WINTER SQUASH
(IU/3.5-oz. serving)

	Baked	% RDA	Boiled	% RDA
Acorn	428 IU	8.5	258 IU	5
Butternut	7,001 IU	140	3,339 IU	67
Hubbard	6,035 IU	120	4,005 IU	80
Spaghetti	110 IU	2	110 IU	2

Source: *Composition of Foods: Vegetables and vegetable products,* Agriculture Handbook No. 8-11 (USDA, 1984).

DIETS THAT MAY RESTRICT OR EXCLUDE THIS FOOD
Sucrose-free diet

BUYING THIS FOOD
Look for: Firm, heavy squash is smooth and unblemished skin. *Acorn squash* should have a wide-ribbed, dark-green shell. The longer the squash is stored, the more orange it will become as its green chlorophyll pigments fade and the yellow carotenes underneath show through. *Butternut squash* should be a smooth, creamy brown or yellow. *Hubbard squash* has a ridged and bumpy orange-red shell flecked with dark blue or gray. *Spaghetti squash* is smooth and yellow. If the squash is sliced, the flesh inside should be smooth and evenly colored.

STORING THIS FOOD
Store winter squash in a cool, dry cabinet to protect its vitamins A and C. Squash stores well. Hubbards, for example, may stay fresh for up to six months, acorn squash for three to six months.

Do not refrigerate winter squash. Winter squash stored at cold temperatures convert their starches to sugars.

PREPARING THIS FOOD
Wash the squash and bake it whole, or cut it in half or in quarters (or smaller portions if it is very large), remove the stringy part and the seeds, and bake or boil. Baking is the more nutritious method since it preserves the most nutrients.

WHAT HAPPENS WHEN YOU COOK THIS FOOD
When you bake a squash, the soluble food fibers in its cell walls dissolve and

the squash gets softer. Baking also caramelizes and browns sugars on the cut surface of the squash, a process you can help along by dusting the squash with brown sugar. If you bake the squash long enough, the moisture inside its cells will begin to evaporate and the squash will shrink.

When you boil squash, its starch granules absorb water molecules that cling to the amylose and amylopectin molecules inside, making the starch granules (and the squash) swell. If the granules absorb enough water they will rupture, releasing the moisture inside and once again the squash will shrink.

Neither baking nor boiling reduces the amount of vitamin A in squash since the carotenes that make squash yellow are impervious to the normal heat of cooking. Vitamin C, on the other hand, is heat-sensitive. Cooked squash has less vitamin C than raw squash does.

HOW OTHER KINDS OF PROCESSING AFFECT THIS FOOD
Canning.   According to the USDA, canned "pumpkin" may be a mixture of pumpkin and other yellow-orange winter squash, all of which are similar in nutritional value.

MEDICAL USES AND/OR BENEFITS
Protection against some forms of cancer.   According to the American Cancer Society, deep-yellow foods such as acorn, butternut, Hubbard, and other yellow squash that are rich in vitamin A may lower the risk of cancers of the larynx, esophagus, and lungs.

ADVERSE EFFECTS ASSOCIATED WITH THIS FOOD
*   *   *

FOOD/DRUG INTERACTIONS
*   *   *

YOGURT
(Acidophilus milk, buttermilk, kefir, kumiss, sour cream)

NUTRITIONAL PROFILE*

Energy value (calories per serving):	Moderate
Protein:	High
Fat:	High
Cholesterol:	Moderate
Carbohydrates:	Moderate
Fiber:	None
Sodium:	Moderate
Major vitamin contribution:	B vitamins, vitamin D
Major mineral contribution:	Calcium

ABOUT THE NUTRIENTS IN THIS FOOD

Cultured milks are fermented products. Their lactose has been digested by any one or two of a number of strains of bacteria that produce lactic acid as a waste product. The lactic acid coagulates proteins in the milk to form curds that thicken the milk. *Acidophilus milk* is pasteurized whole milk cultured with *Lactobacillus acidophilus.* If you add yeast cells to acidophilus milk, the yeasts will ferment the milk, producing *kefir* or *kumiss,* which are low-alcohol milk beverages. *Cultured buttermilk* is pasteurized low-fat or skim milk cultured with *Streptococcus lactis. Sour cream* is made either by cultur-

*Values are for yogurt made with whole milk.

ing pasteurized sweet cream with bacteria that produce lactic acid or by curdling the cream with vinegar. *Yogurt* is pasteurized whole, low-fat, or skim sweet milk cultured with *Lactobacilli bulgaricus* and *Streptococcus thermophilus*. Some yogurt also contains *Lactobacillus acidophilus*.

Cultured milk products are an excellent source of proteins considered complete because they contain sufficient amounts of all the essential amino acids. They contain moderate amounts of sugars, but they have no starch or fiber.* They contain butterfat, which is high in saturated fatty acids. Their cholesterol content varies with their fat content; skim-milk products have less cholesterol than whole-milk products.

Like other milks, cultured milks contain moderate amounts of carotenoids that your body can convert into vitamin A. Vitamin A is fat-soluble; low-fat and skim-milk products have less vitamin A than whole-milk products. For example, one cup (8 oz.) whole-milk yogurt has 280 IU vitamin A; one cup of yogurt made from low-fat milk has 150 IU. Cultured milks made from vitamin D-fortified milk contain vitamin D. All milk products are relatively good sources of thiamin (vitamin B_1) and riboflavin (vitamin B_2).

Milk products are our primary source of calcium. One cup (8 oz.) plain, low-fat yogurt provides 415 mg calcium as compared to 300 in one cup low-fat milk. Buttermilk has 285 mg calcium per cup, sour cream 268. Two cups of yogurt or three glasses of a cultured milk a day provide all the calcium needed by normal healthy adults (RDA is 800 mg).

Milk products are also a good source of iodine, which we ordinarily associate with seafood or plants grown near the sea. In fact, dairy products may now be our most important source of iodine. The iodine in milks comes from supplements fed to dairy cattle and, perhaps, from the iodates and iodophors in the agents used to clean the machinery in plants where milk is processed.

THE MOST NUTRITIOUS WAY TO SERVE THIS FOOD

For adults: skim-milk products, without added fruit and sugars. (According to the American Academy of Pediatrics, giving children skim milk products may deprive them of fatty acids essential to growth.)

DIETS THAT MAY RESTRICT OR EXCLUDE THIS FOOD

Controlled-fat, low-cholesterol diet
Lactose- and galactose-free diets
Sucrose-free diet (flavored yogurt or yogurt made with fruit)

---

*Flavored yogurt or yogurt with added fruit or preserves is much higher in sugar and contains some fiber (in the the fruit). Certain gums used as stabilizers in yogurt may also provide fiber.

BUYING THIS FOOD

Look for: Tightly sealed, refrigerated containers that feel cold to the touch. Check the date on the container to buy the freshest product.

STORING THIS FOOD

Refrigerate all cultured milk products immediately. At 40° F, buttermilk will stay fresh for two to three weeks, sour cream for three to four weeks, and yogurt for three to six weeks. Keep the containers tightly closed so the milks do not pick up odors from other foods.

PREPARING THIS FOOD

Do not "whip" yogurt before adding to any dish. You will break the curd and make the yogurt watery.

WHAT HAPPENS WHEN YOU COOK THIS FOOD

Cultured milk products, which are more unstable than plain milks, separate quickly when heated. Stir them in gently just before serving.

HOW OTHER KINDS OF PROCESSING AFFECT THIS FOOD

Freezing.   Cultured milk products separate easily when frozen. Commercially frozen yogurt contains gelatin and other emulsifiers to make the product creamy and keep it from separating. Freezing inactivates but does not destroy the bacteria in yogurt; if there were live bacteria in the yogurt when it was frozen, they will still be there when it's thawed. Nutritionally, frozen yogurt made from whole milk is similar to ice cream; frozen yogurt made from skim milk is similar to ice milk.

MEDICAL USES AND/OR BENEFITS

Protection against osteoporosis.   Adequate dietary calcium early in life may offer some protection against osteoporosis ("thinning bones") later on. In one study at the University of Pittsburgh's School of Health-Related Professions, researchers found that the bones of women who drank milk with every meal until they were thirty-five had bones of higher density than women who rarely drank milk. There is, however, no proof that consuming milk or milk products will prevent or cure osteoporosis.

To reduce the levels of serum cholesterol.   People whose blood-cholesterol levels are abnormally high are considered at risk for heart disease, but experts disagree as to the effects of saturated fats in the diet. Patients with hypercholesteremia, a metabolic disorder that influences cholesterol production in the liver, may benefit from a diet low in dietary cholesterol, but there is no in the liver, may benefit from a diet low in dietary cholesterol, but there is no conclusive proof that lowering a healthy person's consumption of dietary cholesterol will significantly change the amount of cholesterol he or she produces. In fact, the effects of the cholesterol in yogurts and cultured milks made from whole milk (which is relatively high in cholesterol) are particularly interesting.

In the late 1970s researchers from Vanderbilt University in Tennessee found that the Masai in East Africa had very low levels of serum cholesterol even though their diet was high cattle blood and fermented milk. In a follow-up study in the United States, research showed that cholesterol levels rose among patients given whole milk but fell among patients given whole-milk yogurt. The explanation appears to lie with the bacteria in the yogurt. According to researchers at Oklahoma State University in Stillwater, some strains of *Lactobacillus acidophilus* appear to assimilate cholesterol in the digestive tract before it can be absorbed into the body. In 1984 the Oklahoma scientists designed a study in which pigs (whose digestive and circulatory systems are similar to ours) were fed a high-cholesterol diet. Some of the pigs were given a strain of *Lactobacillus acidophilus* along with the cholesterol. While the diet raised serum cholesterol levels for all the pigs, the levels went up twice as much among pigs who did not get the *Lactobacillus*. (While different strains of *Lactobacillus acidophilus* have different abilities to absorb cholesterol, the Oklahoma researchers believe that there is at least one such strain that may work in the human gut.)

ADVERSE EFFECTS ASSOCIATED WITH THIS FOOD

Allergy to milk proteins.   Milk and milk products are among the foods most often implicated as a cause of the classic symptoms of food allergy: upset stomach, hives, and angioedema (swelling of the face, lips, and tongue).

Lactose intolerance.   Lactose intolerance is not a food allergy. It is an inherited metabolic deficiency. People who are lactose-intolerant lack suffficient amounts of lactase, the intestinal enzyme that breaks the disaccharide ("double sugar") lactose into glucose and galactose, its easily digested constituents. Two-thirds of all adults, including 90 to 95 percent of all Orientals, 70 to 75 percent of all blacks, and 6 to 8 percent of Caucasians are lactose-intolerant to some extent. When they drink milk or eat milk products, the lactose remains undigested in their gut, to be fermented by bacteria that produce gas and cause bloating, diarrhea, and intestinal discomfort. According to researchers at Oklahoma State University in Stillwater, the *Lactobacillus acidophilus* bacteria added to acidophilus milk and some yogurts may supply lactase, the enzyme needed to digest lactose. Lactase-deficient adults may be able to drink acidophilus-treated milks or yogurts without ill effects.

LACTOSE CONTENT OF
CULTURED MILK PRODUCTS

Acidophilus milk	6 gm/cup
Buttermilk	9 gm/cup
Yogurt (low-fat)	12 gm/cup
Whole sweet milk	12 gm/cup

Source: Briggs, George M., and Calloway, Doris Howes, *Nutrition and Physical Fitness,* 11th ed. (New York: Holt, Rinehart and Winston, 1984).

Galactosemia. Galactosemia is an inherited metabolic disorder in which the body lacks the enzymes needed to metabolize galactose, a component of lactose. Galactosemia is a recessive trait; you must get the gene from both parents in order to develop the condition. Babies born with galactosemia will fail to thrive and may develop brain damage or cataracts if they are given milk. To prevent this, children with galactosemia are usually kept on a protective milk-free diet several years, until their bodies have developed alternative pathways by which to metabolize galactose. Pregnant women who are known carriers of galactosemia may be advised to give up milk while pregnant lest the unmetabolized galactose in their bodies cause brain damage to the fetus (damage not detectible by amniocentesis). Genetic counseling is available to identify galactosemia carriers and assess their chances of producing a baby with the disorder.

FOOD/DRUG INTERACTIONS

Tetracyclines The calcium ions in milk products bind with tetracyclines (Declomycin, Minocin, Rondomycin, Terramycin, Vibramycin, and the like) to form insoluble compounds your body cannot absorb. Taking tetracyclines with acidophilus milk, buttermilk, sour cream, or yogurt makes the drugs less effective.

ZUCCHINI

(Summer squash, yellow crookneck squash, yellow straightneck squash)

NUTRITIONAL PROFILE

Energy value (calories per serving):	Low
Protein:	High
Fat:	Low
Cholesterol:	None
Carbohydrates:	High
Fiber:	Low
Sodium:	Low
Major vitamin contribution:	Vitamins A and C
Major mineral contribution:	Potassium

ABOUT THE NUTRIENTS IN THIS FOOD

Zucchini and the yellow summer squash have sugar, as well as the carbohydrate food fibers cellulose, hemicellulose, pectins, and gums. The seeds and peel are a source of the noncarbohydrate food fiber lignin, which is found in stems, leaves, and seed coverings. Zucchini have a little fat. Like other vegetables, they have no cholesterol. Green and yellow summer squash are moderately good sources of carotenes, the yellow pigment that your body can convert to vitamin A. (The yellow carotenoids in zucchini are masked by its green chlorophyll pigments.) One 3.5-ounce serving of these squashes provides up to 340 IU vitamin A, 7 percent of the RDA for a healthy adult.

A 3.5-ounce serving of raw zucchini has about 9 mg vitamin C, 15 percent of the RDA for a healthy adult. An equal serving of raw yellow summer squash has 8.4 mg vitamin C, 14 percent of the RDA. Summer squash have moderate amounts of the B vitamins thiamin (vitamin B_1), riboflavin (vitamin B_2), and niacin.

THE MOST NUTRITIOUS WAY TO SERVE THIS FOOD

Steamed quickly in very little water, to preserve the vitamin C.

DIETS THAT MAY RESTRICT OR EXCLUDE THIS FOOD

Low-fiber diet
Sucrose-free diet

BUYING THIS FOOD

Look for: Dark-green slender zucchini with pale-yellow or white striping. Yellow crookneck squash should be brightly colored with lightly pebbled skin. Yellow straightneck squash may have either smooth or pebbled skin.

Choose smaller (and therefore more tender) squash. The best zucchini are 4 to 9 inches long; the best crooknecks and straightnecks are 4 to 6 inches long.

Avoid: Limp squash. They have lost moisture and vitamins. Avoid squash whose skin is bruised or cut; handle squash gently to avoid bruising them yourself. Bruising tears cells, activating ascorbic acid oxidase, an enzyme that destroys vitamin C. Avoid squash with a hard rind; the harder the rind, the older the squash and the larger and harder the seeds inside.

STORING THIS FOOD

Refrigerate summer squash, which are perishable and should be used within a few days.

PREPARING THIS FOOD

Scrub the squash with a vegetable brush and cut off each round end. Peel older, larger squash, then slice them in half and remove the hard seeds. Younger, more tender squash can be cooked with the peel and seeds.

WHAT HAPPENS WHEN YOU COOK THIS FOOD

As the squash cooks, its cells absorb water, the pectins in the cell walls dissolve, and the vegetable gets softer. The seeds, stiffened with insoluble cellulose and lignin, will remain firm.

Chlorophyll, the pigment that makes green vegetables green, is sensitive to acids. When you heat zucchini, its chlorophyll reacts with acids in the vegetable or in the cooking water to form pheophytin, which is brown. The pheophytin makes cooked zucchini look olive-drab. To keep the cooked zucchini green, you have to keep the chlorophyll from reacting with the acids. One way to do this is to cook the zucchini in a large quantity of water (which will dilute the acids), but this increases the loss of vitamin C. A second alternative is to leave the top off the pot so that the volatile acids can float off into the air. Or you can stir-fry the zucchini or steam it in very little water so the vegetable cooks before the chlorophyll/acid reaction can occur.

Yellow squash stays bright-yellow no matter how long you cook it; its carotene pigments are impervious to the normal heat of cooking.

HOW OTHER KINDS OF PROCESSING AFFECT THIS FOOD

Canning.   Canned zucchini has about as much vitamin C as fresh-cooked zucchini.

MEDICAL USES AND/OR BENEFITS

Protection against some forms of cancer.   According to the American Cancer Society, deep-yellow vegetables, rich sources of vitamin A, may offer some protection against cancers of the larynx, esophagus, and lungs.

ADVERSE EFFECTS ASSOCIATED WITH THIS FOOD

*   *   *

FOOD/DRUG INTERACTIONS

*   *   *

BIBLIOGRAPHY

BOOKS

AMA Drug Evaluations, 5th ed. New York: American Medical Association, 1983.

American Dietetic Association. *Handbook of Clinical Dietetics.* New Haven: Yale University Press, 1981.

The American Heart Association Cookbook, 4th ed., rev. New York: Ballantine Books, 1986.

Arkin, Freda. *Kitchen Wisdom.* New York: Holt, Rinehart and Winston, 1977.

Ashley, Richard, and Heidi Duggal. *Dictionary of Nutrition.* New York: Pocket Books, 1976.

Berkow, Robert, M.D. (ed.). *The Merck Manual,* 14th ed. Rahway, N.J.: Merck, Sharp & Dohme Research Laboratories, 1982.

Briggs, George M., and Doris Howe Calloway. *Nutrition and Physical Fitness,* 11th ed. New York: Holt, Rinehart and Winston, 1979.

Conry, Tom. *Consumer's Guide to Cosmetics.* New York: Anchor Books, 1980.

Cook, L. Russell. *Chocolate Use and Production.* New York: Books for Industry, 1972.

Coulson, Zoe (ed.). *The Good Housekeeping Cookbook.* New York: Good Housekeeping Books, 1973.

Davis, Adelle (ed. by Ann Gilroy). *Let's Stay Healthy.* New York: Harcourt Brace Jovanovich, 1981.

Deutsche Forschunganstalt für Lebensmittelchemie. *Food Composition and Nutrition Tables 1981/82,* 2nd ed. Stuttgart: Wissenschaftliche Verlagsgesellschaft, 1981.

DeVore, Sally, and Thelma White. *The Appetites of Man.* New York: Anchor Books, 1978.

Farb, Peter, and George Armelagos. *Consuming Passions.* Boston: Houghton Mifflin Company, 1980.

Floch, Martin H. *Nutrition and Diet Therapy in Gastrointestinal Disease.* New York: Plenum, 1981.

Freydberg, Nicholas, and Willis Gortner. *The Food Additives Book.* New York: Bantam, 1982.

Gilman, Alfred Goodman, Louis Goodman, and Alfred Gilman. *The Pharmacological Basis of Therapeutics,* 6th ed. New York: Macmillan, 1980.

Griggs, Barbara. *Green Pharmacy.* New York: Viking, 1981.

Grosser. Arthur E. *The Cookbook Decoder.* New York: Warner Books, 1981.

Hampel, Clifford A., and Gessner G. Hawley. *Glossary of Chemical Terms.* New York: Van Nostrand Reinhold, 1976.

Harris, Marvin. *Good to Eat.* New York: Simon and Schuster, 1985.

Jacobs, Morris B. (ed.). *The Chemistry and Technology of Food and Food Products.* New York: Interscience, 1951.

Jacobson, Michael F. *Eater's Digest.* New York: Anchor Books, 1976.

Krupp, Marcus A., and Milton J. Chatton (eds.). *Current Medical Diagnosis and Treatment 1983.* Los Altos, Calif.: Lange Medical Publications, 1983.

Krupp, Marcus, A., Milton J., Chatton, and Lawrence N. Tierney, Jr. *Current Medical Diagnosis and Treatment 1986.* Los Altos, Calif.: Lange Medical Publications, 1986.

Levey, Judith S. (ed.). *The Concise Columbia En-*

cylcopedia. New York: Columbia University Press, 1983.

Lewis, Walter H., and Memory P.F. Elvin-Lewis. *Medical Botany.* New York: Wiley, 1977.

Lust, John. *The Herb Book.* New York: Bantam, 1983.

Macia, Rafael. *The Natural Foods and Nutrition Handbook.* New York: Perennial Library, 1972.

McGee, Harold. *On Food and Cooking.* New York: Scribner, 1984.

Morris, Dan and Inez. *The Complete Fish Cookbook.* Indianapolis: Bobbs-Merrill, 1972.

Paul, A. A., and D.A.T. Southgate (eds.). *McCance and Widdowson's The Composition of Foods,* 4th ed. London: Her Majesty's Stationery Office, 1978.

Pinckney, Cathey, and Edward R. Pinckney. *The Patient's Guide to Medical Tests.* New York: Facts on File, 1982.

Quimme, Peter. *The Signet Book of Coffee and Tea.* New York: New American Library, 1976.

Rombauer, Irma S., and Marion Rombauer Becker. *The Joy of Cooking.* Indianapolis: Bobbs-Merrill, 1984.

Rosengarten, Frederic, Jr. *The Book of Spices.* New York: Jove, 1981.

Spock, Benjamin. *Baby and Child Care.* New York: Pocket Books, 1976.

Steiner, Richard P. (ed.). *Folk Medicine: The Art and Science.* Washington, D.C.: American Chemical Society, 1986.

Subak-Sharpe, Genell J. (ed. dir.). *The Columbia University College of Physicians and Surgeons Complete Home Medical Guide.* New York: Crown, 1985.

Toxicants Occurring Naturally in Foods, 2nd ed. Washington, D.C.: National Academy of Sciences, 1973.

Tyler, Varro E. *Hoosier Home Remedies.* Lafayette, Ind.: Purdue University Press, 1985.

Waldo, Myra. *The Complete Round-the-World Meat Cookbook.* New York: Doubleday, 1967.

Whalen, Elizabeth M., and Frederick J. Stare. *Panic in the Pantry.* New York: Atheneum, 1975.

Windholz, Martha (ed.). *The Merck Index,* 10th ed. Rahway, N.J.: Merck & Co., 1983.

Winter, Ruth. *A Consumer's Dictionary of Food Additives.* New York: Crown, 1978.

Zapsalis, Charles, and R. Anderle Beck. *Food Chemistry and Nutritional Biochemistry.* New York: Wiley, 1985.

PERIODICALS

"A ban on treated apples," *The New York Times,* July 26, 1986

"Acidophilus: Milky bane to cholesterol?," *Science News,* August 24, 1984

"ACS releases dietary guidelines aimed at reducing cancer risk," *Medical World News,* March 12, 1984

Adams, J. B., "Color stability of red fruits," *Food Manufacture,* February 1973

"Alcohol and the heart," *Science News,* June 1, 1980

"Alcohol and migraine," *The New York Times,* June 18, 1985

Allman, William F., "Aspartame: Some bitter with the sweet?," *Science 84,* May 1984

Ames, Bruce, "Dietary carcinogens and anticarcinogens," *Science,* September 21, 1983

Anderson, Duncan, "Bacon smells good again," *American Health,* May-June 1982

Anderson, Karl E., and Attallah Kappas, "Drug effectiveness: Diet shows new importance," *Health Spectrum,* Summer 1983

"Another case against unpasteurized milk," *Tufts University Diet and Nutrition Letter,* September 1985

"Another hazard in undercooked pork," *Science News,* July 19, 1986

"Antibiotics in meat: What to do about it," *Tufts University Diet and Nutrition Letter,* November 1984

"Are you sure you're getting enough iron?," *Tufts University Diet and Nutrition Letter,* October 1985

"Aspartame critics persist, recommend avoidance

during pregnancy," *Medical World News,* February 27, 1984

Aungst, Bruce J., and Ho-leung Fung, "Inhibition of oral lead absorption in rats by phosphate-containing products," *Journal of Pharmaceutical Sciences,* April 1983

"Bacon producers permitted to use vitamin E additives," *The New York Times,* July 6, 1985

Barnett, Robert, "Garlic, the raw and the cooked," *American Health,* January-February 1986

"Beef fat alert lifted a bit," *Tufts University Diet and Nutrition Letter,* January 1986

Behre, Linda M., "Calcium and hypertension—what's the connection?," *ACSH News and Views,* January-February 1985

——— "Sulfite food additives: To ban or not to ban," *ACSH News and Views,* May-June 1986

"Benefits of eating fish," *Tufts University Diet and Nutrition Letter,* July 1985

Bock, S. Allan, "The natural history of food sensitivity," *Journal of Allergy and Clinical Immunology,* February 1982

Boffey, Philip M., "Diet sweetener risk is being reassessed after new research," *The New York Times,* August 21, 1984

——— "New study ties coffee drinking of 5 cups daily to heart disease," *The New York Times,* November 12, 1985

Brewer, Stephen and Pat Sims, "Raves of grain," *American Health,* May 1985

Brock, Carol, "Citrus," *The Daily News* (N.Y.), January 18, 1984

Brody, Jane, "Monounsaturated fats can help lower cholesterol levels," *The New York Times,* April 24, 1984

——— "Personal Health," *The New York Times,* August 16, 1982; November 7, 1984

Brown, Ellen, "Nutritionists let fish off the hook," *USA Today,* June 20, 1984

Bryant, Nelson, "Mushroom articles revive an appetite," *The New York Times,* May 25, 1985

Buckley, Rebecca H., "Food Allergy," *Journal of the American Medical Association,* November 26, 1982

"Burgers: Fatty patties vs. extra-lean," *Science News,* August 10, 1985

Butera, Jay, "Mares eat oats and does eat oats, shouldn't you?," *American Health,* September 1984

"Butter lovers: The news isn't all bad," *Science News,* November 30, 1984

"Can plantains prevent ulcers?" *Hospital Tribune,* December 19, 1984

"Cancer from mushrooms," *Science News,* July 15, 1978

Chase, Marilyn, "Raw milk: Essence of good health or an invitation to food poisoning?," *The Wall Street Journal,* May 30, 1985

"Chicken soup and the common cold," *Mayo Clinic Health Letter,* October 1984

"Chinese salted fish linked to cancer," *Science News,* June 29, 1985

"Coffee and the job: Heartfelt insults?," *Medical World News,* November 23, 1985

"Coffee boosts pain-free walking time for patients with chronic stable angina," *Medical World News,* March 12, 1984

"Coffee consumption and risk of fatal cancers," *American Journal of Public Health,* August 1984

"Combining coffee, theophylline may increase risk of CNS side effects among asthmatics," *Medical World News,* December 12, 1984

"Copper: Whipping egg whites into shape," *Science News,* May 12, 1984

"Court orders HHS to rule on raw milk," *Science News,* May 26, 1984

"Crusty proteins are hard to digest," *Science News,* June 30, 1985

"Curing bacon: Fat on the fire," *Science News,* March 12, 1985

"Drug interactions update," *The Medical Letter,* February 3, 1984

Duke, Jim, "Vegetarian Vitechart," *Quarterly Journal of Crude Drug Research,* 1977

Dusheck, Jennie, "Fish, fatty acids and physiology," *Science News,* October 9, 1985

"Easter egg blues," *Science News,* September 1, 1984

Eckholm, Eric, "Warnings issued on eating shellfish that is uncooked," *The New York Times,* March 13, 1986

"Eating away at cancer risk," *Science News,* February 25, 1984

"Endorphins: New types and sweet links," *Science News,* August 27, 1983

"'Exhibit A' in the case against feeding animals antibiotics," *Business Week,* September 24, 1984

"FDA to ban sulfites from fresh produce," *Science News,* August 17, 1985

"Fiber analysis tables," *The American Journal of Clinical Nutrition,* October 31, 1978

"Fiber's role in food and fitness," *Tufts University Diet and Nutrition Letter,* July 1985

"Fish oil compound for sharp vision. . . and migraine relief," *Medical World News,* July 8, 1985

"Fish oil for prevention of atherosclerosis," *The Medical Letter,* November 12, 1982

"Fish oil may ease arthritis pain," *Medical World News,* July 14, 1986

"Fish oil's CAD benefits may protect diabetics," *Medical World News,* August 25, 1986

Folks, David G., "Monoamine oxidase inhibitors: Reappraisal of dietary considerations," *Journal of Clinical Psychopharmacology,* August 1983

"Food flavours: The Yong recipe," *The Economist,* August 16, 1986

"Food poisoning," *U.S. Pharmacist,* April 1983

Franey, Pierre, "Step by step: Squid without tears," *The New York Times,* July 2, 1986

Fries, Joseph H., "Chocolate: A review of published reports of allergic and other deleterious effects, real or presumed," *Annals of Allergy,* October 1978

"Garlic, not to be sniffed at," *The Economist,* February 15, 1986

Glaros, Tony, "Oyster blues," *Restaurant Hospitality,* August 1985

Goldman, Peter, "Coffee and health: What's brewing?," *The New England Journal of Medicine,* March 22, 1984

Goleman, Daniel, "Peril is seen for babies whose mothers ate fish with PCBs," *The New York Times,* July 22, 1984

"'Good' chemicals in beef and garlic," *Medical World News,* February 11, 1985

Gossel, Thomas A., "A review of aspartame characteristics, safety and uses," *U.S. Pharmacist,* January 1984

——— "Fecal occult blood testing products," *U.S. Pharmacist,* April 1986

Greenberg, Richard A., "I'll have my bluepoints cooked, thank you; Raw shellfish may be dangerous," *ACSH News and Views,* January-February 1984

——— "Industrious ingredients," *ACSH News and Views,* March-April 1983

Hager, Tom, "Food for the heart," *American Health,* April 1985

Hall, Stephen S., "Deflating beans," *Science 84,* July-August 1984

"Hamburger beefs up cancer protection," *Science News,* December 22 and 29, 1984

"Heart disease: Let them eat fish," *Science News,* May 11, 1985

"Heart risk termed lower with fish in diet," *The New York Times,* May 9, 1985

Heller, Linda, "Science puts the pressure on calcium," *American Health,* January-February 1984

Henderson, Doug, "Cookware as a source of additives," *FDA Consumer,* March 1982

"Here is why some of us don't drink milk," *Mayo Clinic Health Letter,* July 1985

"'Hidden' sodium and fat in cheese," *Tufts University Diet and Nutrition Letter,* March 1985

Hinds, Michael de Courcey, "Assessing effects of food treatment," *The New York Times,* March 31, 1982

"Honey and infant botulism," *Science News,* July 15, 1978

"Illness traced to treated milk," *The New York Times,* February 15, 1985

"Irradiated pork: long-awaited arrival," *Tufts University Diet and Nutrition Letter,* October 1985

"Irradiation of pork is approved," *The New York Times,* January 15, 1985

"Is olive oil right?," *Tufts University Diet and Nutrition Letter,* May 1986

Jenkins, Nancy Harmon, "All briny, all tasty and all oysters," *The New York Times,* March 5, 1986

——— "These vegetables merit more praise and less boiling," *The New York Times,* November 13, 1985

Kennedy, Cynthia Chandler, "New light on beans," *Diabetes Forecast,* March-April 1986

Kolata, Gina, "Testing for trichinosis," *Science,* February 8, 1985

Koopman, James S., et. al., "Milk fat and gastrointestinal illness," *American Journal of Public Health,* December 1984

Krysnowek, Judith, "Sterols and fatty acids in seafood," *Food Technology,* February 1985

Langseth, Lillian, "Soft drinks: The great American beverage," *ACSH News and Views,* June 1982

Lehmann, Phyllis, "Food and drug interactions," *FDA Consumer,* March 1978

Levey, Gail A., "Chic beans," *American Health,* March 1986

Londer, Randi, "Chili burn, caveats of fire," *American Health,* March-April 1983

Mahoney, C. Patrick, et. al., "Chronic vitamin A intoxication in infants fed chicken liver," *Pediatrics,* May 5, 1980

Marano, Hara Estroff, "Shellfish off the hook," *American Health,* March-April 1983

McCabe, Beverly, and Ming T. Tsuang, "Dietary consideration in MAO inhibitor regimens," *Journal of Clinical Psychiatry,* May 1982

McGee, Harold, "Tainted cheeses: How dangerous?," *The New York Times,* August 27, 1986

"Measles prevention," *Morbidity and Mortality Weekly Report,* May 7, 1982

"Measuring your life with coffee spoons," *Tufts University Diet and Nutrition Letter,* April 1984

Meister, Kathleen, "Dietary strategies for lactose intolerance," *ACSH News and Views,* November-December 1983

———— "Frozen foods: As nutritious as fresh?," *ACSH News and Views,* January-February 1984

"Milk consumption associated with asthma and migraine," *The Nutrition Report,* March 1984

Miller, Brian, "Ban asked on sale of raw milk," *The New York Times,* April 11, 1984

Miller, Julius Sumner, "Physics in the kitchen," *Science Digest,* August 1975

Molotsky, Irvin, "U.S. issues ban on sulfites' use in certain foods," *The New York Times,* July 9, 1986

"Monoamine oxidase inhibitors for depression," *The Medical Letter,* July 11, 1980

"Monounsaturates to prevent CHD?," *Medical World News,* April 22, 1985

"Mumps vaccine," *Morbidity and Mortality Weekly Report,* November 26, 1982

"Mushroom poisoning," *The Medical Letter,* July 20, 1984

"Natural food ingredients—effects you'd never expect," *Tufts University Diet and Nutrition Letter,* March 1985

"New crop of PKU victims: babies of successfully treated girls," *Medical World News,* November 23, 1981

Omark, Johanna M., "Bottled water—healthier than tap?," *ACSH News and Views,* March-April 1986

"Pass the olive oil," *Science News,* April 6, 1985

"Pass the shellfish, please," *Science News,* December 7, 1985

"Phytic acid: Fiber's double agent," *American Health,* March 1986

"Poisoning linked to cattle germs," *The New York Times,* September 6, 1984

"Poisons may lurk in the parsnips," *Science News,* September 5, 1981

"Potassium for hypertension?," *Medical World News,* March 11, 1985

"Prevention and control of influenza," *Morbidity and Mortality Weekly Report,* May 23, 1986

Prial, Frank J., "Labeling wine to warn of added sulfite," *The New York Times,* April 2, 1986

Price, David P., "Beef and the cholesterol issue," *Beef Magazine,* March 1984

"The question of milk safety," *Tufts University Diet and Nutrition Letter,* June 1985

"Questions of taste," *Food and Wine,* September 1984, June 1985, November 1985, February 1986

"Reaping more than taste from garlic and onions," *Tufts University Diet and Nutrition Letter*, August 1985

"Safe grounds for hypertensives," *Medical World News,* May 27, 1985

Schneider, Elizabeth, "Great greens!," *Food and Wine,* October 1985

———— "Rare spring pleasures," *Food and Wine,* April 1985

———— "The world of rices," *Food and Wine,* November 1985

Schneider, Keith, "Tiny traces of suspect chemical found in apple juice and sauce," *The New York Times,* January 14, 1986

———— "Should U.S. farmers go cold turkey?," *The New York Times,* January 21, 1985

"Some ounces of prevention that lower heart risk," *The New York Times,* August, 31, 1986

Steinberg, Sarah, "Cancer and cuisine," *Science News,* October 1, 1983

"Sulfites as food ingredients," *Food Technology,*

June 1986

Sullivan, Walter, "Garlic cited for meningitis treatment," *The New York Times,* March 30, 1980

"Sushi lovers: Beware of parasites," *Science News,* March 2, 1985

"Testing for trichnosis," *Science,* February 8, 1985

"The textile industry turns to mushrooms," *The Economist,* December 7, 1985

Thomas, Patricia, "Across the board diet reform for CAD—Is the table tilted?," *Medical World News,* May 26, 1986

"Treatment of hypothermia," *The Medical Letter,* January 21, 1983

"Treatment of lactose intolerance," *The Medical Letter,* July 24, 1981

"Updated advice for a healthier heart," *Tufts University Diet and Nutrition Letter,* October 1986

"Vitamin A: A cancer suppressor," *Cancer Update,* January 1984

Wade, William E., and James W. Cooper, "Monitoring the hypertensive patient," *U.S. Pharmacist,*

August 1985

Walker, J. Ingram, Jonathan Davidson, and William W. K. Zung, "Patient compliance with MAO inhibitor therapy," *Journal of Clinical Psychology,* July 1984

"Water overload a risk for people with epilepsy," *Tufts University Diet and Nutrition Letter,* October 1985

"Where's the potassium?," *Medical World News,* April 22, 1985

"Why sugar continues to concern nutritionists," *Tufts University Diet and Nutrition Letter,* May 1985

"Will milk help quench cancer risk?," *Medical World News,* April 22, 1985

Williams, Linda, "Stalking the Dixie kidney stone: collard greens are prime suspect," *The Wall Street Journal,* April 1, 1985

"You are what you don't eat," *Science News,* June 30, 1984

BOOKLETS AND PRESS RELEASES

American Academy of Dermatology
   "Fish oils may offer relief from psoriasis symptoms," June 26, 1985

American Chemical Society
   "Baking and toasting reduce nutritional value of bread," April 2, 1982
   "Chemicals in cooked beef protect against cancer," December 17, 1984
   "Cook meat with vegetables to avoid warmed-over flavor," April 1, 1982
   "Soybean pies?," April 11, 1984
   "Sweeter sweet potatoes from the garden," September 14, 1982
   "Tips for tastier carrots," September 14, 1982
   "Tips for tastier tomatoes," September 14, 1982
   "What's happening in chemistry (Why weep?)," January 1980

American Council on Science and Health
   "Antibiotics in animal feed: A threat to human health?," 1983
   "Diet and cancer," February 1985

   "Does nature know best? Natural carcinogens in American food," October 1985
   "Irradiated foods," October 1982
   "Low calorie sweeteners: Aspartame, saccharin, cyclamate," July 1984
   "PCBs: Is the cure worth the cost?," 1985
   "Sugars and your health," May 1986

Castle and Cooke Foods
   "Facts on fresh vegetables," 1982
   "Facts on oysters," 1980
   "Facts on pineapple," 1978
   "Facts on tuna," 1978

Cornell University
   "Finally: Microwave directions for blanching vegetables," September 30, 1985
   "Fish every day may help keep the doctor away," September 17, 1985
   "Human ecology research makes strides in improving quality of life," January 22, 1985
   "Nutritional value of microwave-cooked foods is

higher than other methods," October 18, 1982
"Sun exposure may affect your nutrition," April 14, 1986

Hoffmann-LaRoche, Vitamin Nutrition Information Service
"Vitamin losses in food preparation," 1982

National Coffee Association of U.S.A.
"Coffee Update," October 1985

National Diary Council
"Cultured diary foods," *Dairy Council Digest*, July-August 1972
"Newer knowledge of milk and other fluid dairy products," 1982

National Live Stock and Meat Board
"Meat, diet and health," 1983

National Psoriasis Foundation Annual Report, 1985

National Research Council
"Recommended dietary allowances," 9th ed., 1980)
"Alternative dietary practices and nutritional abuses in pregnancy," 1982

Purdue University
"The tooth fairy hates raisins," February 26, 1986

United Fresh Fruit and Vegetable Association
"Citrus," April 1981
"Conserving nutrients in fresh fruits and vegetables," August 1976
"Dietary fiber," 1979
"Folates," September 1976
"Food fats," January 1978
"Leafy greens," May 1980
"The fresh approach to fresh fruit selection and care" (nd)
"The fresh approach to apples, artichokes, asparagus, avocados, bananas, blueberries, broccoli, cabbage, carrots, cauliflower, celery, corn, cherries, cranberries, cucumbers, eggplant, grapefruit, grapes, leafy greens, lemons, limes, mangoes, melons, mushrooms, nectarines, nuts, onions, oranges, Oriental vegetables, papayas, peaches, peas, pears, pineapple, plums, potatoes, root vegetables, special vegetables, snap beans, squash, strawberries, sweet potatoes, tomatoes)"
"Sugars in nutrition," October 1977
"Water," August 1979

United States Department of Agriculture
"Canning, freezing, storing garden produce," Agriculture Information Bulletin 410, 1977
"Composition of foods: Beef products," Agriculture Handbook No. 8-13, 1986
"Composition of foods: Beverages," Agriculture Handbook No. 8-14, 1986
"Composition of foods: Dairy and egg products," Agriculture Handbook No. 8-1, 1976
"Composition of foods: Fats and oils," Agriculture Handbook No. 8-4, 1979
"Composition of foods: Fruits and fruit juices," Agriculture Handbook No. 8-9, 1982
"Composition of foods: Spices and herbs," Agriculture Handbook No. 8-2, 1977
"Composition of foods: Vegetables and vegetable products," Agriculture Handbook No. 8-11, 1984
"Conserving the nutritive value in foods," Home and Garden Bulletin No. 90, 1983
"FSIS facts: Safe handling tips for meat and poultry," FSIS 1981
"Meat and poultry products," Home and Garden Bulletin No. 236, 1981
"Nutritive value of foods," Home and Garden Bulletin No. 72, 1981 and 1985
"Provisional table on the fatty acid and cholesterol content of selected foods," 1984
"The safe food book," Home and Garden Bulletin No. 241, 1984
"The Sodium Content of Your Food," Home and Garden Bulletin No. 233, 1980
Watt, Bernice K., Annabel L. and Merrill, "Composition of foods," Agriculture Handbook No. 8, 1983

University of Texas Health Science Center at Dallas
"Monunsaturated fats shown as effective as polyunsaturates in lowering cholesterol," March 11, 1985

Vanderbilt University Medical Center
"Fish oil findings need further research," May 1986

INDEX

Common chemical reactions in food

Medical conditions affected by food

(For information about therapeutic diets that exclude a specific food, please see the listing for that food on pages 1 through 412.)